Thanks!
BooCat

BooCat
Unleashed

Hang in there BooBaby

The Illustrated Biography of a Cat

Barbara Sharik

Copyright©2010 by Barbara Sharik

ISBN: 978-1-929919-27-7

Camp Pope Publishing
PO Box 2232
Iowa City, Iowa 52244
www.camppope.com

May the best of the past
be the worst of the future.
—An Irish Toast

Always and Forever
for
Theresa
&
In Memory
Of
Tony

Introduction

I'm an autodidact writer with no formal training per se. To overcome what would be obvious, in-your-face, writing weaknesses I write about subjects I know.

I'm not so good at making things up. Fantasy and make believe aren't my forte. Instead, I find it easier to bring humorously to life that which is.

Following this self-garnered advice, it's only natural I choose to write about people in general. Being over the age of consent by a generation or so I write about older people in particular when writing my "Life in the Last Lane" humor *Bastrop Daily Enterprise* newspaper columns and my "Runnin' the Roads" humor *Louisiana Road Trips* magazine columns.

In both, I periodically throw in stuff about animals since I'm an adamant animal lover. I tend to find funny in almost everything, then, tempered by "hearticles," which are pieces and particles of a sporadic broken heart, I shake up all these ingredients and let them spill like die from a cup. Seven-come-eleven in the game of Craps is more like "Oh! Crap" in the game of life.

Although I'm now too old to die young, due to a lack of drive and ambition needed, I know I'll never write the Great American Novel. Still, working for a newspaper I have accomplished a writer's goal—I'm actually getting paid to write. Pittances count as being paid because it's regular and I do pay taxes on it.

People are actually reading what I write. My words may line somebody's birdcage tomorrow, but today somebody's reading what I wrote. I have name recognition. In the grand scheme of things, it's a very tiny bit of recognition, but it's for real. And that's what's important. Granted, the New York Times Book folks don't know my name, but the good people in Northeast Louisiana do.

Reflecting, being allowed to write "Life in the Last Lane" and

"Runnin' the Roads" is an amazing outlet for being who and what I am. I feel like the Grandma Moses of column writing. Of course, even knowing who Grandma Moses is dates me.

I wrote my first serious short story at age ten after reading Jack London's *Call of the Wild*. A certain amount of plagiarism was probably involved looking back, because my characters and my dog hero were similar to those found in London's tale right down to the French Canadian dialog.

I cut my eyeteeth on horse stories penned by Marguerite Henry. My all-time favorite was *King of the Wind*, a copy of which was recently given me by best friend Rose Ross, Sketch Set Art Club and Irvin High School (El Paso, Texas) classmate and fellow Class of 1962 graduate.

As with every young girl of my generation I was a horse lover. What kid during those Days of Yore didn't paw the ground, snort and whinny, galloping up and down the sidewalk? Pretending to be a horse in between hopscotch, jacks and marbles was a natural part of growing up in the 1950s. So was climbing trees, skating with a skate key tied around your neck and riding bikes; spending most the day outside with no fear of being kidnapped and murdered or plied with drugs at the school yard gate. Birds sang, dogs barked, cats meowed and peace was upon us. Consequently, coupled with my dream to be a writer, I penned a collection of horse stories about a black Arabian stallion with a white ring around its eye named Dare Devil. Recalling my love of Henry's books such as *Album of Horses*, I have the fondest memories of meeting Wesley Dennis. He illustrated all Henry's horse books, including *King of the Wind* and *Album of Horses*.

Graced with a talent for drawing and painting horses, Wesley Dennis was a major hero. I lost the postcard autographed drawing received during that visit, which saddens me. But not quite as much as the missing letter from President Eisenhower in response to a poem I mailed to him in 1956. Sometime after 2000, it came up missing. The envelope's return address said "White House" and the postage stamp featured a picture of the White House. There was no mistaking the value.

Bringing thoughts current, one unsettling thought surrounding my ability to render a horse upon paper or canvas is that, now at my age I still draw the same horse I drew fifty years ago. I would think I

Introduction

would be better by now. Perhaps one's peaking isn't based on age.

In any case, while a student at school in Virginia—we were living at Ft. Myer at that time where Dad was assigned to the Armed Forces Special Weapons Project (AFSWP) at the Pentagon—we took a class trip to the farm of Wesley Dennis.

I have never outgrown the joy of reading animal stories; an animal advocate in literature and true life. I watched all the Lassie TV episodes and my favorite dog movie is *Turner and Hootch*. I love that drooling dog.

Not only has my love of animal heroes not faded, but America seems enamored with them too. Animals have popped up in a multitude of mystery novels over the past decade or so. Depicted assisting in solving numerous crimes, they appeal to both mystery readers and animal lovers alike. The intuition these critters exhibit is amazing. Don't be too quick to criticize, chalking these tales up as childish. They're anything but. They're real mysteries with the added buttons and bows provided by a perky pet thrown into the mix.

In my book *The Auntie Chronicles* I've a chapter where a dog solves the mystery of a missing tin. There's also a Chihuahua who's a companion of the heroine barking her way throughout. Then, there's an assortment of books where animals are often added to exclusively warm the cockles of the heart of readers just by virtue of their presence; humanizing the main character as it were. Stephanie Plum in the Janet Evanovich series has a pet hamster for example. And David Rosenfelt's Andy Carpenter has his beloved golden retriever, Tara.

While both dog and cat deciphers are plenty plentiful in Sherlockian crime-solving literature these days, in general, books all about animals are at the height of popularity.

Because not all featured felines and furry fellows solve crimes or fill the slot of civilizing a hero or heroine, some are the stars themselves. They're heartwarming to read about in their own rights. Look at *Marley and Me, A Buffalo in the House* (I love that buffalo), *The Library Cat,* and *Dog Heroes of September 11*.

I've I read everything veterinarian James *All Creatures Great and Small* Herriot has written.

In Kinky Friedman's novels in which he depicts himself as a hapless detecting hero, he uses his cat as a sounding board but is always quick to add, "The cat, of course, said nothing."

vii

Friedman, who had an unsuccessful run for Governor of Texas a year or so ago, earned his fame writing and in performing outrageous off-the-wall songs and socializing with the likes of Bob Dylan and Willie Nelson. According to the flyleaf on several of his many books—and he is a very prolific writer—he "lives in a little green trailer in the heart of Texas Hill Country with cats, an armadillo, five dogs and a Smith-Corona typewriter," and claims to have saved "more animals than Noah" through his Utopia Animal Rescue Ranch. His animals are his heart. You have to admire a man who loves animals so much he set up his own animal rescue ranch.

In other words, there's an emotional as well as monetary success in joining forces with pets in life, literature, and movies. You don't need to be a kid to feel warm and fuzzy watching the movie *Babe*.

Whether or not you read the popular dog and cat crime series, just know that cats and dogs really are smart enough to solve crimes in the right circumstances. Animals lead the blind, sniff out illnesses, wake families in burning homes, get help for injured humans, rescue, search, guard and love. Oh how they love. Unconditionally.

According to Baxter Black, cowboy poet and former large animal veterinarian, "People would understand a lot more about life if they could think like an animal. It's called anthropomorphism, attributing animal traits to humans."

My favorite animal-related quote is by Kinky Friedman: "This country was a better place when the cowboys all sang and their horses were smart." I'm thinking Roy Roger's Trigger and Gene Autry's Champion. Both singing cowboys with smart horses and a part of my early childhood and my coming of age during what felt like a kinder and gentler time. Maybe I deceive myself, but it molded the people of my era in a more substantial way than what is being ingrained into the hearts and minds of today's youngsters.

The sign at my front gate leading down my drive to the last house on the left—actually, the only house, reads, "Young dog, old dog, several stupid dogs. Please drive carefully."

I need one of those plaques that read "One spoiled rotten dog lives here," except it needs to be qualified and read "two dogs and one cat." And that's just inside. Outside, well we already know there are young, old and stupid dogs living there.

You see the paw prints covering me? That's because my cat and

Introduction

dogs walk all over me. And I like it just fine.

So, if you want to talk to your dog and read to your cat, go right ahead. It's not only therapeutic, it beats talking to yourself.

Barbara Sharik 12/25/09

Author's Notes: Overview of *BooCat Unleashed*

Laced with humor and a medley of outspoken old lady opinions formed from a lifetime of experiences while living Life in the Last Lane at my home-place, Wit's End Comedy Club in rural northeast Louisiana, the book *BooCat Unleashed* is a chronicle featuring a thrice-rejected, emotionally conflicted kitten I adopted following the deaths on the same day of my mother and my 13-year old cat.

BooCat Unleashed is an inspirational journey: complicated cat meets complex old woman who together create the glue to patch up glaring gaps, mend rips and tears in each other's emotional psyches. With every stitch sewn, humor flows making the voyage more remarkable than the average human-pet relationship. It could be called a biography of a cat. It's also a handbook for cat owners, rich with accurate facts including cat phrases and superstitions. It's the quintessential animal book touching on an array of creatures and critters crossing the path of the new cat.

Eighteen years since the death of my son, there's a constant lingering ache time cannot erase. Then, because my daughter lives in another state, my siblings and granddaughter several thousand miles away, I exist in a tumbling down country home, my nearest neighbor a very long stone's throw away. My heart broken one time too many, there's no romance in my life.

Despite my mostly solitary life, there's comfort caring for a hand-

Author's Notes

ful of rescue yard-dogs and sharing my home with several old pets ranging from age 8 to 18. And me. Past retirement age, poor health, working a couple low-paying jobs to make frayed ends meet, I accepted that I'd likely be living from paycheck-to-paycheck for the rest of my humdrum life. However, keeping a positive attitude, finding humor in all things, I didn't consider myself in a rut, more a comfort zone. Although keeping company with pets provides contentment, it isn't like watching an early morning sunrise with a lover by my side or vocalizing what's in my heart and on my mind.

Then, in walks BooCat. Once on the scene, my modicum of contentment turns into a roller-coaster ride full of adventure. What started as a household of old pets and echoingly empty rooms, changed overnight. With the adoption and unleashing of BooCat, through a topsy-turvy period of adjustment, both my new cat and I are given second chances. Together, we discover there are no limits on the capacity to give and receive love.

The acquisition of BooCat changed life from ordinary to extraordinary. Since her arrival there are no dull days; everyday a journey into the unknown. She made me rethink having fallen into a rut, letting life pass me by. There was the time she rescued the whole family from the jaws of a poisonous copperhead snake. She beheaded an intrusive mouse housebreaker. Admittedly, she isn't a good bird owner and has a stash of bird feathers known as Boo's Bounty. She's rounded up crickets and even unearthed a millipede. She and Chihuahua TacoBelle enjoy a Mexican standoff vying for the alpha position.

In between she snuggles up to Rosie licking her from one end of her long dachshund body to the other like a Mamma cat with its baby. She has an automatic purr-button activated upon the slightest human touch. She's my seeing-eye cat, leading me from room to room, wrapping herself round and round my ankles. She is love.

The book, an ideal read for animal lovers of all ages, is sprinkled with stories surrounding BooCat's antics. Chapters cover everything from flea circuses, Monarch butterfly migration and the wonderful world of wild birds; ghosts and mysterious orbs, interspersed with delightful dog tales. Every chapter touches hearts and provides entertaining learning sessions. It's filled with referenced and relevant facts not just about cats, but about dogs, birds, butterflies and even fish— all the animals with which BooCat intermingles during her everyday activities while turning our household upside down.

Both sad and tender moments are weaved into this tale of triumph over adversities that will leave readers smiling with pleasure. Unlike many animal stories, this one comes with a happy ending. Tears might be shed along the way, but they are soon overshadowed by laughter at this extraordinary cat's ability to bring magic into the lives of everybody she meets.

The tumultuous emotional existence that was this orphan cat's life, the book will reveal once unleashed, is soon packed to a positive capacity, and at the same time she filled my empty heart and magnified my monotonous life too.

What a cat!

BooCat Unleashed is a combination of genres and categories; a kaleidoscope of all things popular. It is nonfiction and includes continuous, breath of fresh air humor interspersed with attention-grabbing, thought-provoking contemporary opinions.

The modern version of the "everything you always wanted to know" book, it is jam-packed throughout with practical how-to particulars and accurate animal and ecological facts combined with charming old wives tales, legends and lore.

A motivational volume, while generously sprinkled with emotional tears, offers self-help that is certain to equal personal success. It puts forward instructions on how-to over-come disparity.

The book is above all else a make-you-smile feel-good, happily-ever-after biography of a thrice-rejected, emotionally conflicted cat and an old lady who discover life isn't always fair or just but by taking chances and making bold choices, love really can conquer all.

Genre

Because *BooCat Unleashed* does not fit into any single category—it is a blending of many books, this makes it different from any other animal book on the market.

The multitude of subjects covered include, but are not limited to:

Cats: basic cat care, cat superstitions, the origin of cat phrases, cat breeds, cat history, cat quirks and what they mean.

Dogs: Mini tales about many dogs who come into BooCat's life including outside rescue dogs and TacoBelle a Chuihuahua and Rosie a Dachshund.

Author's Notes

Snakes: Witness BooCat saving the family from the jaws of a Copperhead Snake; and learn all about copperheads.

Birds: All about feeding the flocks, what makes Purple Martins unique and all about the two birds that live with BooCat.

Fleas: Everything a pet owner needs to know about the danger of fleas but also, learn about Flea Circuses, flea humor and even a flea poem.

Orbs and Ghosts: The supernatural is touched upon offering food for thought.

Mice: Read "The Night Before Christmas" that includes a mouse in the house.

Governor Jindal: Meet the governor of Louisiana the day BooCat joins the author's household.

Hummingbirds: Are Hummingbirds really Fairies instead of birds?

Monarch Butterflies: No other creature on this earth does what the Monarch Butterfly does—read about this unique phenomenal and irrational event.

Luna Moth: The Luna Moth has no mouth—it's lifespan as a moth is approximately 10 days.

Snail Invasion: Does putting out a pie tin filled with beer eliminate snails?

Contents

Introduction	v
Author's Notes	x
Prologue	xix
1 The Touching of God's Finger	1
2 Crossing the Rainbow Bridge	10
3 Yo Quiero Tacobelle	15
4 Second-Hand Rosie	20
5 Granny's Gizzy	23
6 No Time for Tears	26
7 Ancient Lucky Charms	29
8 Watering the Gladness Garden	34
9 Happiness is a New Kitten	38
10 Rockin' to the Oldies	44
11 Discovering a Castle Called Home	48
12 New Cat Needs a Name	54
13 Carnivora, Felidae, Felis, Catus	57
14 Breathing Easier	63
15 How BooCat Got Her Name	73
16 How Rosie Lost Her Bounce	77
17 Did You Hear the One About Opporknockety?	80
18 Good Help is Hard to Find	84
19 No One Sends Me Flowers Anymore	87
20 The Seeing-Eye Cat	94
21 Wit's End Comedy Club	100
22 More Than "X" Marks the Spot	107
23 The Bold and the Boo-Tiful BooCat is the Bomb	111
24 When Boocat Transforms into Bagheera, the Jungle Book Black Panther	116
25 The Incredible BooCat	126
26 BooCat is Not a Good Bird Owner	135

27	BooCat Quirks	141
28	Sowing Seeds and Planting Daffodils	150
29	Making a Home For BooCat and Family	157
30	Growing the Family	160
31	Training BooCat	171
32	Cats are Venus, Dogs are Mars, and Men are Impossible	182
33	Men Can't Help It	188
34	BooCat is Too Smart to Make Resolutions	195
35	Growing Old Disgracefully	200
36	Candy is Sweet But Not So Smart	204
37	The Fearless Flea	208
38	The Distinctive Dachshund	212
39	Cheeto's Mysterious Road Trip	215
40	The Survival of Buddy	221
41	Edibility Depends Upon the Degree of Scorching	227
42	Just How Contagious is Yawning?	233
43	The Mockingbird	237
44	Laptops and LAP Dogs	242
45	The Cheerful Chihuahua	245
46	Cheap Chihuahuas For Sale	251
47	The Fun of Feeding Flocks and Bird Watching	255
48	The Case of the Missing Genes	266
49	BooCat Would Rather be Fishing	270
50	A Mouse in the House	273
51	Yeek!	277
52	The Saga of the Snail Assault	285
53	Magnificent Monarchs and Lovely Lunas	289
54	My Fids Are My Soul Mates	294
55	The Passing of the Alarm Torch	297
56	Who Turned Out the Lights?	301
57	Almost Sleeping Single in a Double Bed	307
58	Catnapping	314
59	Declaration of Independence	320
60	The Dedicated Dachshund	325
61	How Rosie Saved My Life	333
62	The World Needs More Dog Sense	336
63	If I Didn't Have Dogs	340
64	Priceless Moments	345

Contents

65	What One Day May Bring, Another Day May Take Away	354
66	Night Before Christmas at Wit's End	363
67	Home is Where the Cat Is	367
68	*BooCat Unleashed*: The Movie	373
69	Don't Eat the Yellow Snow	377
70	The Cat Toy	385
71	In the Eye of the Beholder	393
72	Retail Surgery	398
73	A Moment in Time Remembered Forever	403
	Epilogue	408
	Bibliography	412
	Acknowledgment	414
	About the Author	416

BooCat
Unleashed

by Barbara Sharik

Prologue

"A common cat does not exist." (Matt Warner)

The year was 1952—The location, England.

There have been original purebred animals around for centuries. But not all purebreds have been the real thing from day one. Some were manmade, created as it were. Some on purpose, some accidentally. The making of a new breed of cat takes due diligence and determination. There's a bit of experimentation involved. No Bunsen burners and test tubes. No keys and kites. But experimental or accidental nonetheless. Genetics.

One such example of an accidental creation of a new breed happened when a British woman mated a black shorthaired Persian-Siamese hybrid with a Chocolate Seal Point Siamese. With fairytale overtones, a single solid brown male kitten was born from that brief love affair.

Instead of getting mad, the owner got glad. When the mixed-up chocolate mistake grew to adulthood, the owner located another Chocolate Point Siamese and the wedding was on. Accounts of the new breed's origin varies depending on who's relating the tale; some details have either been misremembered or lost in the translation of retelling.

Like a famous chef's secret recipe in the making and baking, this particular cat-story's often been repeated in mysterious and hushed tones. Best that can be discerned, there were a few more exotic pairings where a Burmese entered into the mix with a perfect brown kitten as the end result.

This perfect brown kitten became the first Havana Brown registered in England. It was so-called for its color that so identically resembles the famous Havana cigar.

The name caused some confusion and consternation over the years about the breed's country of original. Folks automatically believed the cat to have come from Cuba. Because of this, the English tried to change the name to Chestnut Brown, but because it had already been well established as Havana Brown, the effort failed.

This perfect brown kitten was the progenitor of the original strain of Havana Browns popular today. According to the Cat Fanciers' Association, in addition, in the United States, other Havana bloodlines were developed using the same genetic principles that included the crossing of Chocolate Point Siamese and Russian Blues as a preliminary point.

Following the trail in the establishment of this new breed, a California breeder imported the first Havana Browns to the United States in 1956. The new breed was first shown in the United States in 1959. It is officially recognized by the Cat Fancier Association (CFA).

Each purebred cat has specifics peculiar to that breed. The Havana has a short-to-medium length, non-agouti coat that's a rich Havana Cigar brown. Even its whiskers are brown and its eyes are large and green.

Referred to as elegant, the breed is intelligent, responsive and spirited. It's playful, yet coy. Quiet, even though the Siamese played a part in its genetic makeup and Siamese are not known as a quiet breed. The Havana lacks the demanding voice of the Siamese. Everything about the Havana is a positive.

Because they're purebred cats complete with pedigrees, Havana's aren't likely to be found loitering in back alleys or available for adoption at the local humane society.

On the opposite pole from the purebred cat is the alley cat. The non-purebred. The common house cat.

Resembling the Havana in every way but color, a young black kitten in need of a home and carries no fancy pedigree, walks into the room.

A domestic shorthair.
The Havana was man-made. The domestic shorthair was cat-made. It just happened. Two strangers in the night and 63 days later, Viola! A domestic shorthair is born May 8, 2009.

Domestics come in many colors. Due to a wide genetic background, they also come in an array of patterns, hair types and physical builds and personalities.

Domestics far outnumber purebreds and to adopt one, often means saving its life.

Whereas the Havana's smooth glossy coat is a rich mahogany or chestnut brown, an apt description of the orphan cat's coat would be a lustrous, slick, glossy, even-shade that's so completely black it shines like a china figurine dipped in a vat of only the finest quality of linseed oil.

The whiskers, nose and pads of its feet are black, just as the Havana's are brown. There's not a single white hair, nor is a tabby pattern discerned under certain light. They're each solidly colored: one black, one brown.

The common house cat's responsive eyes are brilliant yellow instead of the vivid green of the Havana. Each beautiful in their own way.

The black rescue cat's sharp muzzle and long, lithe body with its whiplike tail is again similar to the Havana in every detail but color. Show the two cats side-by-side in silhouette and they'd appear related; as twins, or even as one repeated by trickery.

Both the purebred Havana and the domestic shorthair are quiet. The black cat rarely meows. When it does, it's so soft, hard-of-hearing ears can barely perceive it.

Both cats are sleekly muscled, yet fine-boned, asserting incredible agility and speed. The orphan cat's a perfect predator, displaying an amazing ability to catch whatever prey crosses its path including capturing and killing stray molted bird feathers. Perhaps a Havana Brown would find stalking live prey rather uncivilized, beneath its obvious royal-like manner.

The black cat would beg to differ as to its uncouthness; being an expert at the sport. It's always proud of the abilities at which it excels. No doubt logic would have the domestic declaring, "I'm a cat, after all. Cats catch things."

Personality-wise, the fact that the Havana's described as playful, amusing itself alone with any object that attracts its attention, one would think they were talking about the black cat. Clowning in play, any object will do. Or not. The black cat can leap, swirl and have fun with imaginary objects as well as something tangible.

The Havana is a one-person cat. This trait's found in the black cat as well; whether born and bred or because of its unstable beginning; it would be hard to say. Now that it's found a permanent home, as with the Havana, it's proving to be extraordinarily faithful.

The Havana breed rarely abandons itself to great shows of affection—too dignified to show unadulterated affection and too prim and proper to kill bird feathers. Unlike the Havana, the black cat does show enormous warmth toward its owner; whether a part of its built-in personality or grateful for the rescue, is hard to say.

The Havana Brown is a pedigreed purebred cat. The black cat is not. Even lacking a fancy pedigree, the orphan kitten's got every positive characteristic found in the Havana Brown, plus a few extras. Alley cat genes, it's got all the positive attributes of a purebred cat except the paperwork.

A positive characteristic found in all felines, is maintaining a superb independent spirit while sharing their lives with their human counterparts. There's a certain wildness in every cat that makes them very intriguing and most wonderful.

The Touching of God's Finger

1

"There is honor in being a dog" (Aristotle)

I'm an orphan.

Oh, I wasn't always an orphan. I had a father—a retired Army officer and highly decorated veteran of World War II—who died September 8, 1999. And then my mother died too.

That's when I became an orphan.

The definition of an orphan is a child bereaved of both parents. Does it matter when parents die? Or at what age someone's left parentless? It would seem age is irrelevant. It's the emptiness created with the loss of both parents. Certainly, when parents are gone, one becomes a child bereaved of parents no matter the age.

How did I get here from there? Kinky Friedman calls it stepping on a rainbow. What happened was that thirteen-year-old Hershey Kitty died the same day my Mom did, November 21, 2008. I sort of figured he decided to keep her company on their journey crossing that Rainbow Bridge.

Mom fell asleep the night before and didn't wake up again. Hershey had begun to suffer a few days prior; before we had a chance to visit our pet-family veterinarian. It wasn't a put your finger on it kind of thing, but he acted not quite right. I didn't expect him to die, despite his advanced age.

Because Hershey had lived with me since he was just a kitten, his passing was on a par with Mom's. For all my sixty-four years, she'd been in my life. For all Hershey's thirteen years, I'd been in his.

Mom hadn't been recently ill so her death was a shock. She'd suffered a spell with her heart on several occasions, but always pulled through. It'd been more than seven years since her mastectomy with no recurrences. She'd undergone cataract surgery shortly after the breast cancer discovery and treatment. Prior to these incidents all within the last ten years of her life, she never took even one pill. You could probably count on one hand the number of times she'd visited a physician on her own account. She was amazingly healthy. By age seventy-five, most people are popping pills like candy. She had just turned eighty-four a few weeks before she died.

The first of two heart incidents happened on her birthday, November 6, 2005. She wound up in intensive care and then spent time at a rehab hospital. This experience left her so weakened, it was obvious she couldn't come back home at this time. She needed more constant care than I could provide. Because I worked each day and we lived so far out in the country, Mom would be completely isolated day in and day out. Country living was fine while her health was good. It scared me when it was failing. This was when she moved to Oak Woods Home for the Elderly.

As she recovered and settled in, she was elderly, but active. Mom had virtually lived alone after she and my father divorced and then after each of the children made separate lives for themselves: brothers Michael James "Jimmy" and David Paul and sister Janet Lynn. A very independent person, not necessarily by choice, she stepped up to the plate and managed to hit the ball when necessary.

She came from an era when fathers worked and mothers stayed home and took care of the household and children. Suddenly, when my father left, she had to get a job to take care of herself and the children. By then I was married and living elsewhere.

Many years later history repeated itself and I too found myself left alone with children to raise, necessitating the fulltime job becoming a lifetime job; managing emotionally and financially alone. I knew then what Mom went through; and how difficult it can be when the rug of security is ripped from beneath what had been a steadfast life. Such circumstances leaves one floundering.

1 / The Touching of God's Finger

The worst part is the initial surprise of being dumped by somebody who was to have been your life partner. And through no fault of your own his head's turned one day and you and the children are forgotten. It doesn't matter to how many other people this may happen, in your wildest dreams you never saw it happening to you. It takes a while to recover.

Mom recovered. So did I. The thing is, she was always there for me, even when there was far away. A phone call, a letter, a visit, a physical connection. Emotionally, we were intertwined always in the ways of a mother and daughter; her blood streaming through my veins, the ways of the heart.

If someone fell short reciprocating on occasion it was me. There were times I was selfish with my spirit, too wrapped up in my own life—but she never left me. Because of the miles between us over the years, I may have spent times in my life suffering the out of sight, out of mind syndrome. But not often. Never too often. The three years we were in Germany were the most difficult because to call by telephone was costly. We depended upon letters for constant contact. This was years before cell phones, before bargain International calling and certainly before e-mail.

There was the time my son Tony, at only ten months of age, contracted bacterial meningitis and wasn't expected to live. Because this happened while we were living in Germany, it was particularly frightening. So far from home; but Mom, on the other end of the telephone, gave me strength.

The thing is, she may not have had the answers if I was in need, but her emotional presence was sufficient. Like a rock set on the corner of a picnic tablecloth to keep it from blowing up and away, she held me grounded. Even with lack of her actual material manifestation, the imperceptible bond between mother and daughter that allowed us to invisibly touch from afar enabled me a moment to back up, take a deep breath and punt. Sometimes punting was enough to get me through a bad day. We don't always need a touchdown; sometimes just gaining a few yards will do.

Later in life when she moved to Louisiana at my request, we had quality time together every single day. But before that, when she lived alone, I imagined she had to be lonesome at times. She had her newspapers, her crossword puzzles. She had her other children—Jimmy and Jan were especially attentive. But even still, she had so much time on her hands in a world that waited for no one and catered to no one. She never learned to drive; so she walked everywhere she went. Fortunately, she lived relatively close to the Harundale Mall for many years and worked there following her divorce.

Harundale Mall, built by James Rouse and Company, located at the intersection of Ritchie Highway and Aquahart Road in Glen Burnie, Maryland, was the first climate controlled fully enclosed shopping center east of the Mississippi River. Three-hundred-fifty-thousand square feet located on a twenty-five acre tract nine miles south of downtown Baltimore, it was the second covered and enclosed shopping center in the country to be officially referred to as a mall.

With a fountain and tropical planter at one end and a thirty-five foot tall bird aviary at the other, it was truly an exceptional premier shopping destination. Gone now, a Facebook page dedicated to its memory has been developed where people who summon Harundale Mall up as part of their childhood, their coming of age, visit and reminisce. Mom, me, my brothers and sister, we were there for the grand opening October 1, 1958. So was then Senator of Massachusetts, John F. Kennedy. Dad was overseas; in Turkey.

Walking to and from work no matter the weather, late one night Mom slipped on a patch of ice on her way home after closing the shop where she worked at the mall. She learned the next day that her ankle was broken after she'd walked home on it and spent the night with fever and chills.

Another time she was robbed. She worked at a dry cleaners and shoe repair shop. A man came in the front of the store, reached over and grabbed the cash register and ran out the door with it. This was back when cash registers were large, bulky and heavy. He ended up dropping it when people took chase. While the tale was interesting, it only reminded me how alone she was, and how exposed to the rough and tough elements of life.

And because she never drove she always had to walk every where. Whatever she purchased—milk, bread, potatoes, canned goods—she had to carry all the way home in bags in her arms. Through every sort of weather conditions. It rained. It snowed. It was iced over. The temperatures climbed into three-digits. It was all the same. It wasn't a very easy life in many ways. I wanted more for her. She deserved

1 / *The Touching of God's Finger*

more. She'd sacrificed for each of her children in ways that can never be completely and accurately reckoned. That's why I invited her to move to Louisiana.

And then, her health spiraled and once more, I moved her from her comfortable surroundings into the nursing home. Even though Mom complained on occasion after moving into Oak Woods, because she missed the independence she'd developed over the years, I saw the move as very beneficial.

I contend it was a positive even after she considered herself well enough to be back on her own. She had forgetful moments. They were coming more regularly. Her doctor indirectly diagnosed her with early stages of dementia; nothing so severe as Alzheimer's and far from being advanced. Still, it was starting.

When dementia attacks, the person begins to unlearn everything. When she stopped being able to remember how to set her clock herself, the signs were there.

I would've worried she might leave a pan on the stove cooking. I would've worried she might slip and fall. She did actually spend several hours in the bathtub one day before I became aware of her predicament.

When she didn't answer her telephone, I rushed to her door. The screen was locked and Chuck pulled it loose. She said she hadn't fallen in the tub; she'd sat down to enjoy a bath rather than a shower, and couldn't get back up and out. This wasn't long before her move to Oak Woods. To see a loved one decline tears your heart into a million tiny pieces that never fit back in place again. And then comes the time when there are no do-overs. We don't get do-overs. When a loved one crosses the rainbow bridge, all we have are nagging memories of not having handled everything as well as it should have been handled; and regrets because we didn't.

Being ignorant and being sorry doesn't make it go away. Guilt overrides any excuses.

To have a better understanding and not lose patience when the person you remembered as brilliant, suddenly can't remember how to do something she'd been doing all her life, it's natural to grow impatient. I know I lost tolerance at times and had I been more aware of what was happening, I could have handled everything better. I've read about dementia and Alzheimer's since then, regretting that I hadn't read about these debilitating diseases sooner.

When she forgot, she couldn't help it.

Being at Oak Woods meant she no longer had to cook, do laundry, wheel her trash can to the corner, remember to take her medication or be alone during the day all day every day. Living there opened the door to an emotionally healthy environment. It provided her the opportunity to make many new friends among a variety of people and to participate in daily activities of the best kind. I'm so sad she's gone, but I know she was well cared for and experienced more pleasure during those last several years than she had for many previously.

I of course saw her every single day before she entered the nursing facility. After she moved in I made a point of calling her daily and visiting her often. It was a pleasant experience for both of us. I visited on Saturday mornings to sit with her while she played Bingo. I attended the many special occasions at her side: a Las Vegas Night, the performance of an Elvis impersonator who sang up close and personal to her, Christmas dinner parties together, a Prom Night at which she was all dressed up, hair done, nails polished, and had her photo taken, and more. So many more.

The administrative staff at Oak Woods kept activities ongoing. Singing groups came several nights a week. Because Hank Williams Jr. had married a local girl, creating local ties, his children occasionally came and entertained. The facility had a country store, café, beauty parlor, activity room, cable television in every room, and provided buffet-style meals.

When I first moved to Jones, we joined the Bonita Methodist Church. The ladies of the church were looking for an ongoing charitable project. Having been involved as president of the Non-Commissioned Officer's Wives Clubs in both Germany and Colorado Springs, I shared a successful project idea: we played Bingo with the Veterans in the VA Hospital there. We brought the Bingo game, provided prizes and helped the patients play once a month.

Playing Bingo at Oak Woods was so successful, the Bonita church members are still conducting the games some forty years later. Even my children grew up helping with Oak Woods Bingo. I was very familiar with Oak Woods as a nursing home long before Mom moved in.

Because Oak Woods is animal-friendly and subscribes to the prin-

1 / The Touching of God's Finger

ciple that pet-therapy's a positive thing and that pets have an optimistic effect on human health and psychology, a couple cockatiels chatted cheerfully in the living room style lobby. Mom always stopped to talk to the birds whenever she passed by. Likewise, a number of residents brought their cats and dogs to live with them at Oak Woods. Naturally, dogs needed to be walked, but the staff goes the extra mile to provide for these needs. This practice alone moved the choice of a place for Mom to live way up in my estimation.

It's such a good thing to allow pets. The nursing home is often an elderly person's last home. It's only right they be allowed to share that home with their loving pets if at all possible. Scientists have found residents are less depressed and not so lonesome when allowed animal companionship.

I didn't miss any events, nor did Mom. I was so at ease knowing she was under constant professional care. A burden of worry was lifted. Old and established, a non-profit, with a sterling reputation, many area residents made it their home in their later years.

Usually Theresa and Carla visited on Thanksgiving day. We celebrated this my favorite holiday at my house. But the year before Mom passed away, Theresa and Carla couldn't come until the weekend following Thanksgiving day—a work schedule conflict—therefore, I spent most of Thanksgiving day with Mom at Oak Woods. Everyone came to my house that next weekend.

That day she and I watched the Macy Day Thanksgiving Parade and what had become our favorite Thanksgiving tradition, the Purina Dog Show. The Oak Woods staff did a superb turkey, dressing and pumpkin pie meal with all the trimmings. We made plans to do it again the next year. We both looked forward to it. I'd made arrangements with the kitchen staff; we would eat in Mom's room so we could again watch the dog show and parade.

Best laid plans sometimes go array. Mom died a few days before Thanksgiving. It takes my breath just to think of the emptiness created by her death. It's still my favorite holiday, but it wreaks of sadness with conflicting emotional memories.

As I watched the dog show the next year, no one knows just how much I yearned for Mom to be sitting there with me. We always compared notes and picked the winner. I inherited my love of animals quite naturally. She loved them too.

Just as Easter rips my heart apart because on April 11, 1992—a short time before Easter that year—my son Tony was killed in a traffic accident. This left his everyone—Tony's widow Cindy and three-year-old daughter Alisha, my beautiful daughter Theresa and my husband at the time, Chuck, Mom and I, to sit down to Easter dinner together, but Tony's chair was empty. So were our hearts.

For the years since Tony's death, and now Mom's, these holidays are lacking. Certain things will always remind us of lost loved ones. Fragrances. A song. Holidays. Always holidays.

That first Thanksgiving after Mom and Hershey died, there was only TacoBelle, Rosie, Gizzy and me still standing, so to speak. Theresa, Carla and Lance left afterward to return to their home in Gulfport, Mississippi. Even Chuck, dear sweet Chuck—an ex-husband of the best kind—returned to his nearby abode. Does it sound strange to say I could hear the quiet, the stillness? The quiet was overwhelmingly palpable. It almost smothered me.

How can quiet be so heavy?

Standing in a suddenly empty room that only moments before was full of laughter and warmth, I was suddenly aware of interminable time. Life goes on minute by minute, hour by hour, day by day. Each breath I took was like a ticking clock. Tick-tock. Breathe-in, breathe-out. The very walls that just a moment ago resounded with chatter and cheer, now echoed with hollowness. There were dirty dishes. There was homemade leftover turkey soup in the making on the stove. And there were the pets. But the sounds of silence was deafening.

And so, like a dog shaking off raindrops from its coat, I gave myself a mental shake. With loved ones gone, it could be a time to feel let down after the hubbub of conversation and companionship. I don't dwell on the missing parts. It's not my nature. Instead, I concentrate on the joy shared. It's a matter of self-preservation and self-survival to not let sorrow drag me down to the depths of despair. I'm a survivor if nothing else. I learned the hard way.

Admittedly, the wind's not as strong in my sails with so much quiet all too evident, but, there's always the choice. Misery is optional. So is happy reflection. I don't do holiday blahs. I select reflection.

My prayer: Lord please, a steady breeze.

If there's a moment of warmth in the air, perhaps a swish of an angel's wing, I can sigh in peace. I'm never alone. I wish I believed

1 / The Touching of God's Finger

in ghosts. In spirits. I wish I knew there's another dimension. I don't. But I believe in an inner peace.

I've had some been-there, done-that experiences. While those experiences took my breath away and knocked my socks off, the one thing that kept me going was a sense of humor. Simply put, I cried, but I didn't wallow. I hurt, but I didn't bend over. I limped, but I didn't fall down.

My daughter Theresa is the light of my life. I couldn't have picked a more perfect daughter were I given the choice of selection. I've lost people who mattered to me. No one lives as long as I have, coming in contact with as many people, without experiencing the troubling pain caused by loss. None have distressed and grieved me as acutely as the loss of my son Tony in 1992. It's not right for a child to die before his mother.

In 2002, in the blink of an eye, Jon Darlin' was gone.

Now, in 2008, I've lost my mother too. And my cat.

Eyes blink. People disappear forever.

Tony had so much more life left to live. He should be here watching his daughter Alisha grow; standing at the side of his wife, Cindy.

No one ever made me as happy as Jon. It's as though God sent an angel to take care of me and for seven-hundred-and-eleven days he breathed life into my weary soul, making me happier than I'd been in a very long time. And then God called his angel home.

He loved me. I loved him. I miss him so. I'm better for the experience; but I'm sadder for the loss.

Aging has mellowed me. It's made me more appreciative of little things in life. I know there's always room for self-improvement because it's the biggest room in my house. And so, what defined the end of a happy Thanksgiving that year after the dishes were done and soup was simmering on the stove, was to relax in my favorite chair, make a lap for Rosie and TacoBelle and with Gizzy at my feet, I remembered when Hershey Cat sat on the arm of the chair. I wondered if another cat would ever again sit there.

I ended up philosophizing a bit and settled down to read a good book at the end of the day. I was sorely missing my son, my mom and my cat. And Jon Darlin'.

Tomorrow was another day. I looked forward to tomorrow.

Crossing the Rainbow Bridge

2

"My cat, my dogs, have but one aim in life: To bestow their hearts. And I'm the lucky bestowee." (Barbara Sharik)

Often we take our mothers for granted, until we're grown and are mothers and grandmothers ourselves; then we can see how selfless our mothers were. I know this is an odd example, but it is appropriate. I love potato pancakes and it wasn't until I was grown that I realized how much work this particular dish required of Mom. She'd stand for hours first peeling and then grating potatoes and onion by hand—this was before the days of the Cuisinart—and then over a hot stove, frying enough patties for four kids and Dad to gobble up in minutes. Mom was a great cook. She baked desserts and prepared hot meals every day. I remember snow ice cream. I remember strawberry shortcake for my birthday one year. Homemade with real strawberries and real whipped cream. I remember the best potato salad.

Beds were made, clothes always clean and ironed, school lunches packed and ready, movie money on Saturdays. She attended my basketball games, PTA meetings and supplied me with art supplies when money was tight—and it was always tight. She saw that I got to Brownie and Girl Scout meetings, Sunday school and church and later she bought me the most beautiful yellow prom dress. She did everything for me.

2 / Crossing the Rainbow Bridge

I have this urge to say both thank you and I'm sorry.

Looking back, I most likely took her generous sacrifices for granted. I was a demanding child but Mom always managed. I wasn't spoiled, I was loved. And the advantages she made possible for me by often doing without so I didn't have to, helped mold me into the person I am today. There are no words to express how much I miss her. Bless Hershey for traveling with Mom so she didn't have to go alone.

Hershey Chocolate had a brother, Sterling Silver. Sterling died of a heart attack at age eight, so Hershey was an only cat for many years afterward. Hershey was the epitome of warm and fuzzy, literally. He walked across the pages of my life most surely, but slightly sadder after Sterling stepped on that rainbow. It's getting crowded down around the Rainbow Bridge.

For a long time after Sterling died Hershey wandered through the house yowling. It was a most pitiful cry. Heart wrenching, I know he was searching for his brother; wondering where, after eight years, he'd disappeared to.

It's been said when you die and go to Heaven, all the dogs and cats you've ever had in your life come running to meet you. I'll have to rent a very large space to make room for all the pets of my lifetime. There's also a tale held dear by many pet owners, although the author's unknown, and even the origin cannot be determined. The tale's about a place called Rainbow Bridge and it's just this side of Heaven. When an animal dies, this is where it's said to go.

Wikipedia, the online encyclopedia, credits the Rainbow Bridge as having been written, best guestimate, between 1980 and 1992. The theme of the prose is of a mythological place to which pets go upon death; and it's here, at Rainbow Bridge they're eventually reunited with their owners.

The first Internet mention of Rainbow Bridge was January 7, 1993. A poem was quoted from a 1992 issue of *Mid Atlantic Great Dane Rescue League Newsletter*. In turn, the newsletter credited the article as having been copied from the Akita Rescue Society of America.

Would the real author please stand up. Odd that no one's taken credit. It's such a popular legend.

Our pets aren't provided with a specific final resting place in any of our major religions. It's suggested Rainbow Bridge is similar to

Bifrost Bridge of Norse mythology. In Norse mythology, according again to Wikipedia, Bifrost is a burning rainbow bridge between Midgard, the world, and Asgard, the realm of the gods. It appears in the Poetic Edda, compiled in the thirteenth century from earlier traditional sources. In this prose, the bridge ends in heaven at the residence of the god Heimdallr, who guards it. Scholars have proposed the bridge may have originally represented the Milky Way and have noted parallels between it and another bridge in Norse mythology, Giallarbru. There is no mention of the Bifrost Bridge having to do with animals and beloved pets. The only similarity is the mention of it being a rainbow bridge and connecting the mortal world with heaven.

Having a connection with a beloved pet at time of death was discovered when pyramids were found to contain the mummified remains of pets resting with deceased occupants. People of all walks of life as far back as can be determine, have had a bond with their pets in death as well as life.

The original Rainbow Bridge tale, circulated worldwide and found on many websites, tells of a green meadow paradise located just outside of Heaven before one enters there. Rainbow Bridge is both the name of the meadow and the bridge connecting it to Heaven. It proclaims when a pet dies it goes to the meadow where it's cured of any illness or injury. It runs freely, playing with other pets, happy, except for missing the love and companionship of its owner, who's still on earth.

Upon the owner's death, he or she crosses the meadow on his or her journey to Heaven and there they meet, are reunited and cross the Rainbow Bridge together into Heaven. They are never again parted. It's a comforting belief, obviously an emotional desire. Something to hold onto at a time of profound grief.

Now, had I been conceiving this Rainbow Bridge, with an artist's palette in mind, I'd have taken those plain green pastures and turned them into meadows full of flowers of every color and kind. There'd be trees offering continuous shade beneath an ever-shining sun. Yet, there'd be soft showers of sparkling drops of rain which in turn would create a continuous rainbow. What is Rainbow Bridge without a rainbow?

Fluffy marshmallow clouds overhead would bring out the blue of the sky. Cats and kittens would play underneath hanging Weeping Willow branches filled with lacy leaves weaving in a gentle breeze, the sunlight flickering like the winking of fairies and fireflies. Brightly multi-colored butterflies would flit from flower to flower.

There would be clover galore. Four, five and six leaves, both pink and white varieties. And luck-of-the-Irish shamrocks. Just walking across the clover-filled meadow would be lucky.

Drops of jewel-like dew would brighten each tiny blossom.

There'd be hills to climb, rivers to forge, lakes to splash in. Waterfalls would careen from atop the hills into the lakes below, water droplets splashing like diamonds in the sun. Birds would fly chirping melodically overhead. God's eye would indeed be on every sparrow. There'd be no fences; no pens, no cages. It would be a utopia in which pets would run and play and be eternally happy.

Hey, I think I saw this place in a Walt Disney animated movie when I was a kid. Snow White and Cinderella danced by and there were fireworks exploding overhead.

Because music makes me happy, my Rainbow Bridge would have delightful tunes floating on the airwaves; uplifting, smile-making music such as "Ode To Joy" and "Greensleeves" and "Hallelujah."

In my magic place, animals would never go hungry. They'd never thirst. There'd be no more pain. They'd eternally be warm. They'd live in the lap of luxurious comfort. My version would be like the original with some extras thrown in—a good place. A perfect place.

With health restored to old and ill animals, the hurt or maimed made whole and strong again, every animal making its home at Rainbow Bridge would be content but for one small thing. As with the initial tale, these pets frolicking at Rainbow Bridge miss the special human they left behind. You see, that's the only thing wrong with cats and dogs and birds and each and every pet. They just don't live long enough. There's such a beautiful bond between a pet and its owner; when one's parted from the other, the pain is practically physical.

As with the original legend, every day all the animals romp and play together until one day one animal stops and looks up, bright eyes fixed, seeing something in the distance.

Suddenly, breaking from its playful companions, this animal runs full speed ahead, gaining momentum with each bound, all but flying across the idyllic pasture. You, the owner, have been spotted. You and your pet are reunited. The two of you will never again be parted.

Just as in your wildest dream, you receive lots of liquid sugar from your much-loved pet. You stroke, you pet, feeling the silky soft fur you never thought you'd ever again caress. Your eyes meet and so much joy is exchanged. This pet's been gone from your life far too long but you never forgot. How could you forget a pet so special? You couldn't. You didn't. And your pet didn't forget you either.

And together, in my tale of reunion, as in the original, you cross the Rainbow Bridge side-by-side. Mom and Hershey crossed that bridge together. Sterling, no doubt joined the crossing. Also Mom's beloved Sweetie Pie, a Shih Tzu and predecessor to Gizzy. And one day Gizzy would join the crew on the other side of Rainbow Bridge. Mom will be so glad to have Gizzy with her again. After so many, many years together, Gizzy will be glad too. It can be no other way.

It's a beautiful, heartwarming concept to hold onto.

A paradise where pets await their human owners was previously put forth prior to this bit of prose in *Beautiful Joe* written by Margaret Marshall Saunders and a sequel to *Beautiful Joe's Paradise*. The similarities are many, except in Saunder's story, instead of crossing a bridge, owner and pet continue onto Heaven by way of a balloon.

There's a natural Rainbow Bridge National Monument in Arizona and a Rainbow Bridge legend told by the Chumash People of Santa Cruz Island.

It's important for our psyches that there be some form of closure when a loved one, including a beloved pet, passes. However they travel, the important thing is that they do. Together. And look up. Waiting on the other side of the Rainbow Bridge, stands Mom's grandson and my son, Tony.

Yo Quiero Tacobelle

3

"Do not disturb the sleeping dog." (Alessandro Allegri)

I have TacoBelle, a human Chihuahua in fur clothing. She came into my life during the height of the Taco Bell Restaurant commercials whose campaign featured an eight pound, eleven-inch-tall Chihuahua named Gidget as its mascot. Gidget was famous for saying—because Gidget was a talking Chihuahua—"Yo quiero Taco Bell (I love Taco Bell).

An overnight media sensation, I contend the Taco Bell commercials featuring the little ChiChi dog were the best ever produced by any entity before or since. She was probably the hottest little tamale spokesperson—err, I mean animal— since Spuds MacKenzie barked the praises of Budweiser beer. Never underestimate the public's love for animals.

Kudus to the advertising agency that came up with the idea and bah-humbug to the Taco Bell executive who pulled the plug. It was definitely a surprise move when it was announced that the talking pup that barked "Drop the Chalupa" was being dropped.

What were they thinking?

What they were thinking was that Taco Bell sales were down two years in a row. With a backup and punt, it was hasta la vista little Mexican talking dog. Although there'd been a few protests from Hispanic groups indicating the ads weren't politically correct customers of Taco Bell bought over thirteen-million stuffed Taco Bell dog toys. That sounds like, upon reflection, taco sales may've been down but stuffed animal sales were out the window and over the doghouse roof.

The ads were never intended to be distasteful or derogatory, and luckily, the majority of people didn't take offence. Sadly, this year or last, I read super star Gidget stepped on a rainbow and is now nibbling on Chalupa's at Rainbow Bridge.

All that aside, my own little TacoBelle star had me at "Woof." Or maybe it was at "Yo Quiero." Intermittently, she thinks she's a Rottweiler. Read my door mat: "Protected by a Chihuahua Home Security System. 24-Hour monitoring." This is true.

Poor darlin', she has double hernias. They grew as she grew. I considered surgery, but instead decided not to put her through that if we could control the situation; so far we have.

Actually, TacoBelle probably doesn't realize she herself is a canine. I sometimes have to remind her to wag more, bark less. I decipher the threats she snarls and barks when peering out the window at the yard dogs as something like, "If I was out there instead of in here you'd be Taco filling!"

TacoBelle exhibits the individual characteristics that cause some creatures, large or small, to establish dominance over others. It's a territorial authoritativeness that provides them influence. TacoBelle came complete with this built-in alpha factor factory-installed in her genes. In plain English—and I have to use plain English because I failed to learn Spanish when I had the opportunity—she's a born leader of the pack. Because she's the Alpha pet, everybody else belongs in the Beta group, myself included.

She might be little but that's never bothered her. She thinks she's tough. But tough as she is, she's the number one licker in the house—dousing me with licks of love and liquid sugar on a regular basis. She understands the request: Gimme a kiss, and she will in a heartbeat. With pure pleasure. Fair warning: Don't say it unless you mean it because once a kiss request's voiced aloud, you cannot take it back. You're going to get kissed TacoBelle style.

TacoBelle earned her continuing education degree—in that she continually educates me. I was sitting at the computer and she came to me, stood on her hind legs and pawed my leg, barking loudly and persistently. This was earlier in 2009.

I told her I'd feed her as soon as I reached a stopping place. I talk to her like a person because she listens like a person and appears to understand most human talk. She actually understands people talk better than I understand dog talk. This was a good example of my misunderstanding, when if I'd been paying attention, I'd have known. I thought she was telling me she was hungry. She can be very bossy. When it's bedtime, she's vocal. When she's hungry, she's vocal.

It turns out she's also vocal when there's danger afoot.

She was so persistent, I couldn't concentrate so I gave in and said "Okay." I got up and was heading for the kitchen when she veered off in another direction.

"If you want supper, you better come here," I admonished.

She admonished right back, indicating if I wanted to know what she wanted to tell me, I'd best go to where she was going.

The proverbial light bulb finally went on in my head. Must've been a TacoBulb. I headed toward her and she lead me to one of those sticky mouse pads I'd set out.

Wit's End Comedy Club was surrounded by cotton fields for thirty-five years. That was when Cotton was King. Cotton's fallen from American Grace since it can be imported cheaper than American Farmers can grow it. Never would I have believed cotton wouldn't be king; it'd held that position for as long as it'd been grown all across the South. But now, corn has taken its place.

If you've never been in corn country, you may not realize how suffocating it can be. My house is now surrounded by corn during each farming season. Corn grows high and it's planted thick. All around my oasis it's as though a natural fence has been erected. I can't see out and the air can barely get it.

But worse, after harvesting the corn, the farmer comes back and burns off his fields. For months the little field mice have been dining heartily. Then suddenly not only is their source cut down, but their homes are on fire. They run lickety-split in search of a new residence. Where do they go? My abode. Dog food. Water. A million places to set up housekeeping. Even better, these little rascals can climb up—straight up—the brick walls of my house, chew just the slightest bit of wood where the fascia board meets the brick, and slither into my attic.

Once in the attic, the most ingenious figure out how to get into the lower parts of the walls where they chew their way into my living quarters.

You've seen the cartoon mouse hole at the base of a wall? That's exactly what they look like. These adorable little mice chew right through molding creating a very handsome doorway. Suddenly, they aren't so adorable any more.

But even without that, there are other points of entry. Where a wire comes down into the heating/air conditioning unit room, or in a closet. Stuff them with steel wool and it's good for a portion of the season only. These country mice sharpen their teeth on steel wool.

And thus, I've chosen to use the horribly cruel sticky mouse boards because I can handle them easier than old fashioned mouse trap. And that's where TacoBelle led me. To a sticky mouse board.

Ah, but a mouse wasn't stuck. Instead, a fairly large Rat Snake had apparently followed a mouse into the house and gotten stuck on the board and TacoBelle was alerting me.

Yikes!

Fortunately I was able to locate Chuck and he took care of the situation.

Always, when something unnerving happens regarding reptiles and various and a sundry critters, I wonder if there's a mate, a brother, a sister. Where there is one, could there be two?

Bless you, TacoBelle.

She's my heart. She never asks questions and passes no criticisms. I can say foolish things to her and she never gives me that look I might get from a human companion. Actually, she looks at me like, "Golly, you're a genius. You're absolutely right."

She's not so bad herself.

It's very cool being so adored. Because she piles the adoration on so completely, some folks in this part of the country would say I better be careful or it'll give me the big head.

I've got a habit of bestowing proper names on each of my pets, then I wind up calling them an assortment of love-names based on the moment. TacoBelle also answers to the abbreviated form, Taco. Sometimes I call her TinkerBelle, TeeBelle and just plain TeeTee. Other times I call her TeeBug and Teedle-Baum. Jon called her TockEars. Typical Chichi, she's got oversized Dumbo ears.

3 / Yo Quiero Tacobelle

My TacoBelle was born in March 1998. Another elderly pet. The youngster of the mix is Rosie, a dachshund born in 2002. Rosie was a gift from Jon. Jon, while not the only love in my life, was the love of my life. He took me to the top of the mountain and now I don't want to live in the valley ever again.

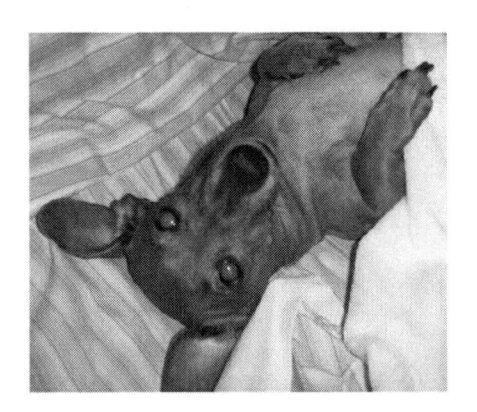

Second-Hand Rosie

4

"Three major puppy concerns: eating, playing and then eating some more."
(Iams)

Jon and I met November 10, 2000 shortly before I was scheduled for my second back surgery. There was an instantaneous emotional connection. Jon and I called it love at first sight. There was a bond formed that only death could sever.

And it did.

Seven-hundred-and-eleven days after we met and became as one in every manner possible—heart, body and soul—Jon, at age 48, on October 22, 2002, the date of my late son Tony's birth (October 22, 1966), suffered a massive heart attack. As quickly as he'd come into my life, he left it.

How did I survive before Jon? How would I survive without him? Somehow I did. But I'll never forget what he brought into my life.

Jon sang to me. He loved to sing and was very talented. Every time he sang the Willie Nelson tune "You Were Always On My Mind," he'd end with "I love you, Barbara." And he did.

He sang me to sleep almost every night. Imagine having someone sing "You Are So Beautiful" to you each night? It made me feel beautiful.

Once he brought me a bouquet of hand-picked wild flowers and said, "I'm your number one fan, Barbara."

He called me Barbara Dear. I called him Jon Darlin'.

Shortly before he died, we were in Monroe on our way to Lowe's Building Supplies when Jon spotted a pickup truck parked on the side of the road with a cardboard sign lettered "Dachshunds For Sale." Jon's Li'l Bit, a black and tan dachshund, died several months into our relationship. I'd also owned dachshunds. They're one of my favorite breeds. We considered ourselves dachshund-people so it was only natural that Jon found it impossible to drive by without checking out the pups. It was even more natural that he was compelled to purchase one. And since the little bitty six-week old puppy was solid red, I named her Rosie, as in "Roses are Red."

Rosie's had to contend with a multitude of love-names—everything from The Rose Dog or RoseBud to Rosalee; from RoseGirl and Rosie-Posey to Second-hand Rosie in honor of having been bought off the back of a pickup truck on the side of the road.

Also, she gets referred to as Bent-Tail Rosie on occasion. Always in loving tones. The guy Jon purchased her from said her tail was broken by her brother while at play. Me and Dr. White are more inclined to think it happened when somebody closed the door on her tail. It has a definite right angled bend in it not too far from the tip end. It doesn't deter from her beauty, but rather just gives her character. Second-hand, bent-tailed Rosie; she's such a sweetie.

Hershey preceded both TacoBelle and Rosie coming into my household. They all got along just fine. Let me clarify that. So long as everybody understood the tiniest critter was the boss, everything was good.

Rosie, a green-eyed sweetheart, developed slightly neurotic tendencies. She's troubled with nasal allergies and Intervertebral Disc Disease, the dachshund back ailment. She adores me above and beyond the normal love of a faithful pet—to the point that I cannot even go into the little girl's room without her following me although I've sworn that there's no back door, that I shall return.

Rosie was pliant and TacoBelle trained her well. As a puppy, at bedtime, Rosie wanted to play before retiring. TacoBelle snarled and Rosie assumed instantaneous invisibility by closing her eyes tight. TacoBelle sniffed Rosie's ears and eyes, turned her back, curled up and went peacefully to sleep.

Within a few minutes I spied Rosie lifting one eyelid, peeking. She turned her head ever so slightly. When she spotted TacoBelle sleeping soundly just inches from her nose, she snapped her eye shut and she too went to sleep. Rosie bowed to TacoBelle's authority: When in bed, do not play. Go to sleep.

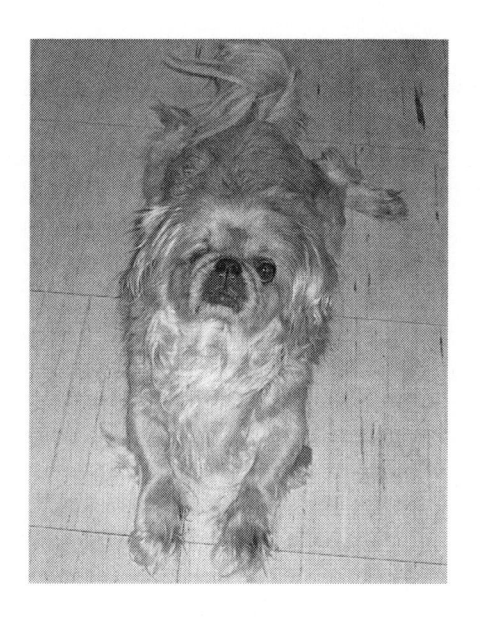

Granny's Gizzy

5

"Dogs lives are too short. Their only fault." (Agnes Sligh Turnvull)

And then there was Gizzy. She came to live with Hershey, Taco-Bell, Rose and me when Mom moved to Oak Woods in 2005. Gizzy was a delight. A Pekingese whose silky coat never developed into show-dog quality—having stayed relatively short—but a Peke nonetheless with all the good Peke traits and attributes.

Sometimes I'd refer to Gizzy, whose real name was Gizmo, as The Gizzard. I also called her Granny's Gizzy and the "One-eyed, One-toed Purple People Eater," although she was neither purple nor did she eat people, purple or otherwise. She was one-eyed, mostly blind. By the way, I never could determine if it's a people-eater that's purple or if its diet was limited to purple people.

Sometimes I called Gizzy the "Deaf, Dumb, Blind Kid" from Elton John's "Pinball Wizard," sung to her in love. She wasn't dumb. It's just that almost everything in life reminds me of a song; including Gizzy's infirmities. My mind tends to run in lyric form much of the time and it's all I can do to speak normally, without tossing in song lyrics.

If I could've sung the multiplication tables I could've learned them. For reasons beyond my meager comprehension, I know the lyrics of a million songs, yet the things teachers pounded into my head faded with time. Perhaps teachers ought to sing their lessons, with children joining in the song. I believe this method would work.

Pekingese dogs originated in the Orient and were popular among royalty. They're still very popular because they're such charming companions. Known for their amusing antics, the breed dates back to 2000 B.C. It's said the Peke was worshipped in the temples of China.

Difficult to picture when thinking of Gizzy because she'd welcome bad guys right along with good guys, but Pekes were often used ages ago as bodyguards of the Emperor. The Peke came to America in 1898 and was admitted to the American Kennel Club (AKC) registry in 1906. So, Pekingese have been around for a very long time.

Gizzy, totally irresistible and always cheerful, was born April 15, 1994. By 2009, she was a very old lady. She'd lost the one eye some years earlier through a mishap with another dog. A cataract developed on the good eye rendering her relatively blind. Although she lost most of her sight and had become deaf, she could still smell an opened a can of dog food and her nose led her right to her bowl.

The worst of all old lady tribulations befalling the kindly little dog, incontinence became a continuing problem. I mopped and I bathed. She peed and she smiled. Then she peed some more.

By the first of August 2009 she started losing her balance. She whimpered on occasion. Once she yowled and became disoriented and scared me wholeheartedly. Eventually, she started running into the furniture she'd heretofore been able to maneuver around despite her failing eyesight. Seemingly, she'd lost that extra guiding sense. Then she began losing weight although she continued to eat well.

Still she smiled.

I cried.

If you've ever seen a dog smile, you know they can and do. Gizzy could and did. Although I knew what needed to be done, I was unable to make the judgment call alone. Just the word euthanize would start my tears flowing. I could not make the one-way trip with Gizzy by myself. I just couldn't.

When sisters Jan and Michele came to visit mid-August, they wisely helped and together the three of us took Gizzy to Dr. Robert White's Mer Rouge Road Veterinary Clinic.

I couldn't stay in the room, but Jan did. Bless her kind and loving

5 / Granny's Gizzy

heart. She'd grown to love Gizzy as much as I did, even though she only saw her a couple times a year when visiting Mom and me from Maryland. She also talked to Mom on the telephone almost nightly. Therefore she heard all about Gizzy's day-by-day antics.

And after all, Gizzy was our sister in a manner of speaking. You don't give up a sister lightly.

The night before the trip to the veterinarian's office, I took photographs of Jan, her eyes red, cheeks wet with streaming tears, as she held a smiling, freshly bathed Gizzy in her arms. I cry still. I will always cry. Gizzy was like the last living vestige of Mom. As long as I had Mom's Gizzy—Granny's Gizzy—I had a piece of Mom. A tangible.

By this time it'd been nine months since Mom and Hershey crossed the Rainbow Bridge together, so when I noticed a slip of paper pinned to the vet's bulletin board reading, "Free kitten" I asked Elizabeth about it.

The note advised the kitten was spayed, declawed and approximately 14 weeks old. Elizabeth, Dr. White's assistant, said her daughter had the cat; she was helping a friend find it a home.

My heart was so torn from having lost Mom and Hershey and now Gizzy, I blurted out that I wanted the kitten—sight unseen. It was one of those impulsive moments I'm a slave to. Mostly I don't regret my impulses, unless it involves spending too much money. And so, we made arrangements to come get the kitten the next afternoon.

Jan, Michele and I had tickets to attend a luncheon that next day where the governor of Louisiana, Bobby Jindal, would be guest speaker. We agreed to pick up the cat shortly thereafter.

No Time for Tears

6

"A house is not a home without a cat or a dog—preferably both."
(Barbara Sharik)

I learned a long time ago not to stop to count the bumps I've stumbled over in the Road of Life. It'd take too long and it'd be disheartening. Even though some knocked me flat on my derrière, to put it graciously, I picked myself up by my non-existent but very sturdy bootstraps and dusted myself off. What're a few scrapes and cuts and bruises if not the stuff from which life's lessons are learned?

And what have we learned children?

Watch where you walk might be a sound answer, except like tornadoes dropping from the sky, wreaking havoc, sometimes there's no avoiding what lies ahead. If it happens, it's best to get over it. The sooner the better.

And so it was with a completely unexpected and totally nasty divorce.

For all my insecurities growing up, at one time I reeked of joyful smugness. In fact, I was probably pretty insufferable as I roosted upon the perch of self-satisfaction. My life was as close to perfect as I could ever imagine; of course I was satisfied, even arrogant.

Born shy, I had to force-feed myself sociable gregariousness, lest I be buried beneath a pile of mediocrity—which I didn't want. I recognized I lacked the spunk and plunk to push myself to super high levels of achievement. I lacked the ambition it'd take to climb over the huddled bodies that'd need to be kicked aside to make way for an ascent of any significance. I was content to be a big frog in a tadpole pond. I had no desire to play leapfrog with the bullfrogs. Not a rut, it was a comfort zone of choice.

Content with a modicum amount of recognition, involved socially locally and appreciated for my contributions and involvements, what I most desired was to be the best wife and mother possible. Borrowing a little piece of heaven and enjoying it here on earth was the script composed for daily airing of my American Dream.

Togetherness was synonymous with us—altogether in our very own happy house on a farm out in the country—a father, mother, daughter Theresa and son Tony, the requisite family pets, a pickup truck for dad, a car for mom, lots of friends. Vacations and meals together, movies on weekends, school activities with the kids, family and friends. Constant contentment. The Cleavers had nothing on us.

My children's father's parents were together forever. Marital longevity was a family tradition. How could I expect anything less? But, idealism shot me down because eventually I came to discover that being happy blinded all my senses. My ears were filled with what they wanted and needed to hear, and weren't so finely tuned to subtle innuendoes. They missed the warning whistle of a marriage smoke detector getting whiffs of something smoldering.

My eyes were so filled with the joy front and center, they missed the pertinent peripherals. Happiness was a gigantic bright light, and I was blinded by that light.

And my heart; oh my heart. It beat in perfect rhythm.

And then one day it missed a beat.

And so, after the mandatory amount of misery a broken heart and shattered life demands, I picked up the pieces and called in all the King's Men and together we put me back together again. That's not to say the rug didn't get pulled out a few more times—like when I lost my son, my Tony, in a traffic accident—but dusting off one's derriere can become a habit and after a time a priceless commodity to have in one's bag of tricks. Eventually, with enough practice, one can become good at dusting. I have.

And laughter. Top among all, the message is to keep laughing because laughter's equally beneficial for smashed souls and whole souls alike.

And chief among all words of wisdom is to remember: Anything cried can be smiled and of course bringing a playful young kitten into the household can increase the opportunities for laughter.

Enter New Cat.

Ancient Lucky Charms

7

"All cats are grey in the dark." (English Proverb: All persons are undistinguished until they have made a name for themselves)

Adding a cat to the household cannot be taken lightly; not if everybody wants to be happy for the rest of their lives. The addition of any pet is a weighty step and as such must be evaluated carefully. Each type pet entails different directions of thoughts, modes of functioning and carrying out the requisite tending requirements, having the means of meeting the proper end results.

In other words, no one should just point-and-pick because when you point-and-pick you've only just begun the journey. When taking on ownership of a cat one must realize right off the bat, right out of the starting gate, from day one, you'll not own the cat, the cat will own you.

Ah, but fear not. That's a very good thing. Trust me.

Cats have specific nutritional needs. They have emotional needs as well. It's vital that owners become familiar with *Cat Care 101*. Cat care is what makes for a healthy life for New Cat and a happy relationship between both parties: you and your cat.

Cats require less time and expense than many pets. Also less room; therefore they're ideal apartment dwellers. They're quite independent yet adaptable to almost any situation. They're clean and easy to care for. Top of the list of attributes, they're very affectionate. Once bonded, and this generally happens upon first introduction, the relationship can last a lifetime.

A dog needs to be walked. A cat doesn't. It's capable of exercising itself, although it naturally enjoys and desires human companionship. There's the kitty litter thing that eliminates midnight walks in the rain a dog requires.

It's proven that stroking a cat lowers the pulse rate and blood pressure, putting cats in the good-for-you health department. There's a sense of comfort and joy, and even security, gleaned from just having a cat purring in your lap. Cats are very responsive. Just remember, their response time and yours may sometimes differ. Cats need their quiet time and privacy, even as you do.

No one actually needs to graduate *Cat History 101* but the more a cat keeper, fellow resident and roommate knows, the better. Cat history's simply icing on the cake in the knowledge department. The rest of this chapter is a simplified drizzle of icing.

Based on ancient drawings, cats have been with us domestically at least four-thousand years. In some cases the cat worked for its living as a hunter of pests and vermin; in others it was worshipped and revered as a goddess.

The cat's had its ups and downs through the centuries. Its worst down period was during the Salem Witch Hunts. That period of time was a huge backward step after having been worshipped in Egypt as cat goddess Bastet around 600 BC, used to fight against evil as the sun god Ra slaying Apep the serpent of darkness around 1500 BC, and as a killer of vermin to keep the food-store safe in the fifteenth century.

What were those Salem Witch Hunt folks thinking?

Unquestionably, that was a backward time for all humanity involved in the insanity of that particular era. Obviously, when it came to the cat and women with cats, participants in the hunt lacked the forward thinking of those who'd come before them in ancient Egypt and around the world. When ignorance blocks out the light of learning, bad things happen in the darkness.

In a nutshell, *Cat History 101* teaches that shorthaired domestic cats were believed to have spread worldwide from Egypt. At a later date, longhaired cats spread from Turkey, Iran and Afghani-

7 / Ancient Lucky Charms

stan. Based on ancient paintings found in India, there's a possibility the domestic cat was already there even before spreading to China or Japan. Much of what we learn historically comes from very old paintings and earliest tomes, antique figurines found in archeological digs, even mummies found within invaded pyramids. Cats have been found in evidence wherever archeologists and historians have explored.

We have shorthaired cats—the goddess cats, the vermin hunting cats—going from Egypt to Italy around AD 4; from there all across Europe and into Great Britain in AD 900; and then brought to the United States by the first settlers in the seventeenth century.

Longhaired cats were taken to Italy from Turkey during the sixteenth century, and from there to Great Britain during the mid-nineteenth century, reaching the United States in the late nineteenth century.

Great Britain received both the Siamese cat from Thailand (Siam) and the Abyssinian from Abyssinia (Ethiopia) during the late nineteenth century.

Probably the easiest of all cats to recognize, the Siamese named for Siam (former name of Thailand), is one of the most ancient breeds. In 1880, the King of Siam gave two pairs of these beautiful cats to the English consul-general in Bangkok. They were then taken to London and presented to the public in a show the following year. Introduced as the Royal Cat of Siam, they were immediately embraced by the people. The first Siamese arrived in the U.S. in 1890, another gift from the King of Siam to an American friend. The Siamese breed's enjoyed non-stop popularity ever since.

Both the Abyssinian, an ancient shorthaired breed, and the Egyptian Mau, are believed to be the most direct descendents of ancient Egyptian cats.

The Manx cat reached the Isle of Mann from the far east during the sixteenth century. The breed's origin's well known and well established. It's also unmistakable and completely recognizable because it is tailless and is a symbol of the Isle of Man throughout the world. The name stands for "cat of the Isle of Man."

During the 1930s the Burmese was brought to America from Burma. In the 1950s the Korat reached the United States from Thailand. In the 1970s, both the Japanese Bobtail from Japan and the Singapura from Singapore, were introduced into the United States.

In a book of poems likely written between 1350 and 1750, illustrations are found of several easily identifiable cats. Unquestionably, a Burmese and a Siamese cat are portrayed, each with their own characteristics depicted. This indicates that both breeds have remained relatively unchanged over the centuries. This obviously signifies that both were separate breeds since ancient times. Burmese cats are sable brown in color, shorthaired and have large round eyes.

Named after a former province of Thailand, the Korat, is another shorthaired breed of which ancient pictures have been found together with the Burmese and Siamese in the Smud Khol, illustrated in the early fourteenth century. In Thailand, the Korat is considered a symbol of prosperity. It's often gifted to important persons and to newlyweds.

If it works and cuts down on divorces, maybe we need to take up the tradition here in the United States.

When the Korat with its beautiful silver blue shorthaired coat and large, luminous, well-rounded green eyes, was first shown in London at cat shows during the end of the last century, cat fanciers were instantly interested. A pair was brought to the U.S. in 1959. The breed was first given official recognition in 1965.

Another of the ancient breeds, the Japanese Bobtail, is believed to bring good luck to any home in which it resides. Good luck statuettes are placed in windows of many Japanese family homes. The statues are made showing a seated cat with one paw raised in a polite salute.

As the name indicates, the Bobtail has a bit of a tail, unlike the Manx which is completely tailless. A proper Bobtail gives the appearance of a bunny tail or a pom-pom. The genetic reason for this is unknown. The Japanese Bobcat was first brought to the United States by returning American soldiers at the end of World War II.

The Singapura's name reflects its place of origin. The breed remains relatively rare, first brought to the U.S. by a couple vacationing in the island of Singapore in 1975. New cats were imported in 1980. As of 1993, it's the smallest recognized breed of cat and features very large eyes and a ticked coat similar to that of the Abyssinian. Very social with a gentle character, the Singapura's also very playful.

Most cats are. It's in their nature.

7 / Ancient Lucky Charms

To sum up, the Korat's considered a symbol of prosperity in Thailand and revered as a lucky charm. The Japanese Bobtail's considered good luck. The Sacred Cat of Burma was once sacred in Burmese temples and lived freely in palaces and places of worship. Egyptians worshipped cats as a matter of fact.

Forget the good luck of a cricket on the hearth, a rabbit's foot in your pocket (ouch!), or finding a penny face-side-up—you want good luck and years of happiness, get a cat.

Watering the Gladness Garden

8

"If you do not own a dog —at least one—there is not necessarily anything wrong with you, but there may be something wrong with your life ." (Roger Caras)

Losing Mom and Hershey the same day was so sad, but it was spiritually reassuring to consider they'd crossed the Rainbow Bridge together.

I didn't want to rush into filling the empty kitty-spot, but after Elizabeth told me about the fourteen-week-old kitten in need of a new home, I was hooked. In fact, I was so completely, irrationally hooked that when handed over to me, I probably should've named her Phonics and been done with it.

Already spayed and declawed, she sounded purr-fect, if you will pardon the play on words. Sometimes I cannot help myself.

That part alone was like one of those irresistibly impossible to ignore bargains—the sale where you can get all the fishing worms you want for a dollar so you ask for two-dollar's worth. Being spayed and declawed with updated shots represented several hundred dollars worth of necessaries already installed in the package.

And free to boot.

I may not like to shop, but I do appreciate a good bargain. This was a good bargain.

Jan, Michele and I made a stop at Walmart prior to picking up the

8 / Watering the Gladness Garden

new kitten. I needed to load up on new kitty supplies. Jan purchased a pretty set of pink and white heart-shaped kitty dishes for the new pet; one for food and one for water.

Jan's a cat-person. She's owned by five cats. She's also a bird-person. She not only has a lot of birds, she operates a bird rescue service. So, being a part of the kitten adoption tickled her animal-loving fancy and gigantic-giving heart.

Michele, who's a member of America's premier professional classical handbell ensemble, Sonos, and tours internationally in addition to teaching handbell lessons and workshops and appears as a clinician at regional handbell events, has no pets. Her lifestyle's currently not conducive to caring for anything more demanding than a couple goldfish. Still, she was caught up in the moment and welcomed being involved in the adoption process as well.

Jan flew into the airport at Little Rock, Arkansas from Maryland and Michele flew in from California. Together, they rented a car and drove the three hours south to visit for a week with me. It was a crowning event in my life. A treasure-filled moment in time that filled me with delightful memories.

I bought a brand new litter box, stocked up on kitten food and various and sundry cat supplies. I wanted one of everything. It was probably just as well I wasn't shopping in a dedicated pet store with a mile-square cat department, but instead was only exposed to a minimum of feline provisions. Lack of cat stuff kept me from being a doddering old cat-woman spending all month's food allowance on silly cat stuff. There'd be time enough for that later.

At the time we made arrangements to adopt this kitten, I hadn't even thought to ask what color she was much less her name, so when Elizabeth brought the sleek, solid black, yellow-eyed kitty from out of the back and handed her over to me, I was pleasantly surprised. She was completely the opposite of my last two cats. Hershey was a chocolate-point Himalayan. His brother Sterling, a silver point. They had very long light tan fur, beautiful blue eyes and as is typical of the breed, flattened faces.

Himalayans were produced by breeding the Siamese—hence the silver and chocolate points—with several longhaired breeds including the flat-faced Persian. Consequently, with discriminate breeding over a number of generations, the distinctive breed was created. Himalayans were recognized as a separate breed in the 1950s.

True to the breed's characteristics although a little shy, both Hershey and Sterling had very warm and affectionate personalities having taken on the personalities of the Persian. Also true to this breed's characteristics, with careful early breeding, they lacked the loud, demanding voice of the Siamese. They were calm and quiet house pets. Except for the constant shedding, I couldn't have asked for more pleasant cat companions.

The good far outweighed any inconvenience of wearing cat fur on my clothing. After all, every cat owner knows that no outfit's complete without cat hair. I keep a pet hair remover roller handy, but usually it's a lost cause. Sometimes I wondered if Rosie's nasal allergies were related to being allergic to long, fluffy, flyaway cat fur.

How many times I've made jokes declaring that every time I vacuumed, I vacuumed up a cat. Or at least the hairy equivalent. A year after Hershey's passing, I still find his hair in amongst that which I vacuum. After thirteen years residing in this house, his fur still flies when stirred.

With dogs that live outdoors, there's a definite shedding time of year. When an animal lives indoors, nature is often confused by artificial heat and cooling. I remember traveling across country one winter with Lady, an adored collie. The heat blowing onto her winter coat as she slept on the car floor coming and going for two full days each way, and then lazing around at Mom's house for a week where a unique heating system created by the installation of hot water pipes beneath the floors warmed the house, Lady began shedding.

This was mid-1969. Mom still lived in Maryland where she was born, spent all her childhood and lived the largest portion of her adult life because she resettled there after my father and she were divorced. It wasn't until years later that I encouraged her to make a move to come live in a mobile home set upon my property. She'd have her independence in her own home, albeit a mobile home, and we'd do things together and it'd be all good for both of us.

Therefore, Hershey and Sterling's coats were in a constant state of shedding to some degree, being fulltime house cats. Neither cat's tootsies had ever touched terra firma. I always have a number of outdoor yard dogs, and to drop a cat in their midst would likely have been disastrous. Therefore, they remained inside.

8 / Watering the Gladness Garden

Although I've had outdoor cats in the past, with age comes wisdom. Like a fish in an aquarium and a bird in a cage, my fervent belief is that all cats should be kept indoors. Cats really don't have nine lives. In the great outdoors they're exposed to much danger. More danger than they can outrun or outlive in too many cases. There are dogs and coyotes. There are cars and trucks. There are cruel and despicable people. Cats are so adaptable to indoor living, there's no reason to keep them anywhere except inside.

Happiness is a New Kitten

"We never really own a cat or dog as much as they owns us." (Unknown)

"Guess what her name is," Elizabeth invited as she handed the black kitten over to me. She said, "I think you'll like it."

A perfect black domestic shorthair, the kitten had a short, very glossy coat. Her eyes weren't typical cat-green, but instead, showstopper yellow. Should a black domestic shorthair be shown in a cat show, yellow eyes are required. Chalk up number one in the perfection column.

Also perfect for showing, the black cat had not one single white hair on her whole body. She was pure black, even her lips, her nose and her foot pads. Did I say she was perfect at first sight? Yes. She was.

Domestic shorthair sounds like a breed, but in actuality it's simply the opposite of a purebred. The most popular type cat is the basic domestic shorthair. In point of fact a domestic can have short, medium or long hair. Colors and patterns vary, as do their physical builds. By and large they're easy to find. Unfortunately, animal shelters are full of them. Unlike their counterparts, purebreds, the domestic's generally free for the adopting. Adopting a domestic, whatever the hair length, is often saving its life.

Factually, very few black shorthairs qualify for entering cat shows

9 / Happiness is a New Kitten

because often they have white hair somewhere on their bodies. Or occasionally the fur takes on a rusty shade in certain light. Some black cat coats will have barely visible, but visible nonetheless, tabby markings.

It's difficult to find a pure-black shorthair, and often one must wait until the kitten's at least a year old to determine for certain whether or not the desired coat color will remain constant.

Okay, so this black cat's only fourteen or fifteen weeks old. A far cry from the mandatory year old date of undisputable coat coloring. Yet, with one look, I doubted very seriously a white hair, a tabby design or a bit of rust would ever be in evidence. This baby was black all over her slender body. She was like midnight without moon or stars unless you count those beautiful yellow eyes. They spoke volumes.

Besides a number of individual breeds, cats come in an assortment of colors. The basic solid colors are black like my new kitten, orange which is usually referred to as red by cat fanciers, dark brown called chocolate like my Hershey's points were, and light brown also called cinnamon. Diluted colors are referred to as blue instead of gray, cream, lilac or lavender and fawn.

All cats are said to carry tabby genes. Under a bright light a ghost tabby marking might be visible even in solid colored cats. New Cat doesn't carry any visible tabby genes under any light. She's black through and through.

Anyone interested in exploring more details in the field of genes will learn, among other interesting facts, that the color-masking gene that allows a white cat to be white by masking all other colors, is also associated with deafness. I'd always heard blue-eyed white cats were almost always deaf. Statistics reveal that twenty-two percent of white cats with non-blue eyes are deaf while forty percent are deaf if they have one blue eye and sixty-five to eighty-five percent are deaf if both eyes are blue. Beautiful blue-eyed cats are almost always deaf. So with every good there's always the possibility of some bad. Such is life.

Tabbies are divided into four basic patterns: spotted, mackerel, ticked, and classic tabby. Tabby markings consist of a pattern formed by a combination of two types of hair. The agouti hairs have alternating bands of dark and light color; and the non-agouti hairs are dark solid colored. A concentration of these dark solid colored hairs is what causes the appearance of stripes and spots in a cat's coat.

Moreover, the colored cats referred to as piebald, has areas of mostly white on their bodies with specific patches of color. They're also referred to as parti-colored. Piebalds are then divided into four categories based on different patterns and various hues.

There's the bicolor with patches of color on head and body; van with patches of color mostly on head and tail; and the mitted cat has white on its paws, chest, belly and back legs. It's not unusual for pet owners of mitted cats, when coupled with black, to name such a specimen Domino or Tuxedo. Former President Bill Clinton and family had a First Cat dressed in this manner and was appropriately named Socks.

The fourth category of the piebald is the locket or button. These cats have only small spots of white on an otherwise colored body.

The tortoiseshell colored cats, often referred to as torties, have coats patterned with both black and red but do come in other versions with other colors. Like the tricolor cat, as many tortoiseshell cats are, they're almost always females. It's another gene thing.

There are more distinctions made that include points, shaded and smoke. Again, my new kitten's easy to identify. She's not tabby. She's not shaded or tortoiseshell. She's midnight black, black as the proverbial ace of spades.

There have been superstitions surrounding cats since time immortal, and most especially black cats. Think black cats—think Halloween. On the other hand, the Egyptians believed cats were gods. Ask a cat owner, and they'll affirm the Egyptians were right.

I grew up hearing if a black cat crosses your path, it's unlucky. I was surprised to read that in some countries, it's believed to be fortuitous to have a black cat cross one's path. In such a case it's advised to immediately make a wish. For every positive, there's a contradiction.

That's like when you and a companion see a one-head-lighted car, you're supposed to say, "Piddiddle. May your wish and my wish never be broke" with little fingers entwined. Silly superstitions; the stuff of growing up.

During my childhood I was told to negate the bad luck of a black cat crossing, I must immediately mark an ex with my foot or turn and go back the other way. Walking under a ladder and having a black cat

9 / Happiness is a New Kitten

cross your path were one in the same according to the philosophy of light-hearted foolish childhood superstitions.

In both Europe and America, the opposite of the black cat, the solid white cat, is viewed by superstitious folks with suspicion.

Who are these people?

I never saw a white cat I didn't fall in love with. Blue-eyed and deaf or not. Of course, I never saw any cat I didn't fall in love with. So you cannot go by me.

There was a time when cats were thought to be familiars of witches; that witches could turn themselves into cats in order to do dastardly witchy deeds. Many a cat died, as did many females falsely accused during the days of the witch hunts. Lack of education, common sense and sound judgment causes much harm. Things haven't changed so much with the passing of the ages. There's still too much of all of the above going on even in today's so-called enlightened society. And it's still causing harm.

There are superstitions about a cat sneezing. Once means good luck to some believers, and to others, it means rain. If it sneezes three times, somebody in the household will catch a cold. You ask me, three sneezes sounds like it's the cat.

If a cat washes its face up over its ears, wet weather is coming. If it washes itself while sitting in a doorway, the preacher will be visiting soon. Licking its tail indicates it'll soon shower. Should a cat sit with its back to the fire, beware, a storm's on the way. There'll be a change in the weather if a cat scratches the leg of a table.

Lacking a local meteorologist or the Weather Channel, I reckon it was left to the housecat to determine what's on the horizon weather-wise. Sort of reminds one of Punxsutawney on Groundhog Day predicting whether or not there'll be six more weeks of winter. We humans come up with some strange stuff, no doubt about it.

Do you suppose when a cat sees its master putting on a raincoat and grabbing the umbrella he and his litter mate confer, agreeing, it's a sure sign of rain. If that's the case, it would appear cats have more sense than humans when it comes to superstitions. Donning a raincoat makes more sense than basing the weather report on tail licking or table-leg scratching.

Sailors are a very superstitious lot. The list of cat-related omens is long. A couple include believing if a cat is heard to meow onboard it indicates there will be trouble, and if the ship's cat leaps about and plays as only a cat can, it's a sure sign that a gale's coming.

Some superstitions claim if a stray cat shows up at your door, you'll receive unexpected wealth. On the other hand, if the stray that shows up happens to be a tortoiseshell cat, you'll be visited by misfortune. It's the old six of one, half a dozen of the other. Take your pick.

Should you hear a cat meowing before traveling, it's advised you go back to see what the cat wants. Otherwise, something really grave could befall you.

There are so many omens and superstitions tied to cats it makes me glad I'm not illogical and gullible and prone to such inanity. Most superstitions make no sense, except perhaps the one that declares "No cat which has been bought will ever be any good for catching mice." The logic behind it being who'd expect some fancy purebred to catch mice?

There might be some merit based on my Hershey and Sterling. Sterling never caught a mouse and Hershey only accidentally caught one during his lifetime.

While many of us wish there was something supernatural within our grasp, the truth as I know it is that I've lived far too many years and seen too much reality in action to ever believe in signs and omens. Now, on the off chance that speaking negatively about such things brings a curse upon my old grey head, I've crossed my fingers. Oh, and I also marked an ex on the ground with my right foot and tossed some salt over my left shoulder. That ought to cover all the bases.

Having nothing to do with good luck, bad luck or her coat color, New Cat is a high energy cat, seeming to be in constant motion. The sailors would sail all around the world with their hatches battened in fear of approaching gales if New Cat was aboard. She's continuously sticking her nose into places it likely doesn't belong. She's the epitome of a curious cat. Somewhere in her mixed genes, might be a sprinkling of an Oriental breed based on her inquisitiveness and energy and her physical build. Yet, her meow's very soft. Definitely not Siamese related.

Of course, I didn't discover the degree of her curiosity until after I took her home and turned her loose. All I could see at first sight was that she was beautiful.

Elizabeth said her name was Maybelline.

9 / Happiness is a New Kitten

Somebody had a Chuck Berry 1950s sense of style. The moment was extra special because of having Jan and Michele with me. We'd shopped the kitty aisle at Walmart, then we attended the luncheon featuring Louisiana Governor Bobby Jindal as guest speaker. That in itself turned into a memorable event. Now we were taking possession of Maybelline. What a special day this had become.

Rockin' to the Oldies

10

"Wanted: Good Human." (Cat and Dog Logo T-Shirts)

Jerry Pye, president of the Chamber of Commerce sponsoring the Governor's Luncheon happens to be my boss, publisher of the Bastrop Daily Enterprise, where I work part time as a humor columnist and staff writer. He had the distinct pleasure of introducing the governor at the onset of his speech. Which incidentally was remarkable. Gov. Bobby Jindal, the youngest governor in these United States, speaks without a single cue card. He's amazing. He's also very brilliant and there's much talk that after President Obama's finished serving as president, Jindal will be next up. I forgive him that he's a Republican (myself being a bleeding heart, left-over hippy-style, idealistic liberal), because he's done much good for the state of Louisiana.

Following the very moving and most enjoyable speech, Mr. Pye added several closing remarks that included introducing Jan and Michele, saying out of the four-hundred-plus people in the audience my sisters had the distinction of traveling the farthest to meet the governor. He invited them to step up and have their photos made with Gov. Jindal.

Hence, it was still with giddy animation, having just left the luncheon, that we stood in front of the counter at Dr. White's office where Elizabeth introduced us to Maybelline. Hearing the kitten's name only added to our gaiety. As we headed home the three of us were singing Chuck Berry's well-known rock-n-roll tune, "Maybelline."

Naturally.

We crooned, "Maybelline, why can't you be true? Ohhh Maybelline... Why can't you be true..."

Halfway through the song, Jan wittily suggested nicknaming the kitty MayBelle. She pointed out it'd match TacoBelle's name quite well.

MayBelle sounded good to me so long as I could refrain from calling her MayBelle Carter and wouldn't start humming Johnny Cash songs. Not that humming Johnny Cash songs is a bad thing. I discovered Johnny Cash when I heard "Ballad of a Teenage Queen" played on a juke box at an ice cream parlor at Ft. Myer, Virginia, probably around 1955–'56. I remember Elvis stealing my heart around then also. Elvis kept my heart for many, many years. Only the new-comer American Idol discovery, Adam Lambert, all these years later has come close to reigniting the fervor Elvis once stirred in me.

It was at that same ice cream parlor I first ate sherbet. Served in cones of orange or raspberry, I don't remember pineapple being available. What a unique taste treat. Singing "Maybelline" stirred my reminiscences and took me on a side trip down Memory Lane.

Sometimes you just have to try a name on for size—a privilege of pet ownership not afforded parents naming a child. The new kitten remained Maybelle-Maybelline all the way home and well into the evening.

To be honest, I had a brand new kitten featured in my mind's eye. I knew this kitten was fourteen or fifteen weeks old, but I guess I didn't remember the size of a cat that age. I was picturing six to eight weeks rather than fourteen or fifteen. Still a kitten, yes, but Maybelle-Maybelline was bigger than I had visualized. I wondered how she'd take to TacoBelle and Rosie since she was old enough to have formed an opinion.

Elizabeth said her daughter had five Chihuahuas. That was reassuring. She was no stranger to dogs. She also said that Maybelle-Maybelline had been relegated to the backyard while the new-home search was in progress.

As an added aside, probably as a direct result of sleeping with dogs and living in the back yard, New Cat came to my house with at least a couple fleas hiding beneath her beautiful black fur.

I also found out the home where she'd originally been destined to live had several dogs in residence. Learning this, I could only assume the new black kitten would be okay with my dogs. The other half of my concern after half a year with no cats to contend with, would my dogs be okay with her?

Fleas are the most bothersome of external parasites. I managed to keep a flea-free house through the use of periodic canine medications and the fact that my inside dogs never ventured out of doors.

At first I saw no fleas on the kitten but noticed she scratched more than a casual itch would necessitate. I get so frustrated when people automatically assume every time a dog or cat scratches it has fleas. You know what? Sometimes a dog or cat just itches and needs to scratch. No fleas involved.

Then one night I spied a flea hopping on the bed. It's very difficult to keep the outside dogs flea-free. Quite logically, the flea could've stolen a ride inside when I stopped and petted the outside dogs. What good are dogs if you don't give them a lot of love and attention? If someone heard me talking to them, they'd think I was a doddering old geezer gal. It's not that I think my furry kids understand what I'm saying, it's just that I'm saying something.

I purchased an all natural flea spray for cats and although it recommended spraying it all over the cat's body, to avoid accidental ingestion, I elected to limit the spray to a few squirts on each of the animal's necks where they couldn't reach with their tongues. There's no poison in the spray but I still didn't want them licking the stuff even if it's all natural. There's a lot of all natural things I wouldn't want to lick.

My logic was if it worked for cats it'd work on TacoBelle and Rosie too. You can't use dog spray on cats, but I didn't believe it'd be a problem to use cat stuff on dogs. I figured if the kitty had fleas, TacoBelle and Rosie probably had them too.

The spray consisted of so many oils it sounded like it belonged on the spice rack at the grocery store: Peppermint, Cinnamon, Lemon Grass, Clove, Thyme, Vanillin, and alcohol. It smelled good too. With all those oils, how could it not? If nothing else, we'd have some fine smelling fleas hopping around the place. But, I doubted its effectiveness. Maybe because I didn't slather them with it. It directed to start spraying at the tail, making sure to spray the entire coat, including legs, tail and underbody. Then with my hand I was supposed to fluff the fur against the way it normally lays, to assure the spray penetrates the fur to the skin.

Okay, so I not only didn't slather, I didn't lather. The directions practically indicated I'd need to bathe the furry kids in the stuff.

I finally made it to Dr. White's office and purchased a stronger dose of meds. Although no one likes using poison on their pets, the fact that fleas can cause anemia, lead to tapeworms, transmit the plague, and many animals are often allergic to the flea-bite itself, there are times when an aggressive treatment is required.

Specifically, cats can catch Feline Panleukopenia Virus (FPV) from a sick cat or from infected fleas. It's so contagious, even if a human handles a cat with FPV, they can transmit this terrible disease to other cats. Approximately ninety-percent of infected kittens under the age of six months old, die. Although there's a vaccine for this deadly virus also referred to as Feline Distemper, you can understand why it was vitally important to rid New Cat of any fleas.

For tiny baby kittens, an infestation of fleas can be deadly because the fleas suck blood and if a kitten's badly infested, it'll cause anemia.

A kitty can also become infected with tapeworms through flea infestation. Tapeworms are parasites that live in the intestines of kittens and cats. Untreated, tapeworm infestation is usually fatal. The premise is, if a cat has fleas, it'll likely have tapeworms.

Fleas may be tiny, but they can be deadly.

Discovering a Castle Called Home

11

"Cats are connoisseurs of comfort." (James Herriot)

To this point, the kitten's life's been like an ongoing road trip, each leg of her journey leading to a new beginning. Considering when I got her she was approximately three and a half months old, with one human year equaling seven cat's, maybe to her all the traveling felt like a lifetime already.

The beginning is sketchy. I've only vague early details given by Elizabeth, of which I admit, I might not have paid strict enough attention considering the mission we were undertaking at that time—saying goodbye to Gizzy.

Little kitty started as part of a litter born about May 8, 2009. I'm picking May 8 because that's my Theresa's birthday, and to have been fourteen weeks in mid-August, this date works fine.

At around eight weeks she found herself in the hands of a veterinarian who administered required kitten shots and declawed her. A home was lined up for the baby cat. It was my understanding that the prospective original owner had lost a beloved pet and in the name of love and wanting to fill a void, her stepsister, the lady veterinarian, obtained this kitty and took care of the above described needs before shipping her to her new home.

There are a lot of pros and cons about having a cat declawed. I've

11 / Discovering a Castle Called Home

had all my housecats over the years declawed. Nary a one experienced problems or suffered emotionally or otherwise as a result. Other than initial pain during healing, and even being spayed or neutered can cause some discomfort, I personally perceive nothing negative—so long as the cat is to remain inside. Therefore, I'm a proponent of declawing.

A main argument against the process is that a cat cannot climb to protect itself after its nails are removed. A cat shouldn't have to defend itself. It should be living happily and safely behind closed doors in a loving home where front claws aren't a necessity. Nor should the cat be living where having front claws or the lack of them is a matter of life and death.

In reality, a cat can still climb, just not as well. It can still protect itself if attacked using the claws on its hind feet in a slashing manner. Actually, the strength of those back legs and the slashing they can mete, is probably much more effective than a swat with a front paw at a time of crisis.

It's been claimed a cat will lose dignity and confidence following such surgery. Silly psychological babble probably posed by animal psychiatrists looking for patients whose owners have more money than sense.

It's also been suggested a declawed cat will stop using its litter box. If an owner notices during the couple days healing process that kitty's paws are overly sensitive or tender, temporarily use shredded newspaper.

I'm not trained, nor do I hold any degrees in an authoritative field, except from the School of Cat-Care, which gives me a leg up to some extent. I personally know from years of my experience that cats adapt nicely following claw removal.

Avoiding the litter box otherwise, or if a cat appears to be suffering from a traumatic experience of some sort, it likely has nothing to do with being declawed. Search for some other cause like a bad little kid carrying it around by its tail or a bully-cat roommate or a sneaky dog eating its vittles. In that case, now you can call a psychiatrist if you want—one for the bad little kid. Most serial killers started their careers by mistreating animals.

No, I didn't say your child's going to grow up to be a criminal. I'm just giving a clue that it's unlikely declawing causes a kitten whose mother taught it to cover up its fecal matter to suddenly refrain from using the litter box. Remember too, cats can be finicky, not just about their diets, but about their potties too. Keep its litter box clean and sanitary at all times. You wouldn't appreciate a nasty bathroom when nature calls; neither does your cat. You don't like visiting a nasty public restroom; neither does kitty.

Here's something I discovered since getting New Kitty. There are contradictory products on the market. There are cat professionals that find cats don't respond well to scented litter. Frankly, I've smelled several litters I wouldn't respond very well to either. I don't buy them. I can barely hear, but I can smell. I've always had a super smeller. New Cat is constantly going around smelling things. Obviously the sense of smell plays an important part in her life. I know certain strong smells can be objectionable, therefore, since she obviously puts a lot of store in how things smell, I don't want to overwhelm her with a too strong unpleasant odor.

On top of that, I read that citrus is a natural deterrent. It advised to spray any verboten area with a citrus smelling product. It is supposed to deter a cat from jumping on furniture or climbing places it shouldn't. The article claimed cats definitely don't like the smell of citrus.

Then, what did I find on the cat product shelf at the store? You guessed it. A citrus-smelling deodorant being sold for the purpose of spraying in kitty's litter box. It promised to keep the litter smelling fresher. I'm thinking it will indeed smell fresher because if cats don't like citrus—it'll stay fresh because the cat very likely will stop using it if doused in citrus.

One of the two is wrong. Either citrus isn't a cat deterrent, or if it is, it doesn't need to be sprayed in the litter box.

It's the consensus of many veterinarians, those who have no hangups about doing the surgery, that declawing a kitten is ideally done between the age of three to fourteen days. The kitten can be back nursing its mom within ten to fifteen minutes at that age. Paws are healed within a few days.

With a cat like New Cat, a dedicated wild-child, if she weren't declawed, I'd have claw marks from floor to ceiling. Normally, only the front paws are declawed, and this is how all of my cats have been. Including New Cat. But hypothetically, if ever a cat was a candidate

11 / Discovering a Castle Called Home

for having all four paws done, she'd be it. She digs in with her back claws and launches herself as she flies all over the house.

Flies—as in "it's a bird, it's a plane, no, it's super cat"—would be the most fitting description of her mode of travel when the devil inside the undomesticated portion of her cat brain engages. In the bedroom she bounds from the bed to the dresser, to the chair, up onto the chest of drawers and back to the bed in a matter of seconds. Her feet, declawed or otherwise, don't touch the floor when making one of these airborne rounds.

Likewise, in the living room. She starts on the floor, leaps onto the couch, soars to the chair and then jumps to the loveseat. Occasionally, one back toenail barely tips the floor but only because of the expanse of space involved. I don't see any wings, but she flies like she has a pair.

Cat claws grow continuously, therefore cats must tend to them constantly. If a cat's nails grow too long, they can become ingrown and painful. A long, untrimmed claw can get caught in something when the cat is making a jump, for example. This can cause the leg to be wrenched and injured. That's why a cat that hasn't been declawed needs a scratching post available.

Besides possibly injuring itself, it'll definitely destroy furniture and curtains and walls. 'Tis the nature of the feline beast. Training a non-declawed cat to utilize a scratching post is essential.

I couldn't attempt to give lessons or advice for such a task. I've no idea how it's accomplished. Cats are smart, but let's define smart. Is smartness measured by trainability or because they've got natural instincts? Thus, maybe it's not so much that a human must train the cat but rather it has to do with luck. Be hopeful you're lucky enough that your cat chooses the correct item to scratch, because by an inborn habit, even a declawed cat will go through the motions of stretching and scratching. It's just a cat being a cat.

While scratching on posts or couches works for containment of the front claws, chewing on the back claws in an effort to keep them clean and growth controlled is the most common method of choice among cats. Hence unlucky cat owners will have their furniture, drapes and walls scratched. Luckier cat owners will beam with pleasure when kitty elects to utilize the scratching post. Ah, but the wisest of all cat owners will have the minor declawing operation undertaken and kitty is welcome to scratch its little heart out. No problem.

Claws can be trimmed by the pet owner of course. Or taken to the vet if the owner doesn't feel comfortable tackling the job. This process is usually done more to blunt the claws than to necessarily shorten them. Blunted nails do less damage to furniture. Of course, declawed paws do no damage at all.

Should an owner elect to clip claws, they should be clipped every week or two. An ordinary nail clipper intended for humans is acceptable when used properly. I've never done it, but I'm told you simply hold your cat on your lap, facing forward. Take your kitty's paw in your left hand and squeeze it gently between thumb and forefinger.

Right about now New Cat will be trimming my nails. With her teeth. Her back claws will be shredding my lap as she escapes from my grip. Because I've no doubt she would escape and leave me bleeding in her wake.

Anyway, if this goes properly (but I know what they say about best laid plans going array so I cannot promise success), neither the clipee-cat nor the clipper-owner should get hurt. The claws should unsheathe and becomes visible. Don't clip the nail so far down it gets into the quick—the pink part. As with clipping a dog's nails, too far down and there can be some bleeding.

Hold the clipper vertically in relation to the claw. Clip. Repeat five times on each paw. Only the front paws need to be trimmed. Good luck.

In the meantime, other friends bestowed the original intended owner of my new cat with a pair of six-week old kittens and a six-week old Chihuahua puppy. Everybody wanted the sad void filled and they were all helping by gifting her with kittens and puppies.

Like the old lady in the shoe with so many children she didn't know what to do, this lady suddenly had so many pets she didn't know what to do either.

Thus, as happens occasionally, with a multitude of pets underfoot—two kittens and the Chihuahua puppy, plus one large old loveable dog—kitty was overwhelmed and admittedly, disturbed. Poor kitty felt eliminated from the loop; she just didn't fit in anywhere.

11 / Discovering a Castle Called Home

Pet owner and animal lover, the lady decided the little black kitten deserved a home where she'd receive more personalized love and attention. Hence, the next stop was to a friend of the friend of the sister of the veterinarian, who agreed she'd try to find kitty another home. With her mom working at a veterinarian's office, she was pretty sure the task of locating a home wouldn't be too difficult. After all, her mom saw cat lovers on a daily basis. It was pretty good odds the right cat lover would come along.

Good hearted with honorable intentions foremost, she put out the word she had a kitten looking for a home, but since she had a basketful of Chihuahuas herself, kitty was relegated to the backyard. By now kitty felt like the redheaded stepchild.

This is where I come in. I saw the note tacked on the vet's bulletin board advertising "Free kitten, about 14 weeks old, declawed and spayed." I wasn't in a rush to replace Hershey until I saw that note. And the next day I wrapped my arms around the newest member of my family and headed for the house.

New Cat Needs a Name

12

"One cat just leads to another." (Ernest Hemingway)

Having passed through households with dogs, Maybelle-Maybelline sauntered in my door with so much attitude, Garfield would've been proud. She didn't even blink when she met resident pooches, Rosie and TacoBelle.

Rosie was nervous. TacoBelle aloof. Fact is, I could almost hear MayBelle-Maybelline saying, "Move over, Girls. There's a new kid on the block."

While I had no problem wrapping my arms around my new kitten, I was having trouble wrapping my tongue around the name Maybelline even though we'd been crooning, "Maybelline, why can't you be true? Oh, Maybelline…" all the way home.

Even Jan's suggestion of calling her MayBelle to match TacoBelle, just didn't seem the ideal moniker for this new baby cat. As I've often said, sometimes you just have to try a name on for size. You can't do that with a human baby, but you can with a new pet. At this point, neither MayBelle nor Maybelline was set in stone, engraved in steel or monogrammed on parchment.

The number one dog name in 2007 according to the ASPCA'S official list, was Max. Veterinary Pet Insurance Company (VPI), a pet health insurance provider, chugged through its data base of more

12 / New Cat Needs a Name

than 450,000 insured pets and found that people-names were more popular than animal-names in 2009.

Animal-names, or example, would be Spot, Fido, or Blackie. From the top-ten dog names, nary a one was a typical canine name. Does this mean we see our dogs as extended members of our people family? Probably. Mine are.

Human names, every one, the top-ten dog names from bottom to top in 2009 were Chloe, Sophie, Daisy, Maggie, Buddy, Lucy, Molly, Bella, Bailey and number one again, as in 2007, was Max.

The top-ten most popular feline names tended to include some human-sounding names, although, contrary to dog names, there were several definite cat names included. Number ten was Charlie, followed by Shadow, Bella, Oliver, Smokey, Lucy, Tiger, Tigger, Chloe, and the number one cat name? Would you believe, the same as the number one dog name: Max.

Note, several other names crossed the cat versus the dog barriers: Chloe, Lucy and Bella. In fact, names from the Twilight book and movie series, such as Bella, were seen as quite popular by several sources in 2009.

The popularity of Max probably stems from the ease for both pet owners to say and pets to comprehend. It's monosyllabic. You name a cat or dog Michelangelo or Anastasia, or even Maybelline, unless you shorten it to Mike and Anna and MayBelle or perhaps May, none of the names will roll off the tongue effortlessly. Your pet will be halfway down the road before he or she figures out you're calling him or her home.

Best to keep it simple using the K.I.S.S. system of "Keep It Simple Sweetie." That way the pet won't get its name confused with a command. Like yelling "No!" and the dog named Joe wags his tail because he thinks you're calling him instead of correcting him. We all know a Joe.

Every year I write newspaper columns about the previous year's most popular baby, cat and dog names. It's always interesting to research and to present to my readers.

Call me an nonconformist but, the last thing I wanted was to name New Cat the number one cat name of year. I wanted something unique, yet a name that rolled off the tongue. Plus, the name needed to fit her personally. Now I see why people used to just call their dog

55

BooCat Unleashed

Spot and be done with it. Creativity didn't play a role back when dogs were called by dog names. But, it's not near as much fun.

Granted, both Maybelle and Maybelline were unique in the world of cat names. But, for me, they didn't roll. Why TacoBelle rolls but MayBelle doesn't might be a mystery, but that's just how it was in my head, which is far from average when it comes to logic.

I did a couple columns about all the dogs that have passed through the White House, identifying breeds and names. This stemmed from when President Barrack Obama promised his daughters they'd get a dog once settled into their new house. As a result, I had names dripping off my tongue, but not rolling off.

Taken from 145,269 cats, *Petfinder's* ten most popular names in 2008 found Lucy as number one. It beat out Molly, but just barely. Molly was number two and Oreo, Kitten, Smokey, Princess, Shadow, Tigger, Angel and Missy followed. In 2006, Kitty was the number one name on the *Washington Post's* survey but was absent in 2008.

Part of the fun selecting a pet name is creatively fitting it to a pet's individual personality. I actually considered the name Cinderella Cookiedough, but for New Cat's color. Cookiedough didn't fit a black cat. If the new cat was a dog, it might've been easier to name her. I could call her Bob Barker or Basil T-Bone. The possible list of dog names is endless. My potfull of outside dogs each have individual names, some creative, some not so much so. Each name I bestowed, fits each dog's personality.

In any case, when the right name for this baby cat pops out of my mouth, I reckoned I'd know it. I'm very opinionated when it comes to cats and dogs. Even lacking opposable thumbs, cats and dogs are smarter than some folks I know. I had a feeling my MayBelle-Maybelline or Miss Kitty (maybe?) fit that smart category very well.

Carnivora, Felidae, Felis, Catus

13

"There are two means of refuge from the miseries of life: music and cats."
(Albert Schweitzer)

Later that night I settled in bed with my book. I cannot go to sleep without reading myself to that state. Likewise, unless I have a companion to chat with, I cannot eat without reading. I probably would have a nervous breakdown should I find myself alone in a restaurant at lunchtime without reading material. My eyes are never not reading if there are written words somewhere within sight. Signs. Cereal Boxes. Everything. And books. Always books.

Books are as essential as food.

I once had to call an ambulance to transport me to the emergency room, and ill as I was, I remembered to grab my book before I was loaded on the stretcher. As I lay in the ER I was able to read, shutting out the smells and noises surrounding me in the place. It's true, you get to be an old geezer gal like me, there's a tendency to become set in your ways. I'd venture to say my reading habits are definitely set in something more substantial than Jello. I've been reading voraciously ever since I discovered how.

My father built me a book case for my bedroom. I still have that bookcase.

I remember the time I was identified by the book.

The day started early. It was a Saturday morning. I'm at my best early. Rosie was running around acting like a Nervous Nellie. I told her it's just a mop. Surely, it hadn't been so long since I'd last mopped that she'd forgotten what a mop looked like.

I had to attend a class later that morning to qualify as Commissioner-in-Charge to work at the polls. I planned to get a bit of housework done first. How much easier to have woke up and settled in with my book and a cup of coffee before heading to the class. But I was determined to cross at least one thing off my To-Do list and that did not include reading half the morning away. Books are my weakness. Reading my downfall.

Louisa May Alcott's quotation could've been written for me: "She is too fond of books, and it has addled her brain."

C. S. Lewis wrote, "I do believe you can never have a cup of tea large enough or a book long enough to suit me." My sentiments exactly.

I've been known to tell the pups, lunch will be ready soon—as soon as I finish reading this chapter. As a result of writing about my love of books and avid reading habits in my newspaper column, I was pleasantly surprised later that day.

After the class, I decided to grab a bite of lunch before heading back home. At a local restaurant, book in hand as always—because as I said, I can't eat and not read—while awaiting my order a lady approached and said, "I saw your book. Are you the lady who writes those columns? You look just like her."

Identified by the book.

Now you might wonder since I went out to eat lunch where I was recognized by the book under my arm, did I finish my To-Do list before attending the poll working class. Nope, I didn't finish. I rarely ever finish the stuff on my list. There are like 200 things on the list. I barely ever make a dent but I always have good intentions. I pave the way with them.

Thinking of To-Do lists reminds me how men and women look at almost everything differently. Very much like the difference between cats and dogs, in fact. Something's always reminding me of

13 / *Carnivora, Felidae, Felis, Catus*

something else. With one thought opening the gateway of my mind to some other thought, my mouth never completely shuts down unless I shut it forcibly. I'm able to babble all day long. It's one of my flaws. Boys and girls start out basically the same. Then the genetics of hormones and chromosomes kick in and by the time a baby's born, gender's pretty much determined. From that moment onward, the gap between the sexes widens.

Based on these built-in X, Y's and Z's, male and female characteristics develop as children grow. Mostly, children learn to speak "Male" and "Female" the way they learn to speak English and Spanish. The difference between each is like a cat's meow versus a dog's bark. While environment, trauma and rote influences both boys and girls, genetics, the X, Y's and Z's, are the bottom-line determining factor in the development of difference.

Women ought to get equal pay for equal work. Most women can do what men do, including all mental and most physical stuff. But, regarding outlook and perception, there's a gigantic dissimilarity. I doubt even Evil Kneival could jump the gap.

Recently, I was privy to a male-oriented discussion of magnetic memo boards.

The female who hung one on the fridge door saw it as a simple means of recording reminders of chores around the house. A handy variation of the standard To-Do list.

The man of the house, on the other hand, opined it to be the introduction of an obnoxious item of menace and contention into the household; a life-changing intrusion. And his pals agreed.

According to the main complainant, the longer the board hung, the longer the list grew—each item added by the wife for hubby's attention.

"It's an exponential form of nagging," my friend Tom C. declared. The men looked at the reminder board as the creation of a monster. It took on Frankenstein proportions.

See how warped men's outlooks can be? Taking the magnetic memo board from the female point of view, it's a magnetically magnificent way to unclutter one's mind. Write it down, then forget it until time to do it. Psychologically, lists make you feel better about yourself. In my case, I'm not a slacker. I'm going to do it. How do I know? Because it's on the list.

Sure, some things on today's list are transferred onto tomorrow's list, and the next day's after that. That's the beauty of lists. Writing down what needs doing is almost as good as actually doing. And it's a lot easier.

In the name of fairness, there are delaying tactics guys could use that'd play an important role in life, limb and marriage retention. Remember the line: "It's on the list." Here's how it works:

In Honey-Do's case, Little Woman asks: "Did you change the air conditioner filter?"

And Honey's-Gonna-Do simply says: "It's on the list." Translating, Honey-Will. Eventually.

You guys can handle it. Tell her: "Bring it on! Lists don't scare me."

That's why they call them To-Do lists. Otherwise they'd be Already-Done lists.

Which, by the way, should only be dragged out in case of sheer self-defense. When the Misses accuses Hubby of never doing anything then the Already-Done list's helpful.

Also, To-Do lists make good bragging points when one or more men gather—they become a matter of male pride. The longer the list, the better. It comes under the heading of Comparing Size (a male bonding tactic).

One guy says: "My list's longer than your list."

The other says: "Yeah? What's on your list?"

So, you see, it's all in how you perceive something whether it's a help or hindrance. One last note on perception: Mainly, all y'all men call it "Nagging."

We women call it "Re-reminding."

Sometimes I feel like a rural hermit, which isn't what I'd planned to be when I grew up. Still, one thing's certain, between my To-Do list, my books, my dogs and my new cat, I don't have time to feel lonely.

Eventually my eyes get heavy, so, setting the book aside (along with thoughts of my To-Do list), let me say that Rosie and Taco-Belle, somewhat old ladies themselves, are also fairly well set in their ways.

Once in bed, they each scooted under the covers mid-way down toward the foot. They were ready for a peaceful night's sleep. They'd had enough of the strange mischievous creature mom brought home.

Make no mistake, domestic cats are cousins of the King of the Beasts. A cat can leap practically straight up into the air from a standing-still position. They're a package of solid muscles. They also have astute smelling and hearing abilities. We speak of a sixth sense; perhaps there are more senses even than that. Anyone having lived with a cat knows what's bundled beneath a cat's fur coat is much more than anything average.

Cats, bears and dogs are all flesh-eaters, putting them into the same order as mammals, the Carnivora. All like animals share distinct similarities among which include clawed toes, fur coats and canine teeth. While cats are members of the Carnivora order, the categories are broken down even more so. Cats are members of the Felidae family. And all domestic cats belong to the same species, Felis catus. From orders to families to species, cats are lastly divided into breeds.

Most purebred cats were originally developed for specific physical characteristics; bred to look pretty in the eye of each beholder. Along the way different breeds evolved different personalities, temperaments and specific characteristics especial to a particular breed. For example, considered the most mellow breeds are the Ragdoll, British Shorthair, Persian, Siamese and the American Curl. This mellowness is as much a part of the breed as the distinctive color, body shape and hair length.

Prior to being adopted by Hershey and Sterling, I'd had more Siamese cats in my lifetime than any other breed. I was always partial to Siamese cats. I airmailed a pair, George and Mr. Jones, to my parents in Massachusetts when the father of my children, a solider in the U.S. Army, and I were stationed to West Germany for a three year tour.

I couldn't stand being catless for three years, so while overseas, we got a Siamese kitten. We had him flown back when we returned to the United States, stationed next to Ft. Hood, Texas.

It's said that tabbies and ginger cats are the easiest to train and black cats, the hardest. Whether that's an old wives' tale—or something a disgruntled dog owner made up—I don't know. What I do know is, speaking from my own experience, a neutered/spayed cat's probably the easiest to educate no matter the breed. Remove the "catting around" portion of the personality, and kitty can concentrate on settling down rather than wanting to roam the streets yowling and cat-calling half the night like a common alley cat.

It's also believed by most everyone who's ever been owned by a cat, that cats aren't really trainable in the truest sense of the word. Not like, say a dog that is bound by love to do its master's bidding. You see, what cats do is train their humans. It's a cat's world and we just live in it. This keeps everybody happy. I know it works for me.

My dogs will chase a ball, bring it back to me pleading that I throw it again. And again.

My cat will chase a ball if she wants to and she'll play with it indefinitely. If she wants to. If I want to toss it again, I can get up and come get it myself. The message she conveys is she's a cat, not a retriever. You want your ball back, get a bird dog.

Recognized cat breeds include the Abyssinian, American Bobtail, American Shorthair, American Wirehair, Angora, Balinese, Bastet, Bengal, Birman, Bombay, British Blue, British Shorthair, Burmese, Burmilla, California Spangled Cat, Chartreux, Chinchilla, Colorpoint, Cornish Rex, Cymric, Devon Rex, Egyptian Mau, Exotic Shorthair, Foreign Burmese, Havana Brown, Highland Fold, Himilayan, Japanese Bobtail, Javanese, Korat, La Perm, Maine Coon Cat, Manx, Munchkin, Nebelung, Norwegian Forest Cat, Ocicat, Oriental, Persian, Rex, Ragdoll, Red Self, Russian Blue, Scottish Fold, Selkirk Rex, Siamese, Siberian, Singapura, Snowshoe, Somali, Sphinx Hairless, Turkish Angora, Turkish Van, York Chocolate, and of course the Black Shorthair, who at this particular moment is nowhere to be found.

A portion of New Cat's particular personality trait is to do things her way whenever and however she wants. She'll be back from whatever adventure she's involved in when she's ready, gracing me with her company as she sees fit. And like a died-in-the-wool cat person, I'll welcome her with open arms and cooing words of admiration. She, on the other hand, will allow me to pet her and administer that adoration. Or not.

Oh yes, it's a cat's world and I merely live in it.

Breathing Easier

14

"People who love cats have some of the biggest hearts around."
(Susan Easterly)

Because all my cats all my life have always purred when contented, I was surprised to read that purring isn't necessarily always a sign of contentment. Purring can also be an indication that a cat's in pain, ill and even dying. It can be a sign of stress—mother cats often purr when experiencing the discomfort of giving birth. It doesn't get much more stressful nor much more uncomfy than when birthing kits in the life of a cat—or in the life of a woman either for that matter.

Also, it is reported by animal behaviorists that cats also employ what is called an anticipatory purr meaning they sometimes purr in anticipation of something they want. That could be before dinnertime, prior to getting special attention from its owner or at the onset of playing a cat game.

The challenge is next time New Cat approaches me and starts purring, I need to stop what I'm doing and figure out what she is anticipating.

This information blew everything I thought I knew about a cat and its purring right out of the water.

Incidentally, kittens can purr when only two days to a few weeks old.

Either homeopathic medication or transcendental meditation, purring is a mental technique to relax and to feel better. It's like the Yoga Guru humming "umm."

Well, not only does a cat's deep, soothing purring vibration make itself feel better, it makes me feel better too. Cats purr at about twenty-six cycles per second, the same frequency as an idling diesel engine, or so I've been told. I know personally nothing about diesel engines and idling cycles, but I do know about purring cats.

Now me? I purr too. I jokingly say when I snore, because I've been told I snore, that I'm purring. Using the term purring sounds more ladylike than snoring.

As it turns out, my snoring was a sign of a serious illness of which I was unaware. Too bad I wasn't more savvy sooner. All the signs were there for several years. By the time I had my diagnoses, some severe damage occurred.

A few days before I picked up my new kitty, I was fitted with a CPAP mask and machine, having been diagnosed with Sleep Apnea. Between the new breathing machine that I wasn't finding comfortable, trying to get into a comfy position so I could relax and read myself to sleep, I wasn't too concerned about the kitty. I figured she'd make herself at home and all would be good.

I remember thinking if I can learn to breathe through this mask covering my nose, wrapped around and binding my head, pushing my nose up and my ears down, and still see to read without getting strangled during the night by the air tubes going in every direction, I too would be good.

Neither Rosie nor TacoBelle seemed to notice any difference even after I donned the darned mask. With a withering glance in the mirror, I was glad I wasn't searching for romance. Unless someone was interested in the extraterrestrial look I'd frighten a good man away.

Read this personal ad: "Wanted. One good man. Must be hard of seeing."

So, head and face wrapped up beyond recognition, book in hand, dogs beneath the covers—no kitty in sight—I assumed she'd found a quiet place to spend the night. After all, it'd been a busy day for her too. She went from somebody's backyard to the vet's office, into a kitty kennel for the day, then into my cat carrier and to my car for a long drive during which she had to listen to the Sharik Sisters singing

"Maybelline, oh Maybelline, why cancha you be true," and finally into a new and strange house where she met up with two nosy dogs.

※

Headlines in the *New York Metro* newspaper read, "Study: Sleep Apnea increases death risk."

Cousin Mike sent the article after I told him I was diagnosed with sleep apnea. I did my research, finding "if left untreated, sleep apnea can result in a growing number of health problems including: Hypertension, stroke, heart failure, irregular heartbeats, and heart attacks."

I've been told my snoring rattled the rafters and shook the rooftop, a symptom. I've also been told I stop breathing while asleep. The diagnosis didn't surprise me, but the seriousness did.

"Severe sleep apnea raises the risk of dying early by 46 percent, U.S. researchers reported," according to an Aug. 18, 2009 *Reuters* article.

Also, according to director of the Comprehensive Center for Sleep Medicine at Mount Sinai, specialist Dr. R. Nisha Aurora, interviewed by the *New York Daily News*, December 29, 2009, "Sleep apnea is a huge public health concern that affects about five percent of the American population—making it almost as common as diabetes."

She reports it as a chronic disorder that seriously impairs quality of life. It also puts patients at risk of other serious and sometimes fatal diseases.

Caused by the collapse of the upper airway during sleep, sufferers experience numerous brief interruptions in breathing—approximately twenty to thirty seconds at a time. Sleep apnea's closely linked with obesity, high blood pressure, heart failure and stroke. People often speak of sleep apnea as though it's simply a nuisance. Instead, it's a serious ailment. Left untreated, it can be fatal.

Let me insert here, that my sweet old lady TacoBelle is experiencing something similar. Tracheal collapse happens to toy and small-breed dogs and it's happened to Taco. It occurs when the cartilage of the trachea, or windpipe, is weak. The windpipe loses its rigidity. This weakness can be aggravated by allergies, such as airborne irritants, obesity and coughing. These in turn can cause the trachea rings to collapse, which causes the trachea to flatten, and then this flattening causes obstruction of the airway. She's not obese, but for whatever other reason, she's suffering from this serious and very scary ailment.

It's more prevalent in older dogs. A honking, gooselike cough's the first sign there's a problem. It causes labored breathing and gagging. Taco usually starts coughing and gagging after barking excitedly. I give her a swallow of children's Benadryl when it's very bad. I don't know if it helps, but she likes the flavor of it, lapping it with obvious pleasure. If it's got anything to do with airborne irritants, the Benadryl should help. It should also soothe her throat.

Our vet gave me some prednisone but warned sometimes steroids can do more harm than good. He admitted an operation for this ailment was far out of his expertise, advising that more often than not, it's done at a teaching hospital.

The National Heart, Lung, and Blood Institute of the National Institute of Health, reported "an estimated twelve-million adult Americans suffer from sleep apnea, the majority of whom are not diagnosed or treated."

I have to ask, if the majority of sufferers aren't diagnosed, how does the NHLBI know there are twelve-million? The National Sleep Foundation puts the number at eighteen-million. Fluffiness, which is how I refer to my deep-skinned condition, agitates the ailment. Fluffiness agitates every ailment. I was seeing the curtailment of angel food cake for breakfast, lunchtime candy bars and suppertime ice cream. Yikes. It's like daddy taking the T-Bird away.

A sleep study revealed I'm among those twelve- to eighteen-million people. Of course, if sleep apnea sufferers are overweight, it's recommended they lose weight.

I know. I know.

There's absolutely nothing that fluffy is good for except warming your sweetie in the winter, and shading him in the summer. With that said, on a positive note, nobody loves a bone but a dog and he buries it.

Fluffy could also be deemed good for making a lap for grandkids and cats and dogs. In that case, Grannies are supposed to be fluffy.

All humor aside, many ailments are traced back to deep skin. My deep skin stems from that skinny little person inside me begging to get out; I have to feed her cookies to shut her up. Now I can't breathe right.

While I joke a lot and say much with tongue in cheek, sleep apnea's no laughing matter. The current most successful treatment besides eliminating the fluff, is the use of a nasal CPAP mask. My cardiologist, Dr. M. Khalil, prescribed using a CPAP machine: *Continuous Positive Airway Pressure.*

It gently blows pressurized room air through the upper airway at a pressure high enough to keep the throat open. Obstructive Sleep Apnea's usually caused when soft tissue at the back of the throat collapses, causing a blockage during sleep. I've got my tonsils and adenoids and that little uvula thing, it's no wonder obstruction occurs. Plus since my last back surgery and arthritis raging in my hips, I am most comfortable sleeping on my back. This is the worst position possible. Sleep apnea sufferers stop breathing repeatedly while asleep, sometimes hundreds of times; which was my case as determined by a sleep study.

According to the December 29, 2009 *New York Daily News* article, the biggest news of the year was a study demonstrating the link between sleep apnea and mortality, and that new breathing devices are in the works. The new devices will likely be smaller, making them more comfortable, and also more effective. I want one.

As is often the case, these new devices are already becoming available in Europe and are still being researched in the United States. My editorial comment is that perhaps they'll eventually trickle down for use in America by Americans. Our country's often slow medically speaking. I never know if it's through caution or if it has to do with monetary gains somewhere down the line.

Look at the healthcare situation for American citizens as opposed to what's provided to all other civilized western countries. No comparison. We die more if we're among the working poor. Companies, made up of people, both of which make a profit from our insurance premiums have the final say in our medical treatments, and that is pretty scary. How much better if it were truly a medical decision instead of a monetary one.

Healthcare reform was passed for the time being. Much more is needed. As long as large insurance companies line the pockets of the other party, the party for the people have an uphill battle.

I ran into such a problem with regards to approaching surgery. My doctor requested a blood test, an EKG and a chest X-ray prior to the surgery. These were not useless or flippant tests requested so somebody would make money. He wanted these tests done before I was anesthetized, verifying I was healthy enough to undergo the surgery. It's in his best interest I don't die on the table. Mine too.

Finally receiving Medicare, the X-ray technician advised Medicare sent notice they'd not pay for a chest X-ray because it has nothing to do with the type surgery I'd be undergoing.

The tech said my doctor wouldn't do the surgery without the X-ray; but Medicare's saying it's not necessary and as such they won't cover the cost. I had to sign papers swearing I'd be personally responsible for the cost of the X-ray my doctor required.

So what else is new?

All my life I've worked and I've paid. I've never received anything from our government, or anybody else for that matter, that I didn't earn. It took me over a year to pay off my ambulance bill the year before because of not having health insurance at that time.

When I underwent cataract surgery, the physician was good enough to allow me to make payments. Likewise, when I purchased hearing aids. Certainly pride enters into the equation. I'd rather work and pay my way so long as I'm physically and mentally able, than to sit on my fluffynutter-butt and expect the government to take care of me. I've no respect for somebody who can but won't. They show no respect for themselves either.

I haven't had health insurance for five years due to the unavailability at my job and the high cost I couldn't handle. I knew I had several health problems developing. I prayed to whatever Grand Pupah in the Sky would listen to please let me hang on until I qualified for my Medicare.

Medicare isn't like Medicaid. It's not free. And it doesn't pay for everything across the board. There are specific guidelines and limits.

I work. I work all the time. I just don't earn enough to pay for additional insurance coverage. My Medicare, although money's been withheld from my salary for years and continues to be withheld, still has a monthly premium attached, plus an annual deductible to be met and it leaves at least twenty-percent to be paid out of my fast-emptying pocket.

14 / Breathing Easier

It is, in essence, a government-operated health insurance program.

The X-ray tech said health insurance companies were much worse than Medicare about refusing payment for various procedures; and he, like me, agreed it's a sad situation when a physician tells a patient what they need but the people we're paying premiums to, say "Sorry Charlie."

I really don't like the idea of a company that's making a profit off me to have the final say, rather than my physician, regarding my medical treatment. Especially when their decision has nothing to do with a frivolous treatment but instead is medically sound. Their decision has to do with the bottom line. Period.

It's time for healthcare reform. While there's too much clamor from amongst the selfish wealthy and the right-wing radicals fearful of government control, a public option would have helped keep private insurance companies a little more honest, so to speak. This president wants health care for the American people. Many American citizens want that too. Unfortunately, the loudest factor, the squeaky wheels who are against it, will probably win out down the road. I won't live to see American people become eligible for the healthcare every other civilized country provides for its citizenship.

My rant of the day. Healthcare reform scares some people. I pray for it. I'm among the working poor without proper insurance. Of course, I pray for it. How long it will be in force before it's voted back out is anybody's guess. The undercurrent is building to wash away the good that could be done.

Check the bankruptcy courts. How many families are forced to declare bankruptcy after losing everything, not because of credit card debt—which is a whole other rant of mine—but instead is due to exuberant medical costs?

By the way, it's speculated there are times when someone peacefully dies in their sleep without any warning and no symptoms to speak of, chances are good the cause was sleep apnea. They stopped breathing and never started again—the little indicator in their brain that normally awakened them failed to kick in.

An outfit out of Monroe contacted me about delivery of a CPAP machine and gear. The young gal who called gave a date and time she'd come to my house. I attempted to give directions but she advised she had a Global Positioning System (GPS). Fine, but I tried to warn her some systems were programmed to turn left at McGinty Road instead of right; be aware.

You know, it's hard to tell somebody something when they won't listen. An hour after she was supposed to arrive, she called. She needed me to come find her. She was lost. Yep, she turned left instead of right, bless her heart.

Rattled and distracted, probably worrying about being late for her next appointment, so that when I complained I was having difficulty breathing through the mask she'd handed me because my nose was stuffy, she said I'd probably need to get a humidifier.

And then she left.

Masks run the gambit from full face, nose and mouth, nose only, to the lightweight nasal pillow design she handed me. With proper adjustment maybe it'd been better. But, ill-fitting at best, it either sliced into my ears and dislocated my nose or slip-slid around. And it's ugly; I even scared myself. As I said, it's a good thing I'm not looking for romance. Coming across looking like an Apollo Seven reject's hardly romantic. Unless you're an extraterrestrial alien.

Probably because the young lady saw a fluffy person, she figured I needed a sizeable mask. Tough to determine a proper fit in five minutes. Here's the thing, the straps cut into the top of my ears. If I tighten the upper straps to get the lower straps off my ears, then the nasal pillows push my nose upward. I always thought little upturned noses were cute—all the cheerleaders had them—but, this wasn't the ideal way to create a perky nose. To endure the mask, I had to loosen it up and wear it on top of and outside my ears like earmuffs.

My mask was too big or my head was too small. Either that or my ears were in the wrong place as opposed to where my nose was located on my face. I planned to tell friends and neighbors when they see me, pay no attention to my dislocated, out of joint, upturned nose and the fact that my ears have been lowered and flattened against my skull. I reckoned in the process of adjusting to the wearing of this life-saving device, it's better my face become a little misshapen and I live to breathe again than the alternative.

Honestly, the first night after I finally got the mask semi-adjusted, I slept through the night for the first time in years. But. Always the abysmal But. CPAP air's an irritant. The irritation dried out my nasal passages and caused bleeding, swelling, excess mucus, congestion and sneezing.

Did I miss anything?

I figured infection was only a day away. And it hurt. I wasn't a good commercial for bestowing the benefits of CPAP treatment. Sleeping all night was being achieved at a high cost of lost comfort and much suffering.

At my wit's end, I called the company to say I was going to the pharmacy and asked what kind of humidifier did I need to get? Turned out, a humidifier's available with the machine and is in fact a critical part of CPAP therapy. Too bad my little lost lady hadn't hooked me up in the first place. Another woman brought one to my workplace the next day. What a world of difference. Moisture saved the day. And night.

Each night I tried really hard to use my CPAP because I wanted to get better. Regrettably, to that point, I hadn't located a comfort zone. Yes. The humidifier worked wonders on the dry nasal passage-problem. But it did nothing for the ill-fitting mask itself.

Resembling a medieval torture contraption, I felt like the Princess and the Pea. My neck was stiff from additional weight. I suffered instant suffocation when the electricity blinked off one night.

Eventually, after sufficient complaining, I got a new mask. The new mask was made specifically for women. Amazing the difference the correct fit makes. I likened it to needing a size 8 shoe but having been forced to wear a size 10 ½ for twenty-two nights. In essence, the oversized clunkers rubbed blisters, created calluses, and caused plantar fasciitis. Better to have gone barefoot than forced to don such ill-fitting shoes—or in this case, headgear.

Imagine if I'd been wearing the new and improved headgear with a humidifier from day one, I'd never have had to suffer like some Gitmo inmate. Believe me, I was ready to tell anybody anything they wanted to know after having spent three weeks bound up in a tormenting torture device. That's not funny, but it's how it felt, night after night. Just light the stake fire and put me out of my misery was the point I'd reached. I don't do pain very well. Especially not long-term self-inflicted pain.

I realize there isn't a mask made that'd be as comfortable as no mask. But, there are degrees of comfort and discomfort. With these degrees, one can make adjustments of acceptance. I understand why some people I've talked said they have masks and machines stuck in their bottom drawer; they didn't wear them because they couldn't find a comfort zone. They'd rather take their chances on the consequences the disease offers. Somebody somewhere needs to invent a better mousetrap.

You know, if men can make it to the moon, why can't CPAP headgear not hurt?

I have to tell you, or anyone who'll listen, getting old was a lot more fun at nineteen than at sixty-five. There's one point I'll make here and now. I've read multiple times that petting a cat can lower an individual's blood pressure. I never suffered from that malady—high blood pressure—until recently. It's no doubt a result of the development of sleep apnea. Now, however, it's become a very demanding problem. Getting it regulated has been difficult.

Therefore, if stroking a cat helps, I believe this little black kitten's just what the doctor ordered. I should be well on my way to recovery. Pardon the pun. She's one very petable kitten.

Good news is that even though she was a bit timid at first, once I started petting her, she quickly warmed up to me and became very affectionate—incredibly so—which warms the cockles of my heart. Also, I feel certain she'll likely outgrow her extreme hyperactivity.

She constantly brushes against me, climbs on my lap, jumps on chair backs where I sit, follows me around and seems very eager to please; in fact she's almost frantic for attention from me. Shadow would make a good name the way she dogs my steps. And I like it. I like it very much.

Because she's so affectionate, despite her kittenish hyperactivity, I was confident she'd calm down as she gets older. Our personalities meshed. This was a positive and because she's so affectionate, she'll likely stay demonstrative and loving. No doubt she at first came across almost frantically desperate because of the unstable, uncertain and insecure road trip she'd traveled since birth. After all, she's thrice-rejected, emotionally conflicted, so we've got our job summarized. We both need each other to make both of us get better.

I'm going to pet her and lower my blood pressure. She's going to like being petted and lower her easily agitated character.

How BooCat Got Her Name

15

"My cat, my dogs, they are my heart." (Barbara Sharik)

All was calm. Sisters Michele and Jan sound asleep after a long day that included shopping for cat paraphernalia, dining and being photographed with Governor Jindal at the luncheon, and adopting the new kitten. TacoBelle and Rosie were sound asleep scooted beneath the covers. Me? I was togged up in my improper fitting CPAP mask, complete with my book, and wondering what the new kitty would think when she saw me in this imitation space mask.

I didn't have to wonder long.

Quite unexpectedly, all of a sudden, a black furry blur leaped straight up from out of nowhere and landed right smack-dab in the middle of the sleeping pups like "Boo!"

Scared them from here to Texas. TacoBelle shot off the bed and didn't come back for three days. She sought sleeping quarters elsewhere.

At that very moment, I renamed the rapscallion "BooCat."

BooCat fit.

She was no Maybelline. She was no MayBelle. She was definitely not a Miss Kitty. She was bad. She was BooCat!

With an explanation point.

Magnificent mouser genes, if it moves, BooCat pounces. That includes wagging dog tails. In fact, she finds all wagging tails irresistible. Including her own.

Rosie eventually accepted BooCat as a rowdy playmate even though occasionally when BooCat gets too rowdy, Rosie hides under the covers. At first, this ruse worked. She was safe under there. Until BooCat figured out how to slip under there too. In essence, she tracked her down. Rosie can run, but she cannot hide.

Rosie accepts BooCat, but I can tell she considers her a nuisance. It startles her when BooCat swats her on the nose just because she can. BooCat's the queen of sneak attacks.

When all the playing is done, BooCat curls up with Rosie, licking her face like a mama cat with a baby. It doesn't matter Rosie's bigger than Boo.

Let me rephrase that. Rosie's larger around. She weighs more. She's longer, discounting tails. But with her short Dachshund legs, she's shorter than BooCat.

There have been legendary animal friendships such as Bambi and Thumper, Milo and Otis, Charlotte and Wilbur, Tiger and Roo. Now there's BooCat and Rosie.

Boo grooms Rosie. They play together. They curl up and sleep together. Boo exhibits a devotion to Rosie that's sweetly phenomenal. It appears to be love at first sight on her part. Rosie's not quite as enamored; but rather more tolerable instead.

Perhaps it's the moving from household-to-household from an early age that caused Boo to forge a close bond with sweet, gentle Rosie.

After BedlamBooCat turned the bed into her private playground, I had to build TacoBelle a fort at the foot before she'd even consider sleeping in the same room with this bad BooBaby. Eventually she overcame her damaged dignity brought on by this intruder. But for quite some time it wasn't such a peaceable kingdom at bedtime.

Fact of the matter, for all of her life TacoBelle's chosen to sleep beneath the covers on the bed. Since this incident, she has never again completely covered up. It's like sleeping with one eye open; if that cat is going to jump on her, she wants to see it coming.

Even still, there are moments when Taco's private haven takes a hit. Constructed from a quilt folded at the foot of the bed in such a way it offers a well in which Taco can sleep safely. That's not to say

15 / How BooCat Got Her Name

it's one-hundred percent foolproof. No place is. We'd need a moat full of alligators for total safety and even then, Boo'd probably figure out a way to thwart the 'gators.

TacoBelle can be curled up, barely visible ensconced in her quilt-constructed fort with the sides folded up high, when BadBoo sneaks up on her, reaches across the quilt-divide and swats her.

Taco wakes with a snarl, leaps out of her sleeping quarters toward the pesky cat, who's stopped inches away, lays back down low with ears flattened. Content that she's made her statement, Taco shakes off the moment. She takes a breath and you can see her muscle relax. She's got the situation under control. But, as she turns around to get back into her private bed, BooCat leaps over her and plops herself into the center. She begins licking her sleek black fur as though she's always been right there. It's one slick move.

That's when TacoBelle makes her way up to my side, curls up, and attempts to fall back into doggie slumber land.

Oh, but the black devil cat's not done yet. Not every night, but fairly regularly, after Taco's been usurped from her fort, relocates at my side, is on the brink of falling back to sleep, Boo abandons Taco's bed—her point's been made and like the Little Engine That Could, she did —and she strolls up beside me mere inches from where Taco's repositioned. She paws at my arm. I move it so she can slip into the crook.

What happens is, with this maneuver, BooCat scoots TacoBelle out of another sleeping spot.

Experts in the field claim cats and dogs don't operate logically. It's not in their makeup. Therefore, it's determined they'll never reach the scale of human intelligence. But, you tell me, isn't some degree of logic playing through Boo's actions?

I think so.

She knows what she's doing and therefore she's doing it. Frankly, I believe pawing at my arm so that I'll make the crook available shows some manner of intelligence on this magnificent cat's part. Not to mention the way she's bumping TacoBelle out of her sleeping quarters. For all the skeptics who declare cats and dogs cannot reason, just tell me, what's BrilliantBoo doing if not reasoning? I rest my case.

This is when TacoBelle goes back to her fort.

What a game we play. BossanovaBooCat's the game master. She

75

writes all the rules. The rest of us are only pawns on her chess board. We don't get to collect two-hundred dollars when we pass Go. We're lucky if we get to pass Go at all.

Except for occasionally playing musical sleep-spot-swaps, in the end, TacoBelle got her groove back. And BooCat adopted Sweet Baby Rose. And the name BooCat stuck. She's unequivocally BooCat.

How Rosie Lost Her Bounce

16

"If it were not for my cat and dog, I think I could not live." (Ebenizer Elliot)

Rosie has reason for not being too rowdy. Besides getting on in years, she awoke May 18, 2007, and her back legs were paralyzed. I rushed her to Dr. White's office and according to X-rays, she'd developed Canine Intervertebral Disc Disease (IVD). The anti-inflammatory Prednisone was prescribed. He was honest and said the ailment could go either way. She could be paralyzed for life, or with medication and a lot of rest, in a month or so, she could conceivably snap out of it.

It's most frustrating that dogs cannot talk; and gut-wrenching because Rosie didn't understand why she was so completely unable to move—her back end was dead weight. And she was in considerable pain. Her pain was my pain.

So even tempered, so sweet, so loving—but also so neurotic, wanting to be with me twenty-four/seven. Her scooting, dragging her back legs, rubbed them raw. Because she'd follow me wherever I went, which was detrimental to her condition, I had to take the sad measure of putting her into a dog crate so she'd rest. To see her so incapacitated and in pain was killing my soul.

I kept the kennel beside my chair but she wanted in my lap. How to explain to a dog that bed rest's required? That this wasn't punishment, it was a necessity?

Dachshunds are more prone to IVD than many other breeds. It has to do with her short legs and her long body. She'd just turned five that May.

After a "ruff" weekend, we visited Dr. Glenn Melton, the other veterinarian in town. As with human ailments, sometimes you feel better with a second opinion and perhaps another suggested means of treatment.

Diagnosed as a stage four out of five, he seriously recommended surgery, but only offered a forty-to-fifty-percent cure rate. The nearest surgeon doing this type operation was located in Little Rock, Arkansas. The saddest thing in the world is realizing I couldn't handle the cost; it was prohibitive. By this time I was researching K-9 carts.

I picked up Rosie and put her in bed with Taco and me at the end of each day. I'd wake at night when I heard her scooting toward the ramp propped against the bed. The ramp makes it possible for Rosie and TacoBelle to go up and down and off and on the bed.

There's a set of wooden pet stairs, but TacoBelle developed double hernias and had a difficult time lifting her hind legs up onto the bottom step; and Rosie grew so long she outgrew them. Chuck stapled carpet to a stout piece of plywood and propped it on the side of the bed where no man dares to go.

Even when the pups are well, operating on all cylinders, a running start is usually required to climb the ramp. Sometimes they slide downward like a runaway snowmobile. But it beats a blank. My bed is quite high off the ground. After my first back surgery, my wonderfully sweet and thoughtful daughter bought it for me. She'd done her research and was assured it would be easier for somebody with a bad back to get in and out of. I love my high bed. But it did require special provisions when I added a couple inside dogs to the household.

I lifted Rosie down to go potty on puppy pads. I was sleep deprived, feeling my age.

Nonsensically, after that first night I told TacoBelle—because I talk to my dogs—to wake me up if Rosie needed off the bed. I didn't want her to attempt to maneuver the ramp on her own.

Guess what? Sometime in the middle of the second night I felt a little dog nose bumping me in the face. It was TacoBelle. Rosie was wide awake and needed lifting off the bed. I know pets pickup on a lot of what we say. And while it's pretty farfetched to think TacoBelle actually comprehended my instructions, it happened. That makes it pretty cool. Forget the lack of opposable thumbs, TacoBelle is smarter than the average person I know.

The next night Taco woke me again around two in the morning.

Martha M. called with encouraging news about her dog's bout and recovery from IVD.

Lucy Z. brought a sack of holistic meds her dog Raja had done well on when it suffered the same ailment. Harry Z. flew Raja to Dallas for acupuncture. Raja recovered.

As an added note, Lucy Zaunbrecher has her own Cajun cooking show on the Public Broadcasting Network (PBS). She's not only a good cook she's a good neighbor too.

It was a grand day when Rosie supported herself on those pitiful back legs for a split-second. Encouraged, I began to dare hope maybe somewhere down this rocky road she'd regain use of her back legs.

On June 3, she wobbled on all fours, taking steps. She eventually developed a sort of hop-along bounce. As she progressed, she wagged her tail and did doggie smiles. I smiled too.

Bear in mind, with her rear legs paralyzed, her tail remained wagless.

Finally one night she gnawed on her red rubber bone before going to sleep. A good indication she was finally feeling better. She'd been in too much in pain to chew her favorite chew-bone.

She had one more bout a year later, but recovered fully excepting a slight hitch in her get-along. But it's working for her. She recovered. So did I.

Did You Hear the One About Opporknockety?

17

"Both dogs and cats desire affection almost more than they desire a tasty morsel—almost." (Barbara Sharik)

Thinking back, one particular incident comes to mind initially involving Gizzy. It was Saturday. There was no reason to rise-and-shine early but Gizzy had other ideas. She needed a Potty Run. When nature calls and the Gizzard barks, I do what I have to do.

Slipping out from under the warm covers, I made my way to the door. Keeping my eyes closed, I was hoping my inner self would interpret this as sleep-walking and thus allow me, once back in bed, to return to the Land of Nod.

Apparently it worked because I re-awakened an hour later and beauty of beauty, I awoke with a dream fresh on my mind. I'd dreamed about writing a column. It was totally bizarre. In my dream I was sitting on concrete steps chatting with a young man whose identity alluded me. He said, clear as day, "The Opporknockety story will make a good column."

The times I've been able to remember what I dreamed are few and far between but some have really been weird. Like the time I dreamed I told Tammi, the lady I work with at Bonita Town Hall, to go tell Mark, the guy who used to be the editor at the newspaper, to call Chuck, who used to be my husband, that Buck, the largest but most

17 / Did You Hear the One About Opporknockety?

loving of my outside dogs, was biting my hand and wouldn't let go.

Tammi came back and told me Mark wasn't coming into work that day.

My domino-effect dream, like the battle lost by want of a nail, with Mark out of the equation, left my hand doomed.

With that news, I had no choice but to wake up.

Awake, my hand hurt but it wasn't from being in a dog's mouth—I'd slept on it wrong. It stopped hurting as soon as circulation was restored. Sadly, not long after that dream, somebody shot and killed three-year-old Buck and his brother Big Red. Also six-year-old Goldie, a spayed female who'd never hurt a fly. They'd apparently gone wandering in our country neighborhood, and their bodies were found less than a mile away in a farm field. They never bothered anyone or anything. But they did enjoy taking an early morning constitutional when the weather was good.

While thinking about the Opporknockety dream, I made a pot of coffee. I fired up the computer and started typing. I knew I shouldn't let an idea slip away.

I dream but seldom remember. Also, once asleep, I rarely move all night long. I've awakened some mornings with the light on overhead and my glasses still perched on my nose and my book resting open across my chest. No wonder I wake up stiff. I sleep stiff. It makes for a most peaceful night for my furry bed-partners too. They settle in for the night knowing their mom won't be tossing and turning and disturbing their sleep. Generally, they also awaken in their same positions all around me.

Wait.

Let me correct that. When this incident occurred, that was the case. Since then, BooCat moved in. Now nobody wakes in the same position they started in. Bippity-Boppity-Boo sees to that.

The dream story was about a famous concert pianist who was scheduled to perform at Carnegie Hall. Preferring his own grand piano, he brought it from home but what with the move, it needed tuning.

Accordingly, the best piano tuner in the world was a guy named Opporknockety from India. The famous concert pianist insisted no one else would do. And so it was, at great expense, Opporknockety was flown to America.

As befitted his reputation, Opporknockety tuned perfectly. After which he returned to India.

The afternoon of the pending concert, stage hands carelessly moved the piano getting it out of tune again. In a panic, the pianist insisted Opporknockety be called back. But alas, Opporknockety, as with any master who's good and knows it, exercised his eccentricity and refused saying, "Sorry. Opporknickety only tunes once."

From this pun my dream took me and my young dream companion into a totally off-the-wall conversation in which I distinctly heard him say he'd recently learned that in an emergency a pen barrel could be used to perform a tracheotomy. Then I heard myself tell him about seeing a segment of the soap opera *As The World Turns,* one summer while still in high school. Where Penny's husband Neil, who was really a doctor but was keeping it a secret, performed an emergency tracheotomy using the barrel of a ballpoint pen and thereby let the cat out of the bag, giving away his true profession. Penny's brother Bob who was married to Lisa, was also a doctor.

Good golly, I thought to myself when I woke up, it's been forty-five years since I last saw that TV show. I found myself wondering if that's what's called long-term memory while I can't remember where I put my car keys five minutes earlier.

Neil let the cat out of the bag.

Next place my mind jumped was to wonder where that expression originated. We know it means to pass along a secret unintentionally. But who first made it up?

Authorities say in medieval England piglets were sold in the open marketplace and often the seller kept his pig in a bag, or poke. The keeping of the pig in a poke made it both easier for the seller to bring to market and for the buyer to take home.

Shady characters have been around for a very long time. Even during the Days of Yore, the shadiest of sellers sometimes tried to trick buyers by putting a cat in the bag because cats were more plentiful and easier to come by than piglets.

If a shrewd shopper peeked into the bag, sometimes the cat, if it was a cat instead of a pig, would get out of the bag. There were also instances when a cat caused such a ruckus that even the cheating merchant was forced to let it out of the bag before he was able to rook some unsuspecting buyer.

17 / Did You Hear the One About Opporknockety?

Another dream remembered was about me inventing a mesh mask. I was still trying to work the bugs out. No pun intended. The mask was for people who snore and consequently sleep with their mouths open. The mask was ideal for snoring campers to prevent bugs flying in their mouths while snoozing in the great outdoors. I dreamt I introduced a deluxe model complete with ear plugs to keep out earwigs.

The night before while in bed reading I spotted a tiny moth flitting around the overhead reading light. Subconsciously I must've feared once I turned out the light, the moth would find me in the dark and fly into my mouth.

BooSkat, where are you when I need you?

Not anything the public's clamoring for, inventing a bug-proof mask in my dream was peculiar. Consequently, considering the topics of my dreams, I long ago determined I don't have psychic powers. I can't see the future in my dreams. Should I happen to recall a dream I can usually attribute it to something that's already transpired—an event, something on television, the plot of a book or something somebody said. My dreams are about remembering the past, intermingled with a vivid imagination.

In any case, opportunity knocked with an idea, even if by way of a dream, and I went with it. I turned it into one of my weekly humor columns. There's no moral here.

Probably next time you see me I'll be the half-blind, semi-deaf old lady buying a lot of cat and dog food and kitty litter and bird and fish food and dreaming nonsensical dreams and dancing as fast as I can,

Truth be known, my goofy dreams probably stem from sleeping with dogs. And a cat.

Good Help is Hard to Find

18

"You can keep your Three-Dog-Nights. I'm partial to Two-Dog-One-Cat-Nights." (Barbara Sharik)

As a child matures, mothers expect them to take on a bit of responsibility around the house. Like making their beds. Picking up dirty socks and depositing them into the hamper sitting alongside.

Occasionally, during the teaching process some moms give up on slovenly kids and do it themselves. As soon as I figured this out, I admit I took advantage of my mom's good-hearted surrender. I should've been making my own bed long before I started. Because I know this now, I'm forever grateful and a little embarrassed too. I wasn't an easy kid to rear.

But, I paid for my raising as the old saying goes because I went through this tumultuous teaching time when turning my kids into tidy citizens. It worked for Theresa. It didn't work for Tony. And it would appear I'm doing it again. Since they live here too, I reckoned I'd put the pets to work. After all, they shed and add to the overall mess. I mean, every time I vacuum, I vacuum up a cat. Like passing on the Olympic Torch, I attempted to pass on the Fantastic Featherduster.

Because it's been said a house isn't a home unless you can write

18 / Good Help is Hard to Find

"I love you" in the dust on the coffee table, my house is about as homey as you can get. If you want you can write the entire lyrics of "Ninety-nine Bottles of Beer on the Wall" and maybe even the words to the "Old Lady Who Swallowed a Fly" on mine. Something needed to be done.

The first time I endeavored to convert the pets to helping out last year before Mom and Hershey died and before sweet Gizzy had to be helped over to the other side, I started with The Gizzard. She just stood there grinning, because at age fourteen, grinning was what she did best.

Rosie, the short-legged, long-bodied, affectionately neurotic dachshund looked pitiful. She seemed to say, "You know I can't reach the tabletop from down here. Besides, dust makes me sneeze."

Ah, and TacoBelle—purebred Chihuahua, ten years old at the time. I dropped the dust rag and approached TacoBelle about changing a light bulb. She responded, "Yo quero TacoBulb! I don't change no stinking light bulbs." Who'd she think she was? Cheech and Chong?

Forget the light bulb, I said. Let's just stick to dusting. She wagged her tail and barked, "Yo quiero! Taco dust? No way!" It seems that spoiled rotten alpha dogs don't dust either. That left Hershey cat, beautiful blue-eyed, long-haired, chocolate-point Himalayan, the closest thing to royalty this side of the Atlantic. He meowed, "Forget the dust. Feed me. Then make a lap. Then scratch behind my ears." Which proves a little dust never hurt anything and while dogs have masters, cats have staff. I'm just here to open pet food cans.

I can only guess what BooCat would say should I suggest she chip in and help around the house. First, I'd have to catch her. Then I'd have to get her attention.

No need expecting any help from SnowBird or George E. Tiel. SnowBird and George have been living below poverty level for so long that the last time I cleaned their cages, Snowbird stopped cooing and started chirping "Where am I?"

I could be wrong but I was sure I heard George say something about squalor and slum lord and then, "You gotta be kidding, right?"

Come to think of it, there's a strong possibility BooBandit would help so long as I assigned her the job of cleaning George and Snow-Bird's cages. She'd like that.

Regarding the bird cages, it's been said country fences need to be horse high, pig tight, and bull strong but when one of George's feathers gets wedged sideways in the skinny tube that carries dirt into the vacuum cleaner's dirt bag it requires a Congressional act, a Phillips screw driver and a college degree to unhook and undo the blockage. What happens is every bit as secure as those country fences.

You smell rubber burning, turn off the vacuum cleaner.

Hard work might pay off in the future but TacoBelle, Rosie, BooCat and me, we all know that idleness pays off now.

Furthermore, George E. Tiel and SnowBird know that the early bird still has to eat worms and the second mouse gets the cheese. Needless to say, the second mouse likely becomes BooCat's breakfast.

No One Sends Me Flowers Anymore

"Animals are such agreeable friends; they ask no questions, pass no criticisms." (George Elliot)

If I didn't sleep with a couple dogs and a cat, I'd be mighty lonesome, because otherwise, I live alone. On the upside, I stay up as late as I want. I own the remote and can watch whatever my little ol' heart desires.

Let me qualify. I can watch whatever I want provided my television can pick up the channel. Since the analog/digital conversion, I'm not a happy viewer. For sixty years I watched TV using rabbit ears and it was free. Television commercial drove TV. The elimination of the availability of analog which rendered thousands of televisions useless is an event I call "The Darkening of America."

I had several televisions. I have one in the spare bedroom. It's a small black and white, but it worked. It no longer works.

There's one in my bedroom that also played the now obsolete video cassettes. It no longer works.

The largest and oldest is in the living room. It's hooked into a VHS player, a DVD player, Karaoke machine, a 50-CD player, an old-fashioned turn table to play records from by-gone days, a radio, and an amp and surround sound speakers. Without a converter box, it no longer works.

There's one in the family room hooked up to a karaoke machine, turn table and tuner. Although it will play DVDs and Karaoke music, it no longer functions as a television.

The one in the kitchen is a small flat screen LCD plasma TV, but new as it is, it's not new enough to have the proper innards required to make the switch from analogue to digital. Without a converter box, it no longer works.

One of my favorite televisions is a little bitty hand-held portable I depended on during tornado warnings. The pets and I could sit in the hallway when a tornado warning was in effect and keep an eye on the weather with the little television set. It played in color, picked up all the channels and a passenger in the car could watch it while driving down the highway. Dead as a doornail, that visual connection to instant weather warnings is gone. Because it no longer works, I purchased a replacement portable handheld TV. The thing is, analog TVs picked up a signal even in a moving vehicle. The new digital portables do not. They must be stationary and they must be where there is a signal available practically next door to where you want to sit and watch. It's not made for use out in the country. It's definitely not made for viewing while sitting in a moving vehicle.

Oh yeah, I also have a black and white combo radio and television alarm, so I could either wake to TV or radio, in my bedroom. The radio still works, but the TV doesn't.

Lastly, there's the black and white television that used to serve as a monitor for a couple outside video surveillance cameras. That's dead in the water too. I'd see and hear who was coming to my door. I'd even check on the outside dogs, but not any more I won't.

Thank you, Congress. And thank you Television manufacturers. Thank you satellite and cable companies. And any one else whose pockets were lined as a result of this secretly slipped-through-the-backdoor activity.

Here's the thing: if your television's non-digital, it was destined to go dark February 17, 2009. End of story. I called this "National Analog Log-Off Day."

Digital television (DTV) is, in semi-simple terms, a telecommunication system for broadcasting and receiving moving pictures and sounds by means of digital signals, in contrast to analog signals used by analog—formerly traditional—TV. DTV uses digital modulation

19 / No One Sends Me Flowers Anymore

data. Digital modulation data is data that has been digitally compressed and requires decoding by a specially designed television set, or a standard receiver with a set-top box, or a PC fitted with a television card.

In plain English, if your TV was analog—and chances are good almost everybody's was— it became a part of the biggest boatload of garbage ever created on one single day. I'm personally left with seven non-working televisions in the blink of an eye, the flick of a wrist, the turn of a screw, the cast of a vote and probably the opening and closing of a couple wallets.

I figure that day at the city dump was busier than Bourbon Street during Mardi Gras. Probably if you listened real close you subliminally heard Don McLean singing about Chevy's on the levees, American Pies and the day the music died.

Me? I sang about the day analog TV died. I visualized a million TVs junked all across America creating Mt. Magnavox. They'd join 8-Tracks, phonograph turntables, wind-up clocks, box cameras, board games, console TVs, reel-to-reel recorders, live operator-assisted corded telephones, movie projectors, and Dos-driven PCs.

Ain't technology grand?

Anger never makes me feel better, so I try not to be too upset that now I only receive two TV channels on a good day on the couple TVs with converter boxes attached. When I moved to the country, a million miles from no where, forty years ago, I thought only receiving three channels was bad. One step forward, three steps back.

No more free antenna TV. Hide and watch. It's just around the corner.

The conversion deadline was signed into law in early 2006. And silly me, I thought our legislators were just signing laws having to do with Saving Time Daily by making the American Robots change clocks back and forth a couple times a year. But by golly, those tricky rascals were also designating our TVs obsolete with the stroke of a pen.

According to Wikipedia, and I quote: "The analog switch-off ruling, which so far has met with little opposition from consumers or manufacturers, would render all non-digital televisions dark and obsolete on the switch-off date, unless connected to an external off-the-air tuner, analog or digital cable, or a satellite system."

BooCat Unleashed

Not surprisingly the ruling was met with little opposition because the average individual didn't know about it. Once we found out, there was nothing we could do but dig deep and buy all new televisions or converter boxes.

Another joke. Coupons offered by our government to save $40 when buying a converter box, limit of two per family. Each family was allowed only two coupons and they came complete with an unreasonably short expiration date. Use 'em or lose 'em. Which would've been fine except the coupons came out before converter boxes were available so by the time they were, the coupons were expired. Then the government ran out of coupons altogether.

Naturally, manufacturers didn't oppose the switch-off. Look at all the TVs they sold. And converter boxes. And new so-called smart antennas. I bought a smart antenna and it doesn't work. Read my lips: "It does not work." You might as well read my lips because you cannot watch my TV.

I never watched much TV despite the TV sets in every room. That had more to do with convenience than volume. But I'm unhappy I can't watch American idol. I used to be addicted. I'm almost weaned, about to get over my withdrawal symptoms. I read a lot while the furry kids sleep a lot.

Just two more things and I'll stop complaining about something I can't do anything about. One thing is that I said I get two channels. I do. But one's a stationary weather map. No writing. No talking. No nothing. Just a map. But it's a legitimate channel.

Why did the world go digital? It's not better.

All my TVs? Useless, every one. Destined for Mt. Magnavox. Naturally, not watching television gives me a lot more time to devote to talking to TacoBelle, Rosie and BooCat. Still and all, for sixty years I watched television. With an antenna. For free. I feel like I'm in a third-world country with only the two channels, and those are iffy because if it rains, they scramble, all of which has nothing to do with living alone.

But, let me add, after my rant about the analog to digital conversion—including a column in the Bastrop newspaper titled "No free lunches and no more free TV," I received a letter from Louisiana Public Broadcasting Programming manager advising a DTV Hotline's available and she'd be happy to have one of the PBS Assistant Chief

19 / No One Sends Me Flowers Anymore

Engineer (whom she said she calls the Digital Whisperer) talk to me or email me about my television reception problems.

Additionally, I heard from my friend Tom C.

I'd spent money on several Smart made-for-digital TV inside antennas that did no good, therefore, I hesitated to spend several hundred dollars purchasing an outside antenna and finding and paying someone to erect it for me. If it didn't work any better than the inside antennas I'd be out a lot more than I could afford to throw away. And I refused to pay for Satellite TV. Like the squeaky wheel, I made enough noise so that Tom C. constructed an outside antenna for me and Chuck installed it.

Tom C. found the antenna blueprint plans on the Internet and built one for the club house at his golf course. Because it worked, he offered to make one for me.

Bless his kind heart. While nobody sends me flowers anymore, one special person sent me an outside TV antenna. Flowers are here today, gone tomorrow. A TV antenna's good until the first tornado touches down. Lord willing, that'll not be anytime soon.

I now can watch four networks and a dozen Louisiana Public Broadcast channels. I'm much happier than I was when I first started lodging complaints that fell on empty airwaves.

When it comes to meals when living with TacoBelle, Rosie and BooCat the biggest dilemma I'm faced with is determining what to steam, simmer or scorch. Still in all, I eat what and when I want.

Obviously, dinner conversation might be considered lacking by some unless you do cat- and dog-speak, which I do. Leftovers become a way of life. But TacoBelle and Rosie don't mind. BooCat's not fallen into the people-food trap; preferring her Purina Kitten Chow best of all. With two exceptions. Cream cheese and dog biscuits. Good Boo.

I think it'd be convenient to have a large trashcan and a vending machine with matching microwave in my kitchen. Most my meals go from the freezer to the microwave to the table and to the trash can. You know, it's heat it, eat it and toss it. Who needs fine china? My china's served its purpose—no pun intended.

If I don't want to clean house, who's going to notice? Definitely not TacoBelle, Rosie and BlaséBooCat. Not only won't they notice, as already determined, they're not going to jump in and help with it either.

The most comfy chair in the living room is mine. It's okay to use up all the hot water when I shower. Is my toothpaste squeezed in the middle of the tube? So what.

I eat the first piece of chocolate in a box of candy. The last one too. Really, since giving dogs and cats chocolate is a no-no, I can eat the whole box. Myownself. The only thing is, after a chocolate orgy, I stay away from the scales. Naturally, TacoBelle, Rosie and BooCat are convinced I make a better lap because I'm fluffy.

It's not ladylike for a woman to snore, sweat or crack jokes about bodily functions, which is okay because, since I live alone, no one knows if I snore or not. Except the furry kids. And obviously they don't care. And if the CPAP machine's doing its job, I don't snore any more anyway.

I used to refer to my snoring as purring. Sounded more ladylike. Whether I do or not, BooBells's purring right along side me and Rosie, with her nasal allergies is sniffing and TacoBelle, who suffers from a Chihuahua trachea problem in her old age, makes her own share of nightly noises.

All together now: Snore, snort, sneeze, cough, purr.

Actually factually, I could sleep on one side of the bed one week, and the other side the next, cutting down on doing laundry so often.

Speaking of sleeping on one side of the bed, on the far side is a tray. On it sits my eyeglass case, notepad and pencil for midnight inspirational ideas, a thermometer leftover from the last time I was sick, a phone book and the telephone and a list of 10-Codes and signals because my scanner's on the other side of the bed. I leave it on twenty-four/seven and much like a coocoo clock, rarely even hear it anymore. I only tune in when something familiar catches my ear. Every now and then one of the dispatchers or police throw in something I'm not familiar with. When you live in such a small place and you come to know almost everybody, a scanner's a good thing.

When I remove the sheets from the bed, I lift the tray, pull the dirty sheet off that corner; same process in reverse to remake it—lift the tray full of necessities, and tuck the sheet corner over the mattress.

I use only half as many towels and half as many dishes.

19 / No One Sends Me Flowers Anymore

I sing karaoke. TacoBelle, Rosie, and BeBopBooCat are my best audience. They don't boo, hiss or howl. They never cut and run. Taco and Rosie wag their tails and are most tolerant. BoogieWoogieBooCat lounges atop her three-tiered Cat Park and looks mysterious. None of the fids* have a clue I can't carry a tune. Dogs love you unconditionally. They really do. Mine are no exceptions. Likewise, BooCat.

My favorite song I sing to BooCephus is Jon Anderson's "Wild and Blue," except I sing Wild and Boo. Rosie gets "How Much is the Doggie in the Window" by Patti Paige and TacoBelle is honored with George Thorogood's "Bad to the Bone" dedicated to her. And when I sing "Yellow" somebody special knows it's for him.

The downside of living alone mostly means I take my own trash to the corner; pay somebody to mow my yard; change burned out light bulbs (because TacoBelle refuses); tote my own groceries into the house and no one sends me flowers anymore.

But I get a lot of liquid sugar kisses from Taco and Rosie and some mighty fine head bunting and purring from BooCoodle.

---

* Furry, fuzzy, feathery kids.

The Seeing-Eye Cat

20

"If anybody has ever had a child, then they know how I feel about BooCat, TacoBelle and Rosie." (Barbara Sharik)

BooCat doesn't think I know where to go unless she leads me, underfoot with every step. She thinks I can't sit unless she jumps in the chair first to show me where and how.

She leads me to the kitchen first thing each morning. I take two steps, she wraps herself around my ankles. I stop walking. She stops wrapping. She unwraps. I take two more steps, she wraps again. I know to walk carefully. It takes us about five minutes to go from the bedroom to the kitchen in the morning. I have to wonder how I ever made it to the kitchen before Boo came along. This is a morning ritual, She's just so overjoyed I woke up and we're going to get breakfast. Together.

She approaches me with her tail straight up in the air, a move that signals a friendly approach. Besides wrapping her tail around my legs, she walks back and forth in front of me.

BooCat rubs up against my legs, wrapping her tail around me, not just to lead, guide and direct me to the kitchen, but it is a complex cat system whereby she's declaring that she likes me. She's greeting me and making friendly contact. It's a cat thing.

She's also marking me as her person. With each rub, she's also picking up my scent. Cats have special scent glands on their temples, the side of their mouths and at the root of their tails.

Experts declare that after a cat rubs against its human, then sits and licks its fur, it's tasting its human. I love my BooDelicious, but not enough to taste her. Good thing she doesn't expect me to reciprocate.

Let me say right here and now, I've lived with animals all my life. I love all my pets. Admittedly, I feel more toward some than others. That's human nature. It'd be good if all love were felt equally, but it just doesn't happen that way.

But my bonding with BooCoo is one of the fastest I've ever experienced with any animal. I'm a love-at-first-sight sort of person with people. I seldom find romance growing if it hasn't sparked at the onset. That's what happened between my heart and Boo. She stole it right from the get-go. Quite simply put, Boo and I are made for each other.

I'd like to believe in Karma and actually practiced it way before I knew it had a name. As a kid I believed if you were mean to someone, or had bad thoughts, it'd come back to haunt you. I never talked bad about a friend because somewhere inside me, I knew it'd backfire if I did. That's the essence of Karma as I understand it. It's a what goes around—both good and bad—kind of thing.

BeguilingBoo and I have some sort of Karma thing going. Like we're meant for each other—our friendship's meant to be. She went from household to household and didn't stay because none of those places were where she was meant to be. She was searching for me. I'm sure glad she found me.

Otherwise, how would I get to the kitchen every morning? But, admittedly, sometimes even with BoomerangBoo's help I run in circles. It used to be when Theresa and Tony were little I'd meet myself coming and going, going, gone. A real saga of circles, to be expected. Mother, Domestic Engineer, community leader and club woman, writer, artist, 4-H Leader, home gardener, Sunday school teacher and one-half household contributor and wife. Until the wife thing broke apart, it was all good. Once that was behind me, it was good again.

After the children were grown and out on their own, my circle running took a different tack. I call it AAADD— Age-Activated Attention Deficit Disorder.

BooCat Unleashed

Mostly it starts in the morning. I plan to sit over whatever book I'm reading and enjoy a freshly brewed cup of hot coffee before starting my day. I've been around long enough so I know a day started in calm pleasantness is beneficial to one's mental well-being for the rest of the day.

That is, until the AAADD kicks in. Alas, BooCat, while an ideal Seeing-Eye Cat in the mornings, can do nothing for my AAADD. Would that she could, but it's mine to suffer alone. She follows me around and keeps an eye on me, but she cannot replenish my thoughts when they get side-tracked. She's good, my little Karma cat, but not that good.

Typical, this happened one day. While the coffee was dripping, I decided to put a load of clothes in the washer. Heading for the laundry room, I heard the outside dogs barking. That reminded me I'd best fill their breakfast bowls. After feeding and petting a passel of happy heads attached to wagging tails, I noticed the sunrise. It was splendid. I have a passion for taking pictures and sunrises are among my favorites.

I rushed back into the house and retrieved my camera, walked halfway up the driveway and started snapping. I've taken some amazing morning photos. The sun rising and casting long shadows from the live oaks in the front yard, the sun aglow looking like fire in the sky, storm clouds illuminated by the rising sun, big white fluffy clouds looking like marshmallow cream.

After the photo session with Mother Nature, all the while being accompanied by an adoring pack of dogs, I continued my journey to the laundry room, only to notice George and Little White Dove needed fresh water.

BarbaricBoo tried to help me with this task. Anything having to do with the birds, she wants to help. As a result, she stays in constant trouble. I believe she believes she's now living at the most amazing house. It's loaded with good cat things: birds, mice, dogs to either play with or torment, and lots of cat toys and cat furniture.

And occasional cream cheese. Earlier I'd opened a stack of club crackers and got an unopened package of cream cheese from the fridge. I planned to nibble on a few cheese crackers when my coffee was done dripping and call it breakfast. I took the package out of the fridge and BoundingBoo came galloping towards me, jumped up in the chair and attempted to take me down. Somehow she got a whiff of the cream cheese even as I took it from the refrigerator, because she was by my side even as it was being opened and she wanted some. Now.

I cut off a small slice, dropped it into her bowl and she was in heaven.

The whole cream cheese thing took place in a mere matter of seconds, and it amazed me. If I didn't know better I'd swear she recognized the silver box as it came from the fridge because she came running even before the slab of cheese was unwrapped.

After her cream cheese frenzy, she and I were at the point of adding fresh water to the birds' cages. I realize I send mixed messages when I tell her she's such a bad little sweet good girl. On one hand I know she means no harm; it's in her genes. On the other, she means harm for the same reason—it's in her genes.

Watering and feeding George and SnowBird made me think I ought to refill the outside bird feeders too. That reminded me I needed to water the hanging baskets outside and the plants on the patio.

What a feather-eating party Boo would have if she was allowed outside. She'd likely consider the bird feeding station BooChef's feeding station. Sparrow a' la mode.

Finally, I put a load of clothes in the washer. By then my coffee was cold so I decided I'd vacuum and mop. Setting the mop bucket in the bathtub, I filled it with hot water, mopped the kitchen, dumped the dirty water, added fresh, mopped the dining room, and continued this routine until all rooms were mopped.

To end this task, before getting side-tracked with something else, I rinsed the mop under fresh running water in the tub only to find the water wasn't draining out.

What's this?

I plunged. I silently cursed. In the end, on hands and knees, I dipped the water out of the tub. You probably already guessed, I didn't have any Draino. All I had were frayed nerves. TacoBelle, Rosie and Boo-Cat found mom on her knees very interesting. Wheels were spinning in their heads (I could smell rubber burning) as they tried to determine if we were on the verge of a new game.

Blast-offBooCat leaped up on the side of the tub and almost, but not quite, leaped in.

She spied the water just in time. She likes pawing at the drip, but she's not ready to take a real plunge yet.

Later, when Chuck stopped by, I told him about the tub. He took a look and returned grinning.

What?

He said I must've bumped the tub stopper lever while filling the mop bucket. He pulled the plug and the water promptly drained. Frustration is missing the obvious.

Because of arthritis making it difficult to turn my head to look out the back window when backing up, and what with a pack of dogs that occasionally find laying on the drive in the path of my new-fangled computerized car ideal, I had Chuck install a backup camera and monitor I'd purchased. The process necessitated he disengage the battery cable to splice a wire and when reattached, the clock had to be reset. That's complicated enough, but the compass also needed to be recalibrated.

Believe it or not, calibrating the car's compass required driving the car in circles until I was dizzy. Every time I tried driving in circles at the corner of my driveway, cars came. Where'd they all come from? Try to drive in circles and it's like Kilbourne Highway became the New York City Freeway.

Finally, I drove round and round in the Bonita Town Hall parking lot at least six times before the computer messaged that the compass was calibrated. I have no idea what anyone who might've seen me thought I was doing. If they knew me at all, they probably didn't want to know. Most likely they'd be afraid to get involved.

So, if I'm not running in circles, I'm driving in them. In fact, I've had to recalibrate the car's compass two more times since then. Circles every time.

And speaking of driving in circles, what's the difference between driving down the road or up the road? I've not determined which is which. If you're coursing south you might say you're going to drive down the road and head up the road if driving north, but what about east and west? Animals aren't so dumb. They don't care if it's up or down, they've got built-in radar and just know which way to go.

Another thing that always befuddles me are man-directions. A man will tell you to turn south or turn west. I say, speak girlie, please. Is that left or right? It took awhile, but I know my left from my right. Pledge of Allegiance: right hand is right; over heart. Wedding ring, left hand is left. Viola!

Which reminds me, not long after I got my it's-new-to-me car, and this was before the first circle saga took place, I glanced at the simulated 747 instrument panel and saw a large bright green "E." Yikes!

My mind went crazy conversing within itself asking "How can it be empty already? I just filled it up. Something's broke."

I turned right on McGinty Road and it went from "E" to "SE." I really freaked. I'm figuring "SE" stands for "So Empty." That is, until I turned into my driveway and the green "SE" turned to "W."

About then I realized "W" doesn't stand for "Whoa! Gas is all gone." It doesn't stand for 'Wise" either. I know. Everybody's figured out by now the car wasn't running on Empty; it was headed East. When I told someone about this they asked if I used to be a blonde, adding once a blonde, always a blonde, even gray-headed. Actually, it's a good thing I was a blonde. Otherwise, I'd have to consider myself just plain stupid. Better a gray-haired blonde than a stupid broad.

Although it's all sexist, it's also all in fun. To quote Hafiz, "There is no pleasure without a tincture of bitterness." Maybe I ought to let the dog drive.

In any case, no matter the color of my hair, at least I learned to tell the difference between running on empty and heading east. Everyday that I learn something new is a good day, satisfying my quench for knowledge.

Wit's End Comedy Club

21

"Happiness is dog shaped, I say." (Chapman Pincher)

Picture a turtle on its back trying to flip over right-side-up. Does anyone else have days like that? I first called my homeplace Wit's End because when you're here, you're there.

There's a reason, actually a never-ending series of reasons, why I selected the name Wit's End. The term, wit's end, can mean being at the end of one's rope, hanging on by a fingernail. That's not why I named it Wit's End, although I've been known to tie a knot at the end of my rope in order to maintain.

Basically, naming it Wit's End had to do with wit as in humor rather than as in half- or as in witless. Then, with the escalation of the wit (as in humor), I tacked on Comedy Club.

Fact is, the longer I hang around here, the more amusing it gets. Therefore, the addition of Comedy Club is appropriate. Now, if anyone asks where I live, I heartily tell them I reside at Wit's End Comedy Club. As a consequence of living at Wit's End Comedy Club, I have those upside-down turtle position days.

Regularly.

Just ask the furry kids.

I remember the time I arrived home from work around nine-forty-five one night. I'd been at the newspaper. I petted a multitude of

21 / Wit's End Comedy Club

heads connected to wriggling-with-joy bodies and wagging tails. I headed inside where I was met by a starving Hershey and a couple hungry hounds. This was before BijouBooCat moved in, adding to the humorousness that is our home.

Dried food is available twenty-four/seven but they expect canned pet chow around six in the evening. Actually, they'd prefer people-food around six each evening, but mostly they get canned. Tonight it was late. They weren't happy biscuit eaters. The biscuits were missing.

I read recently that dry cat food that is high in carbohydrates and vegetable protein can cause health problems. This particular animal columnist recommended giving cats canned cat food such as Wellness, Petguard, Evanger's or Evo. In his article he stated that a cat also needs up to a teaspoon of good-quality fish oil in its food every day, suggesting to begin with one drop and slowly increasing the amount if the cat's finicky.

Well, I didn't find any of those brands at my Walmart and I'm not sure where to find fish oil either. I want to do right by my fur babies but there are so many conflicting reports.

Another guide to feeding cats advised a cat's diet should include a teaspoon or so of vegetable oil each day to keep the coat shining, to prevent constipation and the buildup of hair balls. Maybe that's what the fish oil thing was all about also. It's hard to incorporate oil into the dried food and that's what BooCat prefers; you just have to hope it's included in the ingredients already.

The columnist's reasoning was that while some cats do well on dry cat foods, occasionally there comes a time in their lives when their kidneys or immune systems give out prematurely and they can develop gastrointestinal diseases such as megacolon and inflammatory bowl disease.

BooCee doesn't care much for canned cat food—at least not any of the brands I've offered her. TacoBelle likes Boo's canned food just fine. When Boo turns up her nose and saunters away, TacoBelle sticks her nose into the bowl and inhales. Rosie likes everybody's food—wet or dry, people or pets. She's a glutton.

It's been drilled in my head if I adore my pets, I must avoid giving them much in the way of human food and most especially limit or avoid all fast food, something they beg for should they come within sniffing distance.

Of course since we live so far out in the country there are no fast food places within many miles. Therefore, rarely are they tempted. If I buy a burger, it's usually gone before I get home.

"Smell my breath," is all that's left. And they do. They really do. They can tell mom ate something really good and they didn't get any.

I know there are specific human foods that are a no-no. Like chocolate. It can be fatal, sending dogs into seizures and killing them. Recently I read raisins are verboten, and to go easy on onions and peas, they can give a dog gas. Don't quote me on that. I've had gassy dogs that never ate a pea or onion in their lives.

Realistically, pets have a different digestive system than humans. Their nutritional needs are unlike ours. It's been proven fats are difficult for dogs to digest. Still, I believe if I cook veggies and boneless chicken breast, avoiding fatty accompaniments, that's got to be as healthful, if not more so, than some of what I dump out of a can claiming the "flavor" of chicken or beef.

I make it a point that the canned foods I buy my babies reads "100% Complete and Balanced Nutrition" somewhere on the label.

Yet, when the label reads "flavor" instead of "real" I wonder if that means a factory worker dunked a tough old hen into a barrel of boiling water and then added a teaspoon of that dunked-chicken-water to the batch of other ingredients. That way the company can truthfully say it has the flavor of chicken in the product. I know these big companies are slick and it's always about the bottom line no matter how kind and caring the ad folks indicate they are. The advertising folks are getting paid big bucks too. Yes. I'm skeptical. When you reach my age, you will be skeptical too.

Considering the possibility of a chicken being dunked in water and that water distributed is all but confirmed by what's written right on the label of one brand of canned food. The first listing under ingredients reads: "Water sufficient for processing chicken."

You read that, didn't you? *"Water sufficient for processing chicken…"* ?

No need for the jury to deliberate. The verdict is in. Dunked-chicken-water. Number one ingredient. Water. Sufficient for processing chicken.

21 / Wit's End Comedy Club

It doesn't actually list Chicken. Just water sufficient for processing. And it doesn't say how many chickens. The lack of the plural "s" indicates it is only one chicken. Lots of water. Not much chicken.

I rest my case.

The remainder of the ingredient listing includes: "meat by-products, wheat flour, liver, rice, chicken meal, salt, animal fat, vegetable oil..." along with some really strange-sounding stuff. It winds up including caramel color, onion and garlic extracts.

Hey. I just read onions aren't good for dogs. So what are onions doing in the can of dog food?

I know what I cook for my furry babies is more sanitary and better tasting. Remember what happened several years ago with the on-purpose addition of melamine in pet food imported from China? This stuff ended up in many major brands. Expensive foods were just as affected, as the cheaper products.

I subscribe online to *Google Alerts for Pet Food Recalls*. In the end, thousands of dogs and some cats were adversely affected with many dying. Not to mention, since then there have been recalls involving salmonella and various other problems detrimental to the health of our pets. Most recently, cat food that lacked proper vitamins was recalled. This recalled cat food was allegedly responsible for the death of a number of domestic cats. Domestic cats translates to somebody's furry child. That's heartbreaking.

In October 1999, statistics according to the American Animal Hospital Association, found that about one in every four pet owners feed people-food to their dogs every day. That means, one out of every four pets are very happy because their human owners indulge them. But, not necessarily healthier.

Despite TacoBelle and Rosie's love of all things human, I treat them with less than one percent of their overall diet; more like a treat than a meal.

BooCat prefers dry kitten chow. SmartBoo. Except for one thing as previously mentioned. The only people foodstuff BooCat has ever begged for, stretching her long lithe body from floor to table edge, is cream cheese.

That's my girl!

The only thing I ever shoplifted was a package of cream cheese. I was two or three at the time. Maybe.

Somewhere in my mind's eye and stored in my memory bank, whether I actually recall the incident or if the image is there because Mom told me about it is debatable. The story goes that when I was very young and Mom was buying groceries I disappeared momentarily. I was quickly located behind the butcher's counter. I'd snitched a package of cream cheese, opened it and was taking a bite when I was apprehended, as they say, red handed. Or cream-cheese-handed as it were.

I still crave cream cheese. So does BestBuyBooCat.

I grew up believing cats like milk. Not just dairy goods like cottage cheese, yogurt and cheese, but real milk. Boo doesn't care for any of these things except the cream cheese. But as it turns out, it's just as well that she doesn't care for milk because authorities now say not to give milk to adult cats because it's too difficult for many to digest and can cause diarrhea.

Is there anything we were told when we were growing up that still holds true? If we're not supposed to give cats milk; do mice still eat cheese? Do robins eat worms early in the morning? Are blue birds blue? Is it true what they say about bears in the woods? Is that why all the Charmin Bathroom Tissue advertisements features bears?

Fish is supposed to be good. Cooked mackerel, salmon and any fish except red-met tuna. Red-meat tuna can cause a fatal cat disease called Steatitis. My cousin Mike's cat, Debby Cakes, won't eat anything except tuna. Apparently what he feeds her doesn't consist of red-meat tuna because she's been thriving on it for many, many years.

I have to believe when the pet food can reads that it contains "One-hundred percent complete and balanced nutrition," that it's more than I can provide from my cook stove. In that respect dried and canned is better, even if they do contain dunked-chicken-water.

After filling two bowls with dunked-chicken water-flavored pet food and one fresh bowl of dried cat chow, because Hershey's a part of this story and he also preferred dried food to canned—each in its own separate location for independent dining, I was at last ready for a bite of very late supper myself when a bird flew by.

21 / Wit's End Comedy Club

George E. Tiel and SnowBird were safely ensconced in their cages. I immediately recognized the feathery intruder. Smart little singers, a pair of Carolina Wrens located the only access onto my screened-in patio and hung around like it was their private apartment.

Known for nesting in odd places, the pair built a nest hidden within the flowers on a decorative wreath every Spring, rearing several off-spring. The fly-by bird, worth more than two in the bush, was one of the pair.

I even entered a photograph of a nest the pair built in a wicker trashcan that was actually full of trash, on the patio last year in the *Funky Nests* contest sponsored by the Cornell University Ornithology Department. Checking out the photos entered, it was plain to see birds will build nests everywhere imaginable and even where nobody would imagine.

Sometimes I leave the patio door conveniently ajar so TacoBelle and Rosie can go out there to safely bark their fool heads off at the outside dogs. It's the only time they act like dogs. The rest of the time they are above such doggish activities as barking.

The little brown bird must have found the open door convenient too. It had to have happened early that morning before I left for work. If BlackBeltBoo had been here, she wouldn't have missed it. She's fearless and relentless. Hershey wasn't a hunter—which in this case was a good thing.

My coming home must've stirred up the delightful little bird. It flitted from ceiling fan to light fixture to the aquarium and to this and that for the next forty minutes as I futilely attempted to shoo it outside. I got happy when it lighted atop the opened patio door at one time. But, from there it flew into the kitchen instead of out the door. TacoBelle and Rosie were sure we were engaged in another rousing game. They joined in, smiling doggie smiles and tails wagging. They always get pleasure from the new games mom comes up with.

I called Chuck for help and at one point in frustration he swatted at the bird with his gimme-cap like a butterfly net.

I said "Careful. You'll hurt it," and he said he didn't want to be chasing a bird all night.

I growled at him. He put his cap away.

When the bird flew into the utility room, I swiftly closed the door, limiting its full-house flight pattern. When it landed low enough, I dropped a towel over it. This enabled a safe capture and return to the great outdoors. By then it was eleven o'clock at night.

So you see, it's a laugh a minute around here, and definitely qualifies as the Wit's End Comedy Club.

More Than "X" Marks the Spot

22

"Old age means realizing you will never own all the dogs you wanted to."
(Joe Gores)

The morning after Labor Day, Rosie barked with obvious trepidation; the same way she alerts me when BadBoo is sitting atop the bird cage table. I refer to it as a three-alarm bark.

Of course I'm bound up with my CPAP mask with air tubing wrapped halfway around my fluffy body. I reach for the overhead reading light and flip it on. It takes a bit before I can pull myself into a sitting position due to the above-mentioned mask. It helps me breathe but it sure is confining. Don't get in a hurry. It ain't happenin'.

Finally, unbound, light on, Rosie still barking, I look toward the bedroom doorway. I spied BushwhackerBooCat living up to her name. She was playing with something. She's the world's most playful cat. Because she is so playful, I've gone silly, gotten giddy, and bought her a bunch of cat stuff.

She adores her cat play station and cat furniture and the toys that shake, rattle and roll when she smacks, swats and swipes at them. She sleeps in her bright pink cat cube in my hot pink office while I'm typing and she sleeps atop her favorite of all pieces of furniture, the three storey lounger in the living room, while I read or watch a video.

She climbs in and around the various cubicles and hammocks in the family room entertaining herself for hours. She snoozes on the cat condo in the kitchen. She self-entertains, compliments of all the stuff I've provided her.

The only bad thing—no, no. Let me rephrase that. One really bad thing she did was urinate in the dogs' beds. Just as I have toys scattered around in a half dozen different rooms for her, I have dog beds situated all over the house so that wherever I am, Rosie and Taco-Belle can join me.

And she marked those beds like white on rice.

I'm familiar with Toms doing this, but not little girlie cats. Tomcats are boys and boys are always a bit more randy than girls. You know, boys will be boys? Even the term Tomcat, when applied to human males, refers to a guy who likes the gals—as in "Tomcatting around."

The fact of the matter is, even cat lovers vow that unaltered male cats can make very bad pets. They will spray a foul-smelling urine all over the house, on furniture, folded clothes, even in his master's bed.

The term Tomcat originated in the mid-1700s in England. A book titled *The Life and Adventures of a Cat* is given credit. The book hero was a male cat named Tom. He enjoyed the favors of a multitude of girl cats. I didn't realize books about cats were penned centuries ago. I reckon there have been people who have had a love affair with kitty cats—which included reading and writing about them—for as long as there have been cats.

Cats spend a fair amount of time sending signals, both visual and olfactory. They scratch and leave a scent of sweat from their paw pads. And, they scent mark by spraying urine. This action's more prevalent among tomcats (unneutered males) as I mentioned. There are many reasons for marking. From attracting mates to warning other cats off, to instilling the message: "This is mine. Leave it alone."

Feline head-rubbing, also known as bunting, is a common means of marking a favored person. The cat rubs against its person with its cheek and then its body, usually curling its tail around the person's hand or leg as in a symbolic final embrace.

A sign of affection, it also enables the cat to leave its scent. The rubbing allows odors from large sebaceous glands in its skin around its mouth, chin, ears, anal area and top of the base of the tail to come in contact with the object of its affection. Being rubbed by a cat in such a manner is a good indication kitty's determined you belong to it, therefore you've been marked.

According to cat professionals, urine marking not only signals territory, it either has to do with the breeding season or occasionally, it indicates stress from something such as overcrowding. I had to determine if BeastlyBooCat was marking the dogs' beds because they belonged to the dogs, and if that's the case, was she doing it to mark her territory? Or, was it too crowded?

And then, several signs eventually indicated this new problem likely had to do with her coming into estrus. But wait. The note pinned on the vet's bulletin board said she'd been spayed.

Very long story slightly shorter, in a roundabout way through the Internet networking site, Facebook, the original owner messaged me, revealing BooCat hadn't been spayed after all. She'd been declawed and had up-to-date cat shots, but spaying wasn't done.

I bought BooCat all her own furniture; play stations, cat park, cat condos, cat beds, cat tree, and a variety of cat toys in every single room, so obviously, unless she was the most selfish feline found, this wasn't a takeover-play from fancying TacoBelle's and Rosie's beds. It was a takeover-play of a different sort. Likely more psychological than a simple diagnoses would explain.

BefuddledBooCat was on the verge of coming into season. I saw no discharge but she rolled around on the floor and acted particularly affectionate in ways a cat owner can recognize in association with "coming into heat or season." It was all coming together and making sense: the sudden super affection and the inappropriate marking. An appointment for this necessary operation was made, along with the hope that surgery would eliminate the problem of spraying the dogs' beds because of some sort of warped leader of the pack psychological reasoning inside her beautiful but confused head.

People sometimes erroneously believe a female cat desires kittens. Trust me, a firm proponent of spaying and neutering, cats (and dogs) have no maternal or paternal urges. A momma cat will be the best mamma cat once kittens are born, but there is no maternal desire to have the kittens in the first place.

With that in mind, there is a terrible overpopulation of both cats and dogs. Non-pedigreed cats and dogs are difficult to give away and often wind up in shelters looking for a home if they're lucky or feral if not. By not having cats and dogs spayed and neutered, we can only add to the overpopulation of unwanted pets.

End of sermon. And I hoped also the end of Boo's marking Rosie's and Taco's beds.

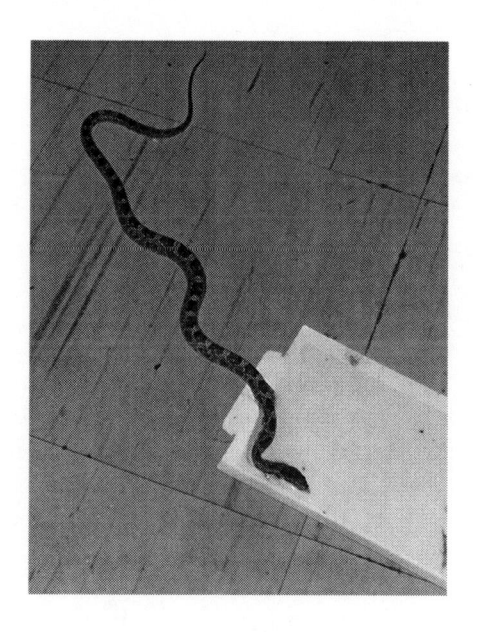

The Bold and the Boo-Tiful BooCat is the Bomb

23

"Don't let the dogs and cat out, no matter what they tell you."
(Barbara Sharik)

I explained how BooCat got her name; why she's no MayBelle or Maybelline or Miss Kitty. Now, let me tell why she's keeping it. She's BooCat from the tip of her black nosey nose to the tip of her switching tail. BooCat's got attitude. She's audacious.

Of all animals known to man, the cat is probably the most mysterious. While independent, haughty, demanding even, cats are mostly serene, patient, unassuming companions. Generally, cats give owners the same respect they expect in return. At least that's the case once they're grown. While still kittens the ballgame's likely quite the contrary. Kittens come wrapped in a package full of mischief. If it moves, they pounce. Built-in mouser genes coupled with killing-curiosity in action.

I read in a little booklet about cats that I picked up at the checkout counter in the grocery store that "very quickly, though, a kitten's vigorous play begins to slow down—usually at about five months."

Say what?

The writer making this bold statement hasn't met BoldBooCat.

The author explains that "experts think the reason for this fall-off in their frolicking is because nature assumes Kitty would already be out on her own, making her living as a hunter—if she were born in the wild."

There you go again. Experts. The author's quoting experts, just as I've done throughout. Who are these experts? There appears to be one on every corner and each one's opinion differs from the expert on the other corner. It appears much depends on which corner you stop at as to what's what when it comes to cats.

Yeah, I say to myself. I can make fun of the contradictory information given from one cat book to the other, but these people are selling their books. That's more than I can say about myself.

What if I called myself a Cat Whisperer? What constitutes becoming a cat expert? Not a veterinarian, but an expert on cat behavior? Is there a college where you go to get a degree? Or is it all learned in the field? By the time I get BooCat raised, I should be eligible for some sort of a degree.

In any case, with regards to this so called frolicking fall-off, obviously Mother Nature and BooCat haven't made such an arrangement regarding playfulness. I can't help but wonder about so-called experts that try to put everything in a box. I believe BodaciousBoo will play until the day she steps on a rainbow. It's just her nature. I've read that Labrador Retriever puppies are more playful longer than almost any other breed; maybe Boo's got a bit of Lab in her makeup.

Cats are clever, opening drawers, boxes, and doors. They'll climb anything high. They crave exploring the unexplored. All cats suffer from insatiable curiosity. Obvious there are occasions when that's dangerous. Hence the "curiosity killed the cat" adage.

I read a cat article claiming originally this saying was "Care kills a cat" instead of curiosity. It said it was first used during the eighteenth-century as a warning that worry wasn't good for anyone's health and could very easily lead to an early grave. Best I could decipher the tie-in with cats is that cats are very cautious creatures. It advised that over time, the word care evolved to curiosity.

To me, this explanation is flawed. I could've made up something far more believable, if I happened to be an expert. But it seems all the corners are already filled. Therefore, it just shows-to-go-you and verifies another old saying: You can't believe everything you read.

The statement may well have begun in the eighteenth-century but tying it to cautious cats and then to claim "care" evolve to "curiosity"

23 / The Bold and the Boo-Tiful BooCat is the Bomb

makes no sense. Cats are curious. They'll play with anything. They can find themselves up a tree due to curiosity, needing a fireman's ladder to get down. They might find themselves stuck in a chimney, due to curiosity. Some of these precarious conditions and situations that a cat's curiosity causes can very well be hazardous to its health.

In addition, cats are fastidious, graceful, supple, delicate yet powerful, solid muscle. Very brave, they'll do battle with animals twice their bulk. They'll also confront critters a mere fraction their size; such as snakes, snails and puppy dog tails.

When the queenly BeauteousBooCat walked into the house, she entered with attitude. Although she's the youngest and the littlest furry creature about, she immediately staked the house as her den. She declared herself the full-fledged leader of the pack.

I get side-tracked so easily, all the walkways at Wit's End Comedy Club need to go left instead of right, up instead of down and sideways instead of straightforward. As I started to say several paragraphs ago before I got side-tracked, the morning after Labor Day, a Tuesday morning, the alarm went off. The sound of country music filled the air. I grabbed my handy backscratcher, reached across the divide between bed and table and punched the snooze button.

Planning to snatch a few extra zee's before rising and shining, I turned over and had just snuggled comfortably when Rosie barked. There was trepidation in her doggie voice much like when BadBoo jumps atop the birdcage table. Both TacoBelle and Rosie tell on her when she gets up there. They're smart enough to know that's a no-no.

With Rosie barking wildly from atop the bed, TacoBelle peering through sleepy eyes, me attempting to get untangled from my CPAP machinery, I finally saw what BoldBoo was playing with. All bravery but no experience caused fear to shoot through my very being.

What BooCat had nabbed registered instantaneously. It caused the hair on the back of my neck to stand up.

Snake!

I got out of bed and Rosie jumped down to lend a paw. TacoBelle wisely watched from a safe distance. I don't give myself points for fast thinking. All I knew was that I had to get the snake out of the house and sooner would be best.

Using needle-nose pliers, I grabbed that sucker by its tail and headed toward the door. Partway, it started to wriggle. Unless you're a snake-ologist, toting a wriggling snake even with pliers didn't make for a happy-heroine moment. Outside, I dropped the snake into a bucket and sighed with relief. After I stopped shaking like a leaf, I took a shovel to the back of its elongated neck and the rest is history.

Best friend Chuck determined what it wasn't: Not a rattle snake, cottonmouth, king or rat snake.

I took it to work and showed it around. Co-worker Tammi suggested a ground rattler. Former Bonita Mayor Mike had no idea. Chief of Police April refused to get within ten-feet. Then Bobby, owner of Bonita Motor Supply next door stated unequivocally, laying the question to rest; it was a young Copperhead.

Copperhead bites are typically not fatal to people, but to a small dog—or a cat—they can be. Of course, checking BraveBoo for injury was the first thing I did once disposing of the snake.

The venom of a copperhead causes local tissue destruction. Secondary infection often sets in. Specialists advise, leave the snake alone and it'll leave you alone. Having the snake in my house, absolutely completely irreversibly negates that advice.

Copperheads bite more people in most years than any other U.S. species but have the mildest venom, according to University of Georgia Professor Dr. Whit Gibbons. His research revealed that most snakes when confronted with a human's presence make every attempt to escape. If escape isn't possible, most snakes will hold their ground and defend themselves.

The difference between copperheads and other species is that, while both just want humans to leave them alone, other snakes will vibrate their tails or, in the case of the cottonmouth, sit with their mouths wide open. These warnings imply they want to be left alone. They're like "Do not disturb" signs. But the copperhead, it strikes first and asks questions later. Their sign is more like "Enter at your own risk." Copperheads have no interest in taking prisoners.

Dr. Gibbon's research indicates that while the copperhead's initial threat display is to strike, it generally injects little venom. A warning, he said it is as though "the copperhead has no intention of wasting valuable venom if it can scare the menace with a minor bite."

At the end of that day I sighed: just another day at Wit's End. Life's

23 / The Bold and the Boo-Tiful BooCat is the Bomb

little surprises

Survival of the luckiest. Bless BooCat. As Randy Jackson of Journey and American Idol fame would say, "BooCat's the bomb." Yes she is.

Boo the Bomb, snake catcher extraordinaire, saved the day. No, I don't know how the snake got in the house and yes, that worries me. A lot.

When Boocat Transforms into Bagheera, the Jungle Book Black Panther

24

"Children are for people who can't have dogs and cats." (Unknown)

And so, with an appointment for surgery scheduled, BooCat and I took another road trip. Back to Dr. White's office to be "fixed." When I picked her up later that afternoon, still groggy, I was in full Mother-Hen-mode. An ominous intuition made me want to stay home from work with my BooChild the next day. I knew I was being silly. You might stay home with a child who's ill, but certainly not a cat just because she's undergone the most natural of all animal operations.

I didn't give into my apprehensions. That was Monday. By Wednesday BooBooCat was coughing.

I'm not psychic. I was being a Mother-Hen. A worry-wart. I was being overly emotional. It was purely coincidental BooCee caught a cat-bug. My common sense told me this is true. But my heart told me something inside lets a mother know when something negative's going to happen; that something is just not right, and especially it lets a Mother-Hen know.

A return trip to Dr. White's office revealed a temperature and upper respiratory infection. As always Dr. White was the picture of concern. His compassion almost scared me when he announced she had a temperature because he looked so serious. He's saved many a pet of mine over the years, and sustained others so their lives were more healthy and fulfilling. His heart is as big as a helium balloon in the Macy Day Thanksgiving Parade. And Elizabeth, his assistant is likewise exceptionally good at what she does. She too is knowledgeable yet all heart. And after all, Elizabeth has a stake in BooCat and her future. She was head of the adoption agency.

Back at home, antibiotics twice a day that incidentally she took like a champ. Even Dr. White commented on her excellent behavior. See, she can be good when it suits her.

As she improved daily from her surgery, stitch removal was the only negative road trip looming ahead. She recovered from her upper respiratory infection about as quickly as she contracted it. I have no idea if it's true that you can't hold a good man down because I haven't known all that many good men, but I do know you can't hold a good cat down and BooCat's one of the best. With each day, she improved and in no time at all she became the original mischievous BionicBoo once more.

In a mixture of candor and honesty, I have to say, as much as I adore BooCat, coupled with the joy she provides, there are days I believe she can best be described as a juvenile delinquent, evolving into the Terrible Two's, on the brink of teenage rebellion.

The very same BalisticBooCat that caught the baby Copperhead snake in our house—thus saving everybody's lives: Mine, TacoBelle, Rosie; probably George and SnowBird too—is responsible for a whole lot of vandalism. She's also responsible for catching an inordinate amount of prey.

I haven't seen a hundred-legged centipede since El Paso, and never a millipede, but BooBagheera found one, saving us again. She located it in the hallway between my bedroom and the main bathroom.

Millipedes are arthropods. They have two pair of legs per segment except for the first behind the head. Whether they add up to a million—or a thousand actually, which is what "milli" means in Latin, I don't know. And, fact be known, I really don't care. What I can say is there are a lot of legs attached. "Ped" means foot.

They're slow moving despite the seven-hundred-fifty legs or so.

Being herbivorous, the majority dine off decaying leaves and other dead plant matter. Some species will prey on small anthropoids, such as insects, centipedes and earthworms. I don't have any idea whether this was a worm or a leaf eater. What I do know is it was where it had no business being. In my house.

Some millipedes are unable to bite or sting, their primary defense mechanism is to curl into a tight coil. There are some species that emit poisonous liquid secretions or hydrogen cyanide gas through microscopic pores along the sides of their bodies as a secondary defense. I wasn't anxious to determine if Boo's catch was poisonous or not.

Centipedes move faster than millipedes. They are predators. Millipedes aren't by nature. In fact, there are people who actually keep millipedes as pets. Is there anything people won't keep as a pet?

Ah, what can I say. I have a dried-up dead Tarantula in a glass aquarium in the bathroom off the game room. It belonged to my son Tony. I inherited it when he was killed. I didn't like the idea of a pet spider, but whether it died of unnatural or natural, causes, I know I didn't purposely kill it.

What's unnatural is that I've not thrown the carcass away. It's a mother-thing. It belonged to my son.

Whether the millipede BooCat caught could or would emit poison, I never discovered. I was just glad Boo wasn't injured when she rescued the family once again from fates worse than stings, bites and maybe even death. I live in the country. Wild things are everywhere, but what are so many doing in my house?

In any case, my BantamweightBooCat's an amazing huntress.

Her hunting talents didn't abate. Next, I rescued a tree frog she captured. If it were an African tree frog, it likely would've emitted a poisonous fluid that would make catchers like BooCat sick. Some of them are known to have a built-in arsenal of poison protection. But, I was fairly certain this little green Louisiana frog wouldn't hurt Boo.

The beautiful little green frog hadn't yet been beheaded or mangled when I caught Boo with it. I rescued it and returned it to the great wilderness that is my yard. Boo sort of shrugged her shoulders and sauntered away. The message she seemed to send was easy-come, easy-go; there's plenty more where that one came from.

※

Wild creatures aren't the only things that could be detrimental to Boo's health. Hundreds of cats are injured or die every year because they've swallowed or tangled with something they shouldn't have. Besides accidentally swallowing the likes of buttons, paperclips, needles, even string, there's the chance of a nosy cat getting a nasty shock from chewing on electric wires.

I know Boo isn't going to get closed up in the fridge, but I never leave the lid of the washer up for fear she might nosily climb down inside and then not be able to get back out. And worse, is the idea of her climbing into the dryer and me not knowing it, tossing wet clothes inside and turning it on. Be like one of those Urban Legends having to do with the poodle in the microwave.

Always remember it is not cruel to keep you cat inside the house. Quite the contrary.

And plants are always worth being wary of. The expression "Don't eat the daisies" is serious business when it comes to cats and nibbling on the foliage. If you've got a poisonous plant, be sure to put it where your cat can never get at it even accidentally.

Only a partial older list, but beware of Amaryllis, Belladonna, Boxwood, Calla Lilies, Daffodils, Daphne, Dieffenbachia (Dumb Cane), English Ivy, Euonymus, Fox Glove, Golden Chain Tree, Hyacinth, Jack in the Pulpit, Jerusalem Cherry, Jimson Weed, Lily of the Valley, Lupine, Marijuana, Mayapple, Mistletoe, Monkshood, Morning Glory, Mountain Laurel, Oleander, Philodendron, Poison Hemlock, Privet, Skunk Cabbage, and Wisteria. If you're a plant person and you have cats, it would be wise to get a more thorough list.

Boo has mouser genes dating back to the Days of Yore. I wear hearing aids and don't hear as well as I once did. Between Meniere's Disease and Tinnitus, I'm lucky I hear at all. At the risk of raising somebody's frustration-dander, there are times rather than ask them to repeat something a third time, I just smile and nod and hope it's the right response.

People have the utmost patience with somebody tapping along

with a white cane being led around by a seeing-eye dog. But ask them for a repeat a time or two, you can gage their changing mood by how loud their voices rise and how red their faces get and how fast their breath comes. With each decibel, the shorter their tempers become. You want to either say "Never mind" or curl up in a ball like one of those millipedes.

I know it's frustrating because even I've been guilty of feeling that particular ire when having to repeat something over again. Deaf people bring out the worst while somebody blind is treated with compassion. I wonder why repeating something a couple times so instantaneously irritates?

Now, there's an interesting subject matter for one of those grants where so much funding is bequeathed it's coming out the researcher's ears. No pun intended.

All this to say, BooCat and her mouser genes get a workout every night. I believe she's hearing mice in the attic. She climbs as high as she can and tries to reach the ceiling. She leaps atop the chest of drawers, balances on the headboard and even climbs and sits on top the bedpost balls, which is an amazing feat in itself. She wants whatever she perceives is overhead. I'm assuming it's the sound of little mousies and not ghosts.

Could it be ghosts?

Occasionally over the years I've heard a rapping noise that makes no logical sense. So, whatever it is that BooCat hears, I don't. My hearing's gotten too bad to hear the scratchy sound of mice scurrying about in the attic. Or ghosts either.

But I do have a number of photographs that have turned up with orbs visible after development. There are several taken on different days of different subjects, but in the same location in the living room, yet the same orbs have mysteriously occurred.

Orbs are a mystery. There is much speculation and no proof one way or the other. Are they dust motes or are they the souls of the dead?

There are so many orbs it's unbelievable in a photos taken of a sunset just a day or so after one of my dearest yard dogs, Boyo, was killed when he was trapped—blocked in by the corn stalks—in the path of a combine cutting corn. He was no more than three feet from our driveway. This location is also near the entrance to the driveway where sadly, over these forty years other pets have been struck by vehicles while carelessly crossing the road.

There's minimum traffic, which logically should make for safety. But, instead of being safe, the animals become complacent, get careless. And the farmers drive so fast up and down my road. Always in a hurry. Give them a straight road and it's difficult not to speed it seems.

In that case, if the orbs represent ghostly visitors, perhaps the dozens of orbs on these photos were lost pets coming to carry Boyo's spirit home to the Rainbow Bridge.

Life's full of inexplicable occurrences. Are orbs the lingering presence on some more subtle level of a spirit from another time? There are many attempts to logically explain authentic orbs on photographs; dust motes being one of the most common suggestions. But none of the explanations have been proven, nor are they scientific. Orbs remain a phenomenon. What they are and what causes them is open for discussion and belief one way or another. Take your pick.

I have felt Hershey's presence.

I felt Jon's nearness for a very long time after his death. He still dances through my dreams on occasion. They are so real. He is so real in them. I waken and expect to find him by my side, hear him singing, see him smiling.

I feel my mother. I believe it's part of the grieving process, and perhaps it's more wishful thinking than actual visits. The mind playing tricks, as minds are wont to do.

I've felt my son, Tony, shortly after he was killed.

Tony was born October 22, 1966 in Ulm, West Germany. From first pain till birth, a mere two-hours and twenty-minutes passed.

His favorite color was purple. He once saved a boy from drowning and was recognized by the Red Cross and the President of the United States.

He belonged to the 4-H, and won a number of awards such as "Best Records" and "Best First Year Boy." He was a Cub Scout.

He collected indian arrowheads and rocks. He loved life and was so excited about everything around him. He was inquisitive and not a little bit hard-headed at times. His wasn't so much the "show-me" attitude as his having to see for himself.

He physically worked hard. Yet and still, he was a dreamer. He had such grand ideas, schemes and plans. And we all thought he had a lifetime to do them in.

Sadly, he seemed to have the proverbial black-cloud hanging over his head. Still he smiled. He was always smiling. He never let adversity get him down.

The love of his life was his daughter, Alisha Danielle. Born January 12, 1989, she weighed a mere two-pounds, fifteen-ounces. She was such a Daddy's Girl. She misses him. Everybody who knew him misses him.

He was killed in a traffic accident less than a mile from our house. April 11, 1992.

Shortly after Tony was killed, one Sunday a picture that had been hanging for years, fell at Theresa's feet as she started to enter the back bedroom.

The wire broke.

Chuck was mowing. He heard someone call his name.

No one was there.

Alisha said she sees her Daddy. She talks to him and reported, "Daddy likes my dress." She held her tiny hand up after being stung by a bee and said, "Daddy, kiss my hand…"

Cindy sees him in her dreams.

It was Tuesday, September 14, 1992, five months from the day of Tony's funeral, he touched me.

Showering, my hair wet, soapy and piled upon my head, I had soaped my face and was washing my neck with my eyes closed when I felt two fluttering puffs of air in quick succession against my forehead.

I opened my eyes, brushing at my forehead, feeling for something tangible. Oddly, my first thought was "Tony."

My hair was still in place atop my head. If it were a Daddy-Long-Legs spider doing push-ups on my forehead, he was invisible.

I held my hand up, reaching over the top of the shower door feeling for air. Had the air conditioner just come on? But there were no vents in the bathroom. And I felt no air stirring.

Two short breaths: puffs. But physical. I felt the air, the breath, the puffs. They were feathery, wispy, real.

This never happened again. It certainly never happened before. But for that moment in time, I know. I do know.

24 / When Boocat Transforms into Bagheera

Tony touched me.

His presence was and is still felt. Always here for those who loved him, having nothing to do with the supernatural, there's a feeling of him. His space isn't empty. He still fills it.

I wish it were possible to stay connected to those we loved but who for whatever reason, had to leave before their time. I'm too much of a realist to allow that thought to linger. The bonds between pets and humans are as strong as any human-to-human bond and I'd like to think there's more to the world than meets our everyday senses.

Back to the mousies running around in my attic, because it's probably mice rather than ghosts that BooPsychic hears. There's a poem written by B. Kliban, whose famous cartoons appeared in Playboy Magazine. His Kliban Cats are known the world over. The poem, it could very easily have been penned by BooCat herownself:

> Love to eat them mousies,
> Mousies what I love to eat.
> Bite they little heads off...
> Nibble on they tiny feet.

Why do we like some things and not others? What's so special about that poem? I have no idea but I have loved that poem since the first time I read it. And I love BooCat. She's so obviously full of super senses, she senses anything that moves and even though she can't reach the ceiling or find her way up into the attic, it was a given that she'd eventually catch a mouse in with the mix.

It's natural when a kitten catches a small rodent like a mouse not to kill it immediately. Often, a young cat will toss the unlucky captive into the air, bat it around, even allow it to believe it's gotten away so she can go through the fun of capturing it all over again. I know that sounds torturous. And it is. The Law of the Fang is riddled with cruelty.

A grown cat usually makes a quick kill. But because Boo's still in the playing stage, I was able to rescue the tree frog. The mouse wasn't so lucky. It joined the Anne Bolynn hall of defamed and beheaded.

BOOCAT UNLEASHED

The rubber thresholds in this old house are worn out so slithering, hopping and jumping things squeeze underneath. And Safari-QueenBoo loves it. I don't. I call her BooBagheera, the Jungle Book black panther. It's a most appropriate name. I don't know if there are any other black panthers in the world of literature that might better describe my BooChild.

I thought about calling her Sheena the Queen of the Jungle, a comic book heroine from my childhood days but until I either locate another black panther in literature, or she becomes the one and only, BooBagheera will do.

BooCat is a skillful predator. Did I mention that she's a cousin to the King of the Beasts? Her playfulness is a natural inborn way to improve her coordination. She won't have to worry about defending herself as an outside cat might, but she's managed to do some earnest hunting within the confines of what should be a safe environment. Suffice to say she's quite a pro but we're not going to mount any of her trophy catches on the walls. Imagine a wall featuring stuffed dead heads of snakes, millipedes, frogs and mice. No thanks.

It's in a cat's genes to stalk, to chase, to bite and paw at objects, both living and dead. Animate, inanimate, and even imaginary, she's been known to chase them all.

Obviously BooCat's a quick and adept learner. Except when it comes to staying away from the caged birds where it's been impossible to disengage her natural instinctive hunting mode. Hung up in second gear, she's not responding to normal teaching methods in this class. She belongs in a special-ed department under the tutelage of someone far more adept at teaching the bad to be good. Is there such a thing as Cat Boot Camp for BadBooCat?

George holds his own through the bars. When she hops up onto the table and gets too close, he squawks. He knows she's bad. Snow-Bird lacks a squawker box but will flap his wings noisily. In any case, I keep a physical eye on their cages.

When BadBoo first leaps onto the table and slinks towards Snow-Bird's cage, I've seen George stick his beak between the cage bars and nip Boo. By then, I'm demanding she "Geddown!"

How long does a kitten stay in the Terrible-Two's phase?

I wonder if BooBaby's mom taught her the basics of hunting prey or if she's self-taught. She excels. Like the night I woke to find her

24 / When Boocat Transforms into Bagheera

bouncing around on the bed batting something from one end to the other. It wasn't a rubber band. And let me tell you, what I saw virtually paralyzed me in fear.

The Incredible BooCat

25

"It doesn't just rain Cats and Dogs—Cats and Dogs reign!" (Barbara Sharik)

There are several cat catchphrases in use for so many years, it's doubtful most folks know the root of their origin. Take There's more than one way to skin a cat. Meaning there's more than one method of accomplishing a task it reminds me of a most amusing *Twins* comic strip by Dave Lochner. Tickling my funny bone forever, this particular cartoon appeared in the *Bastrop Daily Enterprise* in 1998. The first block depicted the mother's dilemma as she picks up the main-dish meat she's planned for supper and says, "Darn. The meat's still frozen."

Not to be dismayed, while inconvenient, readers know this is only a minor setback. After all, she's the mother of twins and has faced worse hindrances. She remarks: "Well, there's more than one way to skin a cat."

In the punch line last block, one twin says to the other: "I don't even want to know how she knows that."

BanteringBooCat likes that cartoon very much but isn't too crazy about the expression itself. The meaning is of course self-explanatory and quite simple even if BooCat considers the statement's pretty horrifying. Obviously there's a history behind the phrase.

One belief is that the term originated amongst cat-fishermen. A catfish is a scaleless fish and must be skinned to prepare it for the fry pot. Hence skinning the cat.

There actually are several methods—more than one way—to accomplish this. Everything from sophisticated catfish skinning boards and special skinning tools to the old-fashioned method of employing a nail hammered in a tree trunk and skinning with a standard pair of pliers, to attacking the task with an electric filet knife after knocking the hapless fish in the head with a hammer. Hang 'em and skin 'em. Gruesome, but factual.

It's best not to spend too much time thinking about how something made its way to your plate if you're squeamish.

The term is also said to refer to an acrobatic trick young boys (and tomboys) of my generation may remember. Mentioned in a 1948 book titled *A Hog on Ice* by Charles Earle Funk, I did the trick myself as a youngster. There was a big mulberry tree right beside where we lived at Ft. Myer, Va., and many of the kids on post spent hours either sitting beneath the tree or climbing it. And that included skinning the cat.

One way was to hang by your hands from a tree branch, or the jungle gym on the school yard or park, draw your legs up through your arms, bringing them over the branch. Then pulling yourself up into a sitting position.

The way I used to do it was to hang by my hands from the branch or bar and draw my legs up through my arms, but not taking them up over the branch. After my legs passed through my hanging arms, I'd drop to the ground, having turned myself inside out. It is sort of a skinning when you consider you're passing your feet and legs between your arms while hanging by your hands from the branch or bar.

You see, there was even more than one way of accomplishing the acrobatic schoolyard trick called Skin the Cat. But, even with that explanation, it's still fuzzy how the trick came to be called skinning the cat in the first place—who came up with the name?

It's supposed that when Ben Franklyn was a child he likely did this trick known even then as skinning the cat although it didn't show up in print until about 1845.

Another record of origin is found in *Random House Dictionary of Popular Proverbs and Sayings* by Gregory Titelman. It states that the term dates back to 1678 when it appeared in John Ray's *Collection of English Proverbs*.

In 1839 the phrase appeared in *John Smith's Letters*.

Seba Smith used the expression in 1854 in *Way Down East; or, Portraitures of Yankee Life*. Smith's use likened more ways to skin a cat as there being more ways than one of digging for money.

In *A Connecticut Yankee in King Arthur's Court*, Mark Twain wrote in 1889, "she was wise, subtle, and knew more than one way to skin a cat."

Research material also credits the phrase as referring to "hoodwinking the gullible." Like the pig in the poke that's actually a cat wanting out of the bag. It's believed cats were sometimes skinned with both the pelt and meat passed off as rabbits at the market.

Similar to skinning a cat was a term used in *Westward Ho!* by Charles Kingsley in 1855 when he wrote "there are more ways of killing a cat than choking it with cream." That one reminds me of the axiom about killing someone with kindness.

The phrase "having kittens" or "had kittens" is an idiom most of us have used at one time or another. Referring to a range of emotions including being in a state of rage, getting upset, even hysterical, to losing one's temper, it's a common saying: "If so-and-so finds out about such-and-such, she'll have kittens."

The best clarification of origin I've located, because every source I sought had the same explanation, is that during the middle ages, or thereabouts, cats were thought to be witches. If a pregnant woman experienced excessive labor pains, midwives claimed the woman had been bewitched. They blamed the severe pains on having kittens inside her womb, clawing painfully.

Magic potions were provided that would destroy the litter so the woman wouldn't give birth to kittens. I'd be willing to bet the magic potions always worked. It's highly unlikely anybody ever gave birth to a litter of cats. Or if they did, it never made the daily newspaper.

BlackmagicBooCat likely would agree, it's best we don't know the origin of some of these strange sayings. So farfetched, even wacky, it might be wise to leave logic out of the equation.

25 / The Incredible BooCat

How about when it rains really hard and we say it's "raining cats and dogs"? There are several thoughts on where that one originated.

One explanation dates back to the 1500s when houses were topped with thatched roofs declaring because the straw roof was the warmest spot in the house, cats and dogs often nestled there. However, in a really hard downpour, the roof likely became slippery and the cats and dogs slipped and fell to the ground below.

You think?

Another theory put forth reports during the seventeenth-century when cats hunted mice in the thatched rooftops, they'd be washed off during a rainstorm and fell onto passersby. Of course this theory doesn't account for, nor address, the dog part of the phrase—unless they were up there chasing the cats.

One more explanation is that the expression dates back to when many city streets were narrow with poor drainage and when a particularly heavy downpour came, poor starving cats and dogs often drowned in the deluge. Following the rain, people found the corpses of these drowned animals in the streets and claimed by golly, it must've rained cats and dogs.

Call them innocents or just plain uneducated, but they believed these dead bodies had fallen from the sky during the rainstorm.

There's mention of cats and dogs in Jonathan Swift's 1710 poem "Description of a City Shower." He writes: "Drowned puppies, stinking sprats, all drenched in mud./ Dead cats and turnip tops come tumbling down the flood."

What does BaloneyBoo say? "Bunkum!" I second that emotion with an explicative of my own: Hogwash.

Bear in mind, a lot of these sayings were created by the same folks who believed the earth was flat. Enough said.

Ah, but before you laugh too much, too hard and too long, when I first moved to this part of the country, I heard old timers call a heavy downpour not just a "Toad Strangler" but a "Fish Rain." They claimed after a torrential rain, fish were sometimes found to be swimming in road ditches. True believers swore the fish fell from the sky.

Naturally, a city gal like me was skeptical.

But, in reality, according to Wikipedia, there's a rare meteorological phenomenon in which various animals have fallen from the sky during rainstorms.

Dorothy? Toto? Is that you, Sugar?

The most common to drop from the sky are fish and frogs. When I first heard about a Fish Rain it was long before Wikipedia was available and nary a word could be found in my *Funk & Wagnells*.

Birds have been found to fall from above when overcome by a storm. Bats can also be overtaken by thunderstorms. I can see more logic in a quarter-sized piece of hail knocking out a bird, sending it crashing to the ground amongst the stormy rainfall, but there's a limit to what makes sense and what doesn't.

Speaking in front of the Society of Natural Sciences, Andre-Marie Ampere, a French physicist it's reported attempted to explain rains of frogs, suggesting that violent winds picked them up and carried them great distances.

A more recent scientific explanation involves waterspouts that are capable of capturing objects and animals, lifting them into the air, and then dropping. Tornadoes have the ability to suck up a pond, letting the water and animals drop elsewhere in what becomes an authentic rain of animals.

Hey! Was that Dorothy and Toto that just breezed by? I vote for tornadoes being the likely culprit of falling creatures. I've read accounts where cows were picked up and dropped during a tornado touchdown. They can pick up whole houses and cars, what's a cat or dog by comparison? Or fish.

"Has the cat got your tongue?"

Let's hope not. While it's come to mean someone's not talking, is too quiet, the idiom dates back hundreds of years ago in the Middle East. If someone were caught telling a falsehood, punishment meant having their tongue cut or ripped out and fed to the king's cats. By the way, thieves had their right hands chopped off. The king's cats got them too.

Why do so many expressions stem from violent activities? It doesn't speak well of our early ancestors.

25 / The Incredible BooCat

Another cat-related expression from dozens is "Catnap," not to be confused with "Catnip."

Catnip is the complete antithesis of Catnap. Catnap is simple. Cats are known for taking short, light naps. Nothing complicated here; that's what's meant when the term's used—taking a short nap.

BooSugar likely takes her catnaps while I'm at work because once I'm home she's wide awake and raring to go. When TacoBelle, Rosie and I go to bed, she comes too. Like the dogs, she's learned the meaning of the words, "Let's go to bed." But most nights, she comes to bed only long enough for Taco, Rosie and I to get situated, then she leaves and usually doesn't return until I turn out my reading light. It's as though she doesn't think I'm serious until I turn the light out. The light going off is her signal to come back to bed for real; until then she has free reign.

Even though she's not ready to settle down right away she's learned the familiar words, "Let's go to bed." With these magic words, Rosie is usually the first to take off toward the bedroom, up the ramp where she stands on her short legs, tail wagging, waiting for the rest of us slow-pokes to arrive.

Rosie also understands "Lay down and I'll cover you up." I keep throws—color coordinated—no matter where we spend time together because when Rosie naps, cold-natured Rosie has to be covered up.

She also comprehends whole sentences like "Go ahead and eat," or "Come over here and eat." I have to tell both she and TacoBelle to come get their food because BooCat by and large beats them to the dishes. They stand back and watch while she chows down. But it's not a serious chowdown. It's more of an "in-your-face" thing because she doesn't eat more than a tiny taste. She obviously likes the power she has over the pups. She's got them waiting for her to get out of the way. And she takes her sweet time. Even if she's not actually eating, she's blocking the bowl. If I weren't so deaf I'd probably hear her chucking under her breath: "Gotcha!"

At this point I have to pick up FatBoo and carry her back to her dish. Over and over, she runs to whichever dog's bowl I'm filling, and sticks her nose in head first. It's like a game with her, not that she wants their food over hers. It's simply that she can so she does. That's just the nature of this bad black beast.

I don't believe talking baby talk to my furry kids is bad for them. Kid behaviorist and authorities used to say it's not beneficial to the learning process to talk baby talk to human babies, although I believe the data's now changed. In the end, the main thing is to talk to the baby, and the pets, a lot. The pets don't need to actually understand the words, it's the essence of the words that's important.

I believe you can never love your child or your cat, dog or any beloved pet too much. Thus, constant chattering, even baby talk, spoken in kind and loving tones is what counts. It works both ways. The love and stimulation I receive back from my pets is part of what keeps me going. Even the parts of me that are failing and falling apart, aren't quite so hard to bear.

In any case, when we go to bed, BelovedBooCat hangs around until everybody gets settled in and then she leaves to go on her nightly forays first. I suppose she's looking for millipedes, mice, snakes and frogs. Anything that moves.

Most obviously she had a successful hunt the night she woke me from a sound sleep bouncing around on the bed, batting something from one end of the bed to the other.

In the dark my first fear was another snake.

I turned on the light, slipped off my breathing machine mask and sat up so I could make a run for it if necessary.

Thank goodness, it was not a snake.

But to my way of looking at things, it was almost as fearful. It was a cricket.

Maybe I was attacked by a cricket in another life because I definitely have a cricket phobia; they have roach bodies. I can barely stand to look at a picture of a roach. It gives me the willies when one of those exterminator trucks with the large plastic roach sitting on top drives by. Roaches and crickets alarm me unrealistically and I get instant goose bumps at the mere sight of either.

Phobias are usually unexplained and uncontrollable. Fortunately, I don't have roaches in this old house but every few years there's a cricket invasion around here. It jumpstarts my phobia just to see a cricket.

25 / The Incredible BooCat

Crickets are from the family Gryllidae, which means nothing to me. They're insects, somewhat related to grasshoppers. I don't much like grasshoppers either but generally, contrary to crickets, they stay outdoors.

Crickets are cold-blooded. Like all other insects they take on the temperature of their surroundings. I guess that's why they're guilty of breaking and entering. They want to come inside to get warm.

And once they come in and get warm, beware if they turn around and leave again. There's this irrational superstition if you see a cricket leaving a house, sickness or death will strike that household.

There are about nine-hundred species of crickets. Eight-hundred-ninety-nine live in Louisiana. Eight-hundred-ninety-eight live in my yard. Except for the ones that break and enter my house.

Something many people are unaware of, and it just proves my cricket phobia has merit: "Crickets are known to carry a large number of diseases," according to Wikipedia. "Most of which cause painful sores but are not fatal to humans."

Disease spreads through their feces, bite or physical contact. Omnivores and scavengers, they'll eat just about anything including clothes in a closet. Don't leave your socks and undies on the floor when you go to bed if you've got crickets in your house. You're liable to find holes chewed in them by morning.

A cricket on the hearth is supposed to be good luck. A cricket in bed isn't lucky. Makes me hurt myself. A cricket chirping means only one thing: it's too close.

It's not enough crickets are said to be harbingers of good luck, it's supposed to be bad luck to kill one. It is thought to bring the cricket killer misfortune.

Only male crickets chirp. A large vein running along the bottom of each wing has teeth much like a comb, and the chirping sounds created by running the top of one wing along the teeth at the bottom of the other wing. To do this the cricket holds its wings up and open so the wings can act as acoustical sails.

So much for the old wives' tale that crickets chirp by rubbing their legs together. I wonder how that rumor got started?

Superstitious native American have reportedly been known to believe it's possible to develop a good singing voice by drinking a liquid made from crushed and boiled crickets. I've never been able to carry a tune. If it takes drinking cricket juice, I never will.

An interesting factoid is that old timers (and smart young whippersnappers) can judge temperatures by a cricket's chirp. Known as Dolbear's Law, temperature in Fahrenheit can be calculated by adding forty to the number of chirps produced in fourteen seconds.

I knew about counting the seconds from the time I saw lightning strike—light traveling faster than sound—until I heard the thunder rumble, as an indication of how many miles away the storm is. But, I didn't know about counting cricket chirps.

As a youngster I read a book about a Japanese child who kept a pet cricket in a cricket cage. Closing my eyes I can almost see the illustrations in my mind's eye in the oversized children's book. Too many books read, too many years gone by, I've forgotten the plot but keeping a cricket for a pet seems a sad commentary.

Different strokes for different folks meaning different cultures have different customs. It's not wrong but it makes me speculate if the little boy named his cricket the Japanese equivalent of Spot? Then, like that ancient Woody Allen joke, I wonder if when the neighborhood bully approaches does the little Japanese kid tell his cricket, "Kill, Spot, kill!"

Get the kid a dog, folks, before the bully steps on the kid's pet and gives him an irreversible inferiority complex.

A real pet, as opposed to a pet cricket, takes care and responsibility. It's been so many years since my Hershey was a kitten, I didn't remember him having so much vim and vigor as No-BoundariesBoo exhibits. Of course when I first got Sterling and Hershey I was a lot younger and better able to keep up, to cope. What seems wild and wooly nowadays might not have phased me fifteen years ago.

BooCat is Not a Good Bird Owner

26

"Put the cat among the pigeons." (British Term: To cause a huge flap or flight. Apparently, when Britain governed India, a popular pastime was to put a wildcat in a pen with pigeons. Then bets were taken to see how many birds the cat would bring down with one paw swipe. Some people will bet on anything and everything)

Cats are said to be most active at dusk and dawn. Kittens are the worst offenders of keeping night hours. This urge to roam is referred to by some as the "feline nighttime crazies."

I know about the "middle age crazies" that strikes many a married man rendering him stupid, there being no cure except divorce from his wife of twenty years and marriage to the young-thing he's gotten goofy over. It's the equivalent of trading in the forty-year old for two twenties.

But I didn't know there was a name for cats liking to roam: "feline nighttime crazies." If a cat's not been neutered or spayed, likely it's known as "catting around."

Many kittens want to play right about the time humans want to go to bed to sleep. This is my BusybodyBooCat. In due course she comes to bed, plops herself in one of several favorite places and goes sound to sleep.

But before that time arrives, she's been known to run around playfully being a BadBoo. Vases of artificial flowers have been plucked, lamps unplugged, curtains unhung. Items that had gathered dust for years now contain teeth marks. She's located lost and missing items that had rolled under chairs years ago. She even tweaked a feather from SnowBird's tail through the birdcage bars.

I've mentioned the two birds, George E. Tiel and SnowBird. George lives happily next door to SnowBird. George talks saying things like "Hello Georgie" and "Pretty Bird." He whistles a most accomplished rendition of "The Mockingbird Aria." There's something else he's been saying for years that sounds almost human, but appears to be in a foreign tongue. Someday I'll record it and get to the bottom of what he's saying. It has an interesting ring and human quality to it but I have no idea what it is.

A really strange moment occurred when I heard what sounded like TacoBelle locked in a closet or basement, except there is no basement. She's barking but it's muffled and far away. I went into panic mode. Where is she?

Wait. Something very strange is going on. There she is. Sound asleep on the bed. She isn't barking.

Yet, I knew I heard her. In fact, when my heart stopped beating like a Tunica Indian tom-tom and I could both breathe and hear again, I swear I could still hear her in the distance.

It was so definitely Taco's bark. I began to suppose another stray dog had been dumped and it must be outside barking for help.

I went to the door, opened it—which woke Taco up. She came bounding toward me and the open door, her tail was wagging. It's not because there's a dog outside. There is no new dog outside. Taco's just happy because the door's open. She always wants to go outside.

I told Taco we aren't going outside, I'm on a mission. Somewhere there's a little dog in distress. I started following the sound. While still muffled, it was getting louder.

And louder.

When I approached George's cage, I found him barking like a little gray and white bodied, yellow headed with orange cheeks, feathered Chihuahua. To this day, whenever the outside dogs or TacoBelle and Rosie bark, he joins in the fray. I never cease to be amazed each time I hear him.

So, what with having a couple caged birds, it's a certainty that bird

26 / BooCat is Not a Good Bird Owner

feathers can be found around them. I won't lie. I'm a slum landlady and conditions aren't always as neat and clean as the birdies deserve. But, on the other hand, I can't help but believe after almost twenty years—George moved in with me in 1992—he'd go into cardiac arrest if he wasn't walking on seed hulls. If I cleaned his cage regularly he'd probably develop a neurosis, become insecure and stop talking and start cursing instead.

And SnowBird? He came to live with me in 2000—he'd think he wasn't in Kansas any more.

Because feathers are available without plucking, BooStalker has made a habit of gathering them together and killing them one-by-one. She tosses them into the air. She chews mightily on them. She bats them about. I can only imagine what she'd do should she ever catch an real bird. It wouldn't be pretty.

The cockatiel's lifespan in captivity is generally given as fifteen to twenty years; therefore George is approaching the longest average given. There are reports of cockatiels living as long as thirty years, so I can hope George and I have many more years together. You see, the only negative thing about our pets is that none of them live long enough.

Cockatiels make good household pets and companions. They by and large normally have sweet dispositions and good temperaments overall. As with any living creature this isn't engraved on a silver charm hanging from the charm bracelet of sure things. Many factors play a part in determining personality

Also known as the Quarrion and the Weiro, the cockatiel is smaller than a cockatoo and belongs in the Cockatoo Subfamily. They are classified as the smallest of the Cacatuidae (Cockatoo family). The cockatiel is the only member of the genius Nymphicus. They are native to the outback regions of inland Australia and are second only to parakeets (Budgerigar) in popularity as a caged pet bird.

Little White Dove, who uses that name only when I sing to him—he's officially named SnowBird—is the same breed most historically described from Noah and his Ark though the present. Think peace—think white dove.

White doves—not white pigeons—are often used in magic acts, but it's the white pigeon that is released at weddings. White pigeons have good homing instinct to return to their dovecote; the white dove doesn't.

White doves are extremely intelligent birds and can be taught simple tricks, as seen on stage with magicians. No magician wants to work with a dumb bird—that in itself is proof positive of just how smart white doves are.

They make excellent pets, are easy to care for, and have an extremely sweet and gentle nature. They do well in a cage or an aviary. Once comfortable with its owner, a white dove will allow itself to be handled. I get so much pleasure listening to SnowBird coo. He's such a gentle soul. He is peace personified. He sets the stage at my house for calm.

Then BooCat comes along and rips that stage apart.

One reason caged birds are more popular than ever before has to do with hand-raising. Hand-raised birds sold as pets is now the norm as compared to twenty or thirty years ago.

When I grew up many families had a parakeet or a canary, but they were relegated to a hanging cage and the prime interaction came when seeds and water were refreshed and when the cage bottom paper was replaced. Before the new wore off, a lot of kids tried to teach their parakeets to talk. Forty-five RPM records were sold at pet stores recommended for use when training a pet bird to talk. Usually the kid ran out of patience before the family bird learned to repeat any of the words. Repetition was the accepted manner to teach a budgie to talk.

At that time having a caged bird was similar to having a large Dieffenbachia sitting in the corner. Often purchased based on color, a bird added a decorative touch to the home, but not much more. Nowadays, birds aren't just for decoration anymore. They are members of the family.

Until a person spends time with a bird, they likely don't realize how much personality birds have. Pet birds can actually rival that of a pet cat or dog in the companionship department and personality-wise. A hand-raised bird comes to think of itself as human just as pet cats and dogs do.

Birds are a big responsibility. For the best return having a bird as a pet, owners must realize they demand a lot of time and in exchange they show affection, become very tame, communicate readily and are as much fun as any other beloved pet. A happy bird is one that's

26 / BooCat is Not a Good Bird Owner

been allowed to interact with its owner. In fact, bird owners should be prepared for bird-bonding.

Birds are finally recognized as being more intelligent than once believed. We used to think when a talking bird spoke, it was just mimicking uncomprehendingly. Admittedly, the first time I heard George barking like TacoBelle, I assumed this was the case. But recent research reveals a talking bird's level of language intelligence is comparable to chimpanzees and gorillas who've learned sign language.

And George knows and understands why and when to bark. He doesn't wait for Taco and Rosie to announce someone's driven up outside. More often than not, he barks before any of the dogs do. Intelligent as well as clever, he's attuned to everything going on around him. He is alert and he alerts me in turn. It's most obvious that he comprehends the point behind barking. It's not simply mimicking. He barks when he's supposed to and he does it before the guard dogs do on many occasions. He put together two-plus-two—a car drives up—and got four—bark.

Birds may learn through mimicking, but their level of understanding what they've learned is what is keeping excited animal behaviorists up at night with smiles on their faces.

BooCat is not a good bird owner. Not yet. Her *Make A Wish* is to eat SnowBird. I don't fool myself thinking it's just to play with him. It's more visceral than that. After she tweaked a tail feather, she proceeded to kill that feather.

A slow learner in this class, I'm having a difficult time teaching her to leave the birds alone. Or perhaps it's not so much being a slow learner as just being a determined cat. Maybe she should be in a remedial class. Or maybe I should be. I'm attempting the impossible. I'm trying to eliminate the built-in, born-in, bird-eating gene. I counted six feathers one day alone scattered about. Boo's Bounty.

I've got to pick them up before I vacuum because as modern a piece of machinery as a vacuum cleaner is, get a bird feather crosswise in the suction tube and you're out of business until you take the whole machine apart and this requires many tools and much patience and a fair amount of cursing because there's no easy access for remedying

139

such an event. And believe me, it's an event. It's like performing major surgery. Getting to the innards is like breaking and entering without the aiding and abetting. Somebody should invent a vacuum cleaner that will handle bird feathers.

As many Facebook friends I've got who are dedicated bird people, because there are thousands and thousands of birders out there, they'd sing the praises (pun intended) of such a magnificent machine and its stock would soar and the bird feather sucker-upper vacuum would outsell all other vacuum cleaners on the market. Sucking up seed hulls is one thing, but if they could handle bird feathers also, wow! Amazing breakthrough.

Forget the mousetrap, invent a bird-friendly vacuum cleaner that doesn't clog up when faced with a bird feather.

I read that if your cat goes where it shouldn't, a common herb called Rue, is sometimes successful as a deterrent. The thing I read advised that Rue is a perennial evergreen shrub with bitter strong-scented leaves. It recommended using fresh Rue, to crush it between your hands and then sprinkle it where you don't want your cat to go.

Torn camphor leaves are supposed to be effective too because cats don't like mothballs. The problem is, these strong scented leaves might not be good around the birds, and it's around the birds BooCat is the baddest of them all.

Instructions recommended using rubber gloves to crush the Rue or kitty might not want to come near you either.

Sister Jan has five cats and dozens of birds. They commingle with no thoughts of murder entering their kitty cat heads. Not so with BansheeBooCat. Honestly, BooCat is starting to comprehend that when I holler "Geddown!" and then add, "Now!" that I do mean now—that I mean business. I've never struck her. I'd never do that, but I have to raise my voice and use the meanest tone I can muster to get her undivided attention. It's not so easy to get Boo's undivided attention when she's stalking the birds. She divides it between George and SnowBird.

When the message is finally digested and she leaps down she rushes to me so I can pet her and tell her she's such a good BooBaby. My kind words are her reward for obeying. Fingers crossed, given time and enough "Geddown's" followed by "Good BooBaby" maybe, just maybe, the birds will find peace again.

BooCat Quirks

27

"You enter into a certain amount of madness when you marry a person with pets." (Nora Ephron)

There are several types of aggression even the most normal cat might exhibit at some time in their lives. Aggression can prove to be a serious feline behavioral problem. Remember, cats have sharp canine teeth. They're quick to move and even quicker to react and can inflict serious damage in a matter of seconds. Children playing too rough with a cat can bring about a pain-induced act of aggression, for example. Painful medical conditions can also be responsible for aggressive behavior.

Some cats are skittish. In that case, fear-induced aggression can be a problem. A cat up a tree might behave aggressively even as it's being rescued. Most aggressive acts have nothing to do with the cat having a mean personality. What a cat lacks in size, it makes up in other ways. It's all a matter of self-preservation.

There are a few times when BooCat exhibits petting-induced aggression. We're having a happy pet-fest, when suddenly she swishes her tail, almost bites the hand that is petting her, jumps down and runs away. Although not desirable, this isn't abnormal. Alas, there's no cut and dried authoritative explanation as to what induces this moment of weird aggression. It would appear the cat has determined,

"Okay, enough is enough," and off it goes.

While this happens with almost all cats at some time or another, with BooCat all I need do is be attuned and keep an eye on her, recognizing when we're beginning to close in on the enough-is-enough petting threshold and when to stop petting. When her tail twitches, her ears lay back and her muscles tense up, it's doubtless time to stop. BooCat's semi-aggressive behavior has never reached the biting stage but part of that could be my awareness and experience with cats—plus her absolute love for me. We've got this mutual admiration society thing going on between us.

BoisterousBoo also exhibits a degree of play aggression toward Rosie. She hides behind a corner, tail twitching, leaps out onto Rosie as she innocently waddles by. She runs, jumps, stalks and pounces. Holding Rosie down with firm paws, she buries her head in Rosie's neck, teeth exposed and in fact bites down. Within split seconds, the bite turns to licking. As unassuming and submissive as Rosie is, I imagine she wonders what just happened.

Other times she knows exactly what happened. If Rosie doesn't want to play at night in bed because after all TacoBelle taught her a long time ago that bed is for sleeping and not playing, in an attempt to stop BullyBooCat from tormenting her by leaping on her, holding her down with her paws, tail switching, proud of her catch, she scoots beneath the covers. Out of sight, out of danger. That worked for awhile. Until BurrowingBoo figured out how to follow poor Rosie under the covers. She plows right in after her. It's the "you can run but you can't hide" thing.

If Boo plays too rough, I intervene. Yet, again, when BooCat's finished horsing around—or is that catting around—she snuggles up with Rosie and licks her like a mama cat with a kitten. She has adopted Rosie as her own private plaything.

Boo loves Rosie so much, licks her so often, from one end of her long red body to the other, when she hacked up a hairball, I swear it consisted of a mixture of both black and red fur: her very own and Rosie Red's.

I mentioned how BamboozleBoo sneakily hides behind a corner and all the while her tail switches and twitches. Dogs wag their tails, cats twitch theirs.

All my younger years I believed when a cat twitched its tail it

27 / BooCat Quirks

meant it was angry and when a dog wags his, it meant he's happy. It's fairly accurate to assume if a dog's wagging its tail, it is happy. But not necessarily is a cat angry when its tail twitches. Depending upon which cat expert's report you read. Naturally it also depends on your own individual cat. This I can safely say with confidence.

There's a faction of cat experts who have broken down and diagnosed the degree of switching and twitching that determines a cat's moods. If a cat switches its tail vigorously, it's said to be angry. If only the tip twitches intently, the cat's very annoyed. But, on the other hand, this also indicates the cat's very happy. And, if the cat switches its tail only occasionally, it's only slightly irritated or perhaps pensive.

Is this conflicting or what? Sort of reminds me of a weatherman. They speak with forked tongues. They report it will be either partly sunny or partly cloudy and before they're done they've covered all their bases so that no matter what the weather does, they were right.

Cat psychologists are supposed to know a thing or two about cats and what cats are thinking—so let's be rational here, who except a cat itself really knows what a cat's thinking?

My point exactly.

Other animal behaviorists reverse all of the above even as contradictory as it is. These experts claim if a cat twitches and switches its tail, it's in a state of conflict—that it wants to do two things at once but each impulse blocks the other. In other words, the cat is emotionally conflicted. You ask me, the cat behaviorists are the ones who are emotionally conflicted.

Okay, so the cat is conflicted. Hey, I've been there. To eat that candy bar or not to eat that candy bar. Thank goodness my tail doesn't start twitching when faced with such a dilemma. I rarely stay conflicted for long. I cease all mental confusion, open the wrapper and munch down.

Wanting to put a modicum of import on what cats are talking about with their tails is confusing because of differing opinions and reports released. The fact is, BooCat switches her tail all the time. I mean, *all the time.* Constantly. She's like a windowless windshield wiper. A metronome. Or one of those perpetual motion desk-top executive toys where you start one ball swinging, it strikes the next and the next and then they swing back in the other direction. Her tail's a perpetual motion appendage.

When she's stretched out with eyes closed and the tip end of her tail flicks back and forth she reminds me of a lion king swatting flies with its royal tail. Except, there are no flies. Yes. She's completely at rest, yet her tail is in constant motion. She's not angry.

She uses her tail for balance as she daringly tight-wire walks across the headboard, and thus it waves backwards and forwards then too. There's no anger or indecision—she's like a high wire walker and her tail's the balance pole.

She moves her tail from side to side when she lays on the bed grooming and licking herself. She does it when I'm petting her. She does it as she watches the birds. She shakes it while she licks Rosie. She switches, twitches, shakes, waves, flicks and wiggles her tail all the time.

If animal behaviorists blame all that erratic movement on anger or even indecision and if that is correct, maybe my BattyBoo need some Ritalin. (Just a joke folks. Just a joke). What I mean to indicate is if anger or indecision is at the base of this behavior, she is a troubled cat.

If her tail twitching and switching and wiggling means she's in a state of indecision, she's an emotional mess, a nervous wreck. If it means she's angry, she's one mad-hatter cat.

You know what? I believe that everything the expert animal behaviorists assert, when it comes to BooCat, is entirely wrong. If the experts who blame it on anger or indecision are correct, Basketcase-BooCat does need some Kitty Ritalin, and that is no joke.

My opinion? She's not switching, she's wagging. BooCat thinks she's BooDog.

To confirm this diagnosis, BooCat has taken a liking to dog biscuits. I drop a couple in the dog dish reserved for treats, and she is the first one to grab one and relocate to a private place where she proceeds to munch down. She leaves crumbs that Rosie and Taco come along and lap up, but for the most part, she eats the whole thing.

One day shortly after Biscuit-eatingBoo discovered dog biscuits, Rosie beat Boo to the bowl and took first one, then the other biscuit, and hid them behind a chair leg. She's no dummy. She was making sure she got a biscuit so she wouldn't be left with just crumbs.

27 / BooCat Quirks

And that's not all. Boo seems to enjoy gnawing on the teeth on the scratching end of my wooden backscratcher. Dogs gnaw. Dogs eat dog biscuits. Dogs wag their tails. Boo has even licked my hand a time or two. Maybe living and sleeping with dogs has given Boodle an identity crisis. Never having the opportunity to peer in the mirror to see that she looks different from Rosie and Taco, she sees them and assumes she's just like them. They are, therefore I am.

More alert than the dogs, she's an amazing watch-cat plus she's the world's first purring dog.

She'll be barking next.

I've taken to calling her Boodle which is a combination of Boo and Poodle.

The only thing I can say for certain is that I'm not wagging the cat, she's wagging me.

When it comes to BooCat's ears, contrary to unusual tail wagging, how she holds them appears to be first class cat behavior and do send normal cat messages. Of course, with BooCat, anything's likely. There are at least five basic ear signals cats send.

Cat owners are familiar with their pet pitching its ears forward and slightly outward. It's a visible pointing. BaffledBooCat does this when she's listening. Like when Theresa and Carla's dogs, Nike and Max, are spending the night, asleep in another room. Boo knows they're nearby and she's keeping an ear out for them. It's a sign of attentiveness.

When BooCat isn't just listening for something, but actually hears a noise like mice or ghosts in the attic, her ears attain an alert mode. They become fully erect and point directly forward.

At times like these, she will also stand up like a Prairie dog or a Bandicoot. She lifts the front part of her body upward, balancing on her haunches and she looks toward the sound with her ears are totally erect and slightly forward.

Cats can hear sounds up to one-hundred-thousand cycles per second. Guess how many cycles per second the sound pitch made by a mouse squeaking is? Yep. One-hundred-thousand. Fancy that. Even dogs can't hear that precisely. Humans certainly can't. Being half deaf

145

BooCat Unleashed

I hear less still.

When Boo twitches her ears I don't know if she's agitated or has a flea or an ear mite or if it's just a nervous tic. I have to trust the flea stuff worked and it's simply a moment of agitation.

Flattening her ears is a defensive mode. It comes during a time of fearfulness; something cats learn from birth. It is recognized as a protective move. They flatten their ears before a cat fight or when under attack in an attempt to prevent the other cat or dog from biting or tearing them.

When ears are rotated in such a way the backs are visible from the front, it's a sign of a very hostile and aggressive animal. BooCat has not had cause to exhibit this particular ear signal. I don't remember if I've ever seen this ear signal in fact, or just read about it.

The ear signal, or manner of holding her ears, like the twitching of her tail, would appear to indicate that my BaffledBoo suffers to some degree of discontent according to cat experts. She often lays them back in a semi-defensive mode. Even as she appears totally relaxed. Twitching tail, ears back. Stretched out. Eyes closed. I know as a thrice-rejected kitten, she is emotionally conflicted to a degree. But, perhaps we place too much emphasis on ears and tails and should instead pay attention to the rubbing and bunting instead. It cancels out the negatives.

Likewise, the purring. BooBaby is the queen of contented-cat purring.

Whiskers, called vibrissae, are important tools in the cat's reserve. It's obvious even to a layperson like myself, they play the roll as another sense organ, like antennae. There are a couple sets—at the side of the mouth in four rows and above the eyes. All twenty-five to thirty of these whiskers are attached to nerves in the cat's skin.

Most cat whiskers grow straight. Hershey's whiskers were curled. Did he sit too close to the fireplace his first winter at Wit's End, scorching and twisting them? I don't know if his curled whiskers were normal or a quirk, but on him they were beautiful. He was beautiful.

Whiskers allow a cat to identify things and keep it from banging into stuff in the dark. Cats have excellent night vision but they don't

27 / BooCat Quirks

see in the dark like Superman with X-ray vision. Whiskers help cats navigate when the light's very poor. In a blind cat, whiskers become its white cane.

I'm always greeted royally by a pack of wildly happy furry friends when I drive down the driveway and up under the carport. I can't imagine life without pets. I babble bubbly baby talk and pat each one on the head at least once before disappearing inside the house.

I know they don't understand what I'm saying. The fact that I'm saying something to each of them, calling each by name, petting and smooching them, that's important. They hear my love and devotion in the tone of my voice.

Once inside I've always been greeted by three more wildly happy furry canine friends, TacoBelle, Rosie and Gizzy. I babbled more bubbly baby talk and patted everyone on their respective heads. They expected to be picked up and smooched, cuddled and coddled.

When finally free of the obligated puppy loving, I moved over to where Hershey Cat sits royally upon the ancient wooden cutting block awaiting his turn. Being a cat he was far too dignified to carry on like the canine crew. Shaking out a snack for Hershey I might tell him—no baby talk for him—I had the best Johnny's mushroom with extra cheese pizza for lunch. He didn't care, preferring his kibbles a little on the fishy side. I explained that outside wasn't safe. Big bad coyotes roamed at night. Chicken- and cat-eating foxes too. Also roughneck dogs, and worst of all, the wheels of automobiles.

My conversations never need make sense. They just had to be carried on in a one-on-one manner.

I miss Gizzy and I really miss Hershey too. Hershey often sat on the windowsill and drooled over the birds in the yard, basic instincts from ancient genes kicking in. Yet he never bothered George or SnowBird. The same cannot be said about BooCat. I think Hershey's reasoning was if it lived inside the house, then it was a pal. That extended even to a stray mouse too. Except once. And only once. The rest of the time, Hershey was a laid-back, live and let live, sort of cat.

I wonder what BooCat would've thought of Hershey? I expect she would have considered him a wimp instead of the royal gentleman that he was.

It didn't take BooCat long to learn to join TacoBelle and Rosie at the door at the sound of my keys rattling in the lock, welcoming me home.

One of the girls now, it's obvious she'd like to be alpha pet but TacoBelle is hanging onto that position. Bossing Rosie around is one thing. Docile Rosie was an easy takeover. But not so with TacoBelle. As with most bullies, they know who to push and how hard and how far. She knows TacoBelle won't put up with her foolishness. She knows because she's tried and failed. TacoBelle may be little, but she's tough. She can go from Chihuahua to Rottweiler in seconds.

An example of how easy Rosie is and how dominant BossyBooCat can be is when I enter the house and all three pets head straight toward me, but should Rosie gain a little momentum and be in the lead, BreakawayBooCat literally body slams her. She boots her out of the way so she reaches me first. She earns the gold medal every time and scores all the points. Of course, if there were a referee on the field, a foul would be called.

Cats are supposed to be unassuming, making great pets for anyone who doesn't demand tricks and constant adoration. It's true what they say about cats and dogs and ownership. You can own a dog, but a cat owns you.

BooCat is far from unassuming. In a manner of speaking, she does do tricks, just not on demand. Nor necessarily for my pleasure. Slightly narcissistic, she does what she does to amuse herself.

One thing I can say, BooCat bestows constant adoration on me. She follows me. She pays attention to my every mood and movement. She has become attached. She'd probably let TacoBelle into her ring of best friends if she'd lighten up a little. Rosie and I are members of the BooCat Club.

SnowBird and George are ex-officio members. That is, members by default. Boo has ulterior motives for wanting them on the roster.

By the way, BooCat just discovered the drip in the bathtub. She is enticed. And why not. It moves. Dripping water drops. She can't resist anything that moves.

With Boo, my secret for successful ownership is to pet her from one end to the other, provide her food of choice, change her litter often, don't expect her to come when I call unless she wants to and let her walk all over me. I treat her as though my entire existence is solely to ensure her happiness. This works. BooCat is a happy cat. And if BooCat's happy, everybody's happy.

Sowing Seeds and Planting Daffodils

28

"Pussyfooting around." (American Phrase: Started as a comment calling attention to how cats, being light-footed, sneaky even and quite stealthy, are when hunting. Dates to about 1893. It has come to mean to tread warily, to refrain from committing oneself, a sort of beating around the bush as it were)

BooCat has come to a good place. I'm happy here. She's happy here too. I've lived here longer than anywhere else. I used to feel sad because I had no roots. Although traveling is a great growing-up experience, now that I'm older, roots are important.

Thinking of roots literally as well as figuratively, and how long I've lived here, reminds me how many years it's been since I was first introduced to the joy of vegetable gardening. Prior to that introduction, I took it for granted that all veggies came in cans. Except for corn on the cob, of course. And lettuce.

Cat and dog food comes in cans. Give us a can opener and we'd survive indefinitely. My early life experience led me to believe all a good cook needed was a can opener and a sauce pan. It wasn't difficult. You wanted peas, you visited the grocery store, bought a can, took it home, opened it. Then you dumped the contents into a pan, set the pot on the stove, added a dollop of butter, some salt and pepper and served them as a side dish when hot. Not a thing wrong with canned peas.

Not until you tried fresh off the vine peas, that is. Ah heaven. Because, when I moved to Jones, overnight I became country through and through and discovered fresh peas picked from the vine. There is nothing sweeter.

I recall thinking, "Look at me, raising a garden. Eat your heart out my city-slicker friends."

Peas and beans, corn, vine-ripened tomatoes, watermelons and cantaloupes, fresh cabbage and lettuce, okra and onions. All fresh. All delightfully delicious.

Thinking back, I recall before the sun rose too high in the sky, when the sugar content was at its peak in the corn, and the dew glistened like diamonds on the waxy cucumbers, I gathered all the delightfully fresh-grown foodstuff from my first garden at Wit's End Comedy Club. How lovely were mornings in the garden at harvest time.

Wait a minute. That sounds poetically perfect, but let's get real. Yes. It was wonderful, but there's a limit to that wonderment. There's reality.

By mid-afternoon, I didn't care if I ever saw another ear of corn and wondered what was so aesthetic about the dew getting the cukes all wet.

I swore the next spring when I bought a package of cucumber seeds, tight and conservative as I am because I hate waste, still I would discard half those little suckers. Just because they packaged a hundred itty-bitty seeds per pack, didn't mean I had to plant all hundred of them.

That first year I learned that one-hundred itty-bitty cucumber seeds produced one-hundred big cucumber vines upon which grew no less than one-hundred cucumbers on each. But that wasn't all. Each of those one-hundred cucumbers on each of those one-hundred vines grown from the one-hundred itty-bitty seeds demanded to be picked each and every single day. Waste not, want not. And once the hundreds of cukes were picked off hundreds of vines, hundreds more took their places. Even a non-mathematician like myself could figure the total sum equaled a lot of jars of pickles and more cucumber sandwiches than I'd ever be able to eat in a summer season.

By the way, prior to planting and raising those one-hundred cucumber plants, like cans of peas, I use to buy pickles in pickle jars already pickled. I never gave a second thought—nor a first for that matter—as to where pickles came from until I learned to make them, learning they were the end result of one-hundred itty-bitty cucumber seeds growing rampantly in some poor soul's veggie garden.

I actually liked making pickles but a family of four couldn't eat a hundred jars in a season. Therefore, I made a tough decision. I determined throwing away half the seeds in each package would be like never missing an opportunity to potty when on a trip—smartly planning ahead. Cucumbers weren't by any means the only culprits. Every seed package produced row upon row of peas and beans. If your back didn't ache and break from picking them, then your fingers would fall off from shelling them.

Oh yeah, that was the first time in my life I shelled peas and beans. I grew to respect the Jolly Green Giant ho-ho-ho-whole-heartedly.

Following the breaking up of the garden plot—which meant getting it ready for planting; planting the seeds and hoeing the weeds—an unforgiving daily duty especially when I realized a hoe is an alien thing that barely fit my hand; then it was time to harvest—which means pick and in the case of beans and peas, shell.

After which this fingerless fool would be faced with phase two—or maybe it's phase four or five—of the veggie-gathering endeavor. I had to "put them up." either in quart jars or the freezer.

It was at that time in my life I recalled with such fondness how a jolly "Ho-Ho-Ho" used to echo through the valley. (Whatever happened to that commercial?)

Besides learning the art of pickle making, I learned how to can tomatoes. We ate sliced tomatoes, BLT's, tomato salad, pickled tomatoes, and tomatoe'd-tomatoes until they were coming out of our ears. I always thought that was just a silly expression. Not so. Tomatoes coming out of ears is the stuff of which nightmares are made of.

But I survived. Although there were moments when I found myself wishing for unassembled snowmen to fall from heaven so I could hang up the garden hoe, each morning I woke up breathing I congratulated myself because I had another opportunity to do it all over again. And I did. Year after year for many years. With no regrets. I wish I had the stamina to do it some more. But the thing is, stuff goes in cycles. Now that I'm an old geezer gal, I'm back to buying my peas in cans and my cukes already pickled. Relegated to the category of "fond memories" I can say the gardening experience wasn't all that bad.

※

Another fond gardening memory relates to an incident I refer to as "The Daffodil Deception."

At this time in life I've probably done about all the planting I'm going to do 'til it is time to be planted. These two acres my house sits on was formerly part of a cotton field and required everything from trees, shrubs, flowers and grass be planted. It all got done and a lovely tree-filled homeplace was created. A little too wild and natural to be featured in *Home and Gardens,* but perfect for raising children, pets and as a fine place in which to grow older.

Now, planting's a been-there-done-that thing. Still, I'll always remember my first ornamental gardening experience.

I'd spent my entire life as a city gal, so when I moved to my oasis, I was such a novice, it was almost sinful. Folks sometimes bestow endearing names on their farms and homesteads and I called this place a couple other names at first—but it outgrew them.

After lining the perimeter with pine trees, in an attempt to recapture a taste of my birth state of Maryland, where I remembered pine trees dotting the woods and roadsides, I called it Whispering Pines. I loved those pine trees even though I was warned pines do not do well in the delta.

The naysayers were right. They developed a gall that spread rampant throughout and eventually had to be cut down. All of them. I struck a bargain with the owner of a lumber company who cut and sold trees to the paper mill. We worked out a deal where he got all the wood and I got rid of my pines. I couldn't very well call my haven Whispering Pines once it became pineless.

I considered calling it Oasis, because it's surrounded by farm fields and indeed, it was my little oasis, my refuge and sanctuary. Then life took a turn and I started referring to it as Wit's End. When life kept taking turns every which way, I added Comedy Club. The name stuck. I don't know how endearing the name is, but it's suitable. When I'm here, I'm there. Stand up, sit down, it's a laugh a minute.

Plant it in a pot and forget it was my mode of operandi when it came to house plants. Mostly I was smart enough to cultivate only the hardiest of cacti—and I've cultivated some mighty hardy ones. Barb's law as applied to my plant jungle was simple—only the hardy survived. I put my plants on a schedule of watering them once a week whether they needed it or not. If they adapted, I'd occasionally talk to them.

So, after having done nothing more green-thumbish than watering those hardy cacti (and complain about the short life-span of everything else), I was appointed chairman of the board of a two-acre yard. Fact of the matter is, this two-acre yard appeared so large, I figured I'd need roller skates to get from one end to the other.

Rude awakening.

Roller skates were out of the question. There was no concrete. Imagine! No concrete. No sidewalks. It didn't seem natural. But, as I soon discovered, living in Jones is the epitome of living in the sticks with a population of very-few-and-widely-scattered. But, in the end, that's what makes it so special. It has nothing to do with hermit ways; I like people. It has to do with breathing, with being surrounded by nature and with the freedom to be. Once I adjusted to the fact that everything requires driving to and from, but once you get back, there is nothing nicer. I love country living.

I'd always admired weedless flowerbeds, pretty lawns and formal gardens. Note the key word: *admired*. I'd spent my entire life surrounded by cement, and here I was, making my home where various species of grasses, weeds and dirt (Whoops! Farmers call it soil), was the norm.

This huge expanse filled my big green citified eyes with its blinding dimensions. Admittedly, when I wrote family and friends, my description of everything probably rivaled that of the proverbial fish story but, for those of you old enough to remember the phrase, it really was bigger than a breadbox.

Because it was formerly part of a cotton field, my yard wasn't exactly a prize place for the kiddies to romp and stomp in. Bare dirt on dry days, yucky mud after a rain. And no sidewalks. Playing marbles is okay in dirt, but what about hopscotch and jacks? Being surrounded by dirt instead of concrete was traumatizing.

Yes. It needed everything. Trees. Grass. Flowers. Sidewalks. Full of enthusiasm at having a home of my own, after sprinkling grass seeds about, I visualized springtime yellow turning wild into idyll. I've always associated springtime with yellow. Forsythias, jonquils, Carolina jasmine, daylilies and daffodils. My first serious planting was to set out daffodil bulbs.

Assuming a prayerful position (and murmuring a few along the way too, I might add), shiny new spade in hand, I dug a small hole.

Trying to keep dirt from falling among the pages, I peered at the instructions in one of the many gardening books I purchased, and carefully positioned the daffodil bulb exactly as pictured.

Half burying it, I scooted back a knee's length and jabbed the spade in the ground again.

And again.

Finally, I reached the end of the row, got wearily to my feet and stretched what I feared would be a permanently cricked back.

Yikes!

I did a double take. I'd just planted one of the crookedest rows of flower bulbs man (or beast) ever laid eyes upon.

I immediately rejected replanting the bulbs. Not even if it would help the United Automobile, Aerospace, or the Agricultural Implement Workers of America. No way would I redo those bulbs.

I settled, instead, on utilizing Barbs' Big Bluff.

Thus it was, when folks stopped by, I put on my most intelligent straight face (I can look intelligent if I have to), adopted the tone of a teacher speaking to sixth-graders, and said, "When flower bulbs are planted in this particular manner, it allows the sun to reach them better."

I contended this method worked on the same principal as "skip-row" cotton planting. I went for the extremely serious look and I never blinked trusting it would impress my neighbors.

Of course, they might have left thinking not only did I not know how to plant flower bulbs, but there was something wrong with my eyes too, what with the utilization of the "serious look."

The truth was, I'd simply become so involved in the task before me, I'd neglected the most important part—to look to see where I was going, or even, perhaps, where I'd been.

Over the years, the bulbs multiplied and though there are still a few visible crooks here and there, it's no longer quite so obvious. Ah, but let a soul mention the crooked row and I immediately don a look of astonishment and ask, "Why, doesn't everybody do daffodils this way?"

Then I smile my sweetest smile. Shuts them up every time.

Making a Home For BooCat and Family

29

"Look what the cat dragged in." (Unknown Origin: Obvious reference to a cat's tendency to bring home its prey, and is used as a derogatory comment upon someone's arrival).

Most the time I would rather be running the roads than staying home dusting. But, as much as I enjoy being on the go, sometimes it's not doable and I'm stuck at home. A free weekend at home usually means catching up on the housework that has piled up higher than a basket of unironed laundry. Naturally, I've got a way to handle a basket of unironed laundry. It's all about taking control of your own situation.

If for some reason a piece of clothing slips by me that requires ironing or dry cleaning—because normally I don't buy anything except perm-press—I relegate it to the laundry basket where it awaits its turn on the ironing board. If it's not been ironed in a year's time, I give it away.

BossBoo approves this method. How do I know? One of her favorite spots, she snoozes in the clothes basket. She knows right from the moment a piece of unironed clothing is dropped into the basket it's not going anywhere and she claims it as part of her bedding.

Actually, right before BooCat moved in, I planned to give the whole basketful away because my iron died. From neglect. I advised friends not to send flowers. Although the iron and I had started our journey through life together in 1962, my mourning period was very brief. I didn't purchase a replacement. I didn't want to be responsible for the death of another useless electrical appliance forty years down the road.

There's a computer-related shaggy dog story instructing the best way to handle housework is to open a new file in the PC and name it "Housework." Next, the file should be sent to the Recycle Bin. After that, simply empty the Recycle Bin.

Computers are amazing. It'll ask, "Are you sure you want to delete Housework permanently?"

You're kidding, right?

With BooCat in my lap purring, she wants very much to help with the process. She likes pressing various keys on the keyboard. She'd walk on the keyboard if I let her. She'd sleep on it too. Anyway, I calmly answer "Yes" and point the arrow and press the mouse button firmly. And it's gone. For good. Just like that.

Nice work if you can get it—or not.

Too bad real housework isn't that simple to eliminate. Real housework is more demanding. I've figured out that the part is equal to some of its whole and that housework is like a milk cow. She won't stay milked, and a house won't stay clean.

Take dusting. What was and what will be is not now, but dust is. It always is. If you don't believe it, try dusting today and then check back tomorrow. The fact is, the shortest distance between two points is either point, meaning you can start dusting in the middle of your house and work outward, or you can start at either end, and by the time you get to the other end, it'll need dusting again. Maybe cats and dogs aren't so dumb. They don't let a little thing like dust disturb them.

So what to do? I've perfected several dusting techniques. If I let dust build up, a couple things happen: One, it protects the surface of my furniture. I'm thinking of patenting this discovery. You've seen people cover their furniture with drop cloths when they're going to be gone from home for any length of time? Built-up dust serves the same purpose. I might make a fortune bottling and selling it to neat-freaks who need some dust in a hurry and don't have time to wait for it to build up.

Second, when and if I decide to remove it, I can pick it up whole,

29 / Making a Home For BooCat and Family

which is easier than dusting with a rag.

You've seen dust motes in a beam of sunlight. They also go dancing in the moonlight.

Therefore, leaving dust sit is medically sound. Unstirred and silently settled makes nighttime sleeping allergen free. No dust motes floating in the air to make me and BooCat sneeze.

A good security measure is not to dust around whatnots and you'll know in a heartbeat if one's missing.

On the other hand, if you move a piece of furniture from one side of the room to the other, replacing the knick-knacks is a breeze provided you haven't dusted. Their places are saved by the lines of dust demarcation.

How often do you dust your television screen? I've got a foolproof formula. When Seinfeld starts looking like the late great humorist Bernie Mac, it's time.

If my ceiling fans are clean, nobody notices. Let them get dusty and that's the first place everybody's eyes travel. My solution—and of course I have a solution—is to keep them on year round. Whirling round and round, no one can see if they're dusty or not.

And the ever inquisitive BooCat loves the whirling. She's a bit of a whirling dervish herself. I can see it in her eyes. She'd hop on a ceiling fan blade at breakneck speed in the proverbial New York minute or in a Nanosecond—whichever is the fastest—if only she could figure out how to get from point A to point B. BooCatCarousel would have her own private carnival ride.

Another trick of the trade developed by years of doing that which is never done, is the burned out light bulb technique. TacoBelle is a staunch believer in this one. She doesn't dust and she doesn't do light bulbs.

Besides keeping ceiling fans running to hide dusty fan blades, burned out light bulbs add to a room's mystique. Shadowiness created by burned out bulbs produces an indistinctness that hides a whole lot of dust. Eventually I do knock down cobwebs but until then, instead of blindfolding visitors, I dim the lights to destroy the evidence by way of camouflage.

I figure the sooner I fall behind, the more time I'll have to catch up. To paraphrase Kinky Friedman and applying it to dusting specifically: Get out the dust rag, wash your hands, and say your prayers, 'cause dust, germs and Jesus are everywhere.

Growing the Family

30

"The cat has too much spirit to have no heart." (Ernest Menaul)

"Oh, no! No! No!" I sat up in bed almost ripping my CPAP mask off my face and my head off my neck. "What have you got, Boo?"

The bed was bouncing. She was tossing something up in the air, catching it and batting it around the bed.

Her bouncy behavior hadn't bothered TacoBelle or Rosie. I guess they've gotten used to her rambunctiousness.

My pulse quickened as I reached overhead to flip on the light switch. I hadn't seen a cricket in over a month. They had either died or were hibernating. Didn't snakes hibernate too?

It could be a mouse. Mice don't hibernate to the best of my knowledge. In fact, in winter they seek warmth with accessible provisions available. Like dog and cat chow sitting out twenty-four/seven; bird food within reach and even with a little chewing ingeniousness, people food.

On the times mice have broken and entered they have found all the above present and obtainable.

So it could be a mouse.

A mouse wouldn't be too bad. I actually like mice. Just not the destruction they do.

Just, heaven forbid, don't ever let it be a full-fledged rat. Rats are big and dangerous and mean as roguish villains; nasty pieces of work.

Why does she have to be such a super huntress?

The night before, she'd slept all night long in the crook of my arm until four-thirty in the morning when she walked up my body, plopped down on my chest and started purring.

It goes without saying, she woke me. But what a nice way to be awakened. Even at four-thirty in the morning.

After the pups and I made our individual potty runs, I scooted Boo over from where she had spread out in my warm spot and pulled the cover up to my neck, advising, "We're going back to sleep." And I turned the light off.

Not until closer to six did we actually rise and shine. By then Boo was sleeping at my feet, scooted up close to Rosie who was buried beneath the covers. TacoBelle was at my side. When Boo didn't reclaim her spot in the crook of my arm, TacoBelle reclaimed hers. When Boo sleeps up under my arm, she usually boots TacoBelle a little lower on the bed. Taco may be alpha dog, but Boo generally sleeps where she wants.

I don't mind when the fids wake me up if I've been purring too loudly, although my CPAP mask pretty well keeps snoring to a minimum on a whole. A couple mornings earlier, I sat up in bed and Rosie came to me and gently stretched her neck and her face so that her long nose almost touched my lips. Her tongue darted out and she barely licked me. She did that twice. She's not a licker, so I guess she considers herself saving my life again—making sure when I stop breathing, that I start again.

I can count on one hand the number of times Rosie has licked me.

So pleasant when we awaken normally. Not so pleasant to awaken to the antics of HuntressBoo.

When the light comes on, Boo stops in mid-play and gazes in my direction.

"What have you got, Boo?" I dare to ask.

As though she understands, she leans down and comes up with her prey dangling from her mouth.

Is that a smile on her face? A Fooled-you-Mom, smile?

It very likely could be because what's hanging from her mouth is nothing more than a rubber band. A safe, non-biting, non-poisonous rubber band.

Sigh.

Because I've disturbed everybody by turning on the light, I speak words of wisdom and love saying what good and smart babies they all are, and that I'm turning out the light now so we can all go back to sleep.

"Nighty-night, Sweeties."

In the dark I feel my heart quieting down. My breath is becoming more regularly. I know it's going to take a moment or three before I'm able to fall back to sleep. One reason I read myself to sleep each night is to shut down my ever-active brain. I concentrate on the characters and plot of a book and that stills the wheels turning internally. Some people count sheep. I read.

I hoped to drift off. I didn't want to turn the light on again and retrieve my book. That would throw my whole sleep schedule off balance.

Unfortunately, sleep didn't come right away because my mind decided to runaway. I found myself recalling what I'd learned in August from my sister Michele about Reinhard.

Coincidentally, when the father of my children and I were stationed in Ulm, West Germany, my brother Jimmy was stationed at Heidelberg and Dad at Bremen. My other brother, David, did a tour in Viet Nam. The Christmas of 1966, just a couple months after Tony was born, both Dad and Jimmy were able to visit over the holidays. All three of us together in Germany at the same moment, spending Christmas together. It was most special. One of my best Christmases ever. That was indeed a moment in time always remembered.

At that time I of course had no idea Dad had met someone and fallen in love with her. My mother was patiently awaiting his return from his tour of duty in Germany. Sister Jan was still a teenager. Mom and Jan were living alone together in Maryland wondering where Dad's next transfer, his new assignment, would take them. That's the life of a military family. Together and apart, at the whim of the Pentagon bosses; orders from headquarters.

The reason Mom didn't accompany Dad to Germany was because brother David and Jan were both still in school at the onset of his reassignment to Bremen. The base Dad was stationed at didn't have American housing or schooling available.

When you're an Army wife you face these situations and do what must be done. He had been overseas fighting in World War II when I was born. He had been stationed in Turkey for a year a few years prior to being sent to Germany for two years. It wasn't a bad life for the most part, but it had its shortfalls. A wife waves her husband goodbye and counts the days until his return. They live off letters of love for the duration. The soldier gets the medals but the wife deserves special commendations also.

Sometimes men return. Sometimes they don't. In this case, when my father returned to the United States, he approached my mother with a request for a divorce. Because I wasn't around her, I missed whatever emotional turmoil she dealt with. I know it must have been very difficult. Jan was there so she wasn't totally alone when her world crumbled. But nothing makes it easier when your husband walks out on you.

In the state of Maryland at that time, a divorce took two years to become final. Thus it was, in the meantime, my new half-sister Michele was born.

Jan said Michele was three years old before she became aware of her existence. I don't recall when I learned of her birth. I have a bad tendency of losing memories if they're unpleasant. Self-protection and self-defense mode kicks in and I forget. Dad introduced Anna, his new wife and child to my family and me after the divorce was final and they'd married. They came to visit. I was only a few years younger than Anna, and accepted her as my father's wife and Michele as my sister. I didn't think in terms of step-mother or half-sister and I fell instantly in love with Michele and felt a friendship develop between Anna and I.

I was glad my father was happy. I wasn't glad my mother was dumped. Such were the mixed emotions situations such as this caused. I maintained a good relationship with my father and Anna and Michele. My mother never felt any animosity toward Anna or Michele but she was bitter for the betrayal she felt from my father. When Tony was killed, by then Mom was living here and Anna and Dad came for the funeral. Everyone got on quite well; Mom was a champ. The only negative being the reason for the family gathering.

By then I was divorced from Theresa and Tony's father. The relationship between us was very strained during the funeral. Of course, there are two sides to every story. The true side—mine, and the lying side—his. He remarried and apparently their relationship was so fragile he allowed himself to agree to have nothing with his own children and the last time he saw or spoke to Tony's widow and child—his only grandchild—was in April 1992. At Tony's funeral.

All the skeletons in all the closets. Likely he cannot even close his closet door. My humble opinion, my closet is fine with room to spare. You see, he hasn't spoken to his beautiful daughter Theresa since April 1992 either. He made some appalling remark after the funeral that he never had a wife named Barbara and he never had a daughter named Theresa, turned to Chuck and shook his hand while saying "Good luck." Evil vibes followed him out the door.

He accidentally sat across from Theresa, Carla, Lance and me in a restaurant a year ago and pretended he didn't know us. We were there first. We watched him and his Bimbo and her daughter and child be seated and our meal was on the verge of being ruined. We wished we had gone to some other restaurant, but it was too late.

The sounds of a heart breaking could have been heard all over the restaurant if you knew to listen for it. I heard it. Bless my sweet daughter's broken heart.

When his father died, a man who had been my father for twenty years too, and Theresa's grandfather all her life, he had the audacity to call and tell me if Theresa and I showed up at his father's funeral he would "call the law" on us. I can say I was stunned. I actually thought he'd developed a brain tumor; he was not the same man who had been a good husband and loving father for those twenty years.

I asked, who is this man?

To this day, I have no idea. Somebody else moved in and latched onto his heart and soul and spoiled them. His granddaughter also suffers confusion, wondering what she did wrong. She was three-years-old when her father was killed. She never had time to do anything wrong.

He was and is a deadbeat dad and nonexistent grandfather. He evaded every responsibility. It was so strange because for twenty years he was a good and honorable man. His about-face is unexplainable.

How could someone go from honorable to dishonorable overnight? Maybe I had been the one married to a stranger; then when he met the other woman, somebody opened the gate and let the dogs out.

In fact he foolishly committed his dishonest feelings to paper August 23, 1981 writing in part:

> First of all, I will say I'm sorry things ended this way for both of us. However, I have no regrets in doing so. We have had a good life together. I hope after this is all over, we can still be friends and respect each other for what we both are. Each of us are individuals. We are two entirely different persons. If you stop and think, we have hardly anything in common.

(And it took him twenty years to determine that? Hah!)

> For some time now, I have started thinking about my happiness and my future. I am admitting the truth to myself and hope to explain so maybe you can understand.

(Yeah, ever since he started sleeping with the Bimbo. In fact, all the while I was visiting my mom in Maryland, I later learned, his Bimbo was sleeping in my bed. You have to know that is sick and unforgivable).

> As I've already told you, I haven't loved you for some time now. It has just been easier for me to say 'I love you' than to explain why I didn't. There is no one else. This is something that has happened to me and my feelings and is the result of no outside influences.

(Watch the man's nose grow Pinocchio-long the longer he types this letter).

A lot of the things I've been doing over the past year or

> so were excuses for me to be away from you because I had become "uncomfortable" around you. Some "for instances" are 1- leaving in the morning to check on farming operations (I know my farming business at all times and would just go drink coffee at the gin or something)
> 2 - Police Jury business (I'm not that interested in helping other people, but it affords plenty of opportunity to be gone).

(You got that part about not interested in helping other people, didn't you? Amazing).

> 3 - Store business (I don't have to stay there and work as much as I do, but it is a safe place to be apart from you).

(The Bimbo worked at the store we owned. Enough said. Interestingly enough, he signed my name on the back of the joint income tax refund and cashed it. And he and the Bimbo each took her husband's and my burial insurance policies and forged our names and redeemed them for the cash value. But, there wasn't anybody else).

> I even considered running for State Rep. That would give me plenty of time to be in Baton Rouge, etc. I don't want to be State Rep. and don't want to serve on the Police Jury anymore after this term is over.

(Funny. When he and the Bimbo moved to Mer Rouge, he ran for Police Jury from that district and lost by the largest landslide ever in the history of local elections for miles around).

> I have admitted all these things to myself and am now telling you in hopes you can understand. For a change I am looking out for my happiness. I have no regrets about the past. I am only looking to the future.
> I don't care about society gatherings or social events. I would rather go out and play in the dirt and mud for instance. We don't like the same kinds of music; you like to read - I like to watch football; you like to talk - I like to

relax and say things when I have something to say; you like to go to museums and other cultural places - I don't; you like for everything to be in its place and all prim and proper - I don't care; you like to be serious all the time and no "F" jokes - I like to joke and have fun most of the time. I am tired of pretending to be happy when in reality I am not happy.

You don't know how much better I feel now that this is out in the open and somewhat off my chest. The children and I even get along better because there is no tension in my mind.

(Self explanatory. My bad. The kids didn't even know they weren't getting along any more than I was aware he was living a lie. I was also unaware he was really an uncouth, coarse, sorry sapsucker beneath the skin he had been wearing for the twenty-plus years I had known him. Give the man an Oscar. When he comes out of the closet, not as a gay man—although I once saw a tendency when he seemed particularly enamored with a male second or third cousin of his—he comes out blazing. He went from admirable to sleazy overnight.)

The only thing you have to understand is I cannot live with you any more. I won't stay with someone I don't love - it wouldn't be fair to me or them... I have made up my mind and as costly as it may be, it will be worth it to me in the future...

The End.

That's all he wrote.

But, no. Actually, it wasn't. He turned mean. I feared for my life. He paid nil for his daughter's college tuition and he paid one month, and one month only, child support for Tony—saying "Take me to court."

He forged my name and the Bimbo forged her husband's name—and they redeemed our burial policies for cash value.

He forged my name on the IRS tax refund, money withheld from my banking job.

He took the set of silverware my father gave me for Christmas the year Tony was born. The list of injustices done is unbelievably long.

He dug up my driveway culvert and moved it to somewhere on his farm land after we were already divorced. This was during the time the Good-Old-Boy network ran the sheriff's office and they simply advised it was a civil matter rather than criminal. No help there.

Looked to me like theft of personal property was criminal, even if the criminal was my ex-husband. There was nothing in the divorce decree that gave him the right to that culvert. If he'd harmed me, I reckon it would have been a civil matter because we were once husband and wife. Makes no sense. Crime is crime.

A good friend obtained another culvert and had it installed for me. I didn't have money to run to court every time the man did evil. He did so much I would've had to keep an attorney on retainer.

No. It wasn't a brain tumor that twisted his personality, but it should have been. It would have been far better. Attending his funeral would have been better than watching the man I had loved and admired turn into a spitefully mean stranger.

But I digress.

When Michele came to visit in August when BooCat was adopted, it had been ten years since I'd seen her. That was at our father's funeral. Jan and her husband Kevin and I attended.

One night during the week Michele and Jan were here, Michele told us something she herself had learned only two years earlier. Why she didn't tell Jan and I sooner, we're not sure. She said she wanted to tell us in person. Whatever her motivation, since the events took place, we were glad to finally learn about them. You can't turn back time. Better late than never. Spilt milk. Platitudes, because it was a shame we hadn't learned sooner and so much valuable precious time wouldn't have been squandered in ignorance.

Without going into too much detail, we learned—Jan and I in August, Michele two years earlier—that we have a brother. Actually, Michele has two—one half and one full. Jan and I have one—half—and another by association.

Anna, Michele's mother and our father's wife, had a little boy by a man who left her before they were wed. Then she met our father and they had a son they named Reinhard. Because my father was still married and on active military duty, when Anna did come to the United States, she left her two sons—one son whose father was our father, making him our half brother—with her mother.

I would like to suppose that when Dad's divorce was final and he and Anna married, they no doubt planned to bring the two sons to the United States also. It would have been the thing to do. In the meantime, Anna became pregnant with Michele.

Time slipping away as it does, when Anna's mother died—the boys' grandmother—because her father was an alcoholic and apparently unable to care for the boys, the state took them and placed them in an orphanage.

I don't now the actual time element or why the boys weren't brought to America to be with their mother.

Reinhard reports the orphanage was run by nuns and he was brutally mistreated and has permanent eyesight loss and scars. I learned he was born a few months before Dad came to visit me and my family that included his new grandson that Christmas in 1966. I never knew until August, 2009, that he had just become a father himself again a few months earlier.

Rein and Thomas were rescued when a caring couple adopted them and took them to their home in Holland where they were raised in a loving family household.

Still, no matter how loving a family may be, when one finally tracks down their real parents—his father already deceased as I understand it—and his mother with no real excuse for abandoning him, it has got to be emotionally tough.

Jan told our two brothers about our half brother. She told her sons and I told Theresa.

The thing that bothered Jan and I the most was that we wish Michele had told us as soon as she learned of Rein and his brother Thomas's existence. So much time wasted.

I wonder if I'll ever meet Rein in person. I'm already an old woman, my health isn't so good and I'm very poor. But we are in touch through the networking website Facebook and via e-mails. He seems a fine young man. Working steadily, a good wife and a couple beautiful children and two dogs. He is the age of my late son Tony. How the world turns and what comes to be, sometimes it seems there is no rationality discernable no matter how hard or how deep or how long you probe.

Better late than never. I have plenty of room in my heart for another brother or two. Hearts are, after all, very expandable.

Training BooCat

31

"If there is one spot of sun spilling onto the floor, a cat will find it and soak it up."
(J. A. McIntosh)

Everybody knows how to select the perfect pet. First, we decide what we want—a cat, dog, bird, fish, hamster or what. I knew I eventually wanted another cat. I thought about another purebred cat. I actually entertained the idea of getting a Ragdoll; based on everything I have read about the breed. The cost, unfortunately was prohibitive.

I knew I wanted a kitten rather than a grown cat because I'd be bringing it into a household with a couple dogs already in residence. I didn't want a feline too set in its ways.

Even though Hershey and Sterling were males and because they were neutered at an early age I never had any negative problems from them, but usually I lean toward female animals.

All things considered, the only solid decision was that I wanted a cat. Eventually. I, in fact, decided I would visit the cat house at the local shelter. I rescue dogs, and a rescue cat would be doing a good deed as well as filling my empty spot.

In the end I didn't go to the shelter, but in a manner of speaking I did do a rescue.

And all the rest of the important things a new pet owner should do? It didn't happen. I didn't check out a litter and pick the most energetic. Nor did I inspect for clear, bright eyes, or a cool, moist nose. I didn't determine if my choice would cower in the corner fearfully, or be overly aggressive. A clinging cat wouldn't be a plus. Most reckless of all, I didn't check for a kitten that showed an interest in me.

I didn't take the normal steps of picking up and holding the prospective pet to determine if it would squirm and attempt escape. I didn't check its weight. I didn't try the toss-the-key-ring-near-the-pet to determine its fear factor. I didn't view the parents, which is often a good gage of what a cat will grow up to look like and how it will behave.

Sure, I know how to properly choose a puppy or kitten but what I did was take the little black fur ball sight unseen into my arms and immediately into my heart.

Just like that.

It worked for me and BooCat.

I don't recommend doing what I did as standard procedure when selecting a four-footed constant companion that very well could be with you for the next ten to twenty years. But every now and then, it is okay to make a concession and break rules. Besides, I had Elizabeth's recommendation that this was a good cat. And Elizabeth ain't no slouch when it comes to animal sense.

New cat home and named and everybody except SnowBird and George E. Tiel happy—and occasionally TacoBelle not exactly overjoyed, our next step is to determine trainability. Hers and mine. Knowing what to do is only half of it. The other half, the main half, is figuring out how to do it.

It's been said for time immortal you can't teach old dogs new tricks. I'm not so worried about teaching my old dogs new tricks. I just want to teach one new cat one trick. I want to teach BooCat not to eat SnowBird.

The booklet read, "If you train your kitten from the first day you get her, you will be able to teach your pet good habits that will last a lifetime."

Dear Author of the above referenced booklet, let me introduce BooCat the Unique. She is a bona fide, dyed-in-the-wool, hardheaded cat with a mind of her own and a will to rival Mt. Vesuvius. Eruption is at her will and her will alone.

31 / Training BooCat

She's not dumb. I didn't say that. She has responded to all the accepted teachings. Her cat toys and furniture—because she definitely has a whole slew of her own furniture— her two litter pans, and her food, water and snack dishes all have specific locations; definite places in this her permanent home. So, there's no problem on that front. She knows each piece of play furniture is hers and hers alone.

She has free run of practically everywhere in our house, but not the kitchen table. She started to climb onto the table once and I shooed her off by picking her up and telling her no while smooching on her so she'd understand getting off the table is a rewardable action and that was the end of that. So, I know she is trainable.

She already knows how to fetch. She fetches bird feathers, rubber bands—which are her all time favorite playthings—and various odds and ends that have heretofore lain lost under beds and chairs for a very long time.

One morning I found an odd sock on my pillow. It was clean. I assumed it was one of the socks that disappear into thin air during the laundry process. And BlackmagicBooCat obviously discovered how to retrieve from thin air. I'm taking that as another positive sign of trainability. Couldn't we do a profitable business going into homes suffering from missing sock syndrome, turn BooCipher loose? Utilizing her phenomenal talents the advertisement would read "Seeking socks? Call BooCat. Sock Salvage and Recovery Inc."

Because of her young age, I realize IttyBittyBabyBoo's kittenish antics are all perfectly normal even if a little on the overactive side. There's every reason to believe the instability she experienced during the first four months of her life—her unstable beginning—that she's exhibiting some negative emotional behavior and with time will disappear. She was thrice-rejected and consequently emotionally conflicted. I have faith love will win over. Hers and mine.

Just as a dog sometimes chews up his master's slippers, newspaper, table leg and house, when left home alone either out of boredom or frustration, a cat can also become bored. There have been bored pet cats that have actually been diagnosed as clinically depressed. The wild-gene within can bring on a built-in restlessness of which even the cat itself isn't aware. It just is.

Forced inactivity of many housecats contributes to feline obesity plus a wide-range of neuroses related to confinement. Cats *should* be confined to a house rather than let out to roam, but there's always that natural desire born and bred and buried deep in a cat's ancestry that spurs it to dream of the nightlife; even a nightlife that it has never actually experienced.

Plenty of love and attention mostly corrects that. Along with having the pet spayed or neutered.

My first impractical idea was to get BooCat her own real tree; erect it in the family room so she could let her cat hair down and feel free. It was on my Gonna-Get list. Pensively, I knew there'd been a time when I was younger and abler that I could have constructed a tree myownself. If my friend Barbara V. can have a fishpond indoors, I figured BooCat could have her own real tree.

Barbara, who, when she and her husband built their new house, constructed within a sixteen-foot long, three-foot deep with waterfall Koi pond. They were fearful if it was outside raccoons and opossums would raid it. They have approximately forty good-sized Koi. So soothing listening to the waterfall and watching the colorful fish wend gracefully through the water she's certain it lowers hers and her husband's blood pressures. I'm sure.

But before I got around to begging, pleading, cajoling or paying somebody to do a real tree for my BooChild, I bought a manufactured "cat tree." From floor-to-ceiling, it features three staggered shelves upon which she can roost. It's not as aesthetically pleasing as a real tree might've been, but it'll do.

Or so I thought.

I have sung the praises of having an inside cat declawed. And I've insisted all cats should be kept as inside pets. I've agreed having a cat declawed can hinder its ability to climb. I boldly have gone on record that a cat shouldn't have to climb to stay safe.

But, now here's the thing. A manmade manufactured cat tree is made on the style of old fashioned—I'm talking forty plus years ago—floor-to-ceiling planters and lamps. The lamps and planters have a central pole and they're spring loaded so they can be wedged in place between the floor and the ceiling. Also the cat tree. While there are three multilevel shelves attached to the center pole, unless a cat has claws to grip and pull itself up to the next two levels, the first level is about as high as it's going to go. Until the tree was brought home and Chuck put it together, I never realized the most obvious: How can

BooCat the Clawless climb straight up and manage to climb out and over the flat shelves? Even with claws it looks hazardously difficult.

A real tree set at an angle would work. Straight up, doesn't.

I've seen fancier—and much pricier—cat trees in pet catalogues that could be maneuvered even clawless. But I don't think the one I bought her can be.

Anybody got a cat with claws who needs a cat tree? Bewildered-Boo has one for sale.

While BooCat no-doubt has these wild-genes in her, she won't have to worry about obesity. She works it off. When we reach a plateau in Boo's life—her age and my time—we're going to learn tricks to keep her from becoming clinically depressed and bored with the whole cat-on-a-lap scene.

Although cats are very independent and known for their aloofness I've had cats who learned some simple things and I have confidence, based on the brainpower BrainyBoo already displays, she's going to make her mama proud.

I read, "With some work, cats can be taught the same tricks as dogs. They will sit up and beg, shake hands and fetch and carry."

Forget that. My dogs don't even do those things. How could I expect my BooCee to?

I always have to keep in mind, a cat might not learn something because I'm teaching it, but is instead doing it because it wants to. I believe this will likely be the case with BooBaby.

And so, the main talent being taught, the trick in the works, is how to be a good bird owner.

She has learned when I tell her to get down from the birdcage table, to do it. Oh, yeah, sure, I had to raise my voice and take on a tough tone and get up and threateningly take a step in her direction to show her I really mean get down, but she has begun jumping down. Then she comes right to me. Like: "See, Mom. I did what you told me."

I always praise her for getting down. I had to raise my voice rather loudly when this phase of training began. It's gotten better. I can tell her "Geddown" in only a slightly louder then conversational voice. Progress. So half the lesson has been learned. She does understand what I am telling her.

The half she hasn't mastered is not getting up in the first place.

BOOCAT UNLEASHED

Now that, that phase of the training operation isn't working out so well. She still gets up every chance she can.

Admittedly, the teaching of Boo-versus-Bird has already taken entirely too long. I knew BanditBoo tweaked one of SnowBird's tail feathers. Later, she got several more. The Boo Bounty pile of tail feathers wasn't completely an innocent result of poor housekeeping and cast-off molted feathers. Several were the real thing. My poor SnowBird has lived in her peaceable kingdom for ten-plus years, tail feathers intact. Now, he's short on them.

I'm frustrated. I feel almost a physical pain of sadness for Snow-Bird.

Boo does get down. She is showing an advancement in the training session. I can only keep trying. I'm not a successful trainer of anything, but common sense advises when I say Please and Thank you that goes a long way. So, my praise when she finally leaps down is a Thank you.

I only hope SnowBird still has a few tail feathers left by the time Boo does learn. SnowBird is such a sweet, loving bird. I can listen to his soft cooing all day long; and when I'm in my home office, I do. His cooing makes me feel as I imagine Barbara and her husband do when watching their Koi swim in their indoor pond.

༺❦༻

The first morning BooCat heard the "cock-a-doodle-doo" she was sitting at her favorite window, peering into the semidarkness. Even my tired old ears caught the sound floating on the airwaves. The sun was just rising, lighting the eastern sky, turning it into a glorious fire in the sky orange.

Chuck built a chicken pen using my metal barn and dog yard panels in the back yard. He got a handsome white rooster, six hens, plus a couple guineas. Within two weeks he collected five dozen eggs.

By the way, guineas are quite fascinating and they run faster than a genuine Road Runner. So far, the couple Chuck has are not very tame; maybe with time they will relax and be less fearful of every movement around them. I don't think even BooCat could catch one if she were given the opportunity to try. You ever see the Road Runner cartoon character. Such speed, dust is left in its wake. Same thing

31 / Training BooCat

with these guineas.

He covered the pen with plastic fencing. Located out in the country, my yard surrounded by open farm fields, the skies are full of soaring, hunting hawks. They are a real and certain threat to chickens. One swoop and Chuck will have one less hen in his hen house.

Not to mention the 'possums, raccoons, foxes and coyotes that roam freely on the outskirts. And the Louisiana Black Bear. As the crow flies, there are plenty thriving in our area as a result of a program instituted by the Wildlife and Fishery folks. Besides showing up in photos on deer cams in the woods, several have gotten turned around and wandered through Bonita and nearby towns. I'm not too worried about the bears bothering the chickens, but I find it fascinating to know they are right around the corner, down a country road and in the woods. But, fascinating as it is, since this program has been so successful, I've taken my last walk through the woods gathering wildflowers and enjoying Mama Nature. BooBear is enough for me face-to-face. Don't really want to meet up with a bear in the woods.

Probably the only critters located in these parts that won't bother the chickens are the armadillos. Poor armadillos bother no one, but because they use their ant-eater snouts to root up grubs and bugs, people have a tendency to overreact when they find their lawns dug up here and there. Out comes the 32 or the shotgun, and outgoes the harmless armadillo. Cruel country bumpkins even laugh at how when shot, an armadillo will leap straight up into the air several feet before dropping dead. That's why I don't want a lawn. I have a yard and the armadillos are welcome to root all they want.

Armadillos have one distinction that actually saved several future generation's lives. In the town of Hamburg, Ark., an Armadillo Festival is held annually. When I first moved to this part of the country, armadillo was served barbecued. Then it was discovered, the armadillo is the only other warm-blooded animal besides man who contracts leprosy. With that little news release, folks stopped eating armadillos. Oh, it hasn't stopped them from shooting them just because they can, but at least they're not ending up on somebody's grill.

Thus far, my dogs have paid no attention to the penned chickens. The pen walls are ten feet tall, and with the protective covering, none of these most common predators should be able to get inside. I can't say about chicken snakes. I expect they can go where they want to go. I advised Chuck to keep a shovel propped nearby his pen just in case.

Bob-a-LouBooCat's ears perked up enthusiastically. Her whiskers twitched. Her body tensed. I could tell she wanted to grab a set of knives and forks and make her way to the chicken yard to investigate. Along the way she probably would have been dancing to the sounds of Zydico music humming Popeye's New Orleans Style Fried Chicken theme song and when she got there I pictured her sending a warning message to the clucking hens that they better do as she says or they might wind up as a couple of feather dusters.

But, since she can't actually see the chickens because her window faces east and the chickens are located to the southwest in the backyard, she only hears the morning crowing of the rooster. Out of sight, sort of out of mind, therefore, the chicken family is granted amnesty. Eventually, like the coocoo of a clock, the crowing becomes background white noise: there but not there.

Ah, but that first day, that first crow, it would have been interesting to have opened a dialog with BooCat—interesting to know what she was thinking. Likely it would have been something like: Read my lips. Chicken soup.

※

BooCat's learned when I say to the dogs it's "time for bed," that it's time for bed. She runs right along with them, leaping up on the bed before they've even half climbed their ramp. Silly thing, sometimes she runs up the ramp just because she can. She rarely lets any experience pass her by.

ScamperingBoo has the "time for bed" phrase down pat but I don't know how best to describe her gait. I think only horses and zebras gallop.

Lope, maybe? Dart, dash, or sprint?

In any case, you can bet she reaches the bed at the same time as the dogs even if they had a head start.

And then there was the time I stepped out of the shower and yelled, "What are you barking about, Rosie?"

I'd heard her bark and bark the whole time I was in the shower. Oh, not nonstop, but a bark, then nothing. Then another sharp bark.

31 / Training BooCat

Then another a moment later.

I stuck my wet head around the corner and peered into the bedroom.

I asked again, "Rosie? What are you barking about?" and then I saw. Rosie was at the base of the bed ramp. RoadBlockBoo was stretched out, languishing, at the top, sprawled half on the bed, half on the ramp itself.

Rose, at the foot of the ramp, would scamper up a couple steps, then waddle back down. And bark. Boo just looked at her.

This scene was repeated a couple times even as I stood there and I could only assume, it was a repeat of what had been going on the whole time I was in the shower and Rosie's barking penetrated the sound of running water.

Stretched out in this manner, Boo appeared three times her regular length. She wasn't acting menacing, she was just creating as barrier at the top of the ramp.

Poor Rosie. Her Doxie dance back and forth was getting her nowhere fast. I know she was distressed over the whole situation, but I have to tell you, Rosie looks so funny when she dances—as that's what it most closely resembles—a few steps forward and several backward. She waddles and bounces and is just so cute.

But she needed help. Poor stymied sweetie.

"Boo," I said.

She looked in my direction. She knows her name.

"Boo, please move. Let Rosie get up on the bed."

Like a cartoon in slow motion, she arose. She stood up taller than Rosie and bigger all over than TacoBelle. Then she stretched typical cat fashion, tail in the air, front feet stretched as far as they could reach, body elongated from normal to triple its length. She yawned, revealing sharp incisors and a pink tongue, eyes squeeze shut momentarily.

She was letting me know she was going to move out of Rosie's way, but she was going to do it in her own sweet time and it wasn't because I told her to, it was because she herownself wanted to.

It was as though she were singing silently, "I am woman, hear me roar."

Eventually, once her point was made, she sauntered to the bottom of the bed and slouched down into catnap position.

Just before she closed her bright yellow eyes it was as though she was asking, "What's all the fuss about?"

In a flash Rosie ran up the ramp as fast as her short legs would allow; onto the bed. She stopped in her tracks, obviously ascertaining whether or not it was truly safe to be up on the bed what with this bad WatchCat on guard.

It isn't often I've heard Rosie sigh; especially with relief. But that's what she did once she determined it was indeed not dangerous any more.

Me? I went back into the bathroom and continued to dry off and get ready for bed.

TacoBelle apparently had gotten situated atop the bed before Boo set up her blockade. She was settled down for the night. She'd been aware of the activity but since it didn't involve her, she wasn't concerned. Eventually Rosie located her favorite spot and plopped down too.

BooCat knows the sound of cat treats being shaken in the container. When she hears that familiar rattle she equates it with a tasty treat and she comes running. She'd probably know the sound of a can opener if we used food requiring one.

She pretty well knows the "come" command, although instead of saying "come" as with a dog, I often use the typical catcall: "Here, kitty-kitty-kitty." She recognizes that this means to come to me. I feel I can safely add that to her bag of Boo tricks.

Did I say BooCat is smart? She is. She is definitely one of a kind cat.

It's possible she's got a teaspoonful of dog genes mixed in with her domestic cat genes.

Instinctively, dogs want to please. Cats are a bit more arrogant, less prone to following orders. But because BooBear is so smart, I believe with dedication and determination on my part, she'll be better than the average cat when asked to do so. Note, I said asked, rather than told? Even a smart, well-trained BooCat will likely only do what I want if I ask, rather than tell. That's not just the feline in her, that's the female—something I understand very well myself.

31 / Training BooCat

Repetition and consistency works with dogs. Cats are smarter than dogs so maybe something similar will work for Boo too.

Since she knows to come when I rattle the treat container, part of my training strategy of calling her name at the same time helped; ensuring she knows her name. I do have an overwhelming habit of calling my furry kids by various love-names and so far, it hasn't proved to be confusing. She does appear to recognizes that her name is Boo. The add-on's are superfluous trimming. It may be Boo-something else, but it's always Boo. She is my Boo. And most amazing is that, unless she's sound asleep and obviously doesn't hear me, I can often simply say her name: "Boo" and she looks up and comes walking over to me.

It's so civilized.

Overall, I've donned my patience cap. I hope to open an extra window of communication between BooCat and me. She already has me trained to do her bidding, now it's my turn to teach her a trick or three.

Cats are Venus, Dogs are Mars, and Men are Impossible

32

"Dogs and cats are smarter than most people I know." (Barbara Sharik)

Thinking about the joy experienced on a daily basis from sharing an abode with my new BooBaby and longtime residents TacoBelle and Rosie, reminds me of the time a friend of mine was having man troubles. She said she just didn't know what to do. Her man wasn't behaving like she thought he should.

I jokingly told her to get a dog because you can train a dog. Maybe not so much a cat, judging by BadBoo's rambunctious behavior, but still, you know right off the bat you can't, under most circumstances, train a man. They're pretty much un-teachable. It's more than the can't teach an old dog new tricks thing. It's more like you can't teach a man any tricks.

She asked. "What about fleas?"

My answer: "Use Frontline. It works."

I explained that nobody can understand a man, but my dogs are easy. As the song says, "easy on Sunday morning," and every other morning too for that matter. When Rosie and TacoBelle stare at their plates and wag their tails it means we love you, feed us. Same with BooCat. And that includes the tail wagging. Remember, her tail's never not flicking, twitching, switching—or like I said, wagging. It also includes rubbing up against me and purring as an added bonus.

When Rosie and TacoBelle look at me, take two steps, look at me again while wagging their tails it means we love you, follow us to the kitchen and feed us. BooCat rubs against my legs and leads me to the kitchen, jumps up on the chair, rubs against me and purrs.

When TacoBelle and Rosie stare at their leashes, wag their tails it means we love you, walk us. Boo doesn't get involved in this dialogue because she has no experience with outdoor life. I'm considering getting her a pretty hot pink harness for down-the-road excursions. If any cat could adapt to walking like a dog, it would be Boo. She is, after all, quite extraordinary.

When TacoBelle and Rosie bring their toys to me, wag their tails, it means we love you, please play. BooCat brings me her chewed up bird feather, drops it at my feet but I doubt she's inviting me to play. Clearly, she's telling me she loves me though. She loves birds too. In a different way from how she loves me.

Simply put, when a dog wags its tail it means I love you. When it licks your hand, it means I love you. No matter what, it loves you. When BooCat rubs against me purring, that means she loves me too.

I told my friend, see how easy that is? My TacoBelle, Rosie and BooCat are always overjoyed to see me. If I leave the room, come back, they're overjoyed all over again. And again. It's amazing to be so loved.

I can actually have a dialogue with Rosie, TacoBelle and BooCat. They listen intently to every word I say. Well, Rosie and TacoBelle listen intently. BooCat lends an ear but isn't so obvious. Cat's, while equally devoted, are a little less demonstrative; but no less loving.

I can tell all of them anything and they never talk back. They don't misunderstand, get their feelings hurt or argue. If I raise my voice, they forgive me because all three of them love me unconditionally. Unconditional love is the biggest bonus and it comes with no strings attached.

A three-dog-night is one that is so cold it takes three dogs curled up together to keep warm. Not to worry. Rosie snuggles beneath the covers on my right side, down near my toes keeping them warm. TacoBelle snuggles mostly beneath the covers on the left side about midway, near my waist keeping that part of my anatomy warm.

BooCat, when she finally settles down for the night has one of two places she sleeps. One is on top the covers, between my knees and my ankles, or else she paws repeatedly, pushing my arm out at the shoulder so she can be hugged in the crook all night while she snuggles. That's my favorite. Snuggle hugs all night long. And either spot keeps me warm.

TacoBelle, Rosie, BooCat and a flannel nightgown is all I need on a cold winter's night. Along with a good book, of course. And socks.

Forever, back as far as I can remember, I've heard heat escapes through your head; wear a hat to keep warm. My head is fine. It's my feet that serve as a degree of freeze-ability. My nose may work like a weather gage; when it's cold, it too is cold. But my feet, when they're cold I'm cold all over.

To keep really warm, I slip on socks before hopping into bed. Should the temps warm up, and I find myself getting overheated? Slip those socks off and I'm fine again. The heat in my body does not escape through my head. It escapes through my feet. I'd be willing to do a study on this subject if Uncle Sam would like to present me with a grant.

Sorry. I'm always reading about the oddest studies undertaken paid for by government funding. And where does government get it's funding? Enter the poor working stiff paying taxes. The working poor. I'm in that category. No tax refunds because I don't have the deductibles. And do they ask me how I want them to squander my money?

Anyway, back to the subject of dogs and cats being better companions than men folk. I admit getting sidetracked is one of my major faults. One thing is always reminding me of something else and I've usually got something to say about everything.

TacoBelle, RoseDog and BooCat eat every bite I give them and never tell me their mother made it better. They never fight with me over the remote. Actually, they don't give a hoot what I watch on TV; just make a lap and they are content.

Thus it is, as a cat and dog owner and lover and pertaining to their overall respective personalities, BooCat is from Venus and Rosie and TacoBelle are from Mars—if I may be so bold as to borrow the concept from John Gray, author of *Men are From Mars, Women Are From Venus*. Which is to say, felines have a degree in femininity and dogs, masculinity, despite a specific animal's actual gender.

My dogs, counting the batch outside in with the mix that includes old, young and several stupid ones, are like four-legged furry fellows. I admit to having a tendency to categorize and stereotype, putting things in neat little slots. There are always exceptions to the rules, but overall, stuff fits. Hence the Venus and Mars reference.

Consider that women rarely spit, but men have been known to. With this rather graphic unpleasant line of thought, recognize, my LadyBoo doesn't drool and slobber, but several of my outside dogs do.

Discounting TacoBelle who, because she's a Chihuahua, is in a league of her own, how many picky-eating dogs do you know? Precisely. Men will chow down on all sorts of vittles in true reckless abandon. Like my outside dogs, set it in front of them, they'll scarf it up. Not so with cats and women. My PersnicketyBooCat will turn her nose and tail up if the bowlful of morsels doesn't titillate her tummy. Rosie is always hungry. She never turns down any offering. She doesn't inhale her food like some hounddawg, but she doesn't have a cutoff valve either. Like her mom, she has a propensity toward becoming fluffy.

Need I point out the similarity between men and dogs and scratching? A dog can absently scratch indefinitely—or is that indefinitely scratch absently—loopy look of pleasure plastered on its face. Likewise, a man. BooCat doesn't scratch unless she itches.

Like bulls in china closets, men and dogs have been known to break stuff. Give Rosie a new toy and she'll tear it to shreds. I haven't found a dog toy stout enough to stand up to Rosie's prowess. If a ball bearing wouldn't break her teeth, that's what I'd give her.

Okay, I have to pass on this one. Most cats, even enticed by catnip rarely do damage. Neither do ladies. BooCat is the exception. She's been known to chew feathers, pluck artificial flowers from containers, unplug lamps and tear down curtains. I'm expecting things to improve as she ages, because normally, like a lady on a dance floor, cats have a natural grace, while dogs and the average man will clomp, stomp, rip, romp and snort. Many, oh so many, on the dance floor will look like frogs in a blender.

Poor BlooperBoo is a little on the klutzy side. Most cats aren't. Will she outgrow it? I don't know. She loves dancing high on the backs of chairs and bed headboards, but she has fallen a time or two.

Because the space between the bed and the wall is tight, there was no landing on all four feet as cats are famous for. A cat can land upright from a fall, but it needs space and time to turn itself right-side-up in mid-air.

When she hears the printer engage, she runs, skips and jumps to investigate up close. Once she stepped over some stuff and fell between the desk and printer stand. She didn't land on her feet.

Over all, with the rare exception, cats are graceful. There's always the exception to all rules. Shoot, even some women lack grace on occasion. Me? I can't dance. I'd never make a waitress. I can't walk and chew gum simultaneously. So I identify with UnbalancedBoo.

And there are the John Travolta's who can dance. But you can see where I'm coming from. Stereotyping to a degree.

Men and dogs rarely play hard to get. BooCat and gals do. BooCat doesn't invite petting from people she doesn't know unless she herownself is in the mood. Make BooCat purr, good for you. But be prepared to draw back a nub when BooCat has had enough.

Rosie, tail wagging wildly, will be all over you begging for a hands-on experience. TacoBelle is a bit more refined, and she picks who she wants to lick. She is a licker. To a fault. But that bunch of outside dogs, now they'll be sniffing, licking and leaping. They never get enough. Cheerfully rowdy.

Most dogs with a ball never give up or give in. They lack the necessary cutoff valve that alerts them enough is enough. As long as a ball's thrown, they'll chase it. It's all about the chase: cars, cookies, cats. Even their own tails. Likewise, it's all about the chase with men too. Think about it.

Another example is the term "catty." It's a female reference only, indicating she's delivering a stinging, verbal blow; her claws are showing. Meow! You see, a cat rarely bites, but has been known to give a stinging, slapping scratch when the need arises.

Whereas on the other hand, a dog can be all loud, blustering bark. It's almost like he is hoping the bark will do the job and the situation doesn't really have to escalate to a real fight and bite.

Lastly, there's the private litter box thing as opposed to the bright red fire hydrant thing and compared to public restrooms. Just as cats require privacy, so do ladies. Men and dogs on the other hand, don't. Peeing off the porch is a rite of passage when becoming a man. This

32 / Cats are Venus, Dogs are Mars, and Men are Impossible

example probably requires no additional or in-depth relative explanation.

A favorite quote on the subject comes from Marie Corelli, "I never married because I have three pets at home which answer the same purpose as a husband. I have a dog that growls every morning, a parrot that swears all afternoon and a cat that comes home late at night."

Pet my dogs and BooCat, and you've got friends for life.

Men Can't Help It

33

"The Cat's Meow." (Expression Coined by Thomas Doegan, American Cartoonist, 1877–1929)

The curtain incident as I refer to it, weakened me momentarily. I found myself wishing I had a regular man in my life. Even though I'm familiar with all of the aforementioned items listed in the last chapter, there are moments when a handy man would be, well, handy.

Actually, I should have known I was in trouble when I lost a sock somewhere between the clothes hamper and the washing machine. Bad enough the dryer eats them, but for one to disappear before being washed was an indication it was going to be one of those days. You know the days I'm referring to, don't you? The upside-down turtle on its back, day.

Fortunately for me, hours later that omen was negated when the missing sock showed up on my bed—bless BooCat, chief detective for Sock Salvage and Retrieval Inc.

My home office has three floor-to-ceiling windows in a row made private with mini-blinds. But in a whimsical moment of decorating the room in hot pink—it was marvelous what stores had available this season in this, one of my favorite colors—I purchased drapes and sheers to carry out the color scheme. Hot pink makes me happy.

So does red, yellow, orange and purple.

It's a proven fact that colors do affect moods. Often without even realizing it, colors have a profound effect on how we feel both mentally and physically. They have power and emotional associations that affect us and can create certain moods—good or not so good.

Nothing new, ancient Egyptians as well as Native Americans used color and colored lights to heal. Colors have various meanings in different cultures, but over all, known as color psychology, researchers agree, colors affects moods.

When Mom moved to Oak Woods, she experienced a major health crisis and it was determined the continuous care would be lifesaving. As she healed, sporadic frustration set in, because she missed her independence. Occasionally there comes a time in an individual's life when independence must be surrendered to the greatest good of their wellbeing.

Giving in doesn't mean giving up, but she did exhibit some blueness. In a literal sense. You see, she had a lovely blue and white bedspread and blue window treatment in her room, but blue was her least favorite color.

The apple not having fallen far from the tree, I understood. Once when I did my bedroom in blue and beige, I found it depressing. I got out the paint brush, splurged on a new spread and accessories and found the peace I sought. That's what happened to Mom.

When Jan visited she bought Mom a new spread, valance, matching lamp, flowers and accessories. Everything featured a patchwork of bright pink, lilac, yellow, green and a smattering of tiny red flowers that matched the prettiest deep red leather club chair and ottoman in all of Oak Woods that my brother Jimmy and his late wife Debbie bought for her.

With the bright, cheerful colors, Mom's whole demeanor immediately became more positive. I credit the bright colors. Blue may represent peace, tranquility, calmness, but it also can be cold, technical and depressing. Introducing festive colors made a difference.

Pink is considered a romantic color, pretty. It, along with its counterpart, red, is a color we pay the most attention to. Red is the warmest and most energetic color in the spectrum. It can actually raise the blood pressure and make the heart beat faster.

I have found if I want to be happy for the rest of my life, I encircle myself with happy colors so that I step into my hot pink office, if I am feeling tired and blah, my mood is suddenly transformed to happy.

Buying new hot pink drapes was one thing, but have you seen the price of curtain rods lately? I opted to make due by stretching an old kitchen rod the length of the three windows and carefully tacking the hangers into the wall. Yes. I know now, screws would have saved the day. But, I was being Miss Susie Homemaker with a hammer and nails. I can hammer a nail straight in almost anywhere. Slam-bam and it's there. But, unless you happen to drive that nail into a stud, sometimes it lacks staying power. It wobbles. Screws work better in that instance.

There's a saying that if something is hard to do but somebody comes along and does it, they must have held their mouth right. With careful, mouth-holding effort, the curtains were hung with about as much permanency as stockings on the mantle the night before Christmas.

In other words, my window treatment glowed perfectly pink in the sunshine so long as no one breathed. Unfortunately, BooCat did.

Innocently wanting to look out the window, when BooCat maneuvered beneath and behind the curtain, the rod slipped out of the precariously hung hanger and dangled lopsidedly by the proverbial miracle thread versus gravity.

It wasn't her fault.

Because the table with two large bird cages sits in front of the window, I endeavored, using a yardstick, to slip the rod back into the hanger across the expanse. End result? Gravity won. Rod and drapes tumbled to the floor.

Forced to slide the birds out of the way, I again attempted to re-install the rod and curtains. I was doing my best to hold my mouth right. I didn't think I needed to get the stepstool. I eyeballed the rod hook. I was on tip-toes. Admittedly, my arms were aching as I reached up over my head and pushed upward and I was wondering when I got so short? Gravity was doing a number on me.

That's when I knocked a decorative, hand painted, antique plate off the wall. It proceeded to bounce off my head. I threw my arms out, dropping the curtain rod and curtains. I reached upward moments after it went downward. I tried my hardest to catch the falling plate. Curtains, rods, arms akimbo, and plate speeding like a bullet downward, I missed. It hit the floor with a loud smash.

Gazing down at the broken plate, I could see even super glue wouldn't help. Gravity won again. It shortened me and it killed my plate.

Viewing the whole spectacle from start to finish, BooCat heard some new words fly out of her mom's mouth.

After one more failed effort, I stashed the curtains until further notice, which brings me to the issue of why I don't have a man with an electric screwdriver handy. It's simple. I've been there and done that and, men being men, you can't live with them and you can't live with them and you're not allowed to shoot them.

For one thing, they are notorious for not listening. Like asking directions? They don't. I'm guessing because men don't want to be told what to do or how to do it, they don't like to read directions much less ask for them.

It's got to be tough being a man. They are expected to know everything. All the time. And some of them think they do. Any doubt? Just ask. But, don't ask a man what he's thinking. It would take too long for him to make something up.

My daughter Theresa put a humorous post on Facebook: "If we can put one man on the moon, why can't we put them all on there?" She quickly qualified that she was only kidding; we would need somebody to lift the heavy stuff.

That made me think about what would happen if men really were on the moon. I figured it wouldn't take long till there were football fields and NASCAR tracks. There would be piles of empty beer cans and pizza boxes scattered about. Sporting goods and hardware stores could be found on every corner. Probably there would be rusted out vehicles sitting up on blocks spotted around here and there. Lighting the sky would be neon signs proclaiming the bar's open. Not to mention, there would be tons of remote controls dotting the landscape.

Want your hubby to mow the yard? Hide the remote control out in the weeds.

It's easy to stereotype. Guys could do a turnabout-is-fair-play and come back by describing the woman's touch. Flowers and trees planted everywhere, a cute little gazebo over here, a nice vine-covered cottage with a white picket fence over there. Frilly curtains in every window. Wall-to-wall carpeting. Everything color-coordinated of course. The horizon would be lined with antique shops and arts and crafts stores interspersed with beauty salons offering manicures and pedicures and a mall or two. Oh yeah, and lots of shoe stores.

If women started from scratch they'd make some stuff different. They'd relocate pharmacies in drugstores to the front of the store so sick people wouldn't have to walk all the way to the back while healthy folks can buy, say candy and cigarettes, at the front of the store. And, women wouldn't put a handicap parking space in the front of a skating rink. They'd tell boys it's okay to ride girl's bikes because the bar thing establishing the difference is just plain silly.

I'll get back to BooCat in a min, since she is who indirectly sent me off on this tangent. I recollect once when an ex discovered he had locked the keys in the car, I wanted to call a locksmith. He insisted he could open it with a clothes hanger and hotfooted it to a nearby store where he begged a coat hanger from the clerk.

He said he could do it, and by golly he did. So proud of himself, grinning ear-to-ear, he stuck the handy hanger under the car seat and said, "I'm hanging onto this hanger. If that ever happens again, I'll be prepared."

Half of you are wondering what's wrong with that. The other half, the women, they know exactly what's wrong. That being said, I've made a mistake or two regarding men. Misjudgment on my part. Which brings to mind the time I attempted to locate the preacher who had married me and my first husband so I could request a refund for what it cost to tie that stringy knot. I'm fairly certain it's illegal for a person to profit from another person's mistakes. And if it's not, it should be. If I do it again, I'm getting something in writing about refunds and money-back guarantees. A Wedding Warranty.

If I knew then what I know now, but I didn't, so I did it again. When I was about half way into that marriage, I called the IRS, asked somebody to send me some of those WD-40's. After the laughter died down, I asked if it would be okay to file "Single" that year. The agent started getting all technical so I clarified I was married, but I wasn't counting on it lasting all that much longer.

My favorite example of manhood in action was the time I was driving down a back country road in Jones and met some guy heading the way I'd just come. I leaned out the window and yelled, "Pig!"

He leaned out his window and hollered, "Stupid!"

33 / Men Can't Help It

Yeah, right. I'm stupid.

In a minute I heard his brakes squeal as he rounded the next curve. Then I heard the big pig in the middle of the road squeal right before the crash. The thing is, men just never listen. Bless their cantankerous hearts.

The important thing, the thing you learn when you've been around as long as I have, is to overlook their shortcomings and accept them as they are. Bottom line: They just can't help it.

BooCat is a lot like that. She just can't help her cantankerousness either.

In any case, the curtains have since been rehung. It was during one of those times when I had a three day weekend and decided to do major house cleaning instead of the usual lick, spit and a promise and a hit and a miss. It felt good boarding the mess-express and creating a path of cleanliness. Rehanging the drapes was included among the major cleaning plan. And so far, BooCat, Demolition Derby Queen, hasn't re-unhung them. I'm sure she would if she could, but I've taken steps to prevent that.

At Thanksgiving when Theresa, Carla and Lance visited, they bought me a new, sturdier curtain rod. Several weeks down the road Chuck installed it properly. All I had to do was retrieve the drapes and sheers from the back bedroom closet and rehang them.

Pulling the bird table from in front of the windows, I slid the stepstool beneath the rod and slipped the curtains in place. What I should have done in the very first place. Life is full of little lessons learned but we rarely learn them without a little grunting a groaning involved first. Or in my case, the discovery that I am no longer five-feet, seven-and-one-half-inches tall in my bare feet, a knot on my head and the loss of a valuable antique china plate.

But even still, the job wasn't without incident. On my first attempt to reinsert the rod into its hanger, I almost cried when it all tumbled in a pretty pink heap among the bird seeds scattered on the floor beneath the bird cages.

Did I say almost?

Alright. I did shed a few tears of frustration because it's so bad what happens when a body gets old and you lose so many natural abilities taken for granted for so many years. Like the simple act of stepping up on a stepstool without fear of falling and hanging up a pair of drapes and sheers.

The second attempt was successful. But it is exasperating what becoming an old geezer gal does to one's psyche. Did I say it was more fun getting old at age nineteen than it is at age sixty-five? Allow me to repeat that, please.

BooCat is Too Smart to Make Resolutions

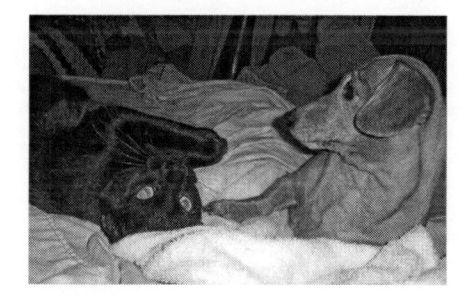

34

"Cats and dogs give paws-itive advice." (T-Shirt)

Having undertaken major housecleaning and re-hanging the drapes and sheers, reminds me of resolution-making time that comes up more often than it used to. It used to take about two years for Christmas and New Years to arrive; now it comes every six months.

I do the usual resolutions, slow learner that I am. I mean, when you resolve to lose weight, exercise and take better care of yourself for forty years, and you don't, isn't there something wrong with that picture? Or the person who keeps making and breaking resolutions?

I often resolve to keep the house as clean as I used to before I became an old geezer gal. A couple of weeks after resolution-making time it is resolution-breaking time.

TacoBelle, Rosie and BooCat are smart. You can bet they don't waste time making and breaking resolutions. Maybe we should stop calling them dumb animals, huh?

The most popular resolutions made each new year are health related: dieting, working out, taking better care of one's self. After years of making and breaking, I've finally learned that to resolve something once a year never works. I can make a resolution in the morning and be fallen flat off my resolution-wagon by day's end. I either need to stop making resolutions altogether and own up to my weaknesses, or get a wagon with steeper sides.

Once I promised to exercise more. I tried jogging. The outside dogs loved it. They ran right along beside me. But I got hot and tired. I sweated a lot. I got blisters. I got leg cramps. I got shin-splints. I got accosted. People laughed at me. Dogs chased me. Cats ran from me.

I thought: *This is healthy? Thanks, but no thanks.*

Once I caught my breath I wrote that resolution off as a lost cause. Yes. I exaggerate. But you get my drift.

Forget the dieting resolution. That one didn't last 'til the water got hot. Or actually, until the cake was done. And gone. Even the crumbs.

Also the cookies.

As I say to anyone who will listen, I've got this skinny little lady living inside me who nags me about being fluffy and I have to feed her chocolate to shut her up.

Also the above-mentioned cookies.

Many broken resolutions behind me, I stopped making major improvement resolutions. They are the first to go. Next I tried minor pledges instead. Things like I will get up when the alarm sounds the first time—no hitting the snooze-cruise. To ensure success with this, I moved the alarm clock several feet away from the bed.

To break this resolution I discovered how to use my backscratcher to reach the snooze-button without having to get out of bed. With my eyes closed.

Another one bites the dust.

One time I promised myself I'd wash the dishes immediately after eating, because sorry to say, when I've only got one glass, one plate and one fork, it's too easy to rinse them off and leave them in the sink. Before I know it, the sink is full. Good intentions pave my way. Unfortunately, my path is littered with dirty dishes.

Another time I resolved to talk less because I've been known to be very opinionated and long-winded. Regrettably, it didn't take long to develop athlete's mouth by sticking my foot in it, breaking that portion of the declaration. I could tell the other half of the resolution was a goner when my listeners' eyes glazed over before I was halfway through my tale.

What?

34 / BooCat is Too Smart to Make Resolutions

Wake up!

Thus determining that making resolutions is useless and I know it, next I came up with a self-improvement wish list. Truth be told, a wish list is probably about as useless as making resolutions with the exception being that with resolutions I resolve to actually do something positive. With a wish list, I just wish I would.

I've heard it said that it doesn't hurt to want or wish. I disagree. It hurts a lot. If wishes were horses, we'd all ride. Well, we'll never all ride nor will all our wishes come true. Still, it's human nature to wish for things, even unobtainable things.

With over sixty years worth of wishes, I'll start at the end instead of the beginning. I wish stores would please wait at least twenty-four hours after I purchase something to put that same item on sale. Nothing makes me feel more like growling than to buy a major item one day and see it advertised on sale the next. Besides putting something on sale, there is the getting it in, in the right color the day you buy.

What I mean is, I looked for things for PrincessBooCat in hot pink because I'm currently in a hot pink mode and stage of life. I found several pink things and added them to her assorted areas in different rooms. But, I was forced to settle for blah and blue and grey and other colors for several other major purchases.

Then, when I went back to get more kitty litter a couple weeks later, there was what I'd already given up and broke down and bought in blah and here it was now available in pink. Skinned my cat, you can bet. I had to stay myself with a major commonsense communiqué, else wise I'd have bought another just because it was pink, when one was enough, even if it wasn't pink.

Growl.

Back to sales the day after, take the "Cash for Clunkers" government program. If I'd known this deal was coming I would have hung onto my blackberry Saturn, "Old Dusty," a little longer. I had hung onto "Old Dusty" for eight years, what would another six to twelve months have hurt? And the interest rate I'm paying on "Old Dusty's" replacement, the successor, would have been a lot less too. Maybe even for a shorter financing term. As it is, I have to work another seven years just to pay for that set of wheels. Unless I die. Then it won't matter, now will it? BooCat can't drive.

I wish I was a stronger shopper, that I didn't have to avoid shopping just to stay sensible. I know my weaknesses. Window shopping is the worst. If I see something I want and can't afford it, it is downright painful. I need Band-Aids. I need crutches. I need to call the Crisis Hotline.

I need *not* to window shop.

On the other hand, when I *do* shop, I want sales. Give me something on sale and I'm putty in the hands of the shopkeeper. I'll buy more than I need just because it's on sale. I bought three woks once. I kept one and used two for gifts. But still, to buy three woks just because they were on sale indicates the extent of my problem.

"My name is Barbara and I'm a Saleaholic" (not to be confused with a Shopaholic).

My best defense is not to go shopping unless it's absolutely necessary.

Another wish. I wish I didn't find myself using the Smoke Alarm as a timer so often. I used to be able to cook without having to throw away burnt-to-a-crisp saucepans and foodstuff reduced to ashes that would break TacoBelle's, Rosie's and BooCat's incisors were I to toss them what's leftover after a three alarm scorcher.

What have I learned? You can put something in the microwave and leave the room. Not so with the cook stove.

I wish I kept neater notes. Always jotting down ideas for columns, something that needs doing at work or a tidbit I want to share with somebody, I'm a fervent note taker. But, I jot my notations on whatever scrap piece of paper is handy. Then I wind up with dozens of little fragments of paper with a word or two scratched on each. It's a rotten system and I know it.

It's like going on archeological digs when I need something on my desk. Or in my purse. Or stacked somewhere. When I find it, I know what it is, but how simple if I'd recorded it in a nice neat notebook. And yes, I actually have several miniature red-covered notebooks scattered around purchased for just this purpose. In my car, my purse, on the kitchen table. Empty, every one.

I wish for self-improvement. My wish list is like a giant To-Do list. I write things down and never get to the bottom because I'm adding more than I'm doing. If I keep working diligently, maybe one day I will reach a degree of semi-fulfillment.

So, here's the thing—broken resolutions and unfulfilled wishes

34 / BooCat is Too Smart to Make Resolutions

don't represent failure. They equal being human. Perhaps I'll make one more resolution, my solution being to make one resolution and make it realistic. That way maybe I could move out of Broken-Resolution-Land by keeping it real.

Maybe BooCat will resolve to behave.

Yeah. Right. When pigs fly. And I'm not making a joke about Swine Flu either.

Growing Old Disgracefully

35

"The most affectionate creature in the world is a wet dog." (Ambrose Bierce)

I always figured I'd grow old gracefully; that I would run the roads indefinitely at full speed ahead, like an agile gazelle.

After awhile, time took its toll and I adjusted to ambling the avenues instead of running them. But, just look at me now. Now, I'm lagging down the lane, looking for a lounger to laze on around every corner. BooCat is still so full of vim and vigor, TacoBelle, Rosie and I have a hard time keeping up with her. Mostly, we don't even try.

I recently said to myself, *I have got to start jogging again.* Then self asked, *When did you do that?* I answered, *When I was a kid.* Well, that ended that conversation. Unfortunately, advancing years have brought on several subtle changes.

For example, while I know a new coat of paint helps an old barn, that's not necessarily so for an old wrinkled brow. Therefore, except for a dab of lipstick to keep my face from fading away entirely, I've forgone the use of makeup I once thought I couldn't live without.

TacoBelle, Rosie and BooCat love me with or without a fake face because smearing on a layer of flesh-colored pasty stuff isn't an added plus after a certain age. It gets lost in the crevasses. Dabbing a bit of rouge on my cheeks creates a clown effect.

The real problem is my body. It's got me growing old disgracefully. The muscles in my upper arms have turned upside down and are now flapping in the breeze. Instead of the spare tire going flat, it's fully inflated. When someone refers to me as Hippie, they're not talking about my liberal views. Thunder thighs have nothing to do with rainstorms. Dresses really do shrunk while hanging in the closet. I've got a few of those stuck way in the back of my wardrobe awaiting a miracle. And, everything hurts. It's all worn out. Carrying a fifty-pound bag of dog food or even a twenty-pound bag of BooCat's kitty litter requires more strength than muscles turned upside down can handle.

I used to rearrange furniture. Gave a new look to the room and I could clean up underneath furniture. Now, the dust bunnies have turned into dust dingoes. Or maybe the dust dingoes ate the dust bunnies. I get too close they growl at me.

Not surprisingly ClairvoyantBooCat doesn't mind the dust and muss and stashes of stuff beneath the furniture. She has found a treasure trove of interesting bits and pieces and miscellany that has been lost for years underneath there. A treasure hunt for her, she doesn't even mind the dust dingoes. She growls right back.

BooCat's favorite plaything is a rubber band. I can loop a half dozen together like making a daisy chain, toss it to her and she will entertain herself indefinitely.

Changing sheets is the most exciting road trip I've taken lately. Let me explain. It's not a difficult task, although it can remind someone with a bad back that their back is indeed bad. I walk around all four corners tucking in the fitted sheet. Next, I have to figure which is the head and which is the foot and flatten out and tuck in the top sheet. By this time, there are at least two dogs and a cat who think making the bed is a game devised for their pleasure, their entertainment.

TacoBelle and Rosie already knew the rules to this game and within minutes of the first bed change after BooCat moved in, she learned too. In fact, she added a few new rules and several fancy moves to the match. She is a master—or should that be mistress—of the sheet changing game. Just as I'm about to tuck in a corner, they scoot under the sheets faster than, well not a greased pig exactly, but as fast as a curious BooCat and a couple peppy pooches.

Blankets have to be fluffed and the spread inserted and smoothed. By the time I'm done, I've walked a mile and been nowhere.

Actually, the bed and blanket game is enjoyed universally by many house pets. My crew doesn't have a patent on it. I can only assume, like much preordained knowledge that comes already installed in the makeup and psyche, knowing the rules of this game is one. You know kids come into the world already knowing how to play peek-a-boo, tag, hide-n-seek—girls knowing hopscotch and jacks and boys knowing marbles. So it must be with cats and dogs and the bed and blanket game.

I received an e-mail from Carolyn of Oak Ridge after she'd read about the fun of making the bed with pets participation in a *Louisiana Road Trips* magazine article. She wrote:

> A little late on this note BUT... I had to laugh out loud when you told of making beds with animals helping. TigerTail, PeterPie and LittleBlackCat are felines most likely to get made up. Or in, as the case may be. All nine pounds of Mr. Curtis and PupPup refuse to budge so the bed looks lumpy. Admittedly, I occasionally screech for everyone to give me five minutes so we can ALL go to bed with fresh sheets. And when one turns around to count 3 dogs and 8–10 cats on/in bed you *know* you should be committed.

Never a dull moment when you have pets.

Replacing a light bulb in a ceiling fixture is major. It's a lot like the curtain incident. In fact, anything that requires a step stool is precarious and heartbreakingly sad. My steadiness-genes deserted me.

Like climbing the steep steps at Gatlinburg, Tennessee to ride the lift—not that I could ride the lift, mind you. If I'd been able to overcome the initial step up I still couldn't ride the lift, and in my opinion, one step up with nothing to hold onto is hazardous to my health. Two steps up is out of the question. But it doesn't have to be up, it can be across. Like the swinging bridge in Colorado Springs.

I don't know what in tarnation happened, and I'm not real happy about it. Oh, it beats the alternative, but why? Why does it have to be this way? It's too late to hope the best of my past might be the worst of my future because apparently I've already surpassed that. Even worse is not being able to pinpoint just when it all went south. One day I could carry dog food and kitty litter and change a light bulb and hang curtains, the next day I couldn't. And now I have to have reparative surgery. And it's all connected to traveling in the last lane of life.

Candy is Sweet But Not So Smart

36

"A kitten is in the animal world what a rosebud is in the garden."
(Robert Southey)

BooCat is keen on looking out the window so long as her hyper-attention span allows. I don't know what she thinks of the outside dogs. I do know what she thinks of the birds she watches. She's one dedicated birdwatcher. She deserves her own pair of bird watching binoculars.

Candy,[†] probably my oldest dog rescued from somebody who was moving to Tennessee and passed to his nephew who in turn passed her on to me, often chooses to lie in front of the floor-to-ceiling windows BooBirdwatcher sits at. Not only is this a perfect bird watching and dog watching window, rays of sunshine blaze through part of the day and Boo likes that. She's a dedicated sunshine sleeper.

Candy appears oblivious to BooCat's presence just a thin pane of glass away. BooCat is curious but not to the point of doing anything more than gazing at the large red-furred body before her. Were either Rosie or TacoBelle in her place, they'd be barking their fool head's off. Boo may believe she's a canine in cat's clothing, but she doesn't bark. Not yet.

[†] Candy stepped on a rainbow from a combination of old age and heartworms, March 2010.

36 / Candy is Sweet But Not So Smart

Candy is the epitome of if three times is a charm, than four times should be something really special. Candy is a chow-mix that came to live with me sometime in 2005 or 2006.

She is one of the reasons I have the sign at my driveway entrance reading *Young dogs, old dogs, several stupid dogs—Please drive carefully.* She's not alone. There have been a few others over the years that contributed to the erection of that sign.

I realize stupid is a strong word. I was taught as a child to never call someone stupid. Imagine, judging by today's standards, to have been reared with rules about language? I never heard either of my parents curse in my presence. Dad was in the U.S. Army, had been to war—he surely knew some bad words. But in our household, nobody cursed and nobody used degrading terms that might hurt feelings. Therefore, ingrained, "stupid" was out. Dad left my mom after a quarter century of marriage, but I have many positive memories of my childhood that included my father.

Still, sometimes you just have to tell it like it is. Sweet Candy—stupid is as stupid does. (Forgive me Mom and Dad).

I feel stupid whenever I have to talk to somebody's answering machine. My tongue gets tangled and my mind goes blank. What's the old saying? My tongue has gotten tangled up on my eyeteeth so I can't see what I'm saying. Or something like that. In fact, talking to an answering machine makes me feel so stupid I figured maybe it affects others the same way.

My answering machine message was created because of the empathy I feel for callers: "If talking to a machine doesn't makes you feel stupid, go ahead and talk to mine. Leave me a message."

Since I don't like talking on telephones, I'm honest enough not to promise to call anybody back. They can leave the message and I might or might not return the call. I can't help it. I've spent a lifetime doing the correct things and now I'm tired.

In any case, certainly, *feeling* stupid and *being* stupid has a clear line of demarcation. Candy crossed that line. So did Noggin.

Most dogs come equipped with better sense than some people, but there's always the exception. This was evidenced several years ago when one of my outside pups somehow got his head, from his shoulders up past his nose, stuck in a piece of four-inch white PVC drain pipe.

Me? I panicked. Failing to remove it with tin snips, we made a flying trip to Dr. White's Veterinary Clinic. Visiting the vet in times of an emergency isn't high on my road trips list.

However, with additional snips from shears and brute force, Noggin was freed from his plastic prison.

My wonderful Boyo, the dog that was run over by a combine, once came home half dead after dark with a beaver snare bound around his neck. His face was swollen, his eyes and tongue bulging. I was able to contact friends Derl and Kitty J. who rushed to my rescue. Wire cutters removed the beaver snare. This wire trap was constructed in such a way it tightened with every move Boyo took. He was being strangled as the minutes passed. It took days before the swelling reduced. This probably wasn't due to stupidity so much as being where he shouldn't have been, sticking his nose into something he shouldn't have been nosing around.

For all those with good dog sense, there are the few, like the car-chasers. They get flipped, bunged up, even run over, and they continue this sport every time a car whizzes by. Some dogs are a wonder unto themselves. I had a beautiful collie some twenty years ago who couldn't be broken until he was broken.

Never learning takes me back to my Candy story. (See how easy I get sidetracked? It's the AAADD thing: Age-Activated Attention Deficit Disorder)

One Saturday morning Candy alerted me to a problem by pawing at her muzzle. Peering in her black-tongued mouth, I saw a stick tightly wedged at the roof. After several failed attempts on my part to forcefully remove it by hand, I rushed her to Dr. White's office. He sedated her and removed the offending woody object.

A couple Saturdays later, she exhibited signs of trouble again. Again, a stick was wedged in the roof of her mouth. Again, we rushed to Dr. White's office. Again, he sedated her and removed the stick.

I figured it was just a fluke. But not so. Obviously a slow learner, I arrived home from work on Tuesday and Candy was pawing at her muzzle one more time. Another stuck stick. When we got to Dr. White's office, he was with another furry patient so Elizabeth hunkered down with a pair of forceps while another lady got behind Candy to keep her still. I held her leash. Elizabeth popped that stick right out and said it was the second one she'd removed from a dog's

36 / Candy is Sweet But Not So Smart

mouth that week. She was amazing.

The very next morning I went out to feed the dogs before leaving for work and again, Candy showed signs of distress. Once more I pried open her giant mouth; she weighs 65 pounds. We loaded up and headed out. It being Wednesday Dr. White wasn't in his office, Every Wednesday he travels to another town lacking veterinarian services. I hustled Candy over to Dr. Glenn Melton's office. Pet owners in our rural parish are very fortunate. We have two outstanding and deeply compassionate veterinarians available.

I wondered if Candy's penchant for chewing sticks could be alleviated if I provided her with a sturdy chew bone, or was the problem dietary? Dr. White had told me it's not all that uncommon; dogs occasionally get sticks and bones wedged in their mouths as it's the nature of the beast to chew stuff.

Associated with Dr. Melton, Dr. Barren treated Candy that day. But this time she had scratched her muzzle deeply by clawing at the stuck stick and required a couple stitches.

Because the problem had started within a couple month's time, we discussed trying a different dog food; something offering extra fiber. Dogs eat grass when their tummy's are upset, maybe she was craving roughage. Not guaranteed to squelch the problem, it couldn't hurt. We discussed providing her a kong-type dog chew toy. Both vets stressed their experiences regarding possible problems developing from rawhide chews. Neither were proponents of rawhide chews. At that time Candy was probably between six to eight years old, so it wasn't a puppy teething problem.

Dr. Barren said Candy was a sweet dog. He didn't add she was a stupid dog, like not the brightest fluorescent in the fixture. With a bit of humor, he said if she keeps this up I might have to learn how to pop sticks out of her mouth. Regardless, I now have both Dr. White and Dr. Melton's phone numbers in my speed dial.

The Fearless Flea

37

"I do honor every flea on this dog." (Ben Johnson, *Every Man In His Humor*)

Thinking about Candy and how illogical she was in connection with chewing on sticks brings to mind how some things simply aren't logical. Like, have you ever noticed when someone sees a dog scratching they automatically assume the dog has fleas? It never occurs to them that the dog might just itch. And scratch.

I don't think the same itch-plus-scratch-equals-fleas applies to cats. Maybe it's because you rarely see a cat scratching in public, whereas a dog makes a living letting it all hang out. Whatever, whenever.

On the other hand, find a flea on your dog and you itch all over. Your scalp itches. There's a crawling sensation down your back. Under your arm. You feel fleas all over your body. You need a shower. Or flea powder.

Thinking about fleas, a common denominator when you have cats and dogs, reminds me of the time my tenth grade math teacher exposed the class to what he said was an example of logic as taught to lawyers. I've forgotten the multiplication table but I remember the truth according to logic as proven by the flea.

You get this flea (stop scratching). Place it in the palm of your hand. You say: "Jump flea!"

The flea jumps. Obviously he heard you.

37 / The Fearless Flea

Then you pull out the flea's legs. (Sorry. I forgot to warn some of this stuff might be graphic in nature). Anyway, you remove the flea's legs. (Call in a surgeon if you are squeamish).

Again you say: "Jump flea."

The flea doesn't jump. It sits there as though it doesn't hear a word you're saying. Therefore, logically speaking, the flea hears through its legs.

I've met folks who hear through their legs. Or not at all. Namely ex-husbands.

Forced to speak to the side of his head because he was faced forward watching TV, I used to wonder if his ear-hair twitched, did that mean he heard me?

Fleas, with or without ears, are a health hazard for cats and dogs. People too. Although they are dangerous disease-carrying creatures, there was a time in our historical past when the lowly flea was well regarding, playing a part in the entertainment field.

Currently a lost art—and it's just as well—up until at least the 1970s, there were Flea Circuses in operation in both the United States and England.

Fleas were attached to miniature carts and other objects where they performed circus acts as part of circus sideshow attractions. To view the tiny Flea Circus, it was common practice to provide viewers with Fresnel Lenses to better see the tiny hopping insects perform.

Because the natural lifespan of the flea is very short, training fleas was an ongoing process. Not to mention, some of the circus acts performed were quite hazardous to the flea's health, adding to the short lifespan.

Fleas, as pointed out in the case of lawyerly logic, are prone to jump. Therefore, part of training process for flea circuses required teaching the flea not to jump—but not by removing its legs. The tiny insects were kept in a container with a lid; the theory being if the flea jumped, it would bump its head and eventually either expire from a concussion or learn to stop jumping. Never underestimate any of God's creatures. What hasn't been thought of probably doesn't exist.

Once these little rascals were trained, a collar constructed of a thin gold wire was carefully wrapped around its neck. These leashes were then attached to the various props making up the circus.

An example of a flea circus act was for a flea to kick a lightweight cotton ball around, giving the appearance of juggling or playing ball. The trick was to infuse the cotton ball with camphor, a chemical used to repel fleas. Naturally the little chained-up flea would kick at the foul smelling ball. I'd kick too.

Born to jump, a flea's legs are very strong. As part of the circus act, the flea's muscular legs made it possible for them to move objects much larger than they were.

According to Wikipedia, the first record of performing fleas was by watch makers who were demonstrating their metal working skills.

The first advertisements of Flea Circuses were found as early as in 1833 England. Actually, Flea Circuses were a main carnival attraction until 1930.

As late as the 1960s, Flea Circuses made their rounds in the United States, while the Flea Circus at Belle Vue Amusement Park in Manchester, England operated through the 1970s.

Odd as it may sound, dead fleas have been used as an art form when painted. Most well known is the Mexican Flea Bank and the Wedding Party that can be seen in Tring Natural History Museum.

Another flea circus entertainment featured fleas playing miniature musical instruments. This act was achieved by gluing tiny replica musical instruments to the fleas themselves. The fleas themselves were in turn glued to the base of a miniature circus enclosure—sort of a diorama. Next, the enclosure was heated. When the fleas sought to escape the heat, the impression of playing the musical instruments was conveyed to the viewer.

Ouch.

Where does amusement end and cruelty and inhumanity begin?

There were Flealess Circuses. These flea circuses, as they were also called, gave the appearance of using real fleas, but they didn't. Not in the same sense as the common flea circus did. Fleas were still involved, but they weren't glued or chained up. Instead, the method involved a variety of electrical, magnetic and mechanical devices used to enhance the exhibits. Along with the powered apparatuses, which were actually accountable for all the acts, loose fleas were released in the exhibit to keep up the impression of performing fleas. A bit of sleight of hand so to speak.

Lastly, not all flea circuses required callous cruelty to fleas. Some

Flea Circuses really did not contain any fleas whatsoever; everything being nothing more than an illusion. These circuses were much like the illusion presented when a magician cuts a girl in half or pulls rabbits from an empty hat. The trick was all in the eye of the beholder.

And with all that in mind, who would ever have imagined that somebody would write a poem about the dastardly flea? An ode to a flea is one piece of literature pet owners won't much care for. Yet, Augustus De Morgan wrote about fleas in much the same way my tenth grade teacher used the flea to exhibit logic. Morgan exhibits an absurdity in *A Budget of Paradoxes*:

> Great fleas have little fleas upon their backs to bite 'em,
> And little fleas have lesser fleas, and so ad infinitum.
> And the great fleas themselves, in turn, have greater fleas to go on;
> While these again have greater still, and greater still, and so on.

The Distinctive Dachshund

38

"Ask not for whom the dog barks and the cat meows;
they bark and meow for thee." (Unknown)

BooCat has embraced SweetBabyRose as her very own combination plaything, companion and baby doll. Except for the usual puppy chewing, until Rosie discovered the pleasure of pillow mutilation, and seriously wrecked a couple throw pillows, she was a perfect puppy. Fortunately, ingestion of my throw pillows phase passed with only one significant loss; a hand-sewn, counted-cross-stitched throw-pillow. I sewed it so if I ever feel energetic and so moved, I can resew another. It was pretty, the face covered with intricately designed butterflies in assorted colors. But, stuff happens. She has more than made up for her discretionary chewing.

Thus, due to Rosie's otherwise sweet disposition, I lived with the loss. Also, my motto is that there are no bad dogs.

About here many people—particularly pit-bull dog owners—add there are only bad owners. I must clarify. There are bad dogs. There are bad dog owners also. I know it appears contradictory. The statement that there are no bad dogs would need to be qualified in detail when referring to specific dogs; but in general, there are no bad dogs. Purebred dogs have specific personalities that have been bred into them. A pointer points even without training. A retriever retrieves. A

Doxie digs the badger out of its hole. A squirrel dog trees. Therefore, it stands to reason a fighting dog has these genes awaiting release. And perhaps the term "bad" is not correct. But, the nature of certain dogs are geared toward certain activities. Beware. Don't kid yourself.

Back to normal training. Very few puppies, like children, are perfect before you get them trained. Of course, also like children, some never do get trained. Rosie's not one of those incorrigible dogs; she trained well and has a beguiling nature and a personality to make any dog-owner proud.

Then suddenly, at what should have been a more mature age, around sixteen-months, which I think in dog years is supposed to be old enough for a dog to know better, Rosie took a backward step. She digressed. I brought home a purple squawking stuffed dog toy and she adopted it immediately. Adopting a dog toy as her very own doesn't sound on the surface like a problem; but read on.

When I got Rosie the doggie toy-box was already full of Taco-Belle's toys, therefore, I never brought home a toy specifically for Rosie, there being plenty for her to chose from. For all that time she made do with Taco's cast-offs, her hand-me-downs; toys Taco had outgrown. Having read Dr. Spock during child-rearing days, I admit to a moment of remorse, wondering, had I deprived this wonderful little dog of something vital to her development? Could this depravation create a dysfunctional dog? Is this why she is now a phobic pooch?

Ah well, even though she was named Rosie as in "Second-Hand Rose," so-called for having been bought off the back of a pickup truck, I knew she hadn't been deprived. Yet, that fleeting feeling of guilt swept over me when I saw the delight she took from having her first very own dog toy.

When Jon Darlin' spotted the hand-lettered cardboard sign tacked to the side of a pickup truck: *Dachshunds*. He pulled over to the side of the road, hopped out, crossed the street and as I watched, he turned back toward me, holding up a tiny reddish brown pup. He was grinning ear-to-ear. Rosie remains a precious gift from Jon since his untimely death several months afterward.

Rosie carried this purple dog toy everywhere; including into bed one night. Usually quick to insert herself beneath the covers, that night she lay at the foot of the bed making her toy squeak and squawk. I indulged her the fun, the noise didn't disturb my reading and I assumed she would tire of playing soon.

Eventually she did. But not until she discovered a way into the innards of that new toy. She pulled stuffing out. Pulling out stuffing is apparently a most exciting pastime for dogs. In Rosie's case it may have brought back puppyhood memories from her pillow chewing days because the next night she brought another toy to bed; one of Taco's oldies-but-still-goodies. She chewed with fervor. It's safe to say I've since collected, picked up and thrown away a ton of fluffy white stuffing from the innards of various and sundry doggie toys that had lived for five years intact; until Rosie went into her second puppyhood.

Rosie is still the sweetest dog anybody could ever meet; it's just her penchant for disemboweling stuffed dog toys that could be bothersome if I so allowed. Which I do not. Even non-dog people want to take Rosie home with them. She's well behaved, is camera-perfect (which means she's beautiful), and absolutely no one can resist her attention. Should she be allowed in a first-time visitor's lap, she immediately lays her head against their chest and closes her eyes with the sheer pleasure of being in that particular lap. It endears her to the lucky individual instantaneously. She's a snuggler.

Rosie was taught from the beginning to behave herself by the grand matron of the family TacoBelle. If in bed at night, when just a little pup, she mistook going to bed as being a time to play, Taco snarled at her and she immediately closed her eyes and assumed invisibility. After a few nights she learned when she got into bed, it meant going right to sleep.

That is, until she discovered the joy of ripping dog toys to death at the foot of the bed. She would make a surgeon proud.

Cheeto's Mysterious Road Trip

"Doggone it! I'm in love." (Happy Slang Expression: "Doggone it!" does not mean somebody's dog is gone or that they lost their dog)

Road trips come in all shapes, sizes and forms. I reckon walking dogs is sort of like taking a miniature nature-filled road trip. Road-tripping with my pooches is good exercise physically as well as mentally. To stroll casually up or down a country road with them at my heels—or more likely me at theirs—is peaceable. I bird watch, wave at passing cars and trucks, and smell the honeysuckle along the way. The dogs bird chase, bark at passing cars and trucks and eat the daisies.

On one walk, a red-tailed hawk swooped down, landing on a nearby fence a few feet away, its eye, no doubt upon a hapless field mouse. When the dogs spotted it, they took off in useless hot pursuit, barking. The raptor left them in its wake, and the field mouse lived another day.

Somehow the number of dogs living at my house multiplied until I'm keeping company with a broad mix of sizes, colors and kinds. My heart is over-extended. I've taken in dogs people couldn't keep, adopted strays, abandoned and dumped dogs, and among the scruffy mix are several I actually bought. Don't ask the headcount unless you wish to be rendered speechless.

One particular yard dog BooCat curiously watches through her favorite window is Cheeto. Cheeto was extra furry—the embellishment of a fur-real fur ball—when born. Her fluffy coat had an orange cast. She was like someone had dumped one of the yummy orange Cheeto snacks out amongst a pile of Plain-Jane potato chips, so naming her Cheeto, while novel, was perfectly suited.

Like most of the dogs eating me out of house and home, Cheeto, a dog of mixed heritage, lacked a pedigree, but she was anything but typical, and certainly not ordinary. The black button nose centering her adorable face called attention to her unique orange coloring. She was beautiful in the eyes of this beholder and her poignant obsidian eyes peered into my soul and love moved into my heart. That is just how it happens sometimes. Love at first sight. An unexplained connection. Like that one special sunrise. Sunrises happen every morning, but one morning one moves you more than the days and weeks before. Same with Cheeto. She was that one special sunrise among many.

Some of the most memorable moments in my life pivot around my dogs and Cheeto is right up there in that department. Not every dog of mine has had a winning personality. Like people, each is different. But, Cheeto struck a special chord in me. While I'm hooked on dogs in general, one or two among my pack seem to get me at first bark.

Enter Cheeto.

With her bone structure I determined she'd be medium-sized and wouldn't grow into a large watchdog. She lacked watchdog genes. She was calm, well-behaved and friendly. She liked being held and handled and responded positively to my attention. A good companion, excellent temperament, Cheeto was well-suited as a lapdog, except for the fact she was on her outgrowing my lap. After getting Rosie and then adopting Mom's Gizzy when Mom moved to Oak Woods, I promised TacoBelle, no more housedogs. Therefore, Cheeto was relegated to live with the outside dogs. Living outside at my house isn't a bad thing. They're each and every one treated like the special friends they are.

The older dogs are the ones that let me tag along on their road trips. The thing is, dogs being dogs, sometimes they take trips without me. The gang has a tendency to wander, play in nearby fields during the wee hours. Usually, they leave en masse and return the same

39 / Cheeto's Mysterious Road Trip

way; usually when they hear the dog food hitting the food bowls. They're never far, but there's something about being free that makes them want to hang around on the wrong side of the fence around the yard. Could be the greener-on-the-other-side thing. Likely that's it. They have a two-acre yard. Yet, they like to lounge just outside the fence in the adjoining farm fields.

Tails wagging, they surround me with childish joy before digging into their chow. If you have a dog that loves you, imagine having a dozen plus.

When Cheeto was three months old, evidently deciding she was old enough to hang with the big dogs, she followed them out of the yard. But, she didn't come back home when they did.

I called her name. I searched. I was devastated. I pleaded with the big dogs to go find little Cheeto; wherever they'd left her; please bring her home. Of course they were clueless. Days passed. No Cheeto. For a very long time, day after day, I'd search the horizon and count heads and just felt so sad.

Early mornings out in the country are my favorite time of the day. I'm forever taking photographs of sunrises having for the most part traded in my oils and canvas for my camera. But, as beautiful as early mornings are, they became so sad with Cheeto gone.

I tried to not worry because there wasn't one single thing I could do to bring her back. Crying over spilt milk, as it were, didn't refill the milk bottle. To dwell in sorrow wasn't constructive. And so, when the dew was still on the grass I'd wax poetic viewing each tiny blade with its own diamond for decoration. I gazed upon the dogs as they lazed in the early morning sunshine. It was easy to see mornings were their favorite times too.

Morning is a time to walk barefoot in the grass. It's a time to braid a necklace from clover; a time to pick a rose and wear it behind my ear. It's a time to glory in the fragrance of honeysuckle, carefully pulling the inner stem through backwards and bringing that so-sweet drop of wild honey to my waiting lips. A time to whisk dandelion fuzz about. A flower, like a smile, is understood in every language.

I thought of the crooked row of daffodils I planted here at Wit's End forty years ago. I'd become so involved in the task before me, I neglected the most important part. I failed to look to see where I was going, or even, perhaps where I'd been. When the daffodils multiplied over the years, the beauty of the yellow flowers every spring almost erased the crooks. Almost.

But they also reminded me no matter how perfect something almost is, there often are crooks. My missing Cheeto was a crook in my heart.

Recalling my first veggie garden and how amazing it was to sample fresh vegetables that hadn't come straight from a can. I gazed with wonder upon the fruits of my labor that first year. Ah, that was before the new wore off. Looking back, although it was a lot of work, it was a time in my life I wouldn't change. I may have been weary at times, but trust me, it was a positive weariness, even though that sounds contradictory. It was a good tired. The kind of tired you feel at the end of a productive day.

Wit's End's a good place. It's my home and not just a house. In fact, to me it's a Southern mansion. There's an old saying: *American by choice, Southern by the grace of God.*

Having a couple acres out in the country lets me have my rescued and adopted dogs. And the dogs wag their tails. They're happy here too.

Everyone except Cheeto.

Cheeto was like my Weeping Willows. I used to play beneath the outer branches of a wonderful weeping willow in my grandmother's front yard back in Severn, Maryland, as a child. It was like being in a fairyland. Wanting my children to experience this same magic, I planted several weeping willows at Wit's End.

I loved the graceful pale green weeping willow branches whispering in the breeze, but I didn't know then that their branches are brittle and though rapid growing, they are also short-lived.

My willows are gone. My Cheeto is gone. Sometimes I weep for my willows. Always, I weep for my lost Cheeto.

And I laugh too. Remembering brings forth a mixture of laughter and weeping. One thing I discovered early on in life is that you make most of your own happiness. You can be happy or sad wherever you are.

Another thing I learned is that you can never truly go back into the past except in your memories. Nothing ever stays the same. Still, you can hold onto yesterday's good remembrances. They can mold and make your tomorrow's better.

39 / Cheeto's Mysterious Road Trip

Bad memories might bruise your soul, damage your dreams, as well as your mind and heart at times, so I've come to realize it's just as well the weeping willows are gone. I don't need any weeping. I only need bees buzzing, the gardenias and magnolias filling the air with their own fragrant brand of music. I only need nature's beauty strumming my heart like a guitar, and the birds singing their sweet song.

So, I became resolved to my little dog being gone.

My prayer is: *Lord please, a steady breeze.*

Then, one evening Chuck came to the door, told me to come outside; he wanted to show me something. What he showed me was a very skinny and bedraggled half-grown orange dog with sparkling black obsidian eyes, a black button nose and a wagging tail. Two months after Cheeto had disappeared, she was back.

She'd been gone two full months during a very formative time in her life. Now, at five months old, she was practically grown. But it was her. Oh thank you, it was her.

Where had she been? How had she found her way back? A mere three months old when she disappeared, a lot can happen during a two-month span in the life of a growing puppy. Chuck believes someone kidnapped her and she finally made her escape. It took a while to allow hands-on and for her to become her former playful self.

She is just fine and dandy once again. I am forever curious about her road trip. I can only imagine what a doggy tale my little orange sweetie would tell if only she could. I have a feeling BooCat would take pleasure in sitting and listening right along with me. After all, there is no doubt BooCat has a road trip story of her own she could relate. Leaving behind the security her mama cat and litter mates provided to the uncertainty that was her life for fourteen weeks

The people she met, the dogs she hung around with, the kittens she came in contact with and the fear and uncertainty she likely felt as she moved from pillar to post.

Cheeto's puppy photograph appeared in an issue of Louisiana Road Trips magazine in reference to taking that doggy-style road trip which makes her a celebrity. She is definitely my celebrity.

She is always the first of the pack to reach the dog food, standing up, front paws propped against the cans showing me where it's stored. I have to invite her to get down and step back so I can open the lid and dip out breakfast. She's a bright and friendly dog. I am so glad she is back home. It is where she belongs.

The Survival of Buddy

40

"Until one has loved an animal, a part of one's soul remains unawakened."
(Anatole France)

Scientifically proven, and I agree wholeheartedly, pets make their owners feel better. Petting a cat or dog has a calming effect, lowering one's pulse. Even high blood pressure drops with a few gentle strokes down the back of one's furry friend. This is certainly one of the main reasons nursing homes and similar institutions welcome therapy animals. Some even allow residents to bring their beloved pets with them when the move in.

I took Gizzy to visit Mom at Oak Woods often and she spent time with Gizzy when she came to my house to visit, but we both decided it wasn't a sound idea for her to attempt full-time care of Gizzy.

Mom loved her Gizzy. Gizzy reciprocated. After all, she and Mom were constant companions for over ten years. But, I worried with Mom's unsteadiness—being required to use a walker and even at times a wheel chair, she might trip over an excited Gizzy. Also, Gizzy might not understand being confined, not being allowed to sit at Mom's feet in the dining room where she would expect Mom to share her meals with her. That's what they did at home, but things would be different in the nursing home. Allowing pets to live in the resident's room is one thing, letting the pets hang around in the dining room would probably not pass health standards.

Mom would need much help to maintain Gizzy on the premises; and together we decided she should stay at my house. Maybe I was wrong. Maybe we should have tried. At least foir awhile. But when Mom first went to Oak Woods, she could barely care for herself, she could not have cared for Gizzy too. Still, I'll never know.

I have to believe at the time it was the right decision. Looking back there are always the maybes and what-ifs. Sadly, it's seldom that we're allowed do-overs.

My BooCat loves being stroked. I'm her mother—whether she sees me as a Mama Cat or herself as a Baby Human, I don't know, nor does it matter. What matters is the relationship itself.

BooCat's feline mom no doubt repeatedly licked her when she was a tiny baby. When I stroke her, it probably feels much the same as when her mom licked her. This is a good thing. BooBaby would automatically equate my motherly stroking with the one who feeds, cleans, protects and loves her.

I've read that even after a cat grows up, it keeps looking at the human who pets and strokes it as its mother, and consequently, it never completely grows up.

Psychobabble aside, I figure BooCat tells herself if it feels good, enjoy it. And she does. I can't imagine BallyhooBoo delving too deeply into the psychological meaning behind petting versus licking and momma cat versus human companion.

Another thing cat psychologists tie back to kittenhood is why a cat kneads your lap like a bowl of bread dough.

BooCat so far is not a kneader, but Hershey definitely was. He would climb upon my lap and start to rhythmically press down, first with one front paw, and then with the other, over and over, slowly. His eyes would close in oblivious hypnotic pleasure. Maybe in his case, the kneading process did take him back to a long ago time when he was just a baby cat. This action is likened to when a cat was a kitten at its mother's nipples, when and where it used its tiny paws to stimulate the flow of milk. Obviously, this is a moment of intimacy between a cat and its owner whether it has to do with babyhood or not.

Why doesn't BooCat do this? Surely when she was a nursing kitten she gently pushed with her paws at her mother's stomach. When an older cat behaves this way, it is believed it is content, recalling some of the best days of its early life. I wonder if there will ever come a day when BooCat retreats to those memories as a kitten; or if perhaps they weren't so happy and thus she chooses to forget?

Talk about unusual explanations, I read the reason a cat licks its fur isn't just to be clean, nor is it just to smooth a ruffled bit of fur. The article advised that the licking helps the cat cool off.

Say what?

I know. I didn't believe it either. The article said since cats don't have sweat glands and since panting helps but doesn't completely solve the problem, in the summer to avoid overheating, cats lick themselves over and over, depositing saliva. Then the saliva evaporates in the same manner as perspiration evaporating on a human's skin does, cooling the cat. Interesting concept. Could it be?

We get our vitamin D from the sunshine, yes, but also from milk and taking vitamin pills. Vitamin D is necessary for our good health. Well, it's also required in the diets of cats. Guess how experts say cats get vitamin D?

No. It's not just from laying in the sun absorbing the rays. It's from laying in the sun and then licking their fur. Sunlight on the cat's coat produces vitamin D. Then the vitamin D becomes lickable. Like taking a vitamin pill via licking, maybe? I don't make this stuff up, folks. I read it and it is attributed to an animal behaviorist and cat expert. I'll have to take their word for it. I have no alternate knowledge to refute this finding. Stranger things happen all around us every single second of every single day.

Why does BooCat like hanging off the edge of every piece of furniture she lazes upon, be it the bed, chairs or her cat furniture? I have dozens of photos featuring her in precarious positions while at ease, which sounds like a contradiction, but it's not. She's like a feline Evil Knievil, bungee jumper, sky diver and daredevil who goes over Niagara Falls in a barrel. Maybe she just likes living on the edge because she can.

In all probability some cat psychologist has covered this audacious predilection of my young cat, but I've yet to discover it. If they don't know why, likely they'll make something up. Then they'll publish their articles and sell their books and be touted as authorities on the subject. I'm not knocking expert opinions. I depend upon them all the time so I'll do the right thing by my pets. But gee whiz, some statements sound so far out it is hard to take it seriously. Like licking the sunshine off its fur. I never thought of sunshine as tangible, nor lickable. But that doesn't mean it's not. Not by a long shot.

But then I wonder, if I'm out in the sun too long and my shoulders and arms get burned from absorbing that very same sun and then if I lick my arms, will I also get my daily dose of vitamin D? I mean, I'm just asking.

BungeeBoo loves rubber bands and strings. Reminiscent of the snake I presume.

Dogs listen. By listening, I don't mean they will follow our every instruction or command unless they've been trained better than I train mine. But, they listen as we speak, a kindly ear so we don't have to talk to ourselves.

Basically, all a dog asks in return is a little TLC (tender loving care). Of course, letting a pet own you requires a certain degree of responsibility. They will need an occasional bath, nails clipped, coat combed now and then, and elimination of fleas, ticks and other pests.

No matter the breed or size, dogs need exercise, fresh water and wholesome food. Once you understand the nature and background of your dog, educate it sufficiently for safety's sake to keep it from harm and become adjusted to living with people while providing a healthy environment, it can fill a blank spot, a void, in your life you may not even know you had.

It's a huge responsibility. But the rewards are even bigger.

Accidents happen and hearts break when you're a pet owner. Take the case of HoneyBunch and Buddy. The old Mamma Dog birthed these two pups around the 4th of July, 2008, along a fence row. She kept them hidden beneath a stand of weeds and wild shrubs. One day she brought them out and presented them to Chuck and me. I picked up HoneyBunch. He picked up Buddy as we came to call each.

We watched as Mamma Dog ducked back into the bushes, speculating she had gone after another fur-ball. Instead, she emerged carrying an old discarded dog chew toy in her mouth. Approaching us, she dropped the rubber bone at Chuck's feet. It was as though she was relinquishing care of the babies to the humans, including their toy.

I doctored them with an over-the-counter (OTC) wormer. Noting they had developed scabies and seborrhea, I doctored them accordingly for that ailment also. I treated them for seed ticks that had burrowed in their ears, between their toes and on their tummies. Living in the bushes had exposed them to too much nature.

Although a trip to the vets was on my to-do list when work and time allowed, time got away until one day I noticed HoneyBunch had lost her bounce, appeared lethargic.

I took her to Dr. Melton's veterinarian office where his exam revealed a serious internal worm infestation. The OTC wormer hadn't done its job. He started a radical course of treatment immediately, keeping her overnight. While little brother Buddy seemed fine, I knew as a litter mate he would need treatment also. I brought him in for an exam the following morning.

Every now and again, someone or something moves into your heart and time has nothing to do with it. These little pups had me at first bark. At first tail-wag. At first sight. So, it broke my heart when HoneyBunch didn't make it. I still feel sad when I think about her. She reminded me of Cheeto, only she was solid white instead of orange. She was more a marshmallow than a Cheeto chip. And she was definitely a honeybunch.

Buddy successfully struggled to get a good footing in life, started his first year off with, if not a bang exactly, than at least with a hope for tomorrow. For a long time his feet and head were too large for his besieged body. He was typical gangly. Even though his fur was still scraggly and sparse so that he looked like the rescue dog he was, he turned out to be okay, growing up into a handsome specimen.

Buddy's photo appeared on the front page of the *Bastrop Daily Enterprise* accompanying an article by Wes Helbling, staff writer, about the importance of preventive treatment for heart worms, which, due to the mosquito factor, is prevalent in this part of the country.

When I looked into Buddy's eyes, even when he was fighting to recover from an assortment of ailments, his eyes were full of tender puppy love, sugary sweetness, and so much natural intelligence. I knew he'd make a super dog.

Aunt Daisy, a tender-hearted dog with a hip birth defect, took him under her tutelage and the end result was all good. Mama Dog suffered from a case of incurable heart worms and is now frolicking in the meadow at Rainbow Bridge, but true to Mamma Dog's wishes, Chuck considers Buddy his pet. Buddy sleeps on Chuck's porch and eats the scraps he throws to him. Chuck needed a dog. Every man does.

Edibility Depends Upon the Degree of Scorching

"Dogs and Cats are People Too." (Unknown Origin)

Every once in a while I'm motivated to cook a real-meal-deal. I mean, like mix together a pile of ingredients and actually use the oven and cooktop. When that mood strikes, I usually call Chuck and share so TacoBelle, Rosie, BooCat and I don't have to feast on my culinary masterpieces for too many days in a row. Masterpieces are not too masterful after the fourth or fifth day. Not to mention, you prepare a humdinger meal and you have dishes to wash for days.

I boiled a pot full of whole potatoes still in their skins and a half dozen eggs for potato salad. My Mom made a humdinger potato salad, so she taught me well and I've always liked making it. Still, it's difficult to make potato salad for one. If you are going to all the trouble of boiling, chopping and mixing everything together with mayo, along with a few secret ingredients, you want to turn out a large bowlful for your efforts. But a large bowl brings you back to the days-on-end leftovers monotony.

Next on my menu was preparation of a killer meatloaf. It had been several years since I'd tackled a meatloaf. It's one of those dishes I grew up eating a lot of because there were four of us kids and Mom had figured out every way possible in which to stretch a package of ground beef; meatloaf being one. So I ate a lot of meatloaf growing up. Hence, while not exactly burned out on it, as it's often put locally, I rarely find my mouth watering for it.

I do crave things. Just not meatloaf. I crave steamed Maryland blue crabs. There's no such animal available around Jones. Sometimes I buy crabmeat and fry up some Baltimore crab cakes, but something's missing. This being Louisiana, I think what's missing is Maryland itself. If there's a difference between the crabs themselves, maybe because the crabmeat I'm buying is "wild caught" in Indonesia instead of the Chesapeake Bay may make a flavor difference.

The new advertisement grabber is to plaster the words "wild caught" all over anything from the sea like that's better than, say Arkansas and Louisiana pond raised catfish or shrimp or crawfish. Advertisers jump on a term and beat it to death, playing on people's vanity. I know pond-raised catfish and I'd rather see those words, coupled with Grown, Raised and Made in America, than Wild Caught in the polluted waters off some foreign shores.

Sam Walton, founder of Walmart, used to have signs plastered all over his stores Made in America" or "American Made" or similar variations. Red, white and blue symbols were everywhere. You didn't take two steps in a Walmart without having America in your face. American Pride ruled.

I expect he's turning over in his grave now that everything in his stores has been imported from China. Check it out. Walmart now sells dishes that are not microwave safe. I didn't think there was such an animal anymore except metal and an uncracked egg.

The microwave oven came about as a by-product of another technology. Around 1946, Dr. Percy LaBaron Spencer was involved in radar-related research with the Raytheon Company. It's said Dr. Spencer walked past a magnetron vacuum tube being tested and a candy bar in his pocket melted. During the next several days he experimented with popcorn kernels that popped and an egg that exploded fully cooked.

Spencer was left, not with egg on his face, but with a brilliant idea: If microwaves can melt candy bars, pop corn and explode eggs from within, can it cook other foodstuff?

And as they say, the rest is history.

In 1947, the first commercial microwave oven hit the market weighing fifty-pounds and costing five thousand dollars. The food industry, restaurants and vending companies recognized the potential of serving fresher food with less waste equaling money saved. Other industries found endless uses—drying ceramics, paper, tobacco, flowers, etc.

First called the "Radarange," twenty-five to thirty years later, microwave ovens were on the way to becoming a household appliance as common as the toaster. By 1976, they were in 52-million American kitchens. I bought mine in 1975.

As an aside, Dr. Spencer was inducted into the National Inventors Hall of Fame Sept. 18, 1999.

All that said, as I started complaining about barely being able to find Made in America products in America, sometimes I find myself thinking we're dismantling progress instead of making it. And it has everything to do with losing our American Pride. When first introduced, not all dishware was microwave safe. By the time it would be an oddity not to have a microwave oven dishes, plates, cookware, all became microwave safe.

I have enough dishes to last several families a couple more lifetimes, but despite this overabundance of everything from fine china and everyday stuff to packages of paper plates, I'm occasionally compelled to buy something just because it's red.

My kitchen is red.

Recently, when I saw some really pretty dishes in just the right shade of red in some sort of melamine, I bought a couple place settings. I'm of the opinion mealtime should be relaxing and enjoyable. Eating from a pretty plate—even if I've got my nose buried in a book the whole time—gives a certain ambiance. It's sad enough to eat alone night after night, to counteract I almost always sit at the table with my meal served on something pretty even though it creates dishes to wash. Which leaves us asking the age-old question: if birds have little birds and fishes have little fishes, why oh why can't sinks have little sinks instead of dirty dishes?

The point is, before you buy new plates and saucers no matter how pretty they are, don't wait until you get home to peel off the price code label that is stuck smack-dab in the center covering vital information. Peek under that label before you leave the store.

Read carefully. You glance and see the words "Microwave Safe" and stick it in your basket but if it's made in China, read again. Don't miss the definitive word "Not."

If you're never going to use your new dishes in the microwave, fine. Otherwise, beware. Since so many of the dishes on the store shelves aren't "Made in the USA" mostly they read: "Not Microwave Safe."

Would they melt or just leak melamine into your food—the stuff that killed thousands of cats and dogs when added to pet food a few years ago after having been imported from China? On top of that, many recommend "Dishwasher Safe: Top Shelf Only."

Is this regressing? I think so. Maybe America needs to rethink its importing of everything for the sake of a dollar

But whatever sells. That's all that matters to the seller it would seem. Free enterprise, entrepreneurship or capitalism. Call it what you will, but be aware of the consequences. And if the seller can convince the American buyer, they're happy, who cares about the long-term affect? It's all about the short-term get it while the getting's good attitude. Truth in advertising and quality doesn't have to enter into the equation.

Anyway, all that having been said, besides real Chesapeake Bay Blue Crabs instead of crustaceans wild caught off foreign shores, I crave hotdogs on a bun with mustard, onions and sweet pickle relish and absolutely no chili whatsoever— just like I used to eat at the ballpark. Even though I fix my hotdog with the right ingredients, ever since the Colts left Baltimore, hotdogs don't taste the same.

I crave Italian Cream Cake and homemade custard pies but I'm too lazy to bake either very often although I do bake homemade almond biscotti's at least once a month. And I will note here that one time I decided to melt my butter instead of creaming it. This doesn't work. Take my word for it.

You melt the butter instead of manually creaming it, then the mixture, while warm, is too runny. To correct this, I added more flour than the recipe called for. Then, as a result of too much flour, the cookies were too flaky and biscotti's aren't supposed to be flaky. When I sliced and turned them out to be returned to the oven for additional baking, they were falling apart. Yikes!

Oh, they still ate good, but they weren't typical biscotti's, that I can tell you.

Additionally, I crave homemade vanilla pudding. That's about the only craving I can handle without a backlash of sadness or because I'm too lethargic most of the time. Homemade vanilla pudding is easily

41 / Edibility Depends Upon the Degree of Scorching

prepared in the microwave yet I seldom have sufficient milk on hand.

When you're just one person, you find milk is the biggest waste of money. Unless you've got a large box of cereal and plan to eat cereal every single day several times a day for the next couple days, milk sours practically overnight. I don't care what the date stamp reads, it won't keep. I've never emptied the last drop into a cereal bowl, or even a dog's bowl—because by the time I'm part way down to the bottom of the container, it's foul.

My friend Rose said organic milk lasts longer but the couple grocery stores I have access to don't carry anything but the largest size. I do buy small sized cartons of milk when I buy milk and that's a better solution—at least not so much curdled milk is getting poured down the drain in cottage cheese-like clumps coupled with that sour-milk odor that will knock you socks off. But, then, by the time I get the urge to prepare cooked pudding or a custard pie, there's not enough left in the tiny carton.

I need to get coordinated.

You see, another problem is that I live twenty-five, thirty-miles from the nearest grocery store. I've learned over the years to plan somewhat ahead. I keep a running list posted on my fridge because there is no jumping in the car and running to the store at the drop of a hat. Between the high cost of gasoline and the wear and tear on the vehicle plus the high cost and wear and tear on my old geezer gal body—the draining of energy—I shop for large supplies at a time. Thus, milk is just not one of those plan-ahead products because of its propensity toward fast spoilage.

Anyway, I whipped up meatloaf and potato salad and called Chuck to say, "I'm cooking." The pets were getting pretty excited. They were accustomed to my sticking mini containers in the microwave, but they were observing some wholehearted kitchen maneuvers in the making.

I decided to do a can of *Original Seasoned with Bacon & Brown Sugar Baked Beans* made from an old secret recipe passed down and so closely guarded by generations of family members that even the dog will not tell it.

There are two recommended ways to heat these magnificent beans: microwave or stovetop. Because I was feeling like Susie-Homemaker, I bypassed the microwave and dumped the can into a pan, turned on the burner, and left the kitchen. Which is okay to do when you're using the microwave, but not so smart when you have a pan on the burner.

Edibility depends upon the degree of scorching. I managed to save the pan with elbow grease, Ajax and a Brillo pad. Well, a couple Brillo pads, actually.

So, while char-flavored baked beans is reminiscent of cooking outdoors over a wood fire, that ought to do me for awhile. When you almost burn the house down cooking canned baked beans, it's time to move back to TV dinners and the microwave. Even the dogs refused to eat the burned beans.

By the way, despite Rosie's Pavlov style behavior, her several neurosis that would fill a dog psychologist's calendar for years to come, and despite her constant begging for food using the barely-able-to-contain-herself, bouncing-her-long-low-self up-and-down and back-and-forth (aka the Doxie Dance) while staring at me with pleading written all over her beautiful face, and after I run out of tidbits to share I'll say "That's all" and she will walk away contented that she has solicited from me every last morsel available.

Her comprehension of whole sentences spoken in ordinary conversational tones amazes me. Ingrained, I find I still have old fashioned ideas that dogs understand only one word commands; when by now I should know they know what I'm saying at all times. The fact is they know but only chose to react to that which most appeals.

So far, except for dog biscuits BooCat isn't interested in dog chow. And except for cream cheese, she fancies no more than a sniff of people food, preferring dried cat food best. TacoBelle and Rosie don't care if I cook healthy or not. TacoBelle, Rosie and I already did the hale-and-hearty diet thing. Now we're old enough to be junk food junkies. Rosie is the youngest, discounting BooCat of course, and even she feels entitled. We've earned the right to eat what and when we want.

Also, although we don't know what it was exactly, we know we miss transfat. In the name of eating healthy, they took it out of everything. Including popcorn. Buttered popcorn that doesn't get your fingers greasy is just wrong.

Just How Contagious is Yawning?

42

> "Which is more beautiful, feline movement or feline stillness?"
> (Elizabeth Hamilton)

Is there somebody out there willing to award me a grant so I can study why cats hang upside down? Why they like to sit way high up? Why the edge of the bed, a dangerous precipice, makes them feel alive and well and happy while their heads hang low and one false move would have them testing the landing-on-all-fours theory? There are government funds spent on a lot more goofy studies than why cats choose to live on the brink, as it were. Sign me up.

I read about a study testing the art of yawning on man's best friend. Don't even ask me why such a test would be conducted. It ranks up there with a bunch of other stupid tests somebody is bilking somebody else out of, getting paid big bucks to conduct, in my humble opinion.

But what the hey. I've got a pack of furry friends, so I decided I'd do my own yawn test free of charge.

The word "yawn" is derived from Old English meaning "a reflex of simultaneous inhalation of air and stretching of the eardrums, followed by exhalation of breath," according to Wikipedia. And I didn't even need to conduct a study to learn that tidbit.

An empathizing thing, it had long been agreed yawning is contagious, which is where the doggie yawning study comes in. Because of my penchant for learning, I decided to delve into the cause of yawning. Fifty years ago, everybody declared yawning was induced by lack of oxygen. It was undeniable. An undisputed fact.

Now they say the theory that lack of oxygen is responsible for uncontrollable yawning hasn't been scientifically substantiated. This totally blows a lifetime tidbit of knowledge right out of the trivia section of my brain.

How do you think that makes me feel? I've been around so long I've learned and unlearned so much stuff it makes my head spin.

Take coffee. It's good for you. No, it's bad. Okay, now it's good again. Same thing with eggs. One a day is on the old fashioned seven basic food groups. Then it was found one a day was not so good. Cholesterol came into the picture. Bad cholesterol of course. Because there is good cholesterol also.

I've seen televisions go from one channel that went off the air at night followed by a test pattern, to several networks and a bunch of channels all for free, to the new digital television eliminating free-antenna TV. It goes forward from good to great to bah-humbug backward.

And so, down through my long lifetime there has been one announcement after another contradicting what I thought I knew but didn't. Yawning facts is a prime example.

You know who the *they* are that keep changing everything around, right? They are the authorities on every subject under the sun, referenced more than any other source and therefore considered indisputable. I mean, how do you dispute an anonymous they? I've been quoting they say all my life.

Anyway, lately they say nervousness or stress has been speculated as a reason for yawning. I don't yawn when I'm nervous or stressed. I do yawn when I'm sleepy. Therefore, I still believe yawning is related to being tired, sleepy, and occasionally bored.

In 2007, researchers from the University of Albany suggested yawning might be a means to keep the brain cool. Say what?

Does this mean that people who yawn are hot-heads? Or does that theory mean in my case, my brain overheats when I'm sleepy since that's when I yawn most?

Another theory is that we yawn to stabilize pressure on either side of the ear drums. Does that mean getting sleepy makes my eardrums destabilize? I have Meniere's Disease and Tinnitus. Could something so simple as yawning be a future treatment for these debilitating diseases? For something so natural, yawning sure is confounding.

Non-human yawning isn't new. Snakes, for example, according to scientific snake doctors, yawn after a meal to realign their jaws, and to expand the trachea for respiratory reasons.

For whatever reason, BooCat, and in fact all cats, tend to yawn all the time. She also catnaps a lot. And purrs. And she doesn't believe the old adage that you must cover your mouth when you yawn or your soul will escape. Neither do I. I cover my mouth if I yawn in public out of politeness because nobody wants to peer down my throat. And I don't want anybody peering either. Not unless I'm saying "Ah" for my Doc.

BooCat is far smarter than those researchers.

In this dog versus yawning study, the University of London proposed that the contagiousness of human yawns passes onto dogs, indicating our pampered pups have the capacity for a basic level of empathy.

Like duh! Anybody who has a dog knows they are stuffed full of empathy. Fuller than most folks I know. Here's what we have: a bunch of brainiacs who haven't much common sense and never owned a furry pet in their lives so they haven't a clue, yet they come along and want to make statements of facts like they've just discovered the origin of fire.

The analysis observed that seventy-two percent of the dogs studied yawned when a human yawned in front of them. The study revealed twenty-one out of twenty-nine dogs immediately yawned also but it *had* to be a genuine yawn or those doggies in the window were having none of it.

I decided to try this contagious yawning theory on my pooches. I woke Rosie up to get her attention but before I could yawn, she yawned. So, of course I yawned. Then she yawned. And so did I. Yikes! We were having a yawn-fest.

Give Rosie a silver star.

I moved onto TacoBelle. I looked her straight in the eye and yawned nosily. Eerily human in every way, she looked back at me like she thought I'd lost my ever-loving mind. She continued to hold my gaze long after I turned away embarrassed for attempting to engage her in something so silly as a yawn test.

My domestic dogs don't make good Guinea Pigs, which incidentally, yawn in a display of dominance or anger, bearing their impressive incisor teeth, often accompanied by teeth chattering, purring and scent making. Ah, but Guinea Pig yawning is a whole different useless study.

By the way, while BooCat yawns often, she doesn't do it on cue. And George and SnowBird don't do it at all.

The Mockingbird

43

"A cat is a puzzle for which there is no solution." (Hazel Nicholson)

The state bird for Louisiana is the brown pelican, which is fine for southern Louisiana (or it was prior to the BP Oil Spew). If ever a state considered being divided into north and south, it should be Louisiana. The cultures are quite different from one end of the state to the other. If we ever did divide, I'd propose the mockingbird be our North Louisiana state bird. After all, we don't have brown pelicans up around these parts, but we do have mockingbirds. In fact, the mocking bird serves as state bird for Florida, Texas, Mississippi, Arkansas, and Tennessee. It's also the mascot of the University of Tennessee at Chattanooga.

My other choice would be the Wild Turkey, which would probably make the hunters jump for joy, but would break my heart. But, surely if it were the state bird, it would become off limits to hunters. No more turkey season. How cool would that be?

I've been collecting Wild Turkey stamps since they were first printed, similar to the Duck Stamps. I've amassed sixty-three different wild turkey stamps contained in three large frames, just ordered a new frame and a half-dozen more different and varied wild turkey stamps.

I actually wondered if I ought to continue my collection. It started in 1970-something, so it has taken forty years to fill three frames; will I live long enough to fill another? At the last minute, I decided to think positively and I ordered it.

I believe it was Thomas Jefferson who originally suggested the Wild Turkey as the official bird of the United States; but the Eagle won out.

Realistically, although they didn't always, mockingbirds now reside in almost every part of the United States. Even though the mocker isn't colorful, its singing makes up for anything it might lack in brightness. Colorful or not, it's a striking bird. Its plumage is medium-gray on the upperparts with a pale breast and belly with prominent white wing patches, and white edges to its long tail, which are especially visible in flight. Legs and bills are black.

Both male and female mockingbirds are identical in color and juveniles are light brown with a speckled breast. The similar Loggerhead Shrikes and mockers are sometimes confused at first sight. The shrike shows more contrast in its plumage and has a black eye mask, or stripe.

The mockingbird got its name honestly. Using its rich, warbling voice, these songsters mock the songs of other birds. Around here, where there are no Nightingales to listen to, the mockingbird will do just fine, thank you very much. They sing at night when the moon is bright. And they sing with style.

It has been noted that mockingbirds, both male and female—because both sing equally—tend to repeat each phrase three times before moving on to another. The mockingbird will not only mock other birds, it imitates the croaking of toads and frogs, barking dogs, squeaky wheels and rusty hinges. It has even been known to copy the sounds of a piano being played.

George E. Tiel, my pet cockatiel mimics TacoBelle's bark along with a mixture of human sentences and words, and also mimics the songs of wild birds, including the resident mockingbirds. George whistles a most beautiful rendition of something I call "The Mockingbird Aria."

The mockingbird's official call, when not singing its copycat Mockingbird Aria, or mimicking all surrounding noises, is a sharp *chack* or *chair*.

There is the song "Mocking Bird Hill" and in Harper Lee's book

43 / The Mockingbird

To Kill a Mocking Bird she says it's a sin to kill one. It's a popular bird.

Courtship is a springtime event and the male mockingbird sings around the clock, usually from a very high perch. In my yard I see and hear him sitting atop the couple of utility poles providing electricity and nightlights to my house. I have to chuckle at his clownish antics; jumping up in the air and waving his wings.

Once he attracts the attention of a female, together they construct their nest in the shape of a large bulky cup with twigs, leaves and grass, lined with such material as rootlets, animal hair and moss. By and large, they are built low in shrubs or thickets.

Commonly, the female mockingbird lays three or four eggs and she incubates them for about two weeks. Both parents feed the babies for twelve days when they fledge. They continue to feed them for approximately two more weeks, giving them time to learn to fend for themselves. There's nothing sadder than to find a baby bird that's fallen from its nest before time to fly, and doesn't survive.

BooCat practically drools when she sees the mockers outside her favorite window. Of course she drools when she sees the sparrows too. She drools when she sees any and every bird. Written all over her, there is not much she would enjoy more than setting up camp out under the Grancy Greybeard tree where a half dozen bird feeders hang. It would be like going out to supper at Popeye's Fried Chicken. Popeye's advertises its bona fide New Orleans style fried chicken and BooCat would likely find the bird feeders a bona fide four-and-twenty blackbirds baked in a pie type cafe—very much to her liking.

One mocking bird that lived in my yard for a very long time could have been the poster bird for the state of North Louisiana. Except for its injured foot, he was quite special. Except for the injured foot, he was otherwise intact. I referred to my resident mockingbird as a he, although mockingbirds are one of the few birds that can't be distinguished by color. Both male and female are like colored.

What made my bird special? He ate dog food with my outdoor dogs. From his own dog food bowl. I've grown used to the mourning doves and even the sparrows sharing dog food with the dogs. But this has been the only mocker to ever do so.

Mockingbirds, fairly large, range between nine and eleven inches long, are year-round residents. They are non-migrating. No other bird possesses all the musical qualities of the mockingbird. He mimics the songs of other birds, often singing them even better than the originals. My humble opinion of course.

Mockingbirds are very territorial, aggressively protecting their terrain against other birds, animals and even humans if they get too close. They are especially defensive of their nests, defending them by pecking and flapping their wings. These aggressive attack generally cease when the young birds have flown.

Mostly polygamous, males have been known to attack their own reflection in a window or mirror, intending to chase away an apparent suitor it perceives to be moving into its territory. I saw this happen when one mocker caught sight of itself in a security mirror on my patio. He went hog wild. No, I'll rephrase that and say he went mockingbird wild. He wanted to do damage to the mockingbird in the mirror, and would probably have hurt himself in the attempt had I not intervened by stepping outside to distract him.

But, while my new best bird friend lived here, he didn't mind sharing his territory with the dogs. To do so allowed him free meals with little or no effort involved.

Normally, mockingbirds eat a long list of foodstuff including insects such as beetles, ants, bees, wasps, butterflies, earthworms, spiders, snails and grasshoppers, crustaceans and small lizards. A mainstay of their diet in winter is often multiform rosehips. Preferring to feed in short-grass areas with shrubby edges, when the mocker raises its wings while fluttering close to the ground, it is usually done to flush out prey.

They are fond of both wild and cultivated fruits and berries, especially in winter. Mockingbirds aren't regular visitors to birdfeeders. Being very territorial, it's usually just as well that they don't depend on birdfeeders. Were that the case, they'd likely defend the feeders from other birds that also need winter food. If your yard has a hungry mocker that does prefer feeding from a birdfeeder, the best way to avoid a problem is to hang several feeders in different parts of the yard. In this way, a territorial mocker can't see and defend them all at once and more than likely, this solution would allow all the little birdies to enjoy winter feedings.

Because pickings are slim during the winter, electing to provide food for mockingbirds is a good thing. They can be enticed by certain

43 / The Mockingbird

foodstuff. Not a part of their standard staple diet, but enjoyed once they discover their availability are raisins, apples, suet, peanut butter and even pieces of baked goods like donuts.

And while these offerings should attract mockers to the yard and help with their winter meals, bear in mind, dog food isn't on their normal list of foodstuff.

I would go out each morning and fill his bowl first. As I filled the dog's bowls only a few feet away, he'd fly over and begin eating. My presence didn't frighten him whatsoever. The dogs and bird got along fine too.

One Sunday morning I went out to feed everybody and didn't see him. He was such a constant presence, I immediately missed him. Then I spied him basking in the sun, perched on the bottom step of Chuck's camper trailer. He was fluffed up and settled down comfortably with a beam of sunlight falling on his feathers. I wish I had thought to snap a photo because it was such an unusual sight. I rarely ever see birds relaxing at ground level. It made me smile.

Mockingbirds mate for life. I've no idea what happened to his mate. He spent that winter all alone—just him and the dogs. I assumed he was one of the same mocking birds that lived in my yard for a number of years; they're long-lived and once take up residence, stay year round.

I hoped perhaps a mate would find her way to the yard that next spring. But, one day he was gone. There are other mockers living in the yard. I would like to think he's one of them, that his foot healed.

But I doubt it. None of the mockingbirds living in the yard eat dog food. If he were still here, he'd still be sharing his meals. Whether his injured foot made him susceptible to a mishap, I don't know. I just know, my mocker flew the coop and I miss him.

We cannot rescue all the wild things, but it does no harm to rescue what we can and to wish we could rescue the rest.

Laptops and LAP Dogs

"I'm Putty in BooCat's Paws." (Barbara Sharik)

You might think your lap is your own, but not if you are a pet owner.

It was a dream come true; a laptop computer for Mother's Day from Theresa and Carla a couple years ago. The laptop, yes, but I'm also talking about Theresa. She is the most perfect daughter ever. Her personality is one that warmly touches everybody she meets, brightening their lives for having been around her. And mine most especially.

I had wanted a laptop for a long time so I could type my columns anytime, anywhere. I visualized myself relaxing on the patio, typing away when one of my kooky ideas strikes. Or sitting propped in bed late at night, because some of my best ideas come during the midnight hour.

I've always kept a pad and pen beside my pillow. I learned the hard way that if I don't stop and write it down, come morning it will be forgotten even if I had tried to burn it in my sleepy brain. I've had whole column ideas come to me at night. It's a prime idea time. So, a laptop's a good thing.

When time came to try it out, it was too early for bed and too dark for the patio. That meant the living room in my favorite chair.

44 / Laptops and LAP Dogs

I'll always remember the moment like it was yesterday. I settled in comfortably, laptop where it belonged—in my lap.

The thing is, anytime I make a lap Rosie and TacoBelle vie for the alpha position. What a rude awakening when Rosie leaped up, only to be confronted with this strange electronic gizmo in *her* lap.

Tacobelle jumped into the same problem. Except she got high up enough onto my lap to type the words: *"jmk" "edsw."* Those being the keys her two front paws landed on before she did an Olympic-worthy twist in midair.

I had a two-dog lap only, with not enough room for Hershey the cat. At least not simultaneously. Hershey was used to snoozing on the arm of the chair. Therefore, he was curious—he's a cat after all—but not perturbed.

There are doggie beds on the living room floor, but Taco and Rosie only climb into them as a last resort. Like when I'm lapless and in an upright position singing Karaoke to them. Some nights before we go to the real bed, I sing them a couple songs. If you don't think dogs can understand what you're saying to them, think again. They were—and still are—my best audience. They don't boo. (Even now, BooCat doesn't boo either despite her name). They don't jeer. They don't care that I carry my tune in a bucket. They wag their tails and are most tolerant.

They are my biggest fans. Well, actually, they're my only fans, but who's keeping track?

But back to the lap problem. How was I supposed to concentrate on a column when I had two dogs sitting at my feet with hang-dog faces and doggie-tears in their eyes? They were sending subliminal messages—something like: *Mom always lets us sit in her lap; what's this peculiar plastic thing?*

I could see wheels turning in TacoBelle's head, trying to determine if Mom had brought home another pet. She had to adjust to Hershey and she had to teach Rosie the rules when she came to us. But this new thing filling what she considered her private lap appeared a whole different animal. She wasn't a happy biscuit eater.

We must make concessions in our lives. I felt one coming on. It's just possible my laptop wouldn't get used in my lap. I realized I had to concede that Rosie and Taco have squatter's rights and I'd have to do my laptopping at the desk or tabletop instead.

I knew I was going to love my laptop, but I also knew that some things are sacred and it looked like my lap was already spoken for by the fuzzy girls.

And so, I closed up the laptop and set it aside. Then I invited, "Come on, girls. Jump up."

You've never seen two happier pups. Rosie sighed and Taco gave me one of her looks, like, *Who did you think you were kidding, setting that thing in my lap in the first place?*

She was right. Who did I think I was kidding? And now we add BooCat to the lap brigade.

The Cheerful Chihuahua

"Every dog is entitled to one bite, every cat to one scratch."
(Unknown Origin)

Taking a bird's-eye-view, if you'll pardon the pun, at the yard that BooCat, TacoBelle and RosaLee are allowed only to gaze upon from within safe confines, makes a happy home for the outside dogs. TacoBelle used to go outside until she snarled at a larger dog one time too many. Since then, she's not allowed. The results of two different confrontations with larger dogs—otherwise friendly dogs—were three emergency life-saving surgeries, one that included the insertion of a drain tube. When you're four-five pounds and you get in the face, snarling and barking, of several fifty pound dogs, one snap is all it takes to shut you up. And caused a life-threatening event.

Like the rest of America, I saw the Taco Bell commercials featuring that adorable talking Chihuahua and I wanted one. Obviously, I couldn't find one that talked, but the one I got makes herself plainly understood. Adorable, and with ears bigger than any other part of her, I named her TacoBelle. Jon used to call her Tock-Ears.

TacoBelle is supposed to be a purebred Chihuahua, but actually, she's mixed. She's part-human. She communicates with me as no other dog ever has. Her expressions alone convey messages. The tone of her bark is distinct for each different thing she tells me. Occasionally she becomes obviously frustrated that I can't understand what she's telling me. My bad. She knows what she means, why don't I?

When her feelings have been hurt, I've seen her look at me with the most heartrending expression, turn and walk away. No amount of calling brings her back until she's forgiven the pain that something I said or did caused. I've never seen tears fall, but I can always tell when her heart's broken. Probably the only reason I've not seen actual tears is because big girls don't cry and she's the biggest five-pound girl I know.

She entered a household already inhabited by two Himalayan cats, Hershey and Sterling. Even after TacoBelle grew up, the cats were still larger than she was, but fur flew as they leaped off the bed at the sound of her growl from beneath the covers. She had gotten tired of being walked on and learned a throaty growl meant her bluff was in.

From this experience, I believe she learned the power of toughness. As one little kid put it, "She's little, but she's tough."

Indeed, she goes into Rottweiler mode when she feels threatened. Many an unsuspecting individual sees her as tiny, sweet and innocent. They will reach to pet her, only to come close to drawing back a nub. Taco's method of operation is to allow them to get close and then, like a mousetrap, bam! She snaps. She never makes connection, but she makes her point.

This bravado as I mentioned, got her in trouble twice with larger dogs resulting in emergency trips to Dr. White's office so that she is no longer allowed to go outside around big dogs; She never learned their teeth are bigger than her teeth. She sees herself as Cujo and she's not.

Never leave a roll of toilet paper within her reach. She's been known to decorate the bathroom with the skill of a Halloween trickster. She can also shred a tissue or napkin in under ten seconds flat. It takes me a lot longer than that to pick up all the pieces. While she knows no human-taught tricks she has a bag of her own.

And bossy! She is definitely mistress of the household. She lets me wait on her hand and foot. In fact, she insists upon it. Very vocal, she lets me know when she's hungry and wants what's on my plate. Or she might be in my lap playing with a doggie toy and if it falls to the floor, she leans over, spots its location, turns back and paws at my

45 / The Cheerful Chihuahua

hand, urging me to pick it up for her. She does not identify with Pavlov's pup at all. She has a mind of her own. And she uses it.

And bedtime. All her life she has been adamant about bedtime. When she's ready for bed, I best be heading in that direction alongside her. She's a haughty bundle of attitude. She comes to me, stands on her hind legs and paws at my arm, barking. I understand exactly what she's barking.

"Come to bed. Now!"

I can tell her wait a minute, and it falls on deaf tock-ears. She does not stop ordering me around until I start following those orders.

She pushes my buttons.

Then, the opposite extreme, she can snuggle and be the perfect lapdog. Discounting her licks of love. They drive me nuts. Doggie kisses. For twelve years I've tried to teach her not to lick me. But like a metronome, when her tail's wagging, her tongue's licking.

Maybe I've just used the wrong approach. Maybe instead of trying to teach her human-to-dog, I need to reason with her person-to-person. Rosie may be a canine. BooCat may be a feline. But I'd be willing to wager money TacoBelle doesn't see herself as either. She's a mini-me.

Once Taco gets to know someone, their lap becomes her private property. But woe is me and thee before she decides whether a visitor is friend or foe. She'll bark. That's the other thing I've been unable to teach her. "Hush" isn't in her vocabulary. She knows "bed" and she knows "kiss," but she doesn't know "hush."

When Rosie joined the family, she wanted to lie on the bed, chew toys and play at night, but Taco would have none of it. Being in bed meant sleeping not playing. She snarled at Rosie, setting the Alpha thing straight. Rosie still treads lightly around TacoBelle even though they've been together eight years. The little kid was right. Taco is little and she is tough.

In reality, TacoBelle emits an emotional humanness that's uncanny. Big, moist expressive eyes speak volumes when she turns them on me, stares, then walks away if I've hurt her feelings. And likewise, on the other extreme, if I've made her happy, the love within her eyes is overwhelming. Her emotions are exuberant and very evident.

All in all, I'm lucky TacoBelle lets me live with her because she's actually the best bad dog that's ever owned me. She has a lot of favorite pastimes including sitting outside on the screened-in patio and bird watching with me. Unlike BooCat, she's not drooling over the birds, but I bet she would enjoy a good chase.

One of the oldest breeds native to the Americas, the Chihuahua can be traced back to the early Olmec, Toltec and Aztecs of Central America and Mexico. There are carvings depicting these dogs from the ninth century A.D.

Actually, historians say Chichi's were originally raised as a delicacy, enjoyed by nobility. Chichi on a stick. Not funny. Even after the Aztecs conquered the Toltecs, the little dog served as a source of food, of hair and as a beast of burden according to some sources. There was a time they were even used as sacrificial offerings. Not a good way to fill out the family tree. It's a wonder the breed survived at all, considering.

Regarding the future of the little dogs, when Hernando Cortez came along in the 1500s and plundered the Aztecs, apparently they managed to escape to the Mexican countryside where they evidently scavenged enough to keep them alive. Surviving much like any other wild canine, it's speculated they probably ate birds, reptiles, rodents and even insects.

More than three hundred years later the Chihuahua as we know it, came to be recognized as something more than meat and a sacrificial object. In the late 1930s and early 1940s, when the rumba dancer Xavier Cugat appeared with his little dogs in movies and on TV, these little pups caught the public eye.

Chihuahuas, the smallest of the toy breeds, have unique personalities and are quite the little characters. TacoBelle radiates personality plus.

She's also quite economical. She hardly eats enough to notice; except over the years, she's gotten a lit more picky than she needs to be. She wants more of what I'm eating, and less of what I dump in her bowl. Ah, but not to worry, Rosie will eat what's in Taco's bowl and what I have also. Even if TacoBelle turns her nose up at something, it won't go to waste.

Chihuahuas have good points, and of course some not so good. Besides not eating much, because they're tiny they don't take up much space and don't need much in the way of grooming. Being little, they're perfect apartment dwellers and don't require a lot of exercise.

Drawbacks include not being known as effective protective dogs.

They've got a lot of heart but not much in the way of physical prowess. Although they might alert their owner of an intruder, they can do little more than snap, snarl and bark defensively Likely it'll only make the intruder laugh his fool head off.

They're considered by some to be yappy little dogs, but unlike certain other breeds, Chihuahua people don't deem them as such. The only time TacoBelle yaps is when somebody she doesn't know comes to visit. Then, yes, she can be yappy. To the point of annoyance. She has a keen sense of hearing and warns me of the approach of a stranger or of an unusual sound. Must be the big ears.

That is, she does unless she's sound asleep. In that case the only thing that wakes her is when BooCat walks on her. And in that case, she wakes up snapping and snarling. BooCat leaps off the little dog, gives herself a shake and continues on her path as though to say, "Sorry, I didn't see you." And likely, she didn't. TacoBelle, like her sister Rosie, sleeps beneath the covers.

In between, Taco is very quiet. Unless of course she's relating some important fact to me. Like that it's bedtime or she's hungry or there's a big dog out in the yard.

Chichi's aren't good hiking dogs; they're too tiny to keep up for very long, although they have plenty of heart. That's not to say they don't want to go with you when you go to the state park into the great wild blue yonder. TacoBelle loved going camping with Jon and I. She, like all Chihuahuas, loved the warmth of the sun and would spend hours basking. But if we went for a very long walk, she preferred to make the trip in our arms.

On the downside, according to Chihuahua authorities, they have been known to get underfoot and trip people, which will never happen with TacoBelle. She came with built-in radar in the name of her own self-preservation. She's never gotten underfoot. Discounting being bitten by a couple different outside dogs on a couple different occasions when she got in their faces, thereby revoking her outside privileges altogether, she's stayed safe.

Chihuahuas are also susceptible to cold weather. There are also several medical conditions peculiar to the breed. Still and all, they are very intelligent little things and are very attentive and seem always willing to please.

Of course, in Taco's case, she's so spoiled she expects me to please her more than she expects to please me. But it works out. We've got a mutual admiration thing going on. She's rather independent and isn't a neurotic lap dog. She's bossy, but she's good company. Not to mention, TacoBelle can anticipate my moods and feelings. She's happy when I'm happy and I believe she can even sense my grief. She's an excellent companion—better than some husbands I've had.

Naturally, because they're small, Chichi's can easily become injured from a variety of happenstances—larger dogs as happened to TacoBelle twice—rowdy children, falling objects, wild animals and even hawks and birds of prey.

I read a startling news account of a falcon dipping down from the sky and in mid-flight, grasped a tiny Chihuahua with its talons, lifted the tiny canine up and up and almost away. Fortunately, the dog was on a leash with its master because they were walking in a park. The owner was able to pull the dog from the bird's grasp. It was injured but not killed. With the hawks circling overhead dining on field mice and keeping an eye on Chuck's chickens, how safe would little tiny Taco be if she were allowed to wander alone outside? I shudder to think.

On this same subject, I digress momentarily remembering that not only Chihuahua's are in danger from raptors. A distressing story released in 1998 about how singer and actress "I Got You, Babe" Cher lost a beloved tabby cat. Her kitty was snatched up and carried off by a huge owl.

According to eye-witnesses, one of Cher's cats, frightened in a thunder storm, ran off and was seen being scooped up clutched in an owl's talons. These large owls feed on rabbits and other cat-sized mammals, so theoretically, the possibility of this occurring, rare as it sounds, might be more commonplace than we realize. Another reason to keep cats in the house. And Chihuahuas also.

Cheap Chihuahuas For Sale

46

"Another dog day afternoon." (Slang Expression)

Speaking of Chihuahuas, and how I simply had to have one because I was emotionally moved by the Taco Bell commercial dog hero, reminds me how, around Christmas of 2008, it was a "here we go again" moment.

Puppy dog impulse buying was on the rise. It came with the popularity of box office hit, *Beverly Hills Chihuahua*. At that time, animal rescuers expected every kid seeing that movie was going to beg mom and dad for a Chihuahua for Christmas, pretty please.

It happened after *101 Dalmatians*. People didn't do their homework; they rushed out and bought adorable spotted firehouse dogs. Had they researched the breed, they would have learned Dalmatians are not apartment dwellers; they're full of energy requiring lots of exercise and training. The result was that Dalmatians galore wound up abandoned in shelters, and way too many had to be euthanized.

Remember the movie *Snow Dog*? Same thing with Siberian Huskies. After this movie hit the theaters impulse buying equaling homeless dogs. Beautiful dogs, but not the perfect pet without perfect training. This isn't new. There were loads of Lassie and Rin-Tin-Tin mid-century pet purchases too.

Collies, because of Lassie, held the trophy for being the most popular breed for a number of years. No one considered the Lassie of movie and TV fame was not just one dog. There were a number of Lassie's, each with their own specialties, making up one super hero dog. While the movie dog sat around in little Timmy's kitchen just awaiting the next crisis, in reality, a collie needs plenty of exercise and a lot of space and being penned up isn't the ideal situation to find itself in, while some frustrated kid says "Sit" and "Shake" over and over.

Chihuahuas were first over-bred at horrible puppy mills that should be banned universally and overbought by folks who fell in love with the petite talking Chichi star of the advertising campaign for Taco Bell restaurants.

I've admitted I was guilty of getting emotional and believed it essential to have a Chihuahua of my very own during the height of that charming TV dog's popularity. I named her TacoBelle with an "e" in feminine recognition as the belle-of-the-ball. I've never regretted adding TacoBelle to my household but, I like to think I knew what I was doing; so many people do not.

Nearly eight-thousand Chihuahuas were available for adoption on petfinder.com even before the release of *Beverly Hills Chihuahua*. Imagine what happened when the rush of Chichi puppy buying wound down and people weren't so happy with their impulsively purchased pups. On the other hand, if everybody wanting a Chichi after viewing *Beverly Hill Chihuahua* would go to this website and adopt an abandoned dog, it wouldn't be so bad. In fact, it would fill two blanks and create a lovely whole.

Unfortunately, most will visit pet stores and want ads, believing they're contracting with reputable dealers, when in fact, often these sellers are churning out pups at puppy mills. Chihuahuas are perfect for this because of their diminutive size; they can be bred machine-like in tiny cages one season after another. There are so many causes we could take up, and stamping out puppy mills is one of them. They are a bona fide form of cruelty to animals.

Chihuahuas make first-rate pets. Exceptional companions, good in small spaces and perfect lap dogs if that's what you want. But, avoid overdoing the lap-princess thing so as not to create a neurotic roommate. Chichi's generally travel well. Extremely intelligent, fiercely loyal, they have personality-plus. On the other hand, they can be strong-willed and because they are tiny and delicate, they aren't an appropriate breed for young children. Children can be too rough. Also, remember, Chihuahuas are house dogs; they can't be tossed outside just because an owner lacks time or patience for proper potty training and expect to survive. They're dogs; they shed. They bark. They need companionship.

If you can resist impulse buying, have done your homework, are sure about what you want and you still want a new furry family member, check out your local humane society. Some of my best dogs started as abandoned, forgotten, neglected and mistreated. With a little love, most of these dogs can be rehabbed. The dog you adopt may not be a movie star, but you can bet it'll be a star at your house come Christmas morn.

A year after the release of *Beverly Hills Chihuahua*, December of 2009, I was listening to a radio broadcast on public radio. The segment reported there were hundreds of Chihuahuas in this particular shelter. Hundreds that needed homes. I couldn't help but wonder if some of these dogs were a result of having been thoughtlessly obtained during the puppy buying frenzy spurred by the Chihuahua movie of last December.

So many unwanted dogs; unbelievable, until you realize how often people react emotionally instead of doing their homework first. Hundreds of Chihuahuas alone at one shelter. Over eight-thousand nationwide through petfinder.com. The accumulation of abandoned and unwanted dogs is a crisis situation.

The radio commentator blamed a lot of the abandoned dogs on the economy. People cannot afford to buy dog food and pay veterinarian bills when thousands and thousands have lost their jobs all across the country. They have to feed their families first, and even a little dog like a Chihuahua has to go. It's about as sad a commentary as I've heard in a long time.

The state of the economy has reached such appalling proportions people are being forced to give up their pet companions because they lack funds to supply pet food due to lost jobs and repossessed homes which means going into a homeless shelter or staying with fiends with no pets allowed. How did we ever let the country get into this situation in this day and age? It all started going downhill during the last administration with official denying publicly that there was a problem looming on the horizon. Now the current president is about to stretch the bootstraps to bursting in an effort to pull everything back in place. That's a challenge when it's been allowed to go so far south for so long.

The Fun of Feeding Flocks and Bird Watching

47

"Dog proud—Say it loud!" (Cheer of Unknown Origin)

There have been several batches of baby wrens raised on my screened-in patio. When they're in evidence, the furry kids—aka as Fids—and I generally cool it until they fledge.

Many, many birds live here at Wit's End Comedy Club. Providing for the birds helps them survive the ever increasing hostilities they face. Besides, few things are as beautiful, as animated and as fascinating as birds. The presence of birds brightens a winter day. They are the color-wheel personified. Musicians of the air, birds sing because they have a song, bestowing year-round music. Birds are springtime. They are love.

In summer, bird families are reared and in winter, searching for food and shelter can become an around-the-clock activity. For generations young rapscallions pondered the promise of catching a bird by sprinkling salt on its tail. It's only after they grow up they realize what's meant by this promise—if a child can get close enough to sprinkle salt on a bird's tail, the salt's irrelevant.

I recall as a very young child, paging through a dictionary making a list of names of every feathered creature I came across from Albatross to Yellowthroat. Early eccentricity, it's a good thing dictionaries were thinner back then. If I'd had a book on birds, it would been less of a task, but realize, I was thumbing, page by page, every single page, word after word, every single word, paying strict attention to each definition in order to verify words referring to birds. It was a daunting task for a youngster, but along the way, I was exposed to many words I'd not have heard otherwise.

I've created a dog- and bird-house subdivision, and in its disordered state, my semi-wild yard is a perfect haven. Almost any bird that stops by can move right in. I don't do formal gardens but I've got bird houses, bird baths and feeders here, there and yonder, interspersed with lots of nest sites and natural habitat.

Plus the mere fact that most birds garner protein from devouring insects and spiders makes an enthusiastic selling point for inviting them to dinner in my yard. Imagine, insect eradication to the tune of cheerful chirping. Partnering doesn't get much better, nor much greener, than that. Keeping it natural in a most pleasant and positive manner. The unwritten contract is: you eat the bugs that would bite me and make me itch and I'll offer you a haven and supplement that insect diet.

My most delightful sighting two summers ago was a pair of Orchard Orioles. The female was a solid colored yellowish-olive-green and the male, not so bright as the famed Baltimore Oriole, was a rusty orange and black; in bird books called chestnut with a black hood. They spent hours gleaning the branches of my Lady Banksia rosebush.

The Orchard Oriole is the smallest of all the orioles. It's regarded as common in the southeast and Midwest, scarcer northward. Yet, this was the first pair I'd ever seen. They are reported to be most commonly seen in orchards (hence the name), on farmsteads and farmyards and along waterways. They are also noted to be found in gardens and yards with scattered trees.

The normal time of departure for males, heading for Central America, is early July. They migrate in segregated flocks. The females and fledglings trail along in late July, giving the fledglings a little more time to sturdy up for the flight. Often, it's time to migrate after having raised but a single brood. Not particularly attracted to feeders, insects are their favorite food. They also enjoy nectar and fruits; generally taking what's available.

47 / The Fun of Feeding Flocks and Bird Watching

There are always Loggerhead Shrikes hanging around the yard. At a glance, easily mistaken for the mockingbirds that also reside in the yard year-round, the shrikes are also known as *Butcher-birds.*

Upon closer examination, there are differences. The shrike's head is large and its hawk-like feeding habits differentiate it from the mocker.

Shrikes have this cold-blooded habit of impaling prey on thorns or barbed wire fences before carving them up for supper. A sure sign that a shrike is in the area would be finding impaled insects, small amphibians, reptiles, rodents, mammals and even small birds—all of which represent its miscellany prey. Shrikes lack the talons of a hawk, hence the use of the convenient thorns and barbed wire.

Once impaled, the rather interesting bird tears its prey apart with its sharp, toothed bill.

Like the mocker, shrikes are year-round residents in my yard. They like the open fields surrounding my house; perching on wires and fences and then swooping down for an attack. They love grasshoppers. I hate grasshoppers. This arrangement automatically makes us friends for life. It's also a plus that they are also fierce snake killers. There are about six thousand species of snakes in the US. Five-thousand nine-hundred-ninety-nine slither around in Louisiana; many in my yard.

There are always Red-Tailed and several other varieties of hawks hanging around the perimeter and outskirts of my yard, beating the little shrikes out of field mice, but seeing Mississippi Kites in flight in the adjoining farm fields is awe-inspiring. They are said to arrive in Louisiana in the middle of April in small parties of five or six. I haven't enjoyed watching any other bird in flight any more than I have these kites. They're graceful yet vigorous. They are aerial feeding specialists. They float on the air. They sail. They circle with ease, giving the impression of playfulness. And then suddenly, they swoop, wings folded, undulating in a shallow dive. They specialize in hunting insects, but discard the insect's exoskeleton, eating the rest.

This wild zig-zag pattern of flying reminds me very much of the flight pattern of a swallow—Barn Swallows and Purple Martins and even Chimney Swifts.

Only once did I see a flash of an Indigo Bunting at my feeding station last summer. The sun hit its feathers just right, and the amazing blue burned itself indelibly in my memory. Breathtaking is the only way to describe it. Perhaps, because they're common for this part of the country, I simply hadn't seen one in the right light before. They're said to appear all black against the light. Also, males change their blue feathers for brown in the autumn.

Unusual. We have an amazing solid blue bird that molts and turns brown in the autumn, then returns in the spring a beautiful indigo blue again. How confusing is that? I dream of seeing another in its full indigo blue dress.

In the *Louisiana Bird Watching* book, it's recommended to watch for them in autumn; but if they molt in autumn, that seems not such a good time to watch. The book also stated that in the spring they are most often first seen feasting on dandelion seeds. They are said to like millet mixes and they also like black-oil sunflower seeds.

And guess what? Black-oil sunflower seeds are the most expensive sunflower seeds for sale in the wild bird food section of the store. Wouldn't you know. Never less than a dollar a pound.

Seeing red-winged blackbird flocks move all during the day in large clouds of birds with flashes of red wings is totally awe-inspiring, yet, I'm guilty of becoming so accustomed to the red-winged blackbird in such ready abundance that it's almost made me lose my awe for their beauty.

Many do live around my homeplace and they're very striking and pleasant neighbors.

Sometimes when finding we're taking something for granted, we need to back up and reopen our eyes. Herons, cormorants and cattle egrets also have lost some of their incredible appeal simply because they are so available. Strange how we let the commonplace, even when it isn't all that common, bore us.

Last summer my Lady Banksia rose bush filled to capacity with Brown-headed Cowbirds, interspersed with various sparrows that

47 / The Fun of Feeding Flocks and Bird Watching

never leave. In fact there are so many sparrows living in the yard that every bush growing on my oasis are filled to capacity with a variety of the little birds. They fill bush after bush at roosting time, feed from the dog food bowls and like living at Wit's End as much as I do.

The Lady Banksia rose bush sits a few feet from BooCat's favorite viewing window. She spends hours sitting there in her private theater in the round bird watching.

In elementary school I first read about cowbirds and found them most intriguing. They lay their eggs in the nests of other, smaller birds, leaving their chicks to be raised by the unsuspecting adoptive parents.

The story is that cowbirds followed herds of buffalo roaming across the country, their main diet being the insects stirred up by the buffalo.

Because the buffalo were always on the move, the cowbirds didn't have time to build proper nests and hang around rearing their chicks. Therefore, they did what worked best for them. They deposited their eggs in other bird's nests and kept on truckin' with the buffalo. This lifelong habit is referred to as to parasitize. The downside is that cowbird chicks are generally larger than the nest-mates and often out-beg for the food being supplied.

Should a songbird recognize the cowbird egg for what it is, she'll either remove it or in some cases, build a new nest overtop of the offending egg.

The males hanging around in my large rose bush were shiny black with dark brown heads. The females were a dull grayish-brown. There were more females than males in the group that stopped by. I wondered if they'd taken time to lay eggs in the nests of the sparrows that are scattered about in my yard.

Woodpeckers live in my yard. In the early morning I repeatedly hear a rat-tat-tat only to find the redheaded and redbellied fellow sitting atop the creosoted utility pole. At first I was left thinking, hey, bird, that pole has been treated with creosote and likely, no bugs would have bored into it. Then because there's a night light attached, I thought perhaps bugs had accumulated overnight and were still hanging around, providing breakfast for the redheaded bird.

Next thought: Maybe the woodpecker was sending a message to his girlfriend with this drumming. The tom-tom-tom can be heard from one end of the yard to the other.

A family lived for many years in a hollow of one of my maple trees until a storm took down that dead section. Best I can determine one or more are residing in and around a live oak in the front yard. They have this tendency to move to the backside of a tree in the habit of squirrels, so I often only garner a glimpse at a time. Illusive, although I have managed to snap several photos of my resident bird.

They eat on hopper, platform and wire mesh feeders and fancy sunflower seeds, corn, tree nuts, suet and fruit. I put out food said to be of their liking at the feeding station, but have never glimpsed them feeding there. One male spent a lot of time in my Chinese Chestnut trees last season.

Years ago we fed birds breadcrumbs. It was all we knew. Then one day I heard breadcrumbs and rice, once wet, could expand inside a bird's tummy and because birds don't burp, would explode in a cloud of feathers. Yikes! Probably a bird-brained urban legend, but I stopped feeding birds breadcrumbs. Nowadays, most brides request celebrants cast handfuls of birdseed or rose petals instead of tossing rice. An ecological change with the welfare, health and safety of our feathered friends in mind.

47 / The Fun of Feeding Flocks and Bird Watching

With the popularity of feeding birds, it's most fortunate that bird food for wild birds is a thriving industry and premium rations that provide these colorful songsters with good nutrition is readily available.

Cardinals eat from all feeders, feasting on seeds, fruit, berries and nuts. The few times we've had snow—because we don't get it very often in these parts—the cardinals against the frosty white is a sight of which I never tire.

Bluebirds prefer platform feeders or feeding on the ground. They like suet, fruit and berries. I have several bluebird houses erected in an open area in my yard. I also provide suet, but the last batch I bought—eight blocks for the price of six—have gone largely ignored by all the birds visiting the feeding station. In fact, it would appear the birds would rather eat dog food than the suet. It winds up getting moldy and having to be discarded.

Friendly finches partake from any type feeder and thrive on thistle, birdseeds, fruit and suet. Every year in the spring, there are flocks of goldfinches that pass through the nearby town of Bonita. I have yet to have them visit my yard, though.

Mockingbirds aren't seed-eaters but enjoy suet, peanut butter and fruit such as raisins and grapes; with the rare resident partaking of dog food.

All my life prior to moving to Jones, I've lived where blue jays stay, so it's odd that they have never taken up residence in my yard here. Blue jays warn other birds of danger and consequently other birds feel secure when a jay is around. According to bird books, blue jays fancy peanuts in the shell, striped sunflower seeds and crushed eggshell.

The mourning doves are ground eaters. Here at my personal wild bird preserve, especially during the winter months, both the doves and sparrows vie for dried dog food, sharing side-by-side with the dogs. I'm partial to the doves. They have the sweetest cooing sound of any songbird. Peaceful, they make me happy.

They are everywhere. While some doves migrate, those living here at Wit's End are year-round residents. The only thing that disturbs them is Dove Season in September. I hate Dove Season.

I live out in the country and ruthless hunters have this idea they can come right into my yard where the doves are living peaceably in abundance, and fire away. I have a problem every year.

Doves are said to be powerful fliers, and although I've seen some fly across the farm field by my house on rare occasions, mostly I never think of them as such. They seem to mostly be perched along the power lines overhead or waddling around on the ground nibbling.

I hear my SnowBird carry on a cooing conversation with the wild doves outside, especially in the early mornings.

Then there are the exquisitely bejeweled hummers. To watch a tiny hummingbird's aerial dance among the flowers is incredible. Feeding three to five times an hour, consuming up to half their weight in nectar, these awesome avian acrobats are easy to court. Store-bought nectar feeders will bring them in droves. What would make me really enthralled would be to locate a hummer's nest. They must have nests in the nearby vicinity because once they settle in, they're constantly at the feeders. Chuck's in charge of the hummingbird feeders every year.

The only hummingbird east of the Great Plains is the Ruby throated hummingbird. Chuck and I spend hours sitting out near where he hangs the hummingbird feeders from the Chinese Chestnut tree branches. I've managed to snap some beautiful photos, my only regret that I don't own a long range lens for better close-ups.

The migration habits of the Ruby throats are every bit as fascinating as the birds themselves. Imagine such a tiny little bird making its way all the way to the Gulf of Mexico, where it overflies nonstop to winter in Central America. And then back again. Year after year.

At the beginning of last spring, I purchased a unique Purple Mar

47 / The Fun of Feeding Flocks and Bird Watching

tin birdhouse fashioned in the style of a castle. It featured multi-compartments with red roofs and red balconies. Erected high up in the air the martins immediately began circling. Several pair moved in the same day Chuck put it up for me.

I sighed with blissful relief because after handing over the check, I started thinking of this majestic birdhouse as a *Spontaneous Combustion* purchase.

I bought it spontaneously. The cost combusted my checkbook.

Usually I'm fairly level-headed because I work too hard for the money, but every now and then, I let my emotions overrule and move me more than my common sense does.

It didn't take long before I could look up, view a unique experience, an outdoor environmental show. With clouds for a backdrop, soaring with remarkable wild grace, were flashes of purple as the purple martins caught flying insects in the sky. Looking like lovely purple ballerinas dancing way up high, only the trapeze was missing in the heavenly circus of stars. It was most satisfying to have these beautiful birds locate at my house.

No other bird in North America has a closer association with humans than the Purple Martin. They are the only bird species in the eastern half of North America that depend one-hundred percent on human-supplied housing in which to nest. Like the *Spontaneous Combustion* bird house mentioned above.

In the Southwest, west of the Rockies, Purple Martins nest only in old woodpecker cavities. In the Pacific Northwest they nest in gourds and in single boxes rather than the multiple roomed houses used elsewhere.

This seems so strange. Why would the same species of bird live so differently in one part of the country to another? It's like the California Martins are too snooty to cram up in a high-rise multi-apartment building. And what's with the woodpecker cavities?

These fascinating birds have specific space requirements that must be supplied by folks wanting to establish a Purple Martin colony. The multi-roomed birdhouse should be placed in the center of the largest open spot available, about thirty- to one-hundred-twenty-feet from human housing. There should be no trees within forty- to sixty-feet. Housing height should be between ten- to seventeen-feet.

The only problem I've had are with House Sparrows attempting to usurp the Martins' abodes. In some areas there is often a problem with European Starlings who not only will take over the birdhouse but will kill the Martins. My current solution is a second Martin birdhouse—not quite so fancy as the *Spontaneous Combustion*—mounted not quite so high up in the air. This is my Sparrow Decoy Birdhouse. It looks, tastes and smells like a Martin house but it's for the Sparrows to inhabit so the Martins can have the fancy house set several feet higher up. And it works. Only a yard or so apart, the Martin house is packed full of Martins, the Sparrow Decoy Birdhouse is full of Sparrows.

Martins winter in South America, mostly Brazil. They return each spring to the same nesting area. They reach my yard between February 1st through March 1st generally. The adult males come first, returning to their former nesting boxes, followed by the females, year after year. It is last year's subadults that colonize new sites.

Then, at the end of summer, these beautiful birds head back to South America around the end of July, about three weeks after the young leave the nests. Like many migrating birds, the adult males leave first followed later by the females and youngsters. They are all gone by the end of August.

Along the way, a sight that must be breathtaking, the birds gather together into an enormous flock for their migration back to South America.

Lest this chapter turns into a bird-watcher's guide, I'll close it out with mention of only one other bird that comes every winter on a regular basis bringing with it, to me, so much pleasure. Jones, with its rice fields and waterways full of aquatic plants and seeds is a part of the migration flight path of the Canada Geese. Their honking fills the air as they pass over. They settle in fields all around the house and although residents see them year after year, hundreds and hundreds, we never tire.

Imparting pure pleasure just by virtue of their presence, wild birds

47 / The Fun of Feeding Flocks and Bird Watching

are the pets I look at but don't need to touch. Bird-watching brings a solitary joy but it's also twice as enjoyable when Chuck joins me as we keep track of the various birds we spot. It's so rewarding.

For us it's a cross between part-time entertainment and a fulltime hobby. It's our introduction to *Nature 101*. I've invested in an array of books dedicated to identifying birds. Another both beneficial and lovely thing is TacoBelle, RoseGirl and BooCat obviously, each for their own reason, like watching with Chuck and me sitting on the screened-in patio. TacoBelle finds a ray of sunshine and stretches out. She snoozes happily.

Rosie looks for a lap.

BooCat lounges as long as she can, then I smell rubber burning It's her brain churning because BooCat no doubt sees herself as the BirdCat of Alcatraz. The smell of rubber burning comes from the tumblers in her brain turning, trying to figure out how to escape these screened-in walls, how to get out of Alcatraz, out to where the wild birds are.

Oh sure, BooCat's mouth waters, but she'll get over it. One day she will become civilized. I have faith.

By the way, there's a possibility that hummingbirds aren't really birds at all. Rumor has it they are actually woodland fairies. I have discovered the magic.

The Case of the Missing Genes

48

"The saddest of sights in a world of sin is a little lost pup with its tail tucked in."
(Arthur Guiterman, "Little Lost Pup")

"Where's my sock?" I ask. "BooCat! I know you took my sock; where is it?" Naturally she doesn't answer, nor does she bring it to me. That's what happens when I foolishly leave a pair of socks sitting on the living room floor actually believing I'll sooner or later put them in the hamper.

I should've done it sooner because later, one of them is missing. I'll likely find it eventually, but at this moment, I have no idea where it went. I only know who the culprit is that snatched it. Three guesses, and the first two don't count. Oh yeah, and the thief's initials are BooCat.

On top of the missing sock, I've searched high and low for several other missing items. Like smoke, they've dissipated into thin air. I know I used to have them. Several of them. I'm talking about my genes. No. Not my Calvin Clines or my Levis. I'm talking about my Cooking Genes, my Cleaning Genes. Also my Color-Coordination and Everything-In-Its-Place Genes.

They were so much a part of me, I even drove my first ex-husband crazy. He said so in his farewell missive, and I quote, "You like for everything to be in its place and prim and proper—I don't care. I

48 / The Case of the Missing Genes

would rather go out and play in the dirt and mud."

Likely he got just what he wanted and is wallowing in it now. Enjoying the squalor he craved. After all, the bimbo he ran off with, her father's occupation was garbage man and this was long before they came up with the fancy title, Sanitation Engineer.

Meow.

I reckon my BooCat claws are showing, but he started it. And he definitely ended it. Be careful what you ask for.

It's too bad he can't see me now. While I'm not out playing in the dirt and mud, hardly anything's in its place and prim and proper any longer. He'd indeed feel right at home. I'm leaving my legacy beneath the furniture in the form of dust bunnies and discarded dog biscuits.

I rarely make the bed before I leave for work in the morning, other than a slight straightening, because there are two dogs and a cat still snoozing on it when I slip out from beneath the covers.

Several times a week I have to sort through the pile of mail I've deposited on the unused dining room table. Junk mail, advertisements, and catalogs I dare not look through for fear of impulse buying.

When I used to run the vacuum, I'd vacuum up a cat, or at least enough cat hair to equal a cat. The late Hershey left a trail wherever he settled. I don't know how much of a hairy mess BooCat will make, if any. She has such short, sleek hair, it may be hardly worth noticing. That is, so long as I wear black.

I've kept a clothes brush handy for years but I'm also a firm believer that no outfit is complete without cat hair. After all, what's a little cat hair when your cat, like your dogs, loves you unconditionally? Nothing's nicer than having BooCat snuggle up and purr contentedly while I sit reading in the evening. Hershey always preferred the chair arm. Boo's a fan of heights—she's partial to the back of the chair and her tri-level living room lounger.

I've thought about it and wonder how should I properly gage when it's time to do housework? What are the housework markers? Looking back, I do have several definite indicators that cause me to stop writing columns, stop reading books, stop sitting outside and commiserating with the dogs and birds and BooCat and instead, clean house.

I'd rather be doing all the above, but there comes a time when it's give-in or take the chance of being buried alive beneath the mess. At my age time flies and has nothing to do with having fun. I vacuum and mop one day and seven days later, just like clockwork, it's time to do it again.

Crossing the threshold at Wit's End Comedy Club is like entering an archeological dig where one enters at their own risk. Which is why I don't enter very often.

When there are no dishes left in the cabinet and there are more dishes in the sink than in the dish drainer, it's time. But you know, only washing dishes when absolutely necessary, you'd be amazed how far a bottle of Dawn dishwashing soap goes. You wash dishes every day, you're buying dish detergent weekly. You try my method, dish soap lasts for months.

Unless you've got time to run out and buy a three-pack, when your sock and undies drawer is down to lint only, it's time to wash a load of clothes. Okay, you're not going to save on laundry detergent because when you get around to doing the laundry, you're probably going to have to spend all day doing lots of loads. But the wear and tear on you yourself is worth something. Instead of having to stop and wash, dry, fold and put away clothes every couple days, you do it once a month and one long day is better than a dozen short days, you ask me.

When TacoBelle, Rosie and BooCat start taking the sheets off the bed by themselves, I know it's not because they want to play the sheet-changing-game. Although they enjoy the process considerably I know another week has gone by and we have to change them again.

Mostly I keep the ceiling fans turned on year round for camouflage but when the blades get lopsided from the weight of dust, and the twirling starts flinging dust bunnies across the room, and they get eaten by the dust dingoes, it's time to clean the fan blades The dust dingoes have settled in for the duration. I toss them a chew bone now and again just to keep them happy.

You can leave one or two light bulbs burned out in the ceiling fixture. The dimness buys time by hiding the obvious and in turn creates the perfect ambiance. But when the last bulb in the chandelier burns out, it's time.

Then, much to my dismay, I start replacing fresh light bulbs and the glare gives the whole game away. And nobody is going to believe I'm letting the dust stack up to keep it from making me sneeze; that I

48 / The Case of the Missing Genes

can just pick it up when thick enough instead of stirring it all around with a dust rag. Also, no one believes the theory that dust protects the tabletops either. I thought it sounded plausible but then, I'm probably part of the people who can be fooled part of the time.

I've managed to wear out several microwaves since I discovered it's simpler to pop a single serving frozen entree in the microwave than to prepare a whole meal on the stovetop. A whole meal entails peeling and cutting up potatoes, preparing a can of something or another, frying a slab of some sort of meat which results in no less than three dirty pans, a paring knife and cutting board, stirring and serving spoons and a plate on which to serve the end results. At the very least.

Then after spending thirty- to forty-five minutes poring over a hot stove and five minutes eating I've got to dig out several containers in which to store leftovers. Microwave versus all that? Why, there's no comparison.

I guess when you reach a certain age, priorities change. What was so important once, gets relegated to a lower position on the totem pole of precedence's. And so, since I've misplaced my cooking and cleaning genes, I don't suppose it matters if I ever find them again. I've acquired a different set.

They are my enjoy-life-while-I-am-living genes. They are also my procrastination genes, because I figure I can always clean the house when I can't do anything else. And most the time, I can surely find something else more enjoyable to do than to vacuum up a cat and create a bunch of dirty dishes that only means spending another thirty minutes elbow deep in dishwater.

Oh, for heaven's sakes. I found my sock. It was on the bed. That's where BooBandit deposits all her treasures and her prey. I have a feeling that's where she was headed with that baby Copperhead, had Rosie not alerted me first.

But, considering how besotted I am over BooCat, I probably would've told her what a good kitty she was even if she had brought the scary snake to bed. As it was, I told her she was a good kitty even as I was picking it up with needle nose pliers and heading out the door.

BooCat Would Rather be Fishing

"Gentlemen of the Jury: The one absolute, unselfish friend that man can have in this selfish world, the one that never deserts him, the one that never proves ungrateful or treacherous, is his dog."
(Sen. George Graham Vest, "Eulogy on the Dog")

The fish tank doesn't intrigue BooCat as much as the birds do, but it's not gone unnoticed, nor unexplored. Fortunately it has a lid cover on it or she'd likely be fishing every day, not that she hasn't tried. She has. I've caught her up on top of it several times.

The fact is, BooCat and I have this dialog, but it's mostly one sided. I'm perpetually yelling, telling and asking to minimum avail. She shrugs off what I say with a "Were you walking to me?" sort of look.

I say: "Where are you? Are you hungry? Leave the birds alone! Get off the fish tank! Where is my sock? Leave poor Rosie alone. You better leave Taco alone if you know what's good for you. Boo! Stop! Aw, Boo. I love you BabyBooGirl."

And she says: Meow.

I started with a fifty-gallon tank, but reduced down to a twenty-five-gallon. The fifty-gallon still sits empty in my dining room. I have good intentions—those things that line the way to somewhere besides heaven—of taking the tank to the town hall where I work and setting it up. I believe it would make a nice addition to the lobby. Children and grownups alike would enjoy it. Many physician's offices keep tanks of colorful fish for the pleasure of their patients.

I kept a purple Beta Siamese Fighting Fish for many years displayed on my desk and it was always catching the eye of visitors. But transporting this huge tank and stand is easier said than done. Relocating a fifty-gallon tank and stand requires a pickup truck and someone much stronger than I am. Remember, I'm the old geezer gal who can't pick up a fifty pound sack of dog food any more, and barely a twenty pound bag of kitty litter. The tank is far heavier than either of those items.

I downsized for several reasons. One was that the larger tank required replacing two filters on a very regular basis; the smaller tank calls for only one; and filters are really expensive.

When I first set up the tank I purchased my favorite Neon Tetras along with several other brightly colored harmonious fish and the requisite guppies. I added several algae eaters.

But, fish die. And when you pay four or five dollars per fish a big ouch factor is involved. At first I'd replace each fish as it died with another one or two. This got costly. I knew not to mix certain fish with other certain fish because of cannibalism. I've been raising fish for many years; but still, I had bad luck with the Neon tetras—which was what I wanted most of all. A tank full of them.

In fact, I've had ten gallon fish tanks since I was a kid; and have probably had some of every variety of tropical fish available at one time or another, the fact of the matter is, some fish are just trickier to raise than others. I'm also partial to Oscars but they'll definitely eat other fish. In fact, you can hand feed them hamburger, that's how much they like the taste of meaty morsels. But they don't give them away.

Thus, after I'd spent all the money I was going to spend, since most of the pretty fish died, except the always hardy guppies, I decided guppies were good. In fact, because they reproduce regularly, I ended up periodically giving away free guppies to anyone for the asking.

Besides the guppies, the Corydoras and the Plecostomus catfish do fine. Scavengers, I've had several Plecostomus grow over five- to seven-inches long in the large aquarium. In the wild or in an extremely large aquarium, they can grow to ten inches.

Plecostomus are in the category of suckermouth armored catfishes. Their mouths form a sucking disc under their heads, making them well equipped for eating algae, which they do industriously. Like most scum suckers, they are most active at night.

The Corydoras are in the smooth armored catfish family and are highly regarded as bottom feeding scavenger fish. You rarely see them as they tend to be very shy and also more active at night. Interesting gnome-like little fish, I always like to keep at least two in a tank.

I still dream of one day having this fantastic tank full of neon tetras with real greenery. And BooCat? She'll take anything she can get her little paw on. Most fortunate, since the tank has a lid cover, the only thing she managed to "catch" was a package of Algae Wafers. Purchased expressly for the algae eaters in the tank, these little discs provide a balance of ingredients developed to promote proper growth in the herbivorous species. The Plecostomus catfish thrive on it. It's a good thing the ingredients consisted only of a high level of vegetable matter because CatfisherBooCat ate a whole package. Luckily, with no apparent ill effects. I now keep the little cellophane package in a drawer. So far she hasn't figured out how to open the drawer. Don't worry. I'm keeping an eye on her. It's only a matter of time.

Give her time. Just give her time.

This is the type activity that led to the slogan that curiosity kills the cat. Had the product not been harmless, BooCat likely could've become very ill or worse. Her curiosity carries her to places she shouldn't go.

The cat just can't help it.

A Mouse in the House

50

"Young dog, old dog, several stupid dogs. Drive carefully."
(Sign on front gate at Wit's End Comedy Club)

BooCat caught her first mouse. This is an old house and somehow occasional unwelcome and uninvited guests find an opening and make their way inside. For all that, during the thirteen years Hershey lived here, he only caught one mouse. It's not that only one other mouse had ever gotten inside, but that Hershey simply wasn't a mouser.

To explain, I start my tale by saying there was a mouse in the house and Hershey caught it—which was quite extraordinary. At the time it was his first mouse-catch and as it were, it turned out to be his only mouse catch.

You see, he was not a cat-cat; a run-of-the-mill mouser. He was a pampered puss-in-boots kitty. His clawless padded-paws had never touched terra firma in his entire thirteen years of life. He was nine years old when he caught his one and only mouse.

Catching it probably surprised him as much as it did me.

It was around midnight when his mournful meow woke me. I called his name and he came as close as the bedroom door and proceeded to make a twittering-chatter sound much as he did when perched on the window sill viewing a bevy of birdies outside and out-of-reach.

Sitting up in bed I looked over at TacoBelle and Rosie. They were ignoring their housemate totally, dreaming doggie dreams. Dislodging both dogs, I got out of bed to see what was the matter—why all the clatter and chatter.

There, at Hershey's feet, sat a mouse. Stunned, but alive.

A dilemma. What to do about a mouse that was sure to regain its senses soon?

Naturally, I did what any sensible woman would do, which did not include yeeking! I'm pleased to report. I had a white mouse or two over the years as pets so mice didn't alarm me per se. I didn't want them scampering around the house, damaging wherever their teeth chose to chew, nor did I appreciate finding mouse droppings wherever their little legs took them. Having free reign is unsanitary no matter how cute they might be.

Remember the little talking mice in the movie *Babe*? Mice are cute. But destructive. And unsanitary.

I brought home a white mouse once when I was a kid—leftover from a science project. I put it into a suitcase and stuck it up in the top of my closet until such time I could break the news to Mom. Well, when I went to check on the mouse, it had managed to chew its way out of the suitcase. Once this discovery was made, I elected to not ever tell Mom about the part I played in the holey suitcase. I had no idea where the mouse got off to and figured no news is good news, or in this case, telling on myself would be dumb.

Quick thinking on my part, while Hershey guarded the unconscious mouse, I got a wastebasket and plopped it upside down over the critter. Next, I set a boot cricket on top for stabilization; boot crickets being heavy. I patted Hershey on his head, praising him mightily by telling him he was a most magnificent mouser cat. Then I climbed back into bed planning to attend to the mouse come morning. It was the middle of the night, after all.

By the way, a boot cricket is a metal item made for the sole purpose of helping a cowboy, or girl, remove his or her boots. You hook the heel of one boot in between the cricket's antennae and tug while holding the cricket steady with your other foot pressed on the cricket's tail end. With the heel of the boot firmly gripped in this manner you can slip your foot out. It beats sitting on the side of the bed, one leg crossed over your knee while you grab your boot with both hands and tug unceremoniously.

Boot crickets are so called because they are crafted and shaped like a cricket. This is the only cricket that doesn't kick my cricket phobia into high gear. Oh, I do have a little brass cricket replica sitting upon the hearth of my fireplace for luck, and it doesn't bother me. Maybe it's because it's artistically crafted it alleviates the buggish fear I normally get when confronted even with pictures of crickets. Even though I don't really believe a cricket on the hearth is good luck, I figure, why take chances. What's the harm?

Morning came and the mouse was still very much alive. He had recovered from his run-in with Hershey. Hershey may have caught his first mouse, but obviously he didn't know what he was supposed to do with it. I mean, isn't it the norm for cats to kill the mice they catch? And then eat them? Yuck.

Frankly, I'm glad Hershey wasn't a cold blooded killer cat. I wasn't a mouse killer either. I commiserated with Hershey on his kindness. I decided I would wait until I got in from work that afternoon, and then call for male assistance. You know, of mice and men? Ridding one's home of a live mouse seemed like a man's job.

Also, there's this thing called procrastination. Especially when it involves an unsavory task. But, as I started getting ready for work, Rosie climbed out of bed and headed straight for the overturned trashcan. I told her to stay away; a mini-monster was jailed within. To no avail.

Subsequently, in between applying lipstick and combing my hair, I set a chair over the trashcan that was topped by the boot cricket. I certainly didn't want Rosie knocking the homemade jailhouse over and releasing the mouse back into the house, undoing Hershey's amazing good deed.

I stepped back and surveyed the situation. No way was a kitchen chair, even with legs surrounding the trashcan topped by the boot cricket, going to be a substantial deterrent to a most curious and cunning dachshund.

Only one thing left to do. I had to physically remove the mouse from the premises. Once and for all. No putting it off. No waiting for male assistance.

Sigh.

I got the broom, turned the trashcan over, swept the poor little rodent into the trashcan and carried it outside and dumped it over the fence where it scampered off.

Now how hard was that?

I said a silent prayer that it would be so grateful to have escaped a fate worse than death, it would keep heading in the opposite direction and not find its way back inside.

Perhaps it's true, the only good mouse is a dead mouse, but this little rascal was being given a second chance at life. When I left for work, I left Hershey preening himself, TacoBelle still asleep under the bedcovers and Rosie sniffing the spot where the lucky mouse had spent a harrowing night. She was no doubt wondering what the heck happened while I was thinking, all is well that ends well.

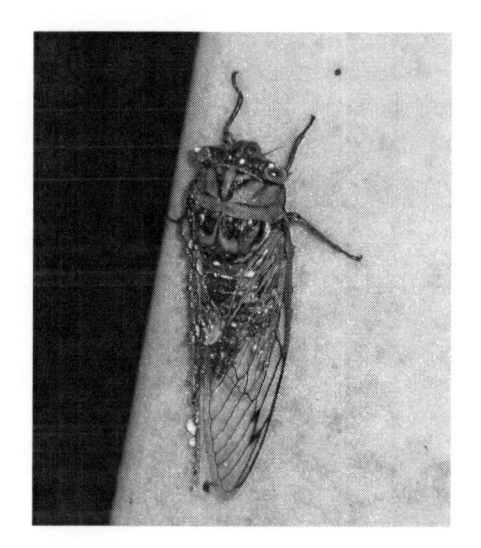

Yeek!

51

"One nation under dog—and cat." (Unknown Origin)

I can recount numerous stories about creepy, crawly things getting into the house. That's the downside of living out in the country. Not that they must come into the house, but they're out there so it's more prone to happen than if a house were located in downtown New York City. Well, then you might have burglars and dog-sized rats breaking and entering. So, whatever. You take your chances every time you rise and shine.

It might be shorter if I list what hasn't slithered, crawled or hopped into my house. Not surprisingly, now that a super-duper watch cat, MissBoo, resides with me, I worry a lot less. After all, she's proven her worth over and over.

Before BooBelle moved in there was the Blue Bell Homemade Vanilla Ice Cream incident. After eating a bowl of ice cream, I set the dish in the sink planning to wash it later. Bad habit. One dish could be washed, rinsed and put away in less time than it takes to say Banana Split but because it's only one measly bowl, it's a lot simpler to walk away thinking one is not hardly worth fooling with. Procrastination personified.

Well, the next morning the bowl was full of little-bitty ants. We're overrun with dangerous, deadly and destructive fire ants in this neck of the woods, but these were old fashioned sugar ants.

What I wanted to know was how did those ants know that ice cream bowl was in the sink? And how did they get in the house in the first place? Where did they come from? Were they just sitting outside the drainpipe awaiting something too enticing to resist? The appearance of ants from out of nowhere is one of life's little mysteries. Ants from thin air—magical.

It's like mosquitoes finding the only hole in the screen so they can swarm inside. Talk about radar, better than anything the Air-Force might develop, bugs and insects have it.

Making matters worse, it's never just one ant or one mosquito. Nope. They invite the whole family. The telecommunication system would make Ma Bell proud. Cell phone providers could take a lesson.

Listen close: "Hey guys. Come on in. There's a hole in the screen over here. Oh and by the way, I smell warm blood."

Every year we have crickets in droves. Again, they're not content to stay outside. How do they get inside the house? They must sit and wait for the door to open and because I'm way up high, and they're way down low, I don't notice them hopping over the threshold. Then, the minute I lay down in bed, I hear them. Their chirping is not music to my ears.

The year TacoBelle moved in—sweet spoiled-rotten Chichi—was a year of a cricket invasion. Heavy-duty invasions happen every few years. The rest of the time there're plenty, just not so many that they crawl up walls and crunch under car tires, turn the ground under street lights black. When that happens, that's an invasion.

Similar to the rising-from-the-ground Cicadas every seventeen years, give or take, the crickets come. Two years ago, it must have been number seventeen for the Cicadas—what I used to call Locusts—arose. As they clambered out of the holes in the ground, several of my outside dogs chased, caught and munched them like potato chips or maybe more like chocolate-covered ants. Enough survived so there were empty shells stuck on trees, the picnic table, and other unusual surfaces.

51 / Yeek!

Back to TacoBelle and the crickets. She trained herself to become a super cricket catcher. Akin to a mouser cat, she'd pounce on a cricket in a heartbeat.

A cricket must have jumped on me in my early childhood; maybe a hypnotist could get to the bottom of my fear. I get goose bumps just seeing one. I don't mind using worms as fish bait, but no way can I do crickets. The best bream bait, but I just cannot handle them. I can barely bear to look at them.

Do you have any idea how long it takes a cricket to die when underneath a bowl on the kitchen counter?

Once I came across a cricket on my kitchen counter. I panicked. I placed a bowl over top of it to await some strong male visitor to remove it from the premises. Crickets are too big to squish—the crunching noise is unbearable—and too scary to catch. Just writing about the crunch shivers me timbers.

It took several days before someone dropped by who I could enlist in my cricket extermination project and I'll be darned if that cricket wasn't still alive. No wonder, like roaches, they've been with us through the eons.

I believe part of my cricket phobia's based on my roach phobia, because if you look at a cricket up close, you'll see a roach's body. Yeek! Ever see the exterminator running around town with a large plastic roach on top of his truck? You can bet I'm not calling him. That big bug creeps me out. Most likely it's a girlie thing.

Ever notice that wasps are perpetually mad at the world? Have you ever met a happy wasp? They fly around with the worst dispositions. You're out there minding your own business, sitting in your lawn chair reading quietly—or you could just as easily be taking sheets off the line—they have a compulsion to dart around your head, coming after you lickety-split. For no apparent reason except that they can. They have acres and acres, the whole wild blue yonder, yet it's like they are duty-bound to hang around you and your book, dive bombing you. And they give no warning. No buzzing to listen for. When they do bite—because it's more a bite than a sting—it happens in a split second but hurts for a very long time.

There's probably a wasp Mafia and their goal is to take out all humanity for invading their turf—which is anywhere they are and everywhere when you live out in the country.

Running barefoot in the clover I expected to get stung by honeybees as a kid. And I did. Those stings were my own fault, but these nasty-tempered wasps are a whole different story. Sitting outside with wasps hanging around is like skinny-dipping with snapping turtles.

One night following a six-inch rain, I flipped on the outside light at half past eleven to check the rising water status. A deluge, the rain spilled over the sidewalk and up onto the screened-in patio and was several inches deep. Beneath the water I spied a snake swimming vigorously. It wasn't that I was concerned whether or not it was poisonous, it was that it had invaded the interior of my home in a manner of speaking. I don't go outside and poke around snake holes, I don't want snakes swimming on my patio.

There were two snakes hanging from the branches of a maple tree in my yard a couple years ago. Even if you don't mind snakes, it felt creepy walking beneath a tree, looking up and seeing a couple of snakes wrapped around the branches overhead. It sort of made me feel like I was in a jungle in South America rather than in my front yard in North America.

I've had snakes clinging to the bricks as they climbed up the wall of the house. I even saw one slither inside a rotten board taking it into the interior walls. Before my hearing got so poor, I heard one rattling outside the carport door. They slither here and there. I've gone to get the mail, peered down and at the base of the mailbox pole, one was curled up. I almost stepped on a beautiful black and white speckled king snake as I walked along the brick walk from my house to Mom's trailer. So I'm used to snakes, but still, it's unsettling every time one appears to be invading my living space.

I got the hoe, intending to remove the trespasser from my patio but when I returned, it was nowhere in sight. This wasn't a good thing. I was thinking before I could let TacoBelle, Rosie, Gizzy and Hershey out, or before I could sit outside with a morning cup of coffee, I'd have to reconnaissance. I spotted a lizard and a green tree frog, but no snake. After a thorough search I could only hope he swam out the same way he swam in.

There have actually been several snakes in this house prior to Boo's famous copperhead snake story catch. One in my bathroom freaked me out because it had to have passed through my bedroom to reach my bathroom. During the night. In the dark. Oh gawd.

I promised myself not to walk barefoot in the night. Of course, there's always the chance that when slipping my feet into slippers, one might be curled up inside. The dark inner toe area of a shoe or slipper would very much resemble a snake hole for a snake out of its element. These are not positive thoughts.

Another time there were two baby snakes in the dining room. Hershey and Sterling cornered them. Not too long before BooCat moved in, a small rat snake got caught on a mouse sticky board. I can only assume he followed a mouse, coming in wherever it did. TacoBelle alerted me to its presence.

Foolishly, I took her extreme irritation and bothersome barking as her wanting supper. Instead, it turned out she was telling me there was a snake in the house. Yo Quiero TacoBelle.

Add spiders to my list of things that make me go Yeek! Years ago I had just settled in for a nice bubbly bath when I discovered a spider swimming amongst the bubbles with me. I'm sure he didn't want to be there any more than I wanted him. Keeping my eye on the uninvited bathing partner, I calmly stood up, stepped out, got dressed, and then yelled, "Help!" I must have been in a state of shock.

Another horrifying experience involving invading spiders happened in my bed, in the dark. More asleep than awake, a feathery whisper tickled my face. This was before the CPAP machine.

Coming totally awake in a flash, I knew some *thing*—not something, but rather, some *thing*, was on my face.

Nothing wrong with my reactions, I brushed at it and sent it flying without wings. Turning on my night light, there it was. Slightly stunned by the flight from my face to the bedcovers, a large spider. A very large spider.

What was it doing in my bed? Worse yet, what was it doing on my head? In my face?

Rosie barely peeked from beneath the covers while TacoBelle, aware of the commotion, popped her head out and tried to pounce on the intruder. Verbally restraining her because I didn't want her getting bit, I tried to squish the spider between the folds of the blanket. And it tried to escape. This incident was also BBC—before BooCat. Had she been present, she would have pounced on it and probably crunched and munched it to boot.

Eight legs gives a spider the uncanny ability to run four-times faster than I could, but I finally sent him to squashed-spiderland.

This meant sleep had to be put on hold, long enough to remove the blanket from the bed. No way could the fuzzy girls and I sleep with a squished spider in bed with us. It made me shudder.

Then my imagination went into overdrive. Suddenly I wondered if the spider had bit me. I'd seen pictures in medical books and on the Internet. If it had bit me, how long would it take for half my face to rot off? Maybe by morning? Surely, if I'd been bitten, I reasoned, I'd be suffering excruciating pain. Therefore, I allowed that I hadn't been bitten. My breathing slowed. I sighed. I was going to be okay. But, I could've been bitten. *Coulda, woulda, shoulda.*

The slang expression *snakebit* was first coined to describe a team, or an individual athlete, that seemed to attract an inordinate amount of bad luck. It's basic jock talk. But over the years it's come to be a common reference to anyone beseeched by Black-Cloud-Fever—the malady associated with having a black cloud hanging over one's head, seemingly causing lots of bad luck.

As a matter of fact, some time after the harrowing incident of the spider traipsing across my face, I was bitten. It was a lot like being snakebit. It is a mighty unlucky thing to have happen and I wouldn't wish it on anybody. Not even my ex.

Wait.

No. Let me rephrase that. I wouldn't wish it on almost anybody. There are a few exceptions. Always the exception.

Continuously pretty self-sufficient, I figured I would be okay using peroxide and an antibacterial ointment. Self-medicating a spider bite is not necessarily wise.

About nine days after being bitten, the bite-site, which was growing and excavating my skin daily, turned a deep purple. Just looking at the bite-site hurt. Besides running a fever, my whole arm started to ache, the bite itself was painful.

The Emergency Room doctor, because it grew much worse over a weekend which meant my doctor's office was closed, wrote a prescription and advised I go to my regular physician if it didn't show improvement within a couple days. It didn't, so I did. He verified by blood test that the infection hadn't entered my bloodstream, gave me an ointment and another antibiotic prescription. He did much more for me than the E.R. doctor and cost about fifteen times less.

One and a half months later, another spot adjacent to the original bite-site erupted. More antibiotics and another blood test. More cash. The overall cost to that point had been almost as painful as the bite itself.

My hand didn't rot off but at the bite-site a large hole developed and a portion of my hand surrounding the bite did rot away. It was a most unpleasant experience.

I didn't actually see the spider that bit me; but it was a clean diagnoses that a spider was the culprit. It may not have been a brown recluse, but it must've been a nasty kissin' cousin. I did kill a black widow once hanging from a web in a dark corner in my bedroom. The first I'd ever seen other than in photographs.

In any case, all things considered and according to statistics I was luckier than some people, as dreadful as the experience was. I lived to tell about the incident.

Having encountered the spider on my face while I was in bed, my mind continued speeding. You ever wake up in the morning and your mouth is dry and you figure you must have been sleeping with your mouth open? Think about that. In that case it would not be a drainpipe the itsy-bitsy spider was going up and down, that would be your windpipe. And I'm dying here just thinking about it.

I debated using the famous fix-all, duct tape—also known as "gray tape"—to cover my mouth before I went back to bed. Even if the spider wasn't aiming for my mouth, had it been open, it could have accidentally fallen in. This visualization was more than my spider-phobia-mind could bear. Could I wrap my head in mosquito netting? And where do you get mosquito netting?

Suffice to say, we never know what's around the corner for us. Or crawling into bed with us. We might feel snug as a bug in a rug—Whoops! Wrong analogy. What I meant to say was, you could feel safe and sound, sleeping the sleep of the just, and along comes a spider, and like Little Miss Muffit sitting on her tufted, he might just sit right down beside you.

Nowadays, even fake spiders give me the willies.

On the other hand, if you leave spider webs hanging in the corners of your carport, they'll catch a million mosquitoes and even a few crickets. Evil begets evil.

The Saga of the Snail Assault

52

"I smell a rat." (An allusion to a cat smelling a rat, according to *Brewer's Dictionary of Phrase and Fable*; commonly used by somebody thinking something isn't right, that something is concealed or hidden.)

This time it wasn't me taking a road trip, it was the snails. No. I don't mean the Mr. and Mrs. Snail family. I mean The Snails. As in a snail invasion. These little road runners road-tripped into Wit's End Comedy Club, where every day is a laugh a minute, and they set up camp.

They weren't the shell-less slugs I remember sprinkling salt on as a kid. I have to think most youngsters participated in that cruel rite of passage. I mean, what kid could resist testing the legend that if you sprinkled salt on a slug it would just dissolve into thin air?

Did it?

I know I sprinkled salt, but the slug either didn't disappear or my safety valve making me forget unpleasant things has kicked in because I don't remember.

These land snail visitors came equipped with little bitty snail shells. Chuck initially noticed them on the trunk of my Chestnut trees. At first glance he thought they were ticks. Upon closer examination—the man needs to wear glasses but won't—he discovered they were miniature pasty-colored snails. Lots and lots of them. Hundreds.

Chuck tends my yard lovingly. It's not groomed to citified-lawn perfection, but it's pleasing. He has a way with Round-up. In its semi-untamed state, shrubs, trees and wildflowers harmonize in a natural wilderness much like a half-tamed colt at play in a meadow.

Birds nest in every tree and bush and judging from their melodious performances, they are the happiest birds in the whole U.S.A. A bird sanctuary and a haven for homeless hounds, it's my refuge as well. My oasis.

Then, whoa! Overnight, snails were everywhere. I looked them up on the Internet and found snail invasions aren't uncommon. Still, this was the first I'd ever experienced in the forty years I've lived in my house that was now surrounded by a snail-covered yard. Because of the dogs and birds I vetoed the notion of putting out snail bait and there wasn't enough of Chuck to go around squishing them like bugs. Truth be told, I never minded snails; I have some in my aquarium. Of course, I never had 10,000 all at once before.

Snails are mollusks. Mollusks range from tiny snails—many of which were in my yard—to giant squid, with clams, mussels, oysters and scallops in between. Bet if you like raw oysters, or fried for that matter, you never thought of them being in the snail family? I know I didn't.

Most mollusks are aquatic, but some live on land like these little guys that cluttered up my yard. I tried escargot once, but because they reminded me of furless fat caterpillars, eating them freaked me out. Or maybe it was guilt stemming from childhood memories involving a box of Morton's Salt.

Anyway, I wracked my brain for a solution. I recalled a fruit fly raid one year when everybody put out vessels of vinegar; the theory being that the flies would be drawn to the vinegar, fall in and die by drowning. The success rate was sporadic, and then failed miserably altogether next time around. I'm thinking the Fruit Fly Attorney General sent out a warning for the little buggers to steer clear of all things vinegary as it could be hazardous to their health.

In any case, the vinegar concept summoned something to mind. From deep within my memory bank, I told Chuck I recollected reading that somebody did successful snail eradication with bowls of beer. The assumption was that the snails would slither into the bowls of beer and drink themselves into a drunken stupor, pass out and drown.

Alright, so drowning by beer may be cruel and unusual punishment in some eyes, but I'd think to a snail it wasn't a bad way to go. Better than being eaten by a Shrike. Or assaulted by salt. Or crunched by Chuck's boot.

Chuck doubted the validity of this method but allowing me my eccentricities—which he is kind enough to do fairly often—he bought a can of Milwaukee's Best.

"How'd you decide which brand to buy?" I asked.

"Because it's the cheapest," and he said he didn't want to waste good beer on bad snails.

I dug out a couple old pie pans. He filled them up with the best Milwaukee had to offer. As he headed home we agreed to meet early the next morning to check out the results. We expected a million-snail-massacre and so it probably served me right for being a party to attempted murder that I dreamed about Chesapeake Bay Blue crabs that night. In my dream, these, my favorite of all seafood, turned into spiders. Eight crab legs became eight spider legs. Yikes! Talk about a nightmare. If crustaceans and spiders are even remotely related, please don't tell me.

But, come morning, the pie pans held nothing more than flat beer. Maybe these snails would've preferred Heineken.

Okay. Chapter Two: Acceptance. How much damage can a few thousand tiny snails do anyhow? Have a chlorophyll orgy on tree leaves? I reasoned that I had plenty of trees. Lots of leaves. Go for it.

Snack on dandelion greens? Persnickety lawn enthusiasts detest dandelions anyway. Perhaps the tiny little snails would develop a taste for Johnson grass and clean up around my chain link fence.

Perchance, they'd mow down Morning Glory vines that keep trying to take hold of my rose bush.

The way I saw it, considering the beer bust—as in fiasco, so please pardon the pun—the mourning doves have gotten so fat sharing dog chow with the pups they look like chickens, so why not let nature take its course? Since I was already feeding a pack and a flock, what were a few more mouths to feed?

At the time, I figured that maybe in a couple days the snails would continue their trip down somebody else's road. To quote Chick Hearn, "No harm, no foul."

BooCat Unleashed

And that's what they did. When nobody was looking, they marched right on down the road and became nothing more than a memory at a junction along life's highway.

Magnificent Monarchs and Lovely Lunas

53

"Let sleeping cats lie." (French Proverb: Meaning to leave things as they are)

Living in the country definitely means sharing space with a multitude of bugs, insects, creatures and critters, but not always bad ones like spiders on your head in bed. One Saturday several years ago a flock of Monarch butterflies, one of the most fascinating insects in the world, covered a couple bushes in my front yard with their beautiful black and orange.

The way BooCat deems everything that moves is moving for her pleasure, she would have had a blast had she been present for the Monarch stopover.

Monarchs breed in the northern United States and southern Canada. Western populations migrate to California, and eastern populations migrate to the Sierra Madre mountains in Mexico to overwinter. The first winter location of Monarch butterflies was discovered in the Sierra Madre mountains west of Mexico City in 1975. It's believed they guide themselves during migration using the position of the sun and the magnetic field of the earth. Amazing is an appropriate way to describe the overall event.

During the summer, female Monarchs lay their eggs *only* on milkweed plants. Within a few days, the egg hatches and a yellow, black and white striped caterpillar emerges, beginning its life cycle.

Monarchs of the fourth generation will live for eight or nine months and travel over two-thousand miles to Mexico; a place they've never been before. Before migrating, they gather in huge numbers at departure points such as Presqu'ile Provincial Park, on a peninsula sticking out into Lake Ontario.

In more exacting detail, since Monarchs cannot survive the cold winter months of the United States and Canada, they migrate over two-thousand-five-hundred miles south and west each autumn to escape the cold winter weather. And then, because larval food plants don't grow in their overwintering sites in Mexico and some parts of Southern California, they must fly back north each spring where the milkweed plant is plentiful.

The Monarchs that live in the eastern states, east of the Rocky Mountains, migrate to Mexico and hibernate in oyamel fir trees. Monarchs that live west of the Rockies hibernate in and around Pacific Grove, California in eucalyptus trees.

Monarchs go through four stages during one life cycle. They also go through four generations in one year. The four stages are the egg, the larvae or caterpillar, the pupa or chrysalis and the adult butterfly.

The four generations are actually four different butterflies going through these four stages during one year until it's time to start all over again.

Are you confused yet? Hang in there.

There's no other creature in the animal kingdom that does what the Monarch does. It's worth following its incredible journey.

Let's start the incredible tale of the mind-blowing journey in February and March from Mexico where the Monarchs have been hibernating. When Monarchs come out of hibernation, each butterfly locates a mate. After that, they begin their marathon migration north and east to find a place to lay their eggs.

Skipping ahead, now it's March and April and the Monarchs have flown the first leg of the exciting excursion stopping when they locate a place to lay their eggs on milkweed plants. The milkweed plant is crucial to the life of the Monarch. It's the only thing Monarch caterpillars eat. Farmers tend to want to eradicate milkweed. Understandably so. But, think twice now that we've come to realize it's the only thing Monarch caterpillars eat. Therefore, if all milkweed is gone, so will the Monarchs be. Over the years there have been living things that have come to be extinct. Let's hope that won't become the fate of Monarch butterflies.

The baby caterpillar eats and grows until it's outgrown its own skin. The caterpillar, after about two weeks, attaches itself to a leaf or stem and then goes through the process of metamorphosis.

Attaching itself to the stem using silk, it transforms into a chrysalis where it spends about ten days going through a rapid change within. Old caterpillar body parts are becoming beautiful butterfly parts through transformation, metamorphosis. The butterfly that emerges from the pupa will, after several hours while its wings dry and harden, fly away.

This is the first generation.

These butterflies will continue the journey northward, feeding on flowers, mating, laying eggs and dying. This takes approximately two- to six-weeks. From these eggs laid, will emerge the second generation. Second generation Monarchs are born in May and June. Again, these same steps are repeated a little farther north and the third generation is born in July and August. Three times in a row, the same exact stages are repeated for each generation.

But now, the fourth generation is slightly different from the first three generations. These caterpillars are born in September and October and go through all the same stages as the first three except that they don't die after two- to six-weeks. Instead, these butterflies begin a migration in reverse, heading back to Mexico and California where they'll live for six- to eight-months in hibernation; after which it will be time to start the whole process over again.

What makes this migration so intriguing isn't just that the Monarchs hibernate using the very same trees every year, but that these are fourth generation monarchs. How do they know what trees to use? Even more astounding is, when these butterflies are born, they have never been to where they find themselves going, yet they know exactly where to go. How do they know? Monarchs are the only insect that migrates to a warmer climate two-thousand-five-hundred miles away.

Since 1986, several of the sites occupied by the overwintering Monarch butterfly have been protected by the Mexican government. There's still a problem with outlaw logging cutting down the trees the monarchs have hibernated in for years.

If these favorite trees are gone, what will happen to the monarchs?

In California, the effects of tourism and poorly planned management and development are a problem. At least seven of the eighty known monarch sites have already been destroyed. Milkweed is widespread and abundant in Canada and the US, but because it's considered a weed, researchers have expressed concern that spraying of pesticides for weed control are killing milkweed plants and may endanger the habitat and food source of the beautiful Monarch butterfly.

At the time the flock of Monarchs visited my yard, I didn't know they were en route to Mexico. Somewhere down near the border, monarchs will meet up and band together making a huge cloud of black and orange as they home into their hibernation spot. It's a awe-inspiring sight. In fact, everything to do with Monarch butterflies is remarkable.

Several months ago, I was visited by another unusual insect that delighted rather than frightened. I came across a Luna Moth. In all my many years of life, I've only seen one other Luna Moth about forty years ago.

As with Monarch butterflies, Luna's also produce generations in a single year. There the likeness ends. In Canada and the far north, Luna's live approximately seven days and only one generation is produced; reaching adulthood from early June to early July.

Two generation moths may be produced in the northeastern United States, the first appearing in April and May and the second seen approximately nine- to eleven-weeks later.

There can be as many as three generations produced by Luna's living in the southern United States. Beginning in March, they are spaced every eight to ten weeks.

Going from egg to larva to pupa and finally emerging from a cocoon into a full-grown moth, is always a fascinating process. When the adult emerges from its cocoon in the morning, its wings are very small and the moth must enlarge them by pumping bodily fluids through them.

At this time the wings are soft and must harden before the moth can fly, an approximate two hour process.

The Luna Moth has a wingspan of between 3.1 to 4.5 inches. They are a beautiful lime green. They generally only fly at night, hence the reason they are very rarely seen.

And here is the kicker. Luna Moths don't have mouths. They don't eat. They emerge as adults solely to mate. The average lifespan is one week.

As with everything on this earth, we have the good, the bad, and the ugly. To me, crickets are the ugly, Monarchs and Luna's are the good and man's indifference is the bad.

When faced with this daily onslaught of bad bugs and wicked snakes, I'd like to ask, "Noah, what were you thinking?"

Here, Noah had the perfect opportunity to rid the world of all creatures bad and useless but by golly, he blew it.

My Fids Are My Soul Mates

54

"Who loves me will love my dog also." (St. Bernard of Clairvaux)

It was probably about two years ago when I had an epiphany. The truth hit me when I asked Tacobelle and Rosie for the third time in a row, "Why don't you pups go outside and play?"—that I'd become the epitome of one of those silly old ladies with pets.

We've all seen them. We've all chuckled over their foolishness. We've all sworn we'd never be one. And now I am.

There's nothing redeeming about the fact that I hadn't asked Hershey why he didn't go outside. He was already out on the screened-in patio. I never had to tell him twice. I didn't even have to tell once. He knows and he goes.

I'd opened the door to the patio and told Tacobelle and Rosie to go outside—enjoy the autumn-like weather. Then I sat down with a cup of coffee. My plan was to eat a Hershey Nut Lover's candy bar and read a few minutes before starting the housework.

Forget the fancy coffee shop lattes, cappuccinos or frappuccinos, just eat a chocolate candy bar with a cup of coffee and you've created your own cup of fresh mocha. Take a bite, then a sip. Melds delightfully.

Dogs and cats aren't supposed to eat chocolate. I deliberated that the best way to secretly pull off this feat was while they were outside. My plan of enjoying my chocolate-coffee sitting at the kitchen table, open book before me, began as I ever so quietly unwrapped my candy bar.

I don't know if it's TacoBelle's tock-ears—Chihuahuas do have over-sized ears—or if it's her super sense of smell, but she either heard the candy wrapper crinkle or smelled the chocolate. She came running. Rosie always lets Taco do the dirty work, reaping whatever benefits Taco begs from me. She was close behind.

It's bad when you can't even eat a chocolate candy bar in your own house. I gave them each a jelly bean and for the second time that day, told them to go outside and enjoy the wonderful weather.

They finally joined Hershey but when I started rearranging the living room, both dogs came back inside and were getting underfoot—whether to help or from nosiness I was clueless.

I do know, and people who know me know, I've said I wasn't going to rearrange any more furniture. The dust bunnies and half-chewed dog biscuits found behind and beneath furniture upon my demise would be the legacy I leave behind.

But. And there's always the but—the exception—I just felt like moving some stuff around for a different look. Old habits die hard. And when moving a chair from here to there, I'd vacuum the accumulation. Both dogs were dogging my every step. Pardon the pun.

While Rosie has no fear of the vacuum cleaner, TacoBelle deems it her duty to protect me from it. Comforting to know my house is protected by a Chihuahua who thinks she is a Rottweiler.

It was at this time I caught myself saying for the third time "Why don't you pups go outside and play!"

And it was at that moment that I knew I'd done it. I'd become a little old lady who talks to her pets like they're human. All doubt was removed.

They share most my food and sleep on the bed at night. I'd already realized several years ago that I'm TacoBelle's staff of one and I'm lucky she lets me live here with her. She's not only the alpha dog, she's the furry queen of my household. Bless her spoiled-rotten little heart.

TacoBelle has ruled this roost for so many years, it is rather trying with BooCat running for election to that position. I won't go into the alpha-pet battle that's currently ensuing between Taco and BossBoo.

It's definitely ongoing since the day Boo strutted in the door and took inventory. By the way, I'm not even anywhere near in the running. My name's no where on the ballot. Nor is the unassuming Rosie. We don't care. Let them battle it out. May the best cat or dog win.

The conclusion is that everybody could benefit from having a dog or cat, or both, or several, when we get older and live alone. They're good company and I can babble away and although my fids may not always listen, it keeps friends and family from accusing me of talking to myself.

I don't know enough about the Theory of Evolution to determine if I believe it or not. There's a part of me that wonders if I evolved from an ape, how come there are still apes that look and act like apes?

While I consider myself spiritual I'm no longer religious. I have deep feelings on the subject that it's taken a lifetime to conclude. Woody Allen once said he was an agnostic and his wife was an atheist, so they couldn't decide how not to raise the children.

In Charles Darwin's theory of evolution, he taught that animals are biological kin to man. Even if this isn't actual factual, how can we not feel something kindly toward other living, breathing creatures? The fact that they are living, breathing, must account for something.

Why can some people find it so easy to open their hearts to animals, and others not? To me, my BooCat, my TacoBelle, my Rosie and my yard full of canines—even my sweet long-lived pet birds—are each my soul mates.

Even as someone who doesn't profess to be religious any longer, if there is a God, I cannot but believe he would surely want mankind (*Man. Kind?*) to respect all creatures that are a part of his creation. I fail to see how people who claim to believe don't see this as a given.

When I look into the eyes of my fids, I see much more than just dumb animals. I see love.

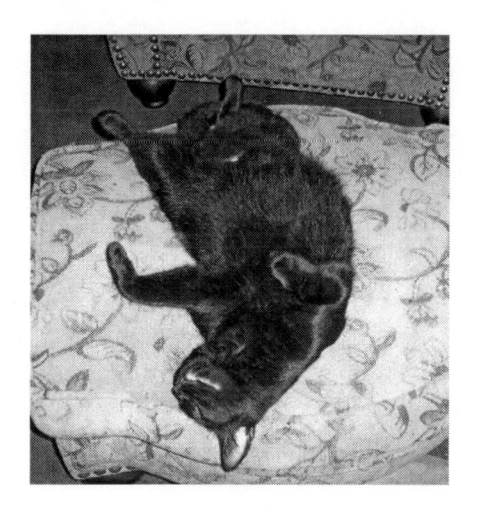

The Passing of the Alarm Torch

55

"TacoBelle and Rosie both had me at BowWow. BooCat got me at Meow."
(Barbara Sharik)

BooCat has inherited Hershey's former job of beating the alarm clock by a minute or two. Hershey would waken me at about five-twenty-nine every morning, workdays or not. It must be a cat thing, because there's no way Hershey passed the legacy on to Boo-Cat. Hershey was sadly long gone by the time BooBaby arrived.

Yet, there it is.

I heard a comedy routine on which the comic said that one day his roommate kept hitting his snooze-alarm from seven in the morning until four in the afternoon. Although part of a joke, I was thinking, that wouldn't be too hard to do. Incidentally, the longest I've engaged mine was from five until seven one morning. Two hours. One-hundred-twenty-minutes. That means I hit it a dozen times. Over a period of two hours, what's twelve times?

That particular incident frustrated Hershey because he took his alarm service duty very seriously.

Usually I only tap the snooze button a couple times. Since my snooze-alarm only lets me doze for ten minutes in between each tap, I have to ask, how can you grab any decent zee's in ten minutes?

My problem was, in an attempt to outwit myself, I put my alarm clock far enough away from the bed so that when the alarm went off, I had to exit said bed to shut it off.

After a few days of this—getting in an out of bed a half dozen times, barely getting any catnapping done before the alarm came back to life every ten minutes—I came up with a solution. I located a long-armed wooden backscratcher and with it, I was able to reach the snooze-button without doing more than raising my head an inch or two from the pillow. In fact, I've gotten so good I can in point of fact, tap it with my eyes closed. The result is that now I can finally get some serious snoozing during my allotted snooze time.

On the other hand, I had a rousing alarm that activated every morning. It was Hershey the cat. He'd position himself several inches from my head shortly before the alarm was scheduled to sound every morning. Being a light sleeper, I felt the vibration when he leapt onto the bed. Then I heard his pleasant purring because he curled up about two inches from my good ear. His tail twitched across my face and made my nose itch. The only way I could de-activate Hershey's snooze-button was to reach out and pet him, whisper a few sugar-filled niceties to show appreciation for his thoughtful attendance every morning.

ThreeAlarmBooCat does it different. She has several modes of operandi. The first and mildest is when she starts out asleep either in the crook of my left arm or sleeping on my legs between my knees and feet. In this case, she runs up my body and lays her head under my chin and purrs. Even with my CPAP mask, I get the message. It's a good message. My cat loving me makes me wake up with a smile on my face.

But, if I'm extra sleepy and don't respond in what she considers an appropriate length of time, she stands up and proceeds to walk up and down the full length of my body. When she reaches my knees or toes, she turns around and walks back up toward my head again. This walking up and down my legs, stomach, chest back and forth almost always ensures no matter how sleepy I am, I am going to wake up.

The thing is, since she's discovered the joy of eating dog biscuits, she's put on weight and she's heavy. She's also persistent. She doesn't yowl. She doesn't even meow softly. She just tramples up and down my body. When she's stretched out, distributing her weight evenly, it's

55 / The Passing of the Alarm Torch

not noticeable. But when she stands up and walks one foot at a time sinking into my fluffy deep skin, it hurts.

So, if sweet purring doesn't wake me, almost always being trodden by the FatCat does.

And still, there is one more action BiguddahBoo resorts to if I don't wake promptly enough to suit her, or if she is attempting to wake me especially early. It involves her leaping onto my body, preferably my chest or stomach, then taking a few steps up close and personal, peering into my face.

The initial landing on my body knocks the breath out of me. Then, when she propels herself off my body, it leaves me expelling a "Whoof!" as air is forced out of my lungs from the force of Boo's back feet lifting off.

Within seconds, she hurdles herself onto my beat-up body again. She is an impatient alarm-torch bearer. If I'd paid attention in math class I might know about centrifugal force and propeller velocity and landing speed so I could better describe what it feels like being awakened by BombLaunchingBoo in the morning.

"Okay, Boo! I'm awake. Stop!"

That's me as I sit up, removing the CPAP mask and gasping for breath, oxygen and air; all of which she's knocked out of me.

Hershey was reliable to say the least. Seven days a week, whether I had to rise and shine or not. Likewise, his predecessor. To a fault.

Hershey was a gentle giant of a cat. MaximumBoo wouldn't know gentle if it came up and introduced itself. She doesn't understand moderation much less gentleness. She does everything to the extreme.

I found out years ago that to wake up to music playing from a radio is much better than to depend on an old fashioned alarm clock that jars you awake with a loud blaring buzz or similar double-digit decibel sounds, startling your whole constitution. Your heart jumps into your throat and your body jumps out of its skin. That's way too much jumping first thing in the morning. Much better to wake to the soothing sounds of music, thereby starting the day gently. Even better to wake to a cat's purring.

There's a down-side to waking to the radio. It's trained me in reverse of most people I know. I have friends who say they cannot go to sleep unless the television's playing. Quite the contrary. I can't fall asleep if it's on because I've been waking to the DJ's voice and music for too many years. Talking wakes me up instead of putting me to sleep.

My go-to-sleep secret is silence and a good book. Forget counting sheep. What do I know about sheep? Concentrating on reading material shuts all the little worries of the day—the sleep-disturbing thoughts—out of my head. It reduces needless fretting. Halts worrying about stuff I have to do the next day. A good book with a good plot overrides the nonessential nonsense that might otherwise keep me awake.

Besides, it's a wise person who never makes tomorrow's problems today's worries. I try to be wise.

Who Turned Out the Lights?

56

"No one appreciates the very genius of my conversation as much as my BooCat, TacoBelle and Rosie." (Barbara Sharik)

I remember one particular Hershey incident. I woke up around four-thirty in the morning and it was pitch dark. Of course, it's supposed to be dark at that wee hour, but in this case, even the lighted dial on my clock was dark. The electricity had gone off and night air was creeping into the house. That's what happens when you live in a totally electric house in the wintertime and the heater stops running. Temperatures drop quickly.

According to the stopped clock on my electric stove, the electricity had ceased to flow at three-forty-five. I made my way to the telephone to dial the electric company by flashlight, which is like adding insult to injury because the phone number for the electric company isn't listed in the phone book in numbers, but rather in letters, spelling out "Outage."

Texters may have no problems with this. I, however, am not a texter. I prefer numbers. It takes me too long to decode which letter is what number. I pressed one number that translated from a letter and five minutes later I figured out the next number and by then I was listening to a dial tone. Ma Bell, like time, waits for no man. Or woman.

Once I figured out which number to push for the letter "O", for the letter "U," for "T," and so on and so forth in the dark with nothing but a very weak flashlight beam which, by the way, required that I hold the phonebook in one hand, the flashlight in the other and use my big toe to press telephone buttons and all the while fighting off the urge to have a nervous breakdown because that would have been easier than this, then an automated voice welcomed me to *Entergy's Outage Reporting System*. The voice instructed me to press the number "one" if I wanted everything in English.

Which I did. Being an English-speaking American. We'll not even go there. I blew my chance to learn Spanish when I lived in El Paso and went to Irvin High School and it was an elective course. At that time I didn't know Spanish would become America's second language or I might've made a concession and learned more than "Quay Paso?" which is likely not spelled right.

I'm not being racist but I do join the ranks of folks who say this is America, speak English please. I applaud people who are fluent in a couple languages but for those of us who aren't, speak English. Please.

I had occasion to call an automated phone number recently with a different approach. Their instructions soften the English-Spanish thing. The voice tells you that you've reached so-and-so and then it immediately switches to Spanish and advises that if you wish to continue in Spanish, press "one."

What they've done is, instead of making English-speaking Americans press the button for English, they are making the Spanish person do the pressing. It's reverse psychology and not a bad idea. If you don't push the button, then the message continues in English. It's more appeasing.

In any case, in this case, the voice from hell next inquired if my phone number was indeed what my phone number is, for me to then press "one." I pressed one.

Remember, I'm in the dark. I can't see the numbers on the dial. All I want to do is report an outage. What I need for moments like this so my hands will be freed up for button-pushing is one of those flashlights on a headband like miners wear.

The brainless voice from hell then advised my account couldn't be accessed using that number. My telephone number was null and void and my account number was required. So guess what? Next on amazing feats expected of me was to key in my account number—which I don't know by heart. If you think pressing "one" is difficult in the dark with one hand holding the flashlight and the other holding the phone, try shining the flashlight at an old electric bill and trying to read your account number, shining the flashlight back at the phone dial, pressing a number, and back and forth until the whole account number has been pushed and the dastardly deed done.

Remember it's pitch dark. It was akin to a wide-awake nightmare. It will do no good to put the outage phone number in my speed dial. I'd still have to provide for all the rest of the requests needed just to tell these folks my electricity is off. If I could be sure the outage is wide-spread I'd just go back to bed and let somebody else do all this button-pushing. But if it's an isolated outage, I needed them to know about it.

I knew immediately what the problem was—why the telephone number wasn't acceptable. When I used to keep the accounting books for the Jones-McGinty Water System I was once asked to supply its telephone number. I did. But since this was a job I worked from my home office, I of course used the only phone number I could connect with the water system. The board members are volunteers and we don't have an official office. And ever since, my telephone number has been tied to the water system as well as my home account and it confuses the automated accounts people.

I no longer keep the books for the water system and would like to have my phone number back but if you think it's difficult reporting an outage by automation you should try to retrieve your phone number. It ain't happenin'.

That done I had to press the number "one" to verify that my name started with V-A-I-L.

Now there's a good one. I'm not a Vail anymore, but I remember the last time I had to change my last name due to the archaic requirement that women take on their husband's last names. I reported the name change. This required having the current bill closed out, being refunded the original deposit of a lesser amount put up under my former name, putting up a new, more costly deposit because everything has gone up, to go with the new name. It is still me. It is still the same house, because the new husband moved in with me and not the other way around. No one even had to turn the utility off. There was no interruption in service. But the name changed and paperwork was created.

I don't care what name my bill comes in. Every single thing that needed a name change, except the social security card, cost money. And stupidest of all, was my Notary Public commission. I became a notary back in 1970. When I was divorced due to no fault of my own, and eventually remarried, I needed to use my new legal name when notarizing legal documents. I notified the folks in Baton Rouge and instead of just changing my name, because I was still the same person after all, they sent me a whole new signed, sealed and dated certificate suitable for hanging. It was signed by the governor at that time. So then, instead of showing I'd been a notary since 1970, now I was starting all over with a beginning commission date of 1982.

And then it happened again. I started over again in 1994 with a different husband and a different name and a new notary commission anniversary date. It changed again. It was as though I had just become a notary for the first time in 1994. Wasted those 24 years in the official record books. When they give out awards for longevity, I'm falling short.

So, nope. I'm not changing my name again. I do not want to be who I was, but how can I afford to be who I really am? One of my biggest complaints about women taking their husband's names is how women become lost in the system as a result. Old school mates can't find you once you've married and changed your name. A major part of a woman's identity is gone everlastingly. Using the school alumni thing as an example, the former classmates knew she was Susie Snowflake, now since Susie has married Frosty Snowman, she is Susie Snowman and lost forever. Look in the phonebook all you want. Search the Internet. Unless you know who she married, you won't find her. She might as well have melted.

So, I pressed one. I'm stuck with that name by a process of elimination of harassment.

Then a different voice, one so faint it sounded like it was coming from the Philippians where it had probably been outsourced. I was advised the electric company was sorry for my inconvenience. At least I think that's what was murmured. And I think she said the power would be restored sometime or another. I clearly heard the voice telling me to push dozens of buttons on my phone dial, but this voice was nothing more than a mumble. Ah, but at least I got the outage reported. It wasn't easy.

I went back to bed, declaring I wasn't going to get up until the lights came back on. Unfortunately, Hershey decided differently. At five-twenty-nine, he was beside me purring. I told him to go away; we were not getting up yet. Then at six-thirty I woke up to his feet planted on my chest and his face in my face as he "meowed" loudly.

Rising, the only thing shining being my flashlight, stumbled out to the living room where I sat in my new club chair and ottoman, flashlight in hand, and read for awhile. That was when Rosie, used to the old recliner instead of my new chair, decided to lose what sense she had and relayed to me that she couldn't figure out how to get into my lap in the new chair in the dark. Dachshunds are said to be smart, but right about then I had my doubts. The only solution was to lift her into my lap. Count to ten. Maybe twenty. Take a deep breath.

Fortunately, the electricity was restored and the lights came back on at seven that morning.

Do I wish I wasn't completely dependent upon an electric company? You bet I do. There's something called a "Hurricane Charge" that's scheduled to be on the monthly bills for ten—yes, I said ten—years. Thank you Katrina. Even 350 miles away, the damage of that devastating storm reaches out and continues to choke all Louisianans long after the fact.

There's also the "Energy Charge" and it's already been on the bills for a number of years. It's almost always more than the actual bill based on wattage used. It has to do with the high cost of oil. Far be it for the electric company not to make a hefty profit and absorb some of these costs. That's one hand. On the other, I don't want to live without electricity. And I prefer it to any other form of fuel. And when the weather is bad, ice storms and tornadoes wreak havoc, the faithful linemen are out on the job restoring power.

Bless their hearts.

Still and all, Louisiana has an elected official who overlooks utility companies but he's asleep at the wheel in this case in my humble opinion.

Always remember, the opinions expressed throughout are mine and mine alone. As my days grow shorter and my memory longer,

BooCat Unleashed

I tend to have opinions on everything and don't mind voicing them even though I recognize the fact that ranting and going off on a tangent does absolutely no good. Still, there are time when I just can't help myself. I'm a lot like BumfuzzelledBoo that way—we're never totally helpless, but we're often hopeless.

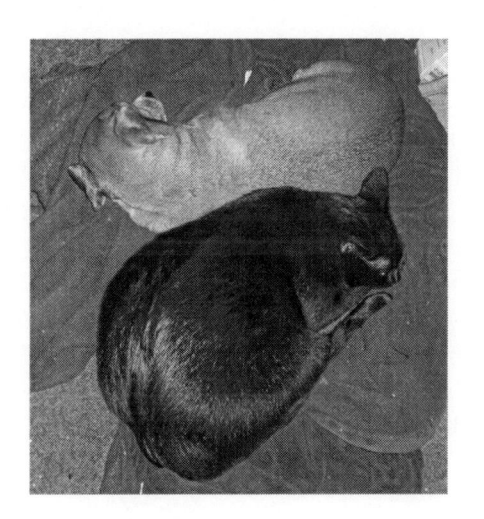

Almost Sleeping Single in a Double Bed

57

"A cat in gloves catches no mice." (Ben Franklin, *Poor Richard's Almanac*; meaning sometimes you cannot accomplish a goal by being careful and polite)

I decided to heat a roll for a quick breakfast, only to find something really strange embedded in the roll. Upon investigation, I found another piece of this strange item in another roll. I swear to you, I believe it was part of a rodent that fell in the vat at the bakery. It shook my faith in mass produced foodstuff. On the other hand, BooCat would've loved it. If memory serves, and sometimes it does, sometimes it doesn't at my age, that bizarre roll is enclosed in a sandwich bag and stashed somewhere in the back of my freezer.

Breakfast abandoned for obvious reasons, I got ready for work and I'm pleased to announce that the rest of the day went fine. Still, in all, one cannot help but wonder about life's little ups and downs. It also leaves one contemplating what it would be like to go through a day without anything untoward happening. What would it be like to have an ordinary day?

I doubt I'll ever know. Probably it would be downright monotonous. Boring even. It was tough-enough to make it through an ordinary day in the past, fat chance ever having one now that BooCat has taken up residence at Wit's End Comedy Club.

No Way José!
Hey, I do know another Spanish word. José.

And thinking of my natural alarm-clock-cats, Hershey of late and BooCat currently, puts me in mind of sleeping single in a double bed.

When you are an old maid, divorcee, widow or spinster—whatever that is—or the male counterpart, a bachelor by choice or otherwise, you might occasionally entertain the idea of becoming attached, finding a companion. But, when you've resided on your own for any length of time, it's pretty easy to get set in your ways.

Considering my attributes, along with my less endearing habits, it has likely become a lost cause to even think about acquiring a two-legged companion on a full-time basis again.

For one thing, I know I snored. I might call it purring but I can only imagine it would still be annoying. Add to that now I wear a breathing machine CPAP mask. It should eliminate the purring but it's scary looking—the sight of which would probably knock any romantic thoughts back into last week.

You saw the movie *Alien* didn't you?

I also leave the light on and read every single night until very late. I prefer absolute silence while reading. No television. I'm not much on idle chatter either. Also, I'm an early riser. Thank you BooCat.

Rosie, TacoBelle and BooBaby sleep on the bed. Wherever they want. Top, bottom, upside or down. And even though I'm not a tosser-and-turner, I won't turn over in the night no matter how uncomfy I might be, because I don't want to disturb BooCat and crew.

When we first get in bed, it feels good to have BooCat climb onto my feet and settle down for the night. She keeps my toes warm. Six hours later, as I slip out of bed for a potty run or to get ready for work, it's not so fine because I can barely stand. My feet are numb. They aren't cold, true, but they aren't okay either.

Rosie always sleeps under the covers. TacoBelle used to. Now she's leery because sometimes BouncingBoo walks on her. She wants her head out from under the covers so she can snarl at Boo. Does BoundingBoo know she's walking on Taco? Probably. It's the kind of thing she would do just because she can.

TacoBelle, whether completely or only partially covered, sleeps on the side of me where a companion might if there were a companion.

57 / Almost Sleeping Single in a Double Bed

This could be a problem.

There's a set of wooden stairs and a wooden ramp beside the bed so they can go up and down easier. Also, I made it known to them upfront that I can't buy anything larger than a king-sized bed. With that established, it was understood there would be no sleeping perpendicular to each other. Nobody would be allowed to sleep stretched out to the fullest extent possible. Even little dogs when stretched lengthwise, can take up a lot of space. Noses pointed straight out at one end and tails straight out the other end to maximize space was disallowed. This would go for a human companion as well.

I ascertained ages ago the secret of letting dogs spend the night in my bed. Any dog wanting to sleep underneath the covers had to get between the sheet and blanket. This way there are no cold noses invading my space during the night and accidentally sending me into cardiac arrest. This would also apply to a human companion.

My sweeties are allowed to beg food from the table. If a human companion gets squeamish seeing a dog lick leftover melted ice cream from my bowl, worrying about germs and the like, I guess he'd better bring his own set of dishes. I generally cook additional tidbits specifically for my fur babies. TacoBelle is the bossy one. Rosie lets her do the begging then partakes of the benefits gleefully. MistressBooCat is pure royalty. I need say no more.

When I get home from work, they get the first hugs and kissie-poo hellos. Anyone else would have to stand in line.

Cat and dog hair have been known to complete an outfit. If somebody doesn't want cat and dog hair on their clothes, all I can say is don't sit on the furniture. Or bring our own cloths brush.

In my household, my pets are people too. To the uninformed, BooCat may appear to be just a cat and TacoBelle and Rosie just dogs. But actually they are my children even though they are short, furry, walk on all-fours and don't speak English as we know it. I understand everything they say. When TacoBelle wants a jelly bean, and she dearly loves jelly beans, she'll make her wishes known in no uncertain words—well, barks. In fact she has an uncanny jelly-bean sixth sense and can locate them even when contained in an airtight tin canister.

I feel guilty if I stay away too long, worrying about leaving my furry kids home alone. When somebody adores you blindly and unconditionally, it's only right you reciprocate.

Because cats are so independent and self-reliant, people tend to take them for granted. It's easy, perhaps too easy. A housecat owner can make sure there's plenty of fresh water, dried food and a litter box and be gone over a weekend without worry. For a short duration, most cats likely wouldn't pine away from lack of attention.

On the other hand, nary a dog owner would leave a housedog home alone. Why?

For one, cats don't require daily walks. Canines do.

Many cat owners don't realize their cat misses their presence on the same level as a dog, but they do. The thing is, a dog sits pining at the door for its master's return. A cat isn't often found pining at the door because they have a different way of expressing their emotions.

Although I'm not one-hundred percent certain about BooCat, I have the feeling it wouldn't be good for her to be left alone any longer than an eight-hour workday. Due to her emotional sensitivities and needy tendencies, unless TacoBelle and Rosie were keeping her company, I don't think Boo would fare so well left alone.

In most instances, it's not that cats don't miss us when we're gone, it's that they can and do amuse themselves in an owner's absence, whereas a dog languishes sadly, waiting at the door. Self amusement can only fill so many hours in the day of a cat. A cat can get bored when its owner is away. But then, a cat can get bored even while the owner is at home. Cats need stimulation; mental and physical.

Without a nanny cam, I can't be sure, but on this subject, my BooCat may be the exception to the cat versus dog sitting at the door awaiting their owners, rule-of-thumb. Whether she is pining doglike, I can't say. But every time I open the door after being gone from the house, she is there. Or if not exactly there, she is seconds and a scamper away. But then, I've determined she's a dog in cat's fur.

As proof that BarklessBoo is part dog, I am reminded of the time when Rosie was asleep under her hotpink throw on her hotpink rug, TacoBelle was sitting nearby and BooCat was peering out the window draped with hotpink curtains while I was typing a few feet away in my hotpink home office. We girls are partial to hotpink.

TacoBelle spied Daisy, one of the outside dogs, as she nonchalantly sauntered past the window. She barked and lunged. She and BooCat simultaneously slammed their bodies with a loud thud into the pane of glass. It was a thousand wonders it didn't crack with the furor these two created. BooCat's paw reached up with a swat-like motion, no doubt cursing the windowpane for being in her way. TacoBelle cursed it too with yappy barking.

Daisy looked over her shoulder at the commotion, and never lost a beat as she continued without so much as a flick of an ear at the disturbance being raised by frustrated TacoBelle and BooCat.

BooCat pining for my return aside, it is essential for a cat's happiness that cats be provided with a wide variety of cat toys that will arouse their natural curiosity and predatory drive. Toys don't have to be fancy or expensive, but they need to be fun as seen through the eyes of a cat. BooKid loves toys. She has an array of store-bought things to amuse her. But Boo is equally happy playing with several rubber bands strung together as she is with a catnip-filled toy mouse.

Unfortunately, it's not easy keeping mouse toys for BooCat, so it's just as well she likes rubber bands. Rosie has never chewed on a human shoe. She doesn't chew on furniture legs. She only chews on pet toys. That includes toy mice. Another bit the dust the other day. I forgot to put it away after Boo finished playing with it. Rosie can't distinguish between a stuffed cat toy and a stuffed dog toy.

Even though cats traditionally spend hours catnapping and chasing imaginary adversaries around the house, they require quality time with their owners. Imaginary adversaries? Or ghosties? With Boothe-Magnificent, I can't say for sure.

An outside cat likely has a healthier psyche, but outside cats don't live as long either. So, keep kitty happy with lots of fun cat toys and spend as much quality time as possible. We do that with dogs, we should do it with our cats too. Cats are solitary hunters but they aren't solitary creatures.

BooCat knows, just as TacoBelle does, that she and Taco can be as bad as they want to be, and I'll forgive them. Although I tell each of them regularly "Don't start nothing and there won't be nothing," they've still got me wrapped around their paws.

You've heard the expression: "Falling on deaf ears." This is what happens to my admonitions in most cases. TacoBell can hear a candy wrapper being opened. BooCat can hear a mouse squeak in the ceiling. But they can't seem to hear when I tell them to behave.

Now Rosie, she's hardly ever bad. It would probably break her heart if I had to scold her for something. So I don't. Even when she demolishes stuffed cat toys. The girl can't help it.

I know I drive all my friends crazy showing them pictures of BeautifulBoo. But she's so photogenic. She could star in her own calendar. She'd be a feline calendar girl. And with the ease of a digital camera, no film, no sending off to be developed, I can take hundreds—and do—and print them on my home computer.

I also know I drive my friends crazy giving them blow-by-blow descriptions of every adorable thing she does—which is just about everything she does. She's so cute. So smart. So perfect. What can I say?

I've not given out T-shirts with BooCat's picture on them. Nor did I send photo Christmas cards featuring the fids this year. But, I'm considering it for next year. Plus I do have hundreds of pictures of each of them posted on my Facebook account.

Animal people are a little cracked. I admit that. Carla had U.S. postage stamps made with Max pictured on them. I have the envelope stamped with Max that she mailed to me tacked to my office wall. I really want some stamps featuring MissBoo.

I remember when BooCat was spayed, I seriously considered calling in sick so I could stay home with her afterward.

Sometimes BooCat makes it problematical to read the newspaper because she plops down right in the middle of it and I just don't have the heart to move her. It's my own fault. I should wait and read it while she's catnapping.

When she's in a particularly loving mood and leaps onto my lap while I'm typing, I just have to stop typing and pet her. She isn't interested in learning to type. She's not one of those cats that walk on the keyboard. She just wants some attention and loving. When she's had enough, then I can get back to the business of typing. But not until then.

There are times when I read in bed and I have to hold my book aloft with one hand, which makes turning pages difficult, so I can pet BooCat with the other.

Do you hear me complaining? No, you do not. It's because someone said, "*Dogs are better than kids because they eat less, don't ask for money all the time, are easier to train, usually come when called, never drive your car, don't hang out with drug-user friends, don't* smoke or drink, don't worry about buying the latest fashions, don't wear your clothes, don't need a gazillion dollars for college, and if they get pregnant, you can sell the pups."

And basically, that goes for cats too. Especially BooCat.

Catnapping

58

"Catnap." (To sleep for a short period of time. The term is in reference to the ability of a cat to sleep frequently and lightly)

Chuck saw something on TV about powernaps and their refreshing powers. A powernap is a twenty minute rest in the middle of the day that recoups and recharges body batteries speedily. This quiet and relaxing nap supposedly reduces stress and anxiety. Of course, if you're napping at work, it could create stress and anxiety if caught by the boss. As always, context is important.

Just ask BooCat. Powernaps work great. She doesn't call hers a powernap, even though it refuels her energy. She calls hers a catnap.

TacoBelle and Rosie take naps too. I don't have the vaguest idea what the proper term is for a dognap. You hear dognap and you think of kidnap, only napping a dog instead of a kid. It happens. After Rosie woke me up the other night sitting on my head, we all spent that next day in need of naps.

I woke up and Rosie was in actuality, sitting atop my head as it rested upon my pillow. She was trembling. A rush of adrenalin shot through my rapidly awakening body. I reached up and touched her and started to ask what is the matter when the brightest bolt of lightning lit up the room through closed curtains and blinds. Simultaneously, a clap of thunder shook the house to its foundation.

When I was a kid and we saw lightning flash, because light travels faster than sound, we would begin counting until the thunder clapped. However high we counted, that was supposed to indicate how many miles away the storm was located. Lightning strike. One-two-three. Thunder boom. The storm was three miles away.

This storm was sitting right on top of the fids and me. I hoped the lightening hadn't struck the house. It sounded like it may have. I've had several run-ins with lightening and wasn't anxious to experience another at 3:15 in the morning.

Rosie isn't fearful of storms; Taco is but not Rosie. Therefore, I don't know if I slept through other thunder and lightning leading up to this mother of all fearsome phenomena's, or if Rosie's sixth-sense sensed it was about to ignite. Rosie has some pretty powerful instincts. She's saved my life a time or two. She's neurotic at times mimicking Pavlov's dog traits, but she's also intuitive and understands almost everything I say to her in human talk. So, she's no dummy.

So, there was Rosie sitting on my head, butting up against the headboard. TacoBelle was buried about as deep as she could go attempting to attach herself to the underside of my left hip. BraveBoo was on my lap. Or where my lap would be if I was sitting up and had a lap. I was stretched out under the covers; she was plopped somewhere around my tummy and upper thigh area.

I expect TacoBelle to be bothered by storms. The older she gets the more they tend to disturb her, causing her to search me out for reassurance and comfort. BooCat hasn't had time to develop storm-phobias. I hope she doesn't. I assumed she was sitting on me because that's what she does. But with Rosie, her behavior was a first. If she was scared, then so was I. She is my indicator of disturbances. If she's nervous, I'm nervous.

Eventually the rumbling of the thunder receded and I never smelled cordite or smoke so I assumed we'd missed a direct lightning strike. In due course we fell fitfully back to sleep until the alarm sounded two or three minutes later.

At least it seemed like only two or three minutes later. Amazing how time flies when you need sleep. And believe me, there are times when fun doesn't even enter into the equation.

During my early years in Jones, following a May afternoon thunder storm, I went outside to pick a first crop of peaches off a tree I'd planted with my own two hands. Actually, the crop was composed of three peaches. But I'd grown them all by myself.

The rain stopped but apparently not all the stormy activity had moved out of the area. From the corner of my eye I saw a flash. I automatically struck at my hair as a natural reflex because I saw a flash out of the corner of my eye. I felt tingling run down my arm. Strands of my hair were actually singed.

Lightning had struck the ground and traveled along and up my body. I was alright, but was left reeling from the close call. It was not a direct hit. More than likely there's a name for traveling or running lightning; something akin to peeing on an electric fence. But whatever the scientific term, it was harrowing and something I've never forgotten.

An early childhood friend had scars on her arm she told me resulted from when she'd been leaning against the refrigerator in the kitchen when lightning struck their house. Like the lightning that ran along the ground, flowing up and out of my body, the bolt that struck her house traveled through water or electrical lines, burning her arm where it was in contact with the metal refrigerator door.

A two-story house not too far from Wit's End, as the red-tailed hawk flies, had a hole knocked into its roof from a lightning strike some years earlier. Another neighbor wound up with a broken mirror when lightening crashed in through the bathroom window and bounced around, breaking it with a resounding frightful crash. Weather warnings include not standing near windows during storms. During electrical storms, it isn't a good time to be standing over the kitchen sink doing dishes. I'm a believer. It doesn't take much to talk me out of doing the dishes anyway.

All this to say, after our harrowing experience with the electrical storm overhead, waking us in the night, all the next day we were in need of a powernap. Our peaceful night's rest was rudely interrupted.

Scientists claim human naps compare to a night's sleep in some memory tasks, but NASA says although naps may improve memory, they do little for basic alertness. The National Institute of Mental Health found mini-snoozes reversed information overload that creates burnout, irritation, frustration and poorer performance, claiming napping could boost performance back to morning levels.

Morning levels? Hey. I've known some grouchy bears in the morning and frankly, I would just as soon they not take a midday snooze.

58 / *Catnapping*

Once a morning growling is enough.

According to what Chuck conveyed, proponents claimed a twenty-minute break can be as effective as three-hour's sleep; that this pause in the day actually allows a body to perform better and improves the napper's well-being.

Being a fan of improved well-being, at the time Chuck was relating what he'd heard about powernapping, I realized I'd been experiencing some form of napping. Unfortunately, it didn't appear to have anything to do with power though. Still, if what he said about napping had any validity whatsoever, my being ought to be about as well as it's ever going to get.

Why? It's simple. My body discovered the fine art of falling asleep sitting in an upright position in my favorite chair in front of the television. Just like BooCat. And Taco and Rosie. We all spend a lot of quality time napping in front of the television set.

I wasn't sure if this newly acquired form of nodding off qualified as a powernap, nor was it a catnap exactly. A powernap involves a break from activity and a catnap is of a more leisurely nature. You grab a powernap in the middle of a busy work day, and take a catnap on the couch on a lazy afternoon. Knowing BooCat it's hard to make this distinction.

So, what was I doing falling asleep in my chair every night the minute I sat down to read or watch television? I had discovered this nap-habit some months ago. It was the period when I'd sit in my chair, especially with an interesting show on television, and the next thing I knew the news was on and I'd missed everything.

I wondered what was going on? This new-found ability to sleep sitting upright in my chair, in the middle of the living room, in the middle of the evening, in the middle of a good book or TV show, was annoying. Suddenly my new bedtime was fifteen minutes after I woke up from spending the evening powernapping in my chair.

Since studies show a little shut-eye helps a body tackle problems and make tough decisions, at that rate, I figured there shouldn't be a problem I couldn't handle. Truthfully, at that time I didn't know if falling asleep in my chair had anything to do with mastering the powernap or not. More likely it had to do with the malfunctioning mechanisms of a worn out body.

And then, I learned about sleep apnea. Hence, a cause for the slipping off to the Land of Nod directly related to the many times I'd awaken at night when I had stop breathing. For the most part, I stopped falling asleep in front of the television, and even worse, fighting the urge to drift off when driving down a boring highway, once I started using my CPAP breathing machine.

I was cured. I saw the ending of every show. It was such a relief.

Until the advent of the semi-annual clock tinkering.

You see, now there's something else afoot with regards to naps—power or otherwise. Just like that, I lost an hour and I can't find it anywhere. I've searched the inside of my eyelids night after night. It appears to be gone forever.

I'm watching the TV show "House" and all through the show he and his crew of physician flunkies have tried everything on this sick kid. Every time they think they've discovered what's wrong, something erupts elsewhere in his body and they change the diagnosis and run more tests or perform another life-saving surgical procedure. You'd be surprised how many diagnosis can be erroneously made in an hour and still Greg House is considered the best diagnostic Doc on TV.

Because there's only about three minutes left of the show, I figure I'm going to finally find out what's wrong with the poor child but the next thing I know, I wake up and it's five minutes into another show. "House" is over.

Did the little boy live or die?

How am I supposed to know? I haven't been able to locate the hour I lost when I sprung the clocks forward a couple weeks earlier in the name of Daylight Saving Time. No matter how many times I drift off it's still non-retrievable. You'd think I'd catch up eventually.

Likely the kid didn't die. People seldom die on "House." If his patients died he would lose his miracle worker status. He'd stop being nominated for Emmy's too. It's frustrating nonetheless. And the fault lies in the irrational tinkering with the clocks twice a year.

The thing is, it's never going to stop. Everybody mumbles grumpily every time we have to go through the process. Everybody says the clocks ought to be left alone. Yet, robot-like we turn them either forward or back so we'll all be in sync.

I don't mind following speed limits. I don't mind paying into Social Security. I don't mind paying Income Taxes even. I don't mind buying affordable health insurance if there is such an animal available. These are all for the good. I don't mind being mandated for everything except this senseless clock turning. The question is, if everybody dislikes it—name me one person who doesn't—then why must we keep doing it?

I suffer from sleep apnea. I used to blame falling asleep at the most inopportune times—like when driving down a boring highway—on sleep apnea. But I'm using a CPAP breathing machine every night and I've conquered that ailment for the most part. So, this recent nodding off while sitting in front of the TV has got to be the fault of the DST thing. That lost hour of sleep.

One of the most apt observations regarding DST was made by an old native American—someone I would have called an Indian Chief before it became politically incorrect to use the term "Indian." A person almost dares not open their mouths for fear of trampling on somebody's delicate emotional toes.

I like what the insensitive old timers used to say: "Call me whatever you want, just call me for supper!" Everybody is so hypersensitive nowadays.

In any case, the old native American asked the point of Daylight Saving Time. When told the reason, he nodded sagely. His lips seemed to quiver with the barest beginning of a smile, but obviously he didn't want to laugh out loud for fear of offending the White Man. After all, you know what happened last time native Americans and White Men tangled.

Wisely, the old Indian said: "Only the Government would believe that you could cut a foot off the top of a blanket, sew it to the bottom, and have a longer blanket."

Way to go, Chief. My sentiments exactly.

Declaration of Independence

59

"Grinning like a Cheshire Cat." (Lewis Carroll, *Alice's Adventures in Wonderland*. Meaning to display a silly smile)

I have yard dogs. Lots of yard dogs. There will always be dogs living out in my yard, demanding attention and food, because I take in strays. Love me, love my dogs. They come with the territory.

I'm a workaholic, holding down several jobs, but not a cleanfreak. Not any more. I might in fact on occasion neglect the house so I can write my columns and this book and read. I have become set in my ways since being one-hundred-percent on my own with the loss of Jon. Life just underwhelms me sometimes. I try to roll with the punches, go with the flow, slide with the sleds. Looking back doesn't make it play forward. Best to get on with life and do my best to savor every little bit that's left. The obituaries tend to have a lot of little old ladies and men in my age bracket slip-sliding away. I'm not anxious to join them. I've still got a whole lotta living left to do.

Yet, I've thought on rare occasions that it might be comforting to share life's little ups and downs with somebody; to have someone other than TacoBelle, Rosie and BooCat to carry on conversations with. They are good listeners, but hey, there's something to be said when someone answers you back with more than a bark and a wag of the tail.

59 / Declaration of Independence

Of course there's Chuck. We were married back in 1982, plus twelve years. We are still best friends but the romance has long since evaporated. We care and we are kind, but there is no passion.

I've not had any passion since Jon died. I've kept one eye open and I have an amazing number of very close male friends, good guy pals, but no ardor.

I've been told the best place to meet a man is at the grocery store. Hang out near the meat department because eventually most men who are shopping will buy a package or two of meat, what with grilling being a manly thing.

Certainly, I'd need to dress warmly; the meat department is refrigerated and I could catch a chill standing around for any length of time. Also, I'm aware I might get some strange looks from the butcher. He might think I'm out to steal a pork chop instead of just looking for a lamb chop to latch onto.

Hanging around the meat market almost seems like commercializing my search for an eligible bachelor. Do I wear a T-shirt that advises "Prime Grade A" or one that reads "Available"?

How's somebody going to know I'm man-hunting and not just lost, confused and dazed? I mean, what's a man to think if he spots me standing around in one department indefinitely?

And what's the conversational ice breaker? If I sidle over and ask a meat question, he's liable to get the impression I can't cook, and everyone knows the way to a man's heart is through his tummy. Sending that message wouldn't be advantageous to the cause.

If I make a cooking suggestion or offer a recipe, he might think I'm a bossy hausfrau. Men just hate that. That's why so many of them won't read instructions when putting something together; it's too much like having somebody telling them what to do. It's the Double D thing. Darned if you do; Darned if you don't.

Would it be kosher to pass out personalized business cards?

Do Singles Ads work? A lot of newspapers have them. I've seen them: "SSF seeks SSM," which interprets as Swinging Single Female seeks Super Single Male.

I've noticed that none of the ads really tell it like it is, such as "TOB (Tired Old Broad) seeking ABG (Any Breathing Guy)."

The odds of meeting a keeper this way are probably about as good as winning the Powerball. Actually, I'd probably have better luck investing my money in lottery tickets.

The Internet is full of singles sites too. It's my understanding that I would upload a photo, tell about myself, which is no easy task in itself; and then sit back to wait, hoping someone will e-mail and love will blossom.

I'd also hope this potential ideal mate isn't a loser at best, or a pervert at worst. Of course, chances are he is. After all, if he isn't, what's he doing searching for romance in cyberspace?

Others advise meeting someone at church, but this seems hypocritical. I mean, I should be attending church services for a spiritual uplifting; searching my soul, not soul-mate searching. I'd be fearful. Attending church with an ulterior motive is like inviting lightning to strike. It's not nice to fool Mother Nature, or God either.

Then there's the bar scene. Everyone cringes at that one, yet it's where many singles shop; another form of meat market. Naturally, if I meet someone at a bar, my next date might take me to an AA meeting.

Sometimes friends like to play cupid and match-make. This might work if you're lucky, but blind dates are scary. Speaking of lucky, I haven't hit it big with the lotto tickets yet. Which is my point exactly.

Anyway, chances are, I'd be introduced to some man and find I can hardly wait till he leaves, instead of meeting some man I can hardly wait till he arrives.

So, do I just wait for a chance encounter? Depend on fate to send someone special my way? Living way out in the country like I do, the chances of any encounters are pretty chancy. We don't even get door-to-door salesmen out here. If someone comes to my door, they are intending to come to my door. There is nothing left to chance about it.

Sometimes I wonder if men face this same dilemma. Is it just as difficult for them to meet women? What's their secret and where do they go to meet women?

Then I start evaluating and I realize a companion would need to be versed in the ways of fending for himself. For example, if I didn't feel like cooking, he would need to be able to. Also it wouldn't hurt one bit if he could mow the yard and take the trash up to the corner once a week. I do that stuff, but I don't always want to.

Because I work hard for my money, I spend it however I want. I

59 / Declaration of Independence

can be so tight I squeak, but if I see something I want, I might buy impulsively. I also spend too much on books and music, including Karaoke music. Which brings me to the part about loving to sing, and since I have the machine and the music, I do it often.

If songs sung out of tune bother you, and they do bother some people, then stay away. Someone said Karaoke is the equivalency of *Redneck Hooked on Phonics*. Probably a silly northerner who has never experienced the relationship one can develop between your frustrated inner singing-side and the Karaoke machine. It's therapeutic.

And BabyBoo, Rosie and Taco fancy having me sing to them. They forgive if I'm not in tune, hit flat notes or get so loud the chandeliers rattle. It's my house and I'll sing if I want to. You would too if you had a Karaoke machine of your own. It actually beats singing in the shower by a country mile.

Jon and I invested in a karaoke machine and a lot of music because he could sing, and did. All the time. Probably one of the most romantic things a gal can ever experience is having her man sing to her. It's a melting moment. We started a karaoke business and went to parties and clubs, doing karaoke for pay.

I'm left with several CDs of Jon singing, I had converted from cassette tapes. I have the machine, music and the mics and memories. Some people go a lifetime and never experience the amazing good love Jon and I shared for a far too brief time.

Now that I've established the joy of singing, let me add I don't like shopping. Except at antique shops or flea markets and actually, I'm just about weaned off them because there's not one single solitary spot left in this house to put another thing. Not one. Not none. Every nook and cranny is full. Every surface is covered with more than just dust.

I've apologized in advance to Theresa and recommended she have an estate sale when I'm gone. She recommended I start selling stuff on eBay.

I don't think wandering around a mall is fun. Window shopping is for folks buying windows. I'm probably not going to be hanging around meat markets either.

I'm never not reading. Books are everywhere in my house. There are bookcases with books stacked two and three rows deep and high in every room, lining walls here and there and up and down the hallway, around corners and piled on tables and chairs and they've buried the pool table. I would rather read than eat. Actually, I read while I am eating. I didn't build this figure by skipping too many meals. And since it's just me and the pets, I eat what I want, when I want. I only make two mugs of coffee each morning. If somebody stops by, I have to do some triculating on how much coffee it takes, versus how much water.

I'd never ask a companion. "What're you thinking?" because now that I'm more mature, I really don't care what anybody is thinking. I don't argue and fuss, but if I say it, I mean it. I'm not subject to depression and am always cheerful; making jokes about all things at all times. Some folks might find this annoying.

This isn't meant to sound like a Singles Ad. I started out thinking a companion might be nice. Then I realized how comfy I am with my own company and that of TacoBelle, Rosie and BooCat, and frankly, I've about talked myself out of the notion. It's better to be alone, alone than to be miserable with somebody.

The Dedicated Dachshund

"The dogs eat of the crumbs which fall from their masters' table."
(Matthew XV:27)

TacoBelle has always been a late sleeper. Rosie wasn't but she's becoming more so as she ages. BooCat is still developing habits and has too much kitten and too much energy to do more than steal a catnap now and again. She plays hard and sleeps hard.

Rosie loves going outside but I only allow her, Taco and BooCat access to the screened-in patio. They don't go out where the wild things grow. Or where all the big dogs are. I fear they would all three be too confrontational for their own good.

As soon as my feet hit the floor each morning, Rosie is off and running to the patio door. Unless I say "Taco, you wanna go outside?" she'll stay deeply buried in doggie dreamland. Like most pets, she knows certain words, and "outside" is one of them.

The other is "bed." They all know that word. When Taco thinks it's bedtime and she hasn't heard me say it's time to go there, she has owned me long enough so I know when she thinks we should all be in bed. She lets me know by coming to me and barking in a specific demanding manner. It's her "Let's go to bed" voice.

If I ask her "Are you ready to go to bed?" she bounces with happy tail wagging and starts heading toward the bedroom, and I had better be following her.

Rosie's attuned to the sounds the computer makes. When she hears me leave a program, she jumps up and starts heading toward the bedroom. Sometimes I have to call her back to tell her, *Not yet*, because I'm just changing from one program to another.

Really, she follows me everywhere, but in the case of the bathroom it's like she's convinced there's a secret exit and I might slip away in the night. She honest to Betsy seemed to think she had to accompany me even though I'd explained time and time again that I've been using bathrooms for years. Her attendance isn't mandatory. My words have always fallen on floppy ears.

And now things have changed. I wouldn't have believed it possible. Before BooCat came to live with us, when I'd go to the bathroom, even if Rosie was sound asleep, she'd wake up and follow me. Now, she only comes to the door and peers in; like she's standing guard. She has passed this particular torch over to the BlackWatchCat, and did so without fanfare.

BooCat, who has her own panel of neurotic habits, comes into the bathroom. She jumps into the bathtub and plays with the dripping faucet until I'm ready to leave this fascinating room. It still surprises me that Rosie's relinquished her long-held position to BooCat. Or perhaps, the job is only being shared.

In any case, sharing the bathroom guard duty has allowed Rosie a little less to worry about.

BooCat finds water dripping in the tub amusing. But then she can spend fifteen–twenty minutes playing with a rubber band all by herself. She's a cat. She's easily entertained.

As I exit the bathroom, I'm trailed by BooCat, who quickly overtakes me and runs on ahead; while Rosie waddles along behind—just so happy I didn't make a getaway.

Rose understands whole sentences spoken in conversational tones. She's very intelligent. Could it be my Rosie has Mensa tendencies, that her hang-ups are signs of genius; like a Canine Albert Schweitzer?

BooCat's motive for following me into the bathroom is different from Rosie's. She's smart enough to realize I'm not going anywhere; that I have to leave by the same door by which I entered. Therefore, it's my consensus that she takes this time just to explore and play. The old curiosity thing.

Boo's taken charge of the bathroom brigade while Rosie stands guard at the door. Rosie seemingly no longer deems it necessary to come all the way into the bathroom because by staying at the door on one side of me, and with BooCee in the tub on the other side, I'm surrounded. Obviously Rosie trusts BrigadierBoo will prevent me from escaping to parts unknown. They are clearly in cahoots. They are working in tandem. It's hilarious.

I'm not surprised Boo likes the dripping water. Normal cats wouldn't care all that much for water dripping on their heads or getting their paws wet. She's not normal. Dripping water is one more thing that moves and she can't ignore anything that moves.

Actually, animal behaviorists insist if a kitten is taught to take baths, they'll enjoy the water. And there is one particular breed that's known for its acceptance of water.

The Turkish Van is said by some sources to "love to swim." Others don't go quite that far but instead believe perhaps the cat simply doesn't struggle when given a bath due to a philosophical acceptance of life's little chores. Still, for this particular breed to be culled from the entire feline bunch with remarks specifically about it in relation to swimming and bathing, seems unusual unless there's truly something to it. Because, after all, why would the Turkish Van philosophically accept bathing more so than any other breed unless there's a preponderance toward this trait?

In any case, I've not given BathingBeautyBoo a bath. Thus far, she remains in charge of bathing herself in the old fashioned cat manner by licking herself. But, she does enjoy batting at dripping water in the tub and doesn't even flinch when some splashes on her head.

What joy these babies bring and especially each with their individual quirkiness. Rosie makes me laugh. She can be so funny. She gets so excited and in her vivaciousness, bounces backwards. It's a real hoot to see her. Very clownish. She's inquisitive, very fun-loving and playful. This is probably why BooCat took to her right from giddy-up.

She's a faithful and loyal companion. She sees it as her duty to protect our home from the outside dogs. Dachshunds aren't considered wimps, by any means. There's a history there to verify this. But while her ancestors may have been grand badger hunters, Rosie is a mellowed down version. Now, don't misinterpret or get me wrong. Rosie is ferocious with a window pane between herself and the outside crew. That window pane is the difference between courage and cutting and running.

As is typical of the breed, she's very clean. She's clever, good-tempered, intelligent and quite obedient and very easy to get along with. I've already established she's slightly neurotic. Well, maybe a lot neurotic. Well, gee, it just depends on how you define neurotic. Okay. So she suffers from a dog's version of OCD—Obsessive-Compulsive Disorder. Or as actual Obsessive-Compulsive humans define it: CDO—because they have to, in their compulsiveness, alphabetize the letters. Case in point, see the above mentioned bathroom thing.

Another obsessive-compulsive thing with SweetBabyRose is how she gets into bed. She's such a creature of habit. If she were human she'd be one of those people who won't step on a crack and it has nothing to do with breaking their mother's back. She would be a hand washer because of perceived germ infestations. She would go back into the house a half dozen times to be absolutely positive that she turned off the stove.

She enters the bedroom door. To the right is the ramp upon which the fids get into bed. But she always (as in every single time) goes to the left. She goes to the left, walks beside the bed, then ducks under the bed, crossing beneath the bed over to the side with the ramp. Then, and only then, she climbs the ramp into bed.

A straight shot if she went right, directly to the ramp, never happens.

And so it is once in bed, once she's finished working enthusiastically on her chew bone and is ready to go to sleep, she always, every single time, walks up to my head, passes above my head walking on my pillow, and then walks down along my left side right on the very edge of the bed, traveling down to my feet, ducking under the covers. During this portion of the trip, to ease this monotonous journey, I generally lift the blanket up so she can slip underneath.

Since her sleeping spot of choice is down around my feet—and everybody has preferences on which side of the bed they like best just as they have favorite chairs at the dining table—she could more easily just walk across the bed and over my feet and legs. I'd be glad to move my legs out of her way so she'd have this straight shot. When she's ready to get out of bed, that's the path she takes; she climbs over my legs and feet toward the ramp. But, to get where she's going upon entry, she always cuts across my pillow above my head and down the left side. What's the difference of getting into bed and getting out?

Is that strange? OCD in action.

Strange doesn't end just getting into bed. We've had the "jump in mom's spot the minute mom gets out of bed even though mom says she'll be right back" thing going on too. For years. Because I occasionally must get out of bed to go potty which is doggie-speak for going to the bathroom, and because Rosie's on my right side blocking me in, I always have to disturb her. I do my best to lift my legs up over and her and not have my derriere bump her nose as I slide out, onto the floor, into my slippers and then it's my turn to waddle—into the bathroom. I always, every single time, tell Rosie: "I'll be back. Don't move."

Of course she does. Night after night. Year after year.

Until now. Now, as with the bathroom thing, she's turned the job of guarding mom's spot to GuardDogBoo.

For all these years, when I came back to bed, Rosie would be sprawled out in my spot. I'd have to shove her out of the way. Generally that meant she'd go to the left; therefore, once I was in bed, she'd have to climb up over my head and pillow and down my right side and back under the covers once again. All the while, because we're so close to the edge, I caution her not to fall off. Luckily, we've not had a tumble off the bed during these weird maneuvers.

As with the changing of the bathroom guard, swapping out the saving mom's place in bed didn't happen overnight.

At first BooCat and Rosie had this thing going on. When I'd return from wherever I'd been (most likely the bathroom) they would both be in my spot. I never heard Rosie tell Boo what to do. BooCat took it upon herself not to miss any of the fun this activity produced.

BooCat has now taken over the activity completely. There's no more sharing. Boo moves into my spot every time and Rosie lets her. She obviously likes the sport. Just as Rosie did.

Sometimes I shove her over out of the way physically. Sometimes she gets covered up when I pull the covers over myself when she doesn't shove so easily. There she is, completely under the cover. I lift the blanket and peer at her. Her eyes are big, but she stays sprawled in apparent comfort. I let the blanket fall down on her. She doesn't move. I lift the cover and peer again. She's perfectly content. Peek-A-Boo seems to enjoy playing "Peek-A-Boo."

The game goes on for several lift-and-peeks until finally, she slowly works her way upward until her head is outside the covers. Her eyes dart about. It's obvious she doesn't feel trapped, because when she finally climbs out from under, it's not in the panic one might expect. She goes gently.

Once completely out from under the covers, in one magnificent leap, she ends at the bottom of the bed where she immediately begins licking her ruffled fur with vigor. That is ruffled as in reality rather than metaphysically speaking. Being beneath covers has mussed her fur. Cat's like their fur to lay neatly. Dogs aren't so persnickety.

And there you have it. A nightly routine between one neurotic Doxie and one strange black cat.

Fortunately, Rosie isn't a licker, but TacoBelle can plant a lick of love on my face quick as a wink. Each pet has their own distinct personalities and are wonderful company. When we are together, it's sort of dancing with woofs; if you will pardon the pun.

A long time ago, I'd promised Taco and Rosie that I wouldn't bring any more strange animals into our house after a disastrous time a couple years earlier. Before Gizzy moved in, who Taco accepted because she had known her for years, I bought a dachshund puppy from a friend of mine. It was supposed to be a dachshund and it probably had dachshund in its bloodstream, but it was rambunctious to a fault.

Sterling stayed above ground for the couple weeks we had this bad boy dog. It was super playful and it played rough. He was klutzy and more than TacoBelle, Rosie, Sterling and I could handle. I found him a new home as soon as possible. By the time he was situated elsewhere, our nerves were totally shot. Thus I made that promise to the girls.

I wasn't too worried about Rosie when I spontaneously brought BooCat home because she's so good natured, but I felt guilty about breaking my promise to TacoBelle.

I knew it was only right to have a talk with Taco. I said, "Taco-Sweety, I know I told you there'd be no more pets."

If looks could wither, my body became wilted and my soul shriveled just by the look she gave me. Her sad eyes spoke volumes.

Taco knew the implications of what I was saying. I saw betrayal in her expressive face. Her all-knowing stare said it all. I knew I'd have to do some very serious petting interspersed with lots of love talk to get back in her good graces. If there was to be peace and happiness at Wit's End, I knew getting back in her good graces was essential.

Taco didn't get her nose too out of joint when Rosie came to live with us. Rosie's personality is pleasant and pliant. Despite the bloodline of being a dachshund, Rosie was not a threat to Taco's peaceful easy life. I suppose one can say there are dachshunds and there are dachshunds.

Rosie is a dachshund. The name means badger hound. In medieval Europe, they were used to "follow badgers to earth," according to the American Kennel Club. There are illustrations dating from the fifteenth, sixteenth and seventeenth centuries showing badgers being hunted by long dogs with short legs.

The name dachshund became the official breed name in the early seventeenth century. The breed always came in both long hair and short hair, called smooth. Rosie's a smooth-haired Doxie. In 1890, a wirehaired variety was registered as a third type.

Badgers weigh twenty-five to forty pounds. To be a successful hunter, the breed needed strength, stamina, keenness and courage. Doxies running in packs, were also used to hunt wild boar. These dogs generally ran thirty to thirty-five pounds. So would the dachshund I brought home that upset TacoBelle, Rosie, Sterling and me so much. He was not a miniature dachshund as Rosie is. In fact, I had doubts if was purebred. Perhaps some stranger in the night made a pass at his mom.

Dachshunds used to hunt smaller game such as foxes, were usually smaller; weighing sixteen to twenty-two pounds. They were also used to trail wounded deer.

An even smaller size dachshund was used to hunt stoat and hare, weighing in at about twelve pounds. Rosie's in this category except she's a glutton and fights the battle of the bulge. It's a family trait. I've also fought that battle and the battle won. She'd weigh around eleven or twelve pounds if she weren't a glutton. Because she has no cutoff valve, she takes after her mother. Yes, I'm her mother and yes,

I'm rather fluffy. Like mother like daughter.

Nowadays, using a dachshund to hunt would be a rarity. They're small enough to live in a house or apartment, yet large and hardy enough for outdoor country living. The smooth-haired coat requires no care whatsoever. They're hardy, vigorous and seemingly tireless. And they're a very affectionate breed.

Perfect description of Rosie, a solid red dog; hence her name. She's a lover, not a fighter, but she's extremely alert. Take the snake incident as a prime example. She's responsive. She's a companion of the utmost. And most of all, she can be so hilarious at play.

How Rosie Saved My Life

"Cat-O'-Nine Tails: Eight kittens and a Mamma Cat."
(Whimsy by Barbara Sharik)

Humans come in kits—ready for assembly. You hope the finished product turns out successfully. We can measure success in many ways but success isn't always about making money. Sometimes it's about finding inner peace.

Maybe you think you're not what you wanted to be when you grew up and sometimes life leaves you feeling like you were folded, stapled and mutilated. Then something happens to remind you life is good.

I was half awake, half asleep, and I felt Rosie walking up along behind me from where she'd been sleeping at the foot of the bed. Since I was lying on my side, facing away from her, she continued her journey up and over the top of my pillow, coming around until she was facing me. I opened my eyes, but it was too dark to see anything more than the red digital numbers on the clock. The alarm hadn't gone off. It was the middle of the night.

I could feel her tail wagging and I reached out to pet her. Then she gave me a couple quick licks of love, turned around and headed back to the bottom of the bed where she went back to sleep, leaving me wondering, what was that all about?

Perhaps I'd been talking in my sleep, or maybe purring—which is feminine for snoring—and she felt the need to come check on me. Whatever. It was an unusual moment. She'd never done that before. It reminded me that kindness can come in all flavors and from any direction.

Life now and then has us so busy we don't take time to smell the proverbial flowers along the way. This is especially true for those of us who are getting up in age. As we age we must promise not to waste time feeling sorry for ourselves.

For most of us, it's within our own capacity to not let quality time fade. Age makes rivers grow wider and old oak trees stronger. It also makes our futures grow shorter and our pasts longer. It gets frustrating when we find we can't do all that we once could and consequently need the grace to accept our lessening abilities. Bitterness comes easy if we're not careful. It's wrapped up with the frustration bow. As a result, we find the need to both sharpen our wit and soften our tongues.

Part of my happiness-philosophy is to always take time to pet my cat and dogs and I guess one of my dogs decided to show her appreciation. Bless my Sweet Baby Rose.

Often, as our eyes grow dimmer, our memories increase. I wrote a poem that says nothing is accomplished by looking back; better to ride the tomorrow-train down a one-way track. It is foolish to waste the precious present because today is only borrowed and tomorrow barely lent.

Too often as we age, and I speak for myself especially, we get this uncontrollable urge to comment on every subject. Talk too much, in other words. Even though we may have been there and done that, we have to be careful not to bore the young folks with all this humongous amount of knowledge we want so bad to impart. Contrary to our beliefs, they might not be dying to hear it. Of course, we can take comfort in that there probably will come a day when they will wish they had listened.

We spend our lives giving away little pieces of ourselves, and for every piece we give away, we generally receive so much more back. Cats and dogs have always known this and most of us humans need to figure it out; the measure of love is to love without measure.

Since that most memorable and touching moment when Rosie

61 / How Rosie Saved My Life

came to me in the night, I was diagnosed with sleep apnea. During a sleep study I learned that I stopped breathing several hundred times in a single night. I now sleep with a breathing CPAP machine.

The fact that Rosie is a miniature dachshund and dachshunds are scent hounds, and as such, they have one of the most highly developed senses of smell; more pronounced than other breeds, it is possible a chemical change takes place in my brain, emitting a specific odor, when I stop breathing. Maybe Rosie's keen sense of smell alerted her to my dilemma.

There's also the chance that another sense kicked in. With sleep apnea, usually one wakes up when something in the brain signals breathing has stopped. But, in some cases, the signal doesn't come. In these cases, people die silently and serenely in their sleep. This is what I think may be what Rosie sensed. She came to me several more times in this same manner before I was diagnosed and started medical treatment. But this first time, it made the biggest impression on me. On that one special night I credit my little RoseDog with waking me back to life. Bless her heart.

The World Needs More Dog Sense

62

"I agree with Agassiz that dogs possess something very like a conscience."
(Darwin, *The Descent of Man*)

It is my firm opinion that humans could use a little more dog sense. If dogs and cats had opposable thumbs, they wouldn't need humans for anything. They could open their own cans of dog food. We could back up and let the dog drive. And they could.

What is said is that what separates humans from canines is the ability to reason. Actually, some dogs can do a better job of reasoning than a lot of people I know.

An example might be when one dog reasons because he's the biggest, he gets to eat first. And the little dogs reason, by golly, he's right. They let him eat first. This reasoning is a cross between logic and the law of the fang; but that blending isn't entirely unreasonable.

If your dog sees you with his leash, it's reasonable that he assumes you're going to take him for a walk. Now human reasoning isn't always so reasonable. Like, using the overused, why are humans the only beings who feel the need to label things as either flowers or weeds when they're all plants with blossoms? Just saying, you know?

Not getting into deep philosophical subjects like trying to figure out why someone votes for a particular politician and not the other, because when it comes to politics, nothing is reasonable or logical;

so let's take shopping with coupons. If someone's a couponer, and I am definitely not, they go through their Sunday paper, clip coupons and with the thought of a dollar off, the reason-button in their brains shorts out and disengages and off they go to the store, purchasing something they don't need—probably spending five dollars they don't have, just to save one dollar. How reasonable is that?

There are lots of examples. Some pointed out over and over, some I just thought of on my own. Is it reasonable for manufacturers to put a light in the fridge, but not in the freezer?

Is it reasonable for clothing manufacturers to install all closures in all women's clothes in the back of the garment? Dresses, slacks, bras—so many open and close in the rear where no human can reach. So why? Are clothing companies dominated by men who hated their mothers and have waged war on women as a pay back? And why do we women keep buying up stuff that's inconvenient. Unreasonable isn't it? Surely given the option, every woman would prefer her bra to open in the front. But they don't come that way very often. All the pretty lacy ones fasten in the impossible back. You either have to be a contortionist or do the slip, slide, turn and adjust thing.

The person who drinks too much, loses all reason. He thinks he's whispering when he is not. He thinks drinking makes him a great dancer and a fine singer. Drinking makes him reason that he is tougher, smarter, faster and better looking than everybody else. Drinking even makes him think people are actually laughing with him.

Dogs and cats are too smart to drink.

I read an interesting description of inner strength. I agree completely. It said:

> If you can start the day without caffeine or pep pills; if you can be cheerful, ignoring aches and pains; if you can resist complaining and boring people with your troubles; if you can eat the same food everyday and be grateful for it; if you can understand when loved ones are too busy to give you time; if you can overlook when people take things out on you when, through no fault of yours, something went wrong; if you can take criticism and blame without resentment; if you can face the world without lies and deceit; if you can conquer tension without medical help;

if you can relax without liquor; if you can sleep without drugs; if you can do all these things, then you are probably the family dog.

In general, dogs live a much less complicated life than humans. Give a dog a chew bone, some kibble and a toilet bowl to drink from, and he's content. Not so for a human. We people think we need bigger, faster cars. Fancier homes. Designer clothes. Gadgets of every sort.

We would think we were starving if we had to eat the same thing every day. An occasional pat on the head just won't do it for a human being. Maybe we should take a lesson from our pets. Learn to live a more simple existence instead of keeping up with the Jones's. Dogs never seem to worry. Most stuff people worry about never happens anyway.

Is a dog smart because he's obedient, does tricks and obeys our every command, or is he showing more intelligence if he thinks for himself? There's no argument that the dog is "self-domesticated." How nice it would be if more people were also "self-domesticated."

Because dogs share a number of social behaviors with us, they give comfort and security in return. They give warmth on a cold night and affection all the time. A dog's role as a companion is probably its most significant attribute.

While a dog's bark is his talk, actually his best language is mute. He communicates with us through body language, showing both affection and aggression. Ever notice that your dog has the ability to understand your feelings and emotions? His keen sense gives him this ability. Wouldn't it be nice if more people had this same capability?

It doesn't take a very big person to carry a grudge and it's impossible to unsay a cruel thing. That's a human thing. A dog just loves you unconditionally, showing the best sermons are lived, not preached. He doesn't care who is right or wrong and he is never too proud to show he's sorry for any wrong done.

A dog knows it doesn't matter who's the first to say good morning, make contact and give love. Just so it happens.

Good dog!

When Theresa and her dog, Nike, a Yorkshire Terrier; and Carla and Lance and their dog, Max, a poodle—my granddogs—came to visit shortly after BooCat came to live with me, I was concerned. I've grown quite fond of my granddogs. I didn't want BooCat to hurt them. As it turned out, they all got along just fine. No ruffled fur.

Both Nike and Max are used to a cat; one lives inside their home with them and one lives right outside the back door; a stray that adopted the family. Apparently Boo didn't see the need to show force or to remind the visiting dogs whose house it is; so it was all good.

They have come back since and the goodwill continues. Good dogs and a good cat makes for a good visit enjoyed by all. All of which confirms what I said before: Humans could use a little more dog sense and if dogs and cats had opposable thumbs, they really wouldn't need humans for anything. But we sure would be lost without them.

If I Didn't Have Dogs

63

"Scratch a dog or stroke a cat and you've got a permanent job."
(Unknown Origin)

Recently, a pet expert on a Public Broadcasting TV show stated what I've preached a long time: Cats should be inside pets only. There's too much potential harm outside. Cats are quick. Cats are smart. But cats don't really have nine lives. It was reassuring to hear an animal expert express my very views.

On the subject of dogs, sister Jan, who has birds and cats but no dogs, sent me an e-mail titled *"If I Didn't Have Dogs."* However, one could substitute cats for dogs in many incidences. And birds too, for that matter. I can pretty much equate most of this dog stuff to my BooCat as well as to TacoBelle and Rosie.

As with many e-mail forwards, there has to have been an original writer somewhere back at the beginning, but the author's name is usually long lost and even in some cases, when attribution is made, it's often incorrect or inaccurate. Anyhow, I have no idea who wrote this tribute to dogs, so I'm taking the liberty of commenting on some of the quotes contained within the original as it reached my e-mail mailbox.

Given that I have a passel of both rescued and selected dogs living at my house, Jan knew I'd take pleasure in reading about how life would be different without dogs.

In part, it said:

"If I didn't have dogs, my house could be carpeted instead of tiled and laminated."

I know that's true. After adopting Mom's fifteen-year-old Gizzy, she became the epitome of accidents happen. Poor old lady dog was deaf and blind, but so full of love, I just kept mopping up after her.

I use puppy pads and have seen TacoBelle walk to the pad, step upon it, and squat. Her front feet are where they should be, but her little Taco-butt isn't. Whoops! Puddle clean up time. I would very much like to be able to remove all the carpeting from my house and replace it with tile. It would be more sanitary and likely Rosie, Taco-Belle and I could breath better. We each have respiratory problems.

And speaking of puppy pads, although BooCat has two litter pans in different parts of the house for her convenience, she has her favorite puppy pad. I know she's the one using it because It gets all crumbled up after each use (and has to be replaced immediately). It is as though she is "covering up" after using the pad just as she does with litter in her litter pan.

BooCat is part dog. From munching down on Hartz Crunch'n Clean dog biscuits to wetting on a particular puppy pad, she definitely has an identity crisis going on.

"All flat surfaces, clothing, furniture and cars would be free of pet hair."

Face it, no outfit is complete without cat and dog hair. Before Hershey stepped on a rainbow, being a long-haired Himalayan, every time I vacuumed, I vacuumed up a cat. I'm still vacuuming up leftover Hershey hair. So far BooCat hasn't begun to shed to any grat degree. I'm sure she will eventually. Being solid black, she'll probably wait until I'm wearing something white. There is a commercial on television advertising a cat hair picker-upper that shows a woman with a white couch upon which dozens and dozens of black cats descend. Each and everyone of those black cats is the spitting image of BooCat. So, if she were to star in her own movie, she has a lot of stand-ins available.

"When the doorbell rings, it wouldn't sound like a kennel."

TacoBelle, around eighty-four in people years, yaps *"It's my house, I'll bark if I want to"* to the tune of Leslie Gore's "It's My Party." She never learned the meaning of "Hush." Obviously she doesn't believe she needs me to tell her it's time to stop barking. She decides when it's time all by herownself.

Thus far, whoever wrote this pet-parable punched dog ownership right on the pedigree. It's purebred actual factual. Puns intended.

"I could sit on the couch and my bed the way I wanted, without taking into consideration how much space several furry bodies would need to get comfortable."

This is true, but I rather like the furry bodies sharing my space. They offer warmth and comfort, both physically and emotionally. We have two-dog and one-cat nights when it's cold. I have trustworthy watch dogs and cat on alert in case of invaders. I have company whenever I want it; an attentive audience of three when I speak or sing. This keeps me from talking to myself and gives me a reason to sing.

"I would have money and no guilt to go on a real vacation. I would not be on a first name basis with 6 veterinarians…"

In order for all my furry babies to eat regularly, I buy one-hundred pounds of dried dog food a week; canned food by the dozen, biscuits and treats. Dr. Robert White and Elizabeth are on one side of town and Dr. Glenn Melton and his staff are on the other. They are on my speed dial. Among my favorite people, they do it out of love and their charges are, as a result, always fair. It is money well-spent. Still, I have to tell you, a third job wouldn't hurt so I could eat regularly too because added to that is cockatiel and dove bird food, wild bird food and fish food. It really doesn't leave much for people food.

Still, I manage.

"The most used words in my vocabulary would not be: Out, Sit, Down, Come, No, Stay and Leave Him/Her/It Alone!"

Candy already thinks her name is No! No! Bad Dog. TacoBelle hears Hush! but she ignores it. BooCat, not a dog but a cat with a dog's mentality most the time, hears Leave Her Alone in reference to poor Rosie.

Nobody listens.

This fact doesn't stop me from ordering everybody around, it just does no good. We cohabitate with the understanding that I can tell everybody what to do and everybody does what they want.

"My house wouldn't look like a daycare center, toys everywhere."

I tried teaching TacoBelle and Rosie and BooCat to put their stuff away when they finish playing, but they never finish playing. Right now, BooBaby is the worst offender. It isn't completely her fault. I keep buying her stuff and we have just about run out of floor space.

Rosie loves chewbones. I have to keep normal dog toys away from her. She has a penchant for disemboweling them. I have yet to find a stuffed dog toy, or even most hard rubber ones, that she does not destroy within minutes. I am talking minutes here. I am on a constant search for the ultimate toy; we have yet to find it.

A ball bearing?

TacoBelle once had a little blue dog-shaped squeaky rubber toy that she adopted and fell into motherly love with and from which she would not be parted. She carried it every step she took. She took it to bed. She loved that little blue baby. It was obsessive. After she was spayed, she lost interest in the little blue dog toy. I believe it was an emotional maternal craving to have puppies; but thank goodness, she set aside the neurosis after her surgery.

BooCat will play with the air, unseen dust motes, sounds of ghosts in the ceiling and mice under the bed. She will play with anything that moves or with stuff she thinks might move. She doesn't even need toys. But, I am a mother who believes in allowing the fids to have plenty available playthings for their entertainment and emotional wellbeing. I have my books, they have their toys. And yes, my books overflow the house, so why not their toys? This is our home after all.

"I wouldn't have to answer the question 'Why do you have so many dogs?' from people who will never have the joy in their lives of knowing they are loved unconditionally by someone as close to an angel as they will ever get."

This last part is pretty self-explanatory. My dogs and my BooCat are a delight. They love me unconditionally. That is how I love them also. Else, I would not put up with potty accidents, yappy barking, constant shedding, eating me out of house and home and sharing my bed and lap every day. We have a mutual admiration society thing going on around Wit's End.

"Remember, D-O-G spelled backwards is G-O-D. How empty my life would be, if I didn't have dogs."

Without my dogs and my cat, I know how empty my life would be. My furry and feathery kids are each and every one a part of my family. My daughter Theresa doesn't mind that she is not an only child. In fact she and BooCat have the same birthday. Theresa isn't the jealous kind.

She knows her spot as number one daughter hasn't been officially usurped. She has her own furry family members. She understands.

What mother could ever ask for more?

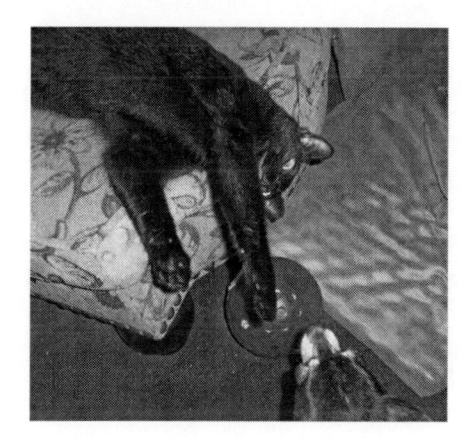

Priceless Moments

64

"*Catacomb (cat-a-comb): Grooming tool for BooCat.*"
(Whimsy by Barbara Sharik)

Each time there's a breakthrough moment between BooCat and TacoBelle, I get happy because there is the ongoing struggle for the Top Dog position in the household between the two of them—a vying for power.

Squatter's-rights awards Top Dog position to Taco, but dogged-determination puts IndomitableBoo right up there neck-and-neck and nose-to-nose. And it was a nose-to-nose moment that moved me one day in January 2010.

We were breaking cold temperature records day after day, and woke up to temps in the teens coupled with snow flurries the day of the momentous incident.

Because it was so cold, the central heater ran continuously. I never heard it shut off and held my breath that it wouldn't break from overuse. Saying he hadn't been really warm for days, I offered a back bedroom and Chuck accepted. He spent several nights because his trailer failed the insulation test. He's always such a good pal, not to mention many years previous, we were married for twelve years. All exes should get along so well. Because we can and do, I think we must be pretty special.

The secret to a successful marriage: separate houses. When nerves are frayed, one or the other can go home instead of running to the divorce lawyer. Just an idea to consider. Faithfulness would still be required, but separate breathing spaces could make a difference.

For all the running the central heat was doing, burning up the kilowatts, my home office where I spend hours typing and where George and SnowBird live, was so very cold I plugged in a small space heater and turned it on; it was imperative the chill be broken or SnowBird would live up to his name by default rather than because of his white feather color.

I was soon going to curtail my typing because it's difficult to type with ice cycles instead of fingers. Still, I needed to write a February column for the *Louisiana Road Trips* magazine a little earlier than usual because I was scheduled for reparative surgery the following Wednesday.

The surgery would help insure more quality living, but I didn't look forward to it. Being female and getting old has its downsides. Being surgically put back together is one of them. My favorite expression that I borrowed from Corinne, a Facebook friend from Nottingham, England, is that I'm "aging *dis*gracefully." The necessary surgery is a prime example.

With the small heater oscillating warm air, BooCat leaped upon a storage box located in such a convenient spot so the heat blew directly in her face and on her body. She settled down for a warm catnap. Rosie was wrapped up from head to toe in her pink throw in the center of the pink rug. I was typing. Shortly thereafter, Queen TacoBelle, the only family member missing, talked and walked herself out of bed from either loneliness or curiosity guiding her to come check out where everybody had gotten off to.

She stopped for me to reach down and pet her head, murmuring a few sweet-somethings which got her tail wagging happily. She sniffed at the blanketed lump that was Rosie. She delicately stepped over a pile of no less than a dozen collected bird feathers—BooCat's bounty.

When a bird loses feathers, is that called shedding or is there another more proper term? Molting? A question for Google. Or more likely, for my sister, Jan, the bird lady of Severn, Maryland. In some cases it's Boo feather plucking.

Walking toward the window, everybody's favorite gazing spot, TacoBelle abruptly stopped in mid-stride. The warm air caught her attention. It was like, "Whoa! Heat!"

TacoBelle is a typical Chihuahua—skinny-bodied, short-haired and thin-blooded—easily chilled. ChiChis need to be kept warm. Taco, true to her breed, likes to lie directly in the sun shining through a window or on the screened-in patio during the summer months. And, along those same lines, she likes to be near a heater in the winter. She likes to be in her own bed when the air is too cool, where she curls up into a round ball, tucking her nose beneath her leg. This gives her a pocket of warm air to inhale, keeping her warm. Both she and Rosie have always preferred sleeping beneath the covers—although since BooCat moved in Taco keeps one eye uncovered, the better to see Boo with—and they both like sharing the warmth garnered from my body; sleeping as close as possible throughout the night.

Taco sat down beside the heater, receiving instant gratification. I saw her turn her head toward BooCat, just inches away. Instead of her usual "Move it, Cat!" snarl, she gently leaned her head in Boo's direction and sniffed. Except for a breath of warm air between them, their noses all but touched.

Taco then turned away, facing the heater once again. BooCat sighed. The moment was priceless.

Two weeks later another moment outshined this one; do these moments just get better and better? More priceless? How many more will come before I can stop marveling with each breakthrough?

Resting in bed, reading. Contemplating rising and shining. Maybe the shine a little tarnished because the morning was so cold, snow having fallen the day before; but shining nonetheless. After all, the sun was making a debut after days of rain and then the snow. People subject to depression from lack of natural light would be reaching for their bottle of pills during this week's weather. I have my own manner of maintaining. I call it filling up the pickle jar.

In any case, if the sun could rise and shine, surely so could I. But, rousing the fortitude meant at least reading to the end of a chapter, a stopping point, before sliding out from under the extra covers.

Once the light was turned on overhead in the morning, BooCat was wide awake. It takes TacoBelle and Rosie a bit longer to revive themselves, especially on cold mornings. Rosie doesn't stir officially until my feet hit the floor, but only on the second time. She's smart enough not to be fooled by false alarms.

If I'm making a bathroom-run and coming back to bed for a moment more of snoozing, I tell her: *I'll be right back,* so as to stay her. The bathroom-run constitutes the first time my feet hit the floor. The false alarm.

I know her so well. And she likewise knows me. She listens and waits. She's fully awake but she's not about to get out from under the covers until getting up is official.

TacoBelle, on the other hand, doesn't even open her eyes. There are occasions she allows Rosie and I to climb out of bed and begin our day before she follows.

In this case, I was nestled all snug in my bed, as has been poetically stated a time or two down through the ages. After awhile Rosie settled back down, realizing Mom isn't getting up yet.

BooCat on the other hand woke up in her usual playful mood. She sniffed at the book in my hand. Paperback, she attempted to sink her teeth into the cover. I'm reminded of a very old friend who was killed in Viet Nam so many years ago, who used to tease his wife if she said or did something silly, telling her: "I buy you books and buy you books, and all you do is eat the covers."

BooCat was trying to eat the cover of my book. I moved it from her curious tasting bite. BitingBoo does a lot with her teeth. She uses them to stay Rosie—not to hurt her but to contain her. I have a couple photographs snapped at just the moment when her teeth appear to be sinking into Rosie's skin and Rosie's look of horror as a result; but seconds later, the teeth, never having broken the skin, release and she begins licking Rose instead. The teeth were just the instrument used to "capture" Rosie, bringing her into the position.

She will gently grab my hand with her teeth to pull my hand to her. It's obviously not an aggressive move; instead it is as though her teeth are serving as another appendage—like an extra hand on a human. Boo is very adept at using her paws to manipulate and coupled with her teeth, she is pretty well able to handle most situations and items of interest. She is one smart CookieCat!

In other cases she uses her teeth as an additional sensory device. For tasting, as it were. She is also a devout sniffer. She smells everything. Coupled with smelling, I catalogue her method of gently biting as kicking in an additional sense as well as an additional utilityware when coupled with the use of her paws. Biting can also be used as a form of protection or as a defense mechanism.

Her book biting desire foiled, she chews on the backscratcher instead. Her oddly human hands—in that they can essentially take hold of items she's interested in further exploring—lifted the backscratcher up and turned it over and over until she managed to shove it off the bed and onto the floor. She quickly lost interest. Out of sight, is out of her devious mind.

Next, she retrieved my ballpoint pen kept in the bedside tray for recording inspirational ideas that strike me at all hours of the night. She herded it off the tray and onto the bed where she proceeded to bat it around. Just as she leaned over, teeth set to sink into the plastic barrel, I do a *Now you see it, now you don't,* bamboozling her.

I put it back on the tray. She went after it several more times before I break all the rules of her game and hide it beneath the phone book. Out of sight, out of mind once again.

BooCat, her off-limits play-pretties removed, located one of her rubber bands. Like an apple tree dropping its fruit and shedding its leaves, she has littered the house with rubber bands. This one flies through the air a time or two before she tires.

BooCat woke up in a playful mood. I could see from the corner of my eye that she wanted to get into something, but didn't know what. One by one, all the good stuff was removed from her grip.

She sat on the side of the bed staring off into space. I was sure the wheels were turning, but I had no idea in what direction they were headed. Down a one-way bad-girl street no doubt.

Eventually she walked over to my prone body, climbed on top and walked the length until she reached my knees, where she finally settled down. Play time was over. Momentarily. Catnap time was here.

On my right Rosie snoozed, her head still out from under the cover; left from when she thought we were getting up. On the left, just inches from where BooCat settled, a sound-asleep TacoBelle. To this point Taco has paid no attention to Boo's early morning activities. And this is what she continues to do. To pay no attention.

Even when BooCat stretched out full length and her head tilted to the side and rested on Taco's back, nothing happened. TacoBelle had to feel the pressure, had to sense at the very least, this wild and wooly baby cat was laying on her, yet she took no heed, paid no attention.

And so, for the next fifteen or so minutes, before I decided I had to get up and make coffee, the two slept soundly while physically touching.

Even when I began to stir, and Boo, Rosie and Taco did also, Taco didn't snarl at the close proximity of Boo. Boo no longer had her head resting upon Taco but she was still a mere inch away.

Another step in the right direction. TacoBelle hasn't thrown in the gauntlet, of this I'm sure. But it would appear her tolerance level ratcheted up a tad and reached a new high.

Another priceless moment.

It's good they are priceless. Nobody around here has any money anyway.

I mentioned lack of sunshine doesn't destroy my emotions. I'd like to say I'm lucky that way but actually it has taken a concerted effort to not let sadness overwhelm coupled with years of self-discipline. What I've learned—and it didn't come easy because it did take years to reach this point and to achieve the ability to maintain control. I've adopted a certain theory and cultivated the recipe for filling up the pickle jar.

My theory is, why worry?

There are only two things to worry about. Either you're sick or you're well. If you're well, there's nothing to worry about. If you're sick, there are only two things to worry about. Either you'll live or you'll die. If you live, there's nothing to worry about. If you die, there are only two things to worry about. Either you'll go to heaven or you'll go to hell. If you go to heaven, there's nothing to worry about. If you go to hell, you'll be so busy shaking hands with friends, you won't have time to worry.

All jokes aside, we basically have only two things to worry about each morning; two decisions to make. Choose to be in a good humor or start the day in a bad mood. Simple choice: Be happy.

Imagine you're breezing along in a good mood and something bad happens? Two choices. Either let the bad thing affect you adversely or learn from it. Mistakes are lessons learned. Simple choice: Misery's an option. So is happiness.

Suppose somebody irritates you? Two choices: Let it annoy you or not. The adage about the glass being half full or half empty gives you a choice. Half full is better. I like to think midway through lunch at McDonald's, I still have half my Big Mac instead of it being half gone. Same thing.

We would all choose to hang around cheerful folks because grouches pull us down, but realistically that's not always possible. Therefore, when faced with grouches, smile at them. Kill them with kindness. Tickle their funny bone. How people affect our moods and attitude is our choice. If we blame our bad mood on somebody else that's laundry without detergent. It won't wash. Our mood of choice is our choice. Maybe we've got to stop and count to ten, but the ball is in our court.

I remember a magazine cover illustrating the "Pecking Order," in four pictures. The first featured an angry boss shaking his finger at an employee. The next showed this employee at home angrily shaking his finger at his wife. The next block had the wife and mother shaking her finger in the face of their child. With nowhere else to go, the last scene showed the little boy shaking his finger at his befuddled puppy dog.

In this emotional domino effect, each person took their frustration out on someone else, which happens too often in our daily lives if we let others determine how we behave.

Curve balls come our way. Life is one big dodge ball game. You don't want to get hit by a train, don't sit on the tracks. For every situation, we have choices. Grin and bear it or get upset. Grinning is better. Turn the other cheek or throw a punch. Getting angry never made me feel better. Revenge isn't a positive. Crack a joke or retort with something negative. Jokes are better. You can pick your fights, or better yet, don't. It takes two to Tango. It also takes two to tangle. Sometimes it's best to keep your mouth shut when in deep water.

When faced with viewpoints and outlooks, choosing the widest and broadest is best. Never let prejudice be part of your makeup. Practice tolerance. Smile every chance you get. Truth be told, if you don't have a good sense of humor, you probably don't have good sense. Don't choose to be senseless. Laugh often. Laugh long. Laugh loud. Laughter is always the best medicine, and always the best choice.

Be kind. Just as too much salt spoils the soup, so does meanness spoil the spirit. Money will buy a fine dog, but only kindness makes him wag his tail. Maintain high values. Don't just make a living, make a life. Enjoy everyday to the fullest. Conquering outer space is fine, but individually, conquer your inner space to discover inner peace.

Surround yourself with good things. Make your house a home. Take up a hobby. Do things you enjoy. Be with people you care about. The only person who will be with you your entire life is you yourself. Learn to live with yourself.

Never be envious; be grateful for what you have. Enjoy the simple things in life. Your character and good name are precious commodities; keep it that way.

Maintaining a positive outlook is especially essential as we grow older. Don't let aging get you down; it's too hard to get back up.

And finally, take a great big empty dill pickle jar. Fill it to the brim with ping pong balls until not another ball will fit.

How full is your jar? All filled up?

If you said yes, try this. Pour in a bag of jelly beans. Shake the jar so they tumble down into all the open spaces between the ping pong balls and not another jelly bean will fit.

Is the jar full?

If you said yes, you're wrong. Sift a bag of cornmeal into the jar. Just good old fashioned Southern cornbread-making cornmeal. It doesn't matter if it's self-rising or not. It doesn't matter if it's white or yellow. Just watch. The cornmeal fills up everything else so that nothing else will fit.

Nothing else will fit, will it?

If you said yes, try this. Pour a couple cans of Hershey's Chocolate syrup into the jar—the kind that makes the best glass of chocolate milk or converts a plain scoop of ice cream into a chocolate Sundae. After which, you will realize once again there was room for something else in what you were positive moments before was a for-sure full jar.

Whether you are young or old, this lesson is straightforward. Think of this pickle jar as your life. The ping pong balls represent important things such as your family, spouse or significant other. They represent your health, children, friends; the things about which you are most fervent. They symbolize things that even if everything else was lost, your life would still be full.

The jelly beans symbolize other things that matter like your house, your job, your car. While meaningful, they are secondary.

The cornmeal is all else—the small stuff. Had you filled your jar with cornmeal first, there would have been no room for ping pong balls and jelly beans. Like life, if you spend all your time and energy sweating the small stuff, you will never have room for things of real worth.

The pickle jar demonstration is a reminder to pay attention to what is most consequential in your life and put these things first. Say nice things to your mate every day. Thoughtless things once spoken aloud can't be unheard any more than a bell can be unrung.

Hug your children and grandchildren.

Broaden your personal horizon; read a good book. Sing a song with the radio—or get a karaoke machine and do like I do, sing my heart out for my own happiness and that of my fur babies. Dance, stroll leisurely, look around and smile always. Don't worry who is right or wrong. Never be afraid to say I'm sorry.

In other words, take care of the ping pong balls first because they are the things that really matter. The rest is just cornmeal mush with a few jelly beans scattered here and there.

And the chocolate syrup? Simple. No matter how full your life is there's always room for chocolate. And remember, there are only two things to worry about. Make the positive choice.

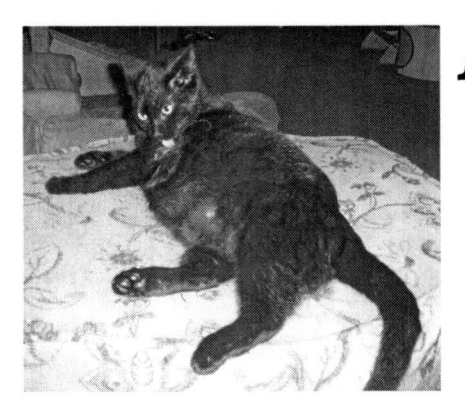

What One Day May Bring, Another Day May Take Away

65

"Who's your doggy?" (Whimsy by Barbara Sharik
—Based on: Who's your Daddy?)

I have to tell you right here and now, Daylight Saving Time confuses me and my BooCat. I realize it's a subject I've belabored fruitlessly for years. I'm at it again. Some of it's my own fault. Not the act itself—I can eventually get all the clocks turned one way or the other—but instead, it's the configuring of the act.

It's a dilemma. Why didn't I pay attention in Algebra class instead of copying off the guy next to me? I managed to partially learn the multiplication table with several little tricks and using my fingers and toes, but there's no easy way to figure out the pi-are-square versus no-pi-are-round thing. I've often admitted I knew the Dewey Decimal System better than the multiplication table.

Mostly, with the multiplication tables you have to give up and give in and commit it to memory. There is this nine table technique,‡ but

---

‡ The Nine Table Made Easy:
Step 1: Vertically list 0 through 9.
Step 2: To the right of each number, starting with 9, list 9 through 0.
0 9 = 9
1 8 = 18
2 7 = 27

65 / What One Day May Bring, Another Day May Take Away

you have to use pencil and paper to work it. If you can memorize certain mathematical equations like seven times seven is forty-nine, then you can work from there using your fingers, but it's still no easy task.

Even to this day I might get to eight-times-two-is-sixteen and then have to count hash marks or fingers. Adding machines and calculators haven't helped the memorizing part, but they have been a blessing for blondes like me. I've always worried about cramming too much into my head; memorizing the multiplication tables probably would have tipped the scale and caused a severe aching of the head.

My teacher took pity and awarded me a passing grade when I finally learned how to spell the word arithmetic. I took the first letter from each word: *A Rat In Tom's House Might Eat Tom's Ice Cream* and was able to spell the word. A-R-I-T-H-M-E-T-I-C. I might not have been able to do it but at least I could spell it.

Just take my word for it when I say I scooted through Algebra I and no colors were flying. I didn't take Algebra II. I never reached the point of needing the mysterious contraption known as a slide rule either. Only really brainy geeks carried them. They had a Slide Rule Club at my school. I wasn't allowed within fifty-feet of the club door. A siren went off if I approached even accidentally. It was humiliating. My photo was found in several places in my yearbook: *Who's Who in Art* and *Scholastically Outstanding*. I've always wondered about that scholastically thing. If it wasn't a mistake somebody must have figured scholars didn't have to be mathematicians.

So, you can imagine what I was faced with when trying to determine if I'd finally get to sleep all night or not when the clocks were turned back, as in *fall back*. I love those helpful ditties. *Fall back* in the fall and *spring forward* in the spring. Sort of like *A Rat In Tom's House Might Eat Tom's Ice Cream*.

---

3 6 = 36
4 5 = 45
5 4 = 54
6 3 = 63
7 2 = 72
8 1 = 81
9 0 = 90

Voila! The nine table mastered in minutes.

Of course, if the powers that be would just leave the time alone, I'd love that even better. Just knowing the fall and spring thing is complicated because it boils down to mathematics which I've already confessed isn't my strong suit.

If BooCat wakes me up at four in the morning during Daylight Saving Time, and then I fall back to Standard Time; turn the clock back an hour, what will happen?

If four becomes three on the clock will it be three when she wakes me?

Or, if because five becomes four, will it be five?

Five would be bearable. Three would not. What I need is for BooCat to wait until five-thirty my time to wake me, whatever time that happens to be. But she hasn't yet. Hershey never could keep it straight either. Friend Rose Ross said her cats stay confused too. So we can't blame it on cats lacking sense; it's the politicians who keep messing with our clocks that lack sense.

I don't suppose with Daylight Saving Time gone for a few months and Standard Time resurfaced, reinstated and rerun, she will know either. She has her own internal clock and it neither falls back nor springs forward. It just is.

I've written a four and I've written a five and a three and drawn a line connecting one to the other with a little arrow going this way and another going that way, trying to make a chart, but honestly, I still don't know how it's going to play out. Where's a Geek with a slide rule when you need one?

I can't count how many times I've heard people say they wish "they" would just stop messing with the time; leave it one way or the other. If I listen real close, I might even hear myself saying the same thing. Whether we lose or gain an hour's sleep makes for a good conversation starter twice a year. As for me, I firmly believe I lose both times of the year when I have to reacclimatize my sleeping and eating habits. You might think an hour makes little difference, but like jet-lag, some folks suffer from time-lag.

I'm looking at the clock, seeing it's 9:30; knowing 24 hours ago it was 10:30 and I definitely should be in bed asleep. I've run around the house and reset all the clocks, except the one in my car. It's already adjusted because I find by the time I dig out the manual and ascertain how to set the clock one way or the other, it's time to change it back;

65 / What One Day May Bring, Another Day May Take Away

so I just leave it as is. For half a year I add an hour in my head and then the other half, I spend my time hoping I don't forget and add the hour that isn't there any more.

I moved my clock far enough away from the bed so I'd have to get up and out of bed each morning, making reaching the snooze button a little less convenient. But it didn't work. I'd get up, careful to keep my eyes closed, hit the snooze, and climb back under the covers. Of course, a mouse trap placed on top of my alarm clock would prevent me from rolling over and going back to sleep when I hit the snooze button. But BooCat would probably snap it and foil my attempt at doing the right thing in the morning.

You see, with the time change I need that additional snooze time. I located my long-handled back scratcher, stuck it under the empty pillow beside me; and then I didn't have to get out of bed. I'd just reach over with the back scratcher, tap the snooze button and go back to sleep, grabbing ten minutes more. Where there's a will, and a need, there's definitely a way. Then I usually do it again, because I *know* that my clock is five minutes fast, so I'm ahead of the game for at least one more tap. I probably wouldn't have to do the snooze alarm thing every morning if we didn't have to keep turning the clock back and forth twice a year.

The hundred year old question is, do we really save daylight when we change the clocks back and forth? If we have to be somewhere at seven, don't we still have to be there whether it's still light outside or not? If we've turned the clocks forward, keeping the illusion of it being lighter later, at least lighter longer as far as our clocks are concerned, doesn't that mean we have to leave the lights on longer, burning more electricity? You can't geaux-green if you're wasting electricity.

Ex-lovers aren't really dying for us to telephone them in the middle of the night, whether it's Daylight Saving Time or not. Little kids who are afraid of the dark still grow into teenagers and want to stay out after dark every night. The sun still rises and sets on a regular basis, so I haven't figured out the logic behind the whole Daylight Saving Time thing.

BrilliantBoo, TacoBelle and Rosie can't tell time. They don't point at their wrists with one paw to ask me the time because they depend on their internal clocks instead. Naturally, because of this, they don't understand why I'm either still in bed or getting up earlier than usual, depending upon the time of the year. I know how they feel. Yesterday we were eating lunch at noon. Today, even though the clock says it's noon, we're eating at eleven. Tell me it's not a hassle to readjust.

Not to belabor the point—Oh yes. Of course I'm belaboring the point. I live to belabor the point. The thing is, once the clocks have been turned, when I wake up in the morning that next day, I'm already an hour behind before I ever get out of bed. Daylight Saving Time. I call it "Fly-Bye-Night."

Still trying to figure out the lose-or-gain-an-hour thing, the more I ponder, the more certain I am that I've lost more than one hour. At bedtime my body knows it's nine at night, even if the clock reads ten. I laid me down to sleep. And couldn't.

I tossed and turned until it really was ten according to my body-clock; and because I'd been tossing and turning so much, it was closer to eleven, body-time, before I drifted off.

The alarm went off at five that next morning, but in body-time, that's four. Having had a difficult time falling asleep the night before, this was way too early to drag my sleep-deprived body out of bed. I'm talking at least two lost hours of sleep, not just one. Even an extra cup of coffee doesn't help. Time-lag in action. Or maybe I should say in in-action.

When I left for work at seven-thirty, which was really six-thirty, it was still the middle of the night. It was dark and the moon was out. We're saving daylight all right; starting the day in the dark so of course there's more daylight at the end of the day. Which, by the way, is going to happen with or without clocks. It's a scientific thing. Longer days and shorter days. It's an ongoing process.

Even a month later, my body still hasn't caught up with my clocks. Have you ever counted have many clocks you have? Not to mention watches. On the oven, the microwave; maybe the coffee pot. Probably one in every room except maybe not the bathroom. Possibly a grandfather clock, a mantel clock and an outdoor patio clock; increasing the count. On the television and VCR too. Most computer clocks automatically set themselves; but computers are smart. Digital ones aren't bad when Daylight Saving Time begins because they are moved forward, but wait until you have to turn them back. You will have to go around twice, through the a.m. cycle, into the p.m., and

65 / What One Day May Bring, Another Day May Take Away

back to the a.m. Anyway, they are everywhere and they all need adjusting.

By the way, folks in Australia tried it to conserve energy. They reported that it didn't work. It only had everyone down under turning lights on earlier in the morning instead of in the evening. Same energy consumed, just at a different time of the day. Yeah. This indicates Australians are smarter than Americans. Their tubs may drain counterclockwise from ours due to the Coriolis Force or Effect, but they've got enough clock-sense to know DST doesn't work.

When you're in the Southern Hemisphere, you'll always curve to the left no matter what direction you go and in the Northern, you curve to the right. So, put that in your toilet bowl and flush it!

Yes. I'm still on the DST thing. And that's another thing—the name. Most dictionaries spell it without the "s" on Saving. The Associated Press (AP) Stylebook, a guide to aid newspapers report uniformly, advises reporters not to add the "s." Yet, when we speak it out loud, many of us do say savings - adding the "s." And as often happens over time, when words or expressions are erroneously used repeatedly, they become acceptable. Already, on many calendars, the event is spelled Daylight-Savings Time with the "s."

But, to find the illogic of adding the "s," try reversing it. A good test of correct English would be to say that we are "saving daylight." Now try it with the "s." Say we are "savings daylight." Unfortunately, even though it's incorrect, Daylight-Savings (with the "s") Time rolls off the tongue more easily.

Anyone who keeps a regular schedule and has a pet or two, though, knows about the uncanny sixth or seventh sense pets have. They sense when it's time for the alarm to go off, or time for you to arrive home from work. BooCat is the cat is in charge of reveille and TacoBelle and Rosie form the designated welcoming committee.

When the clocks were first turned, BooCat wanted to know why the alarm was ding-a-linging so early. The pups wanted to know what took me so long to get home. What can I say? I don't like it any better than they do.

We spend all summer saving time and for what? Just about the time we get used to all the extra daylight we've saved the folks in charge rip the rug right out from under our constitution—meaning our bodily constitution, not the U.S. Constitution—although it figures in there somewhere. Just about the time everyone acclimates, it's time to do the dastardly deed again.

My continuing ranting year-after-year suggestion is to leave it. My message to elected officials is to find something worthwhile—maybe even earth shattering instead of nerve shattering—to vote on instead of messing with America's clocks. I'm certain there are those who would like to be thrifty during the winter months too. Either way, there's still only twenty-four hours in a day.

Here's an idea. Why not standardize Standard Time?

Let me tell you what happened to me one year since I'm on this subject and can't seem to find my way off. I got up at five-thirty one morning twice. I got up at five-thirty, piddled around, put on the coffee and then around six-thirty I remembered I'd forgotten to set the clock back an hour for UDST—which means *Undoing Daylight Saving Time*. So, I turned the clock back to five-thirty and it was like I got up at five-thirty twice that morning. Now, that is no fun whatsoever. It never would have happened if our leaders weren't spending so much time tinkering with the time.

It affects the children too. When we turn the clocks up an hour, then send the kiddies out to the bus stop in the morning, there is no daylight to guide them. Instead of the sun peeping up from beneath the Eastern horizon, lightening and brightening the morning sky; making me and the roosters happy because I can see without turning on the carport light to feed the dogs, it's dark all over again.

I don't have kids to send to school anymore, but I have myself to see off to work. And I have dogs to feed. After floundering around in the dark with dog dishes, feeling my way blindly to the car, with headlights beaming, I drive down the dark road—there is no road as dark as a country road. Along the way the little kiddies are standing in the dark waiting for the school bus. And it's cold.

A little later temperatures will rise with the morning sun; but for now, it is still dark and it is still cold. Poor little munchkins have to leave for school in the middle of the night, and when the days shorten, they will arrive back home in the dark as well. The are like little mole-children.

And why do we do it? I know I'm a constant complainer about the time changing. I complain turning it both forward and back. I want to see it just sit still. I see no saving of daylight. When it's six, it's six.

65 / What One Day May Bring, Another Day May Take Away

Same with seven o'clock.

I took a vote. Two tail-wags and a tail-switch. Three to none. The fids voted to leave the clocks alone. It confuses the heck out of them too.

Intended to promote energy conservation under the Energy Policy of 2005, instead of turning the clocks forward an hour the first Sunday in April and ending the last Sunday in October, in 2007 a new schedule required turning ahead three weeks earlier and one week later. Ben Franklin penned a whimsical essay about the saving of time in 1784. William Willett produced a pamphlet titled *Waste of Daylight* in 1907. Long-story-short, we have sashayed back and forth between DST and Standard Time ever since World War I.

If we can rip the Ten Commandments—which by the way even if you aren't religious makes mighty fine rules to live by—from our courthouses and disallow a crèche on public property and ban prayer in school, then why-oh-why must we abide by this useless clock tinkering?

Not able to do anything about the time change reminds me of another frustrating subject. Several years ago I decided if I lost sixty pounds, I'd treat myself to a tattoo. Hence the other item of frustration. Losing sixty pounds.

Besides eating light, the health gurus recommend exercise to lose weight and be healthy. Burn off the fat. Speed up that heart rate. I wouldn't drive my car faster to extend it's life, so why should I exercise to speed up my heart? How can that make me live longer? Looks like it would wear it out quicker instead. Conserving energy sounds better. Want to live longer? Take a nap. Exercising means pushing to the limit. That hurts. Who said no pain, no gain? You ask me, no pain? Good.

I determined if I wanted a tattoo while I was still living and could enjoy it; I'd have to just do it. Waiting until I lost sixty pounds was a losing proposition, because there is losing and there is losing.

Unless I buy into the weight-losing game, which I never seem to have the mental money to do, I would never have gotten the butterfly tattoo. Like a piece of jewelry that I can't take off, it is tiny and pretty. There are no regrets.

And it is a good thing I didn't wait. Because I would have had to resign the contract with myself. Sixty pounds would have turned into eighty. Yikes. Just think "diet" and I get hungry. Just think "lose sixty pounds" and I "gain twenty."

And so, I turned my clocks forward this spring and I got my tattoo a couple years ago and I do my best not to exercise any more than I have to.

It's okay to have a tattoo and be fluffy too. Would I rather not be so fluffy? Yes. But am I lamenting over what has happened over the years? Nope. If I were, I would give up Blue Bell Homemade Vanilla Ice Cream, cheese cake, Biscotti's, coconut custard pies and angel food cake. But at this time in my life, with less years left than already spent, why suffer?

As I've aged, I've found that *"someday"* and *"one of these days"* tends to lose their importance in my vocabulary. If it's worth seeing or hearing or doing, see it, hear it, do it. Now. Because regardless of what I do with my clock, in just two days, tomorrow will be yesterday.

On top of everything else, as I write this, having only returned to Daylight Standard Time recently, neither BooCat nor I know what time it is any more. One day we are eating lunch at noon. The next day we are eating at eleven o'clock. Or maybe it's one o'clock.

I would just as soon the pro-Daylight Saving Time people be stuck in some dark corner with the anti-Global Warming people. Their sense of logic defies…well, it defies logic.

Night Before Christmas at Wit's End

"The Cat's Pajamas." (The term refers to E. B. Katz, an English tailor, late 1700s–early 1800s, who made the finest silk PJ's for royalty and other wealthy patrons—"Katz Pajamas"— and is used when referring to something outstanding.)

'Twas the night before Christmas,
when all through the house,
not a creature was stirring, not even a mouse.
Everything that could be done was, including me too.
I sighed and plopped in my chair with my doggies two.
BooCat sat upon the chair back, purring by my head.
They were all waiting for me to take them to bed.
The stockings were hung and filled with treats,
like dog biscuits, catnip and doggie sweets.
Cockatiel George had his head tucked beneath his wing,
while SnowBird slept sweetly on his wee bird swing.
Christmas carols were playing in the background,
and I intended to nap to the joyful holiday sound.
This was the first year I didn't put up a tree.
After all, it was just the furry kids and tired old me.
I don't mind putting it up, trimming it all around,
but at my age, I hate having to take it back down.
Later we would nestle all snug in our beds,

BooCat Unleashed

while visions of Christmas dinner danced in our heads.
Suddenly, there arose such a clang and a clatter.
I sprang from my chair to see what was the matter.
From the corner of my eye, I saw movement so quick,
and I knew in a moment, it wasn't Saint Nick.
As I lifted my head and was turning around,
down the table leg something scampered with a bound.
All covered all in gray fur from its head to its toes,
Crumbs spattered its whiskers and coated its nose.
Its droll little mouth was drawn up like a bow,
and the breadcrumb on its chin was white as the snow.
It had a cute tiny face and a little round belly,
that shook like a bowl full of red jalapeño jelly.
A big chunk of cheese was stuffed in its cheek,
so full was it, it could not even squeak.
It was chubby and plump, a right jolly old mouse,
because it had been eating me out of home and house.
More rapid than eagles my pets they came,
as I whistled and shouted and called them by name:
"Now, Rosie! Now TacoBelle! On, BooCat!
Move it! Move it! Hurry! Catch that little rat.
"Hey, sweetie-babies, what's the deal?
There's a mouse in the house, here for a holiday meal.
"It's over in the corner, right near the wall.
Now, dash away! Dash away! Dash away all!"
Its nose may twitch and eyes twinkle and glow,
but by golly, that little mouse just has to go.
Tiny feet pattering, away it flew in a flash,
across the windowsill and up on the sash.
With the three furry kids hot on its trail,
it escaped in the mouse hole by barely a tail.
It disappeared from sight like a magic elf,
and I laughed when I saw it in spite of myself.
Once outside, it scampered quick as a whistle,
Rocketing as swiftly as a guided military missile.
BooCat meowed as she skidded to a stop
TacoBelle and Rosie flopped on the floor with a plop.
Sorry to chase the mouse out in the cold night air,

but it sure ruined my nap in my favorite chair.
"Come, my little fids, it's time for bed,"
I said with a wink of my eye and a twist of my head.
With that little mousie plum out of sight,
I exclaimed "Happy Christmas to all and to all a Good-night!"

I remember as a kid I could hardly wait for Christmas. I don't mind putting up a tree and it's joyous to decorate it, but the taking down is tedious. Of course, had I put a tree up since BooCat moved in, BooCat would have done the honors of taking it down. Trouble is, she probably would have taken it down about as fast as I put it up. She is a one-cat dismantling unit. I have an ex-brother-in-law who has a very profitable demolition business. BooCat would make a prima demolition employee.

BoisterousBoo is never bored. She keeps herself amused and taking down a Christmas tree would have provided her much amusement. Sadly, the holiday doesn't hold quite the same uniqueness it once did. With no little children in the household, the main dish on the menu is missing.

And since I have reached the how-time-flies age, I could have sworn Christmas was just here and here it is again. Naturally, looking at the bright side, at my age, presents I receive won't wear out. Also, I don't need a new holiday outfit, and I have stopped holding in my stomach no matter who walks into the room. All in all, there's not much left for me to learn the hard way, so I'm okay.

Christmas is still a time of harmony. Unless you are amongst the crowds swarming the mall looking for last minute presents. I outgrew enjoying the company of other shoppers a long time ago. Merchants miss me but give me a catalogue and I can get everybody something and never cross the threshold of a crammed store. What with the loss of income due to the Internet that the post office is experiencing, postal workers appreciate mail-order shoppers. I do my part.

Congested stores aside, with traditional gaiety, music filling the air, multicolored lights blinking from one end of every street across America to another, it's all good. Even if I don't have little tiny tots to buy for, I do have my fids. They may not know the reason behind the season but they like getting new treats and toys each year.

In many parts of the country snow flakes flutter and people scurry to and fro bundled in winter coats. Chimney smoke spirals into the night skies and church bells toll in praise of the silent night. It is a hugging good time of the year.

Unfortunately, even my fireplace has been relegated to the back shelf, in a manner of speaking. I haven't had a chimney sweep come check it out to know if it could still burn safe and between the cost of firewood and the physical effort involved with toting it into the house, I just got tired of all it entails. I'm glad I'm not a pioneer woman who not only would have to tote the wood in, but likely have to chop it too. Hey, I'll be a tree-hugger and not waste our precious trees by sending them up into smoke.

The thing about the holidays is the recognition that it is more than just exchanging gifts. In addition to the religious aspect, there is the human one. There are the shut-ins and those living alone. While Christmas can be the happiest of times—the season to be jolly—a person alone is reminded at Christmas of the aloneness more so than almost any other time of the year because of everyone else's surrounding togetherness. Christmas for people alone can be sadly hollow and they are often swallowed up in emptiness.

Theresa never misses being with me at both Thanksgiving and Christmas, even though she lives farther away now. But filling the gap, thank goodness I have my precious pups and Boo. Christmas is so much more than just a day. It is the soul of all little children on earth. And my pets are my onboard children.

Little children, and our furry kids, come into the world lacking hate, discrimination and intolerance. They lack corruption, malice and self-centeredness. Their little hearts come complete with goodness and it is only after they begin to grow and mimic adults that they learn life's negatives.

How good it would be if we all could look at Christmas through the eyes of the little children—and our loving pets—with innocence, sincerity and pure delight.

Home is Where the Cat Is

67

"My fids walk all over me." (Barbara Sharik)

Being somewhere for the longest length of time only earns seniority, not rank. Hardly ever is a new boss appointed from within the ranks of workers. You might climb the levels but only so high. After that, in walks some unknown know-it-all who proceeds to tell everybody who's been there for all eternity just how the horse eats cabbage.

Sure, you find yourself thinking, like he or she *really* knows how things should be done around here—and him or her a newcomer. But, even if they don't know, what they say is now law. What this boils down to is that they have no *need* to know, but there's something you do need to know: How to say *Yessir*. Or in some cases: *Yes'm*.

No, it isn't fair. What in life is fair? Somebody figure that out and they'll have found the key to the universe, the answer to prayer, the holy grail. Maybe even the fountain of youth. Life isn't about just desserts. It's about a whole lot of luck and a little bit of smarts.

Case in point: In walks this new kid on the block—a black wildchild cat. Already established and doing just fine thank you very much are TacoBelle and Rosie. They had the pecking order down just fine. Taco barked and Rosie asked "How high?" Seniority was established.

And there are a couple birds: George E. Tiel and SnowBird who've been managing to manage just fine for years on end too, with no outside interference or intervention by black wild cats. George whistled lovely tunes and even barked. SnowBird cooed.

It worked ideally for a long time. Now everything's changed. Somebody went and appointed a new boss who not only hasn't paid her dues and climbed the ladder, but who's under the impression she's a goddess.

TacoBelle isn't a happy second-in-command. She pretty much had gotten used to being the boss and the demotion causes her to snarl on occasion. Rosie's wary at times but mostly tolerant. After all, she's spent all her life having to put up with, make do, and tolerate living under the command of the little Mexican Boss-Lady Dog. This wasn't much different except that this new boss sometimes plays a little rough. And she wants to play all the time.

If Rosie had met the new boss when she was a young playful whippersnapper pup, this might have been an ideal situation. It might have been fun having a playmate. Now, instead, it's a bit of a bother.

And as such, early one morning I awoke to Taco's snarling and barking and heard the sounds of BooCat bounding off the bed. Obviously, she did one of two things: she either accidentally walked on TacoBelle while going from one end of the bed to the other, waking the little dog into action and noisy discontent; hence the snarling and barking. Or she woke TacoBelle from her sound sleep by batting her tock-ears with her curious paw; also a typical cause of snarling and barking. BooCat cannot not bat at Taco's tock-ears whenever she gets the chance. Does she care that Taco doesn't like it and will snarl and bark? Nope. It's part of the fun. It's called stirring the pot. She loves stirring the pot of chaos stew. The more ruckus she stirs up, the happier she is. Every bark, every snarl, only adds to BooCat's happy dance.

In either case, the little dog woke up snarling and barking and the cat leaped off the bed. BooCat never leaps from fear. No doubt if Bodacious Boo were a human species, I'd have heard devilish laughter emanating from her little catty mouth. She's a tormenting rascal and she cannot help herself.

I turned over and patted Taco, telling her it was okay But because I knew she was innocent of any charges the BooCat might bring against her I didn't tell her to hush. Besides, she doesn't know the meaning of the word anyway. I know she had been sleeping peacefully when BadBoo caused the commotion. I know this because BooCat does it at every opportunity.

It's her form of playing the cat and mouse game. She's the cat and everybody else is the mouse. Might as well pin on the badge because as everybody knows the cat always gets her mouse.

After awhile, I switched on the light and decided to get up to make coffee. Who can go back to sleep once forty years of early rising and shining has been instilled into one's constitution and brain? I was awake. I might as well get up.

As I headed to the kitchen I felt strangely alone. It was almost eerie. Boo wasn't leading my way. She always leads me. She's been leading me from the bed to the kitchen ever since she arrived in this household.

Instantaneous fear wracked my whole being. I stopped in my tracks. Where's Boo?

I cautiously called her name. No BooCat.

I called louder. Still no sign of the little leader of the pack.

Panic mode set in. I called "Here, kitty, kitty, kitty."

Nothing. She always comes when I call *Here-kitty-kitty*.

I searched the house over. She wasn't in the bird room-slash-office. She wasn't already in the kitchen awaiting me to feed her breakfast. I didn't find her in plain sight in the bedroom. She wasn't in the bathtub smacking about water drops from the leaking faucet.

I even rushed to the laundry room to see if the washer lid was up or the dryer door open. No Boo. I called her name with every step of my panicked searching.

She was no where.

I suddenly feared the snarling, barking fuss she and TacoBelle had earlier. Taco snarls. Taco barks. But Taco doesn't hurt. And Boo has the art of dodging the little dog's ferociousness down to a fine art.

When Boo first moved in she leapt to the top of my bed's headboard, leaned across the divide in an attempt to maneuver behind the blinds to the windowsill, and surefooted as cats usually are, she missed her step and fell behind the bed. From my position I couldn't see if she landed on all fours as is said to always happen when a cat falls. When a cat falls, usually they have time and space to flip themselves into the landing on all fours position—in this instance with the headboard and wall blocking her in, limiting any movement, I was pretty certain her descent wasn't one that allowed landing on all fours. She recovered quickly, but the next few times I petted her, when I stroked her one hind leg, she pushed my hand away with her foot. I thought perhaps she'd bruised it.

Had she fallen? Was she trapped under the bed?

I leaned over, lifting the bedskirt and called her again and again. Nothing.

I made the rounds, calling her name over and over from every room in the house. I wound my way back to the bedroom. She had to be under the bed.

"BooCat! Where are you?"

Then I heard a bumping noise coming from beneath the bed.

Due to a bad traffic accident some years ago, both my knees are messed up. My physician recommended surgery to remove bone splinters and crunchy stuff, but as long as I could walk, I elected to pass. As a result, I can't kneel, or put any weight on either knee.

Therefore, I couldn't get down low enough to find Boo. I heard another scrape and knew she was under there. I didn't understand why she wasn't coming when I called; fearing she must be injured.

My breath was coming fast. I felt my blood pressure rising in terror. If something happened to my BooBaby I didn't think I could stand it. I was ready to call Chuck for help. As I was turning to make my way to the telephone, I saw the bedskirt rustle. I stopped. I expected to see a broken cat body dragging itself from under the bed. It was Boo. She slowly crept out from beneath the bed.

I didn't see any blood. She wasn't limping. I grabbed her up and she began purring.

Did I tell you she has an instant purr button? She engaged it. Instant relief. Then I recalled reading cats purr not only when content, but also when hurt, when having kittens and even when dying. Oh my gosh. I couldn't stand this.

I carried her tenderly out to the kitchen, I spoke softly to her and attempted to check her over thoroughly.

I didn't finding any sign of injury.

Maybe it's internal, I feared. My worry-gear was fully engaged.

I gently set her in the chair seat. I stepped back, the better to see

67 / Home is Where the Cat Is

her overall body. She immediately leaped down and ran away.

I called and followed her tracks. She headed for the bedroom and slipped back beneath the bed.

I cried *BooCat, where are you?*
BooCee, come here!
BooBaby, please come back.
What's going on?

Fortunately, she didn't stay hidden from sight for long. Within a few minutes of my reaching the bedroom and beseeching her to please come back, she was already exiting from under the bed. Whatever had caught and held her attention previously, was no longer having any effect on her.

She was out and she didn't go back underneath the bed again. Instead, she came to where I was standing in the bedroom doorway, wrapped her body and tail around my legs and began her usual ritual of leading me to the kitchen so I could feed her. She was her old self: my seeing-eye cat.

There can be only one explanation: something under the bed had her full and undivided attention. I'm guessing a mouse. Maybe. Whatever it was, she either lost it or she ate it. She nibbled on her kitten chow and I sighed with relief.

With the incident over, she took up her position as General Boo-Cat once more. After breakfast, she strolled around the house with the confidence of a true company commander making her rounds.

Leaping back atop the bed, she checked on Rosie who was still fast asleep under the covers. Rosie, bless her little heart, missed the whole emotionally charged event that unfolded while she snoozed.

Taco sat perched alertly in bed while I called and called for Boo, but after she was located, obviously TacoBelle determined whatever was going on no longer mattered to her nor was it worth any more of her time and concern. She settled down in her ChiChi curl.

Following a quick sniff, BooCat skirted Taco's tiny sleeping body, not waking her this time. Then, after jumping down from the bed, Boo's next stop was out to the office and the bird cages where she got up close and personal until I admonished her with the usual "Ged-down, Boo!"

Eventually, the diminutive BooBoss climbed onto her catbed and proceeded to do the thing she does best: catnap. Her household kingdom was under control. Under her eminent control.

I was still bumfuzzled, wondering what had been under the bed that so captured her attention that she ignored my calls. Whatever it was, so long as it doesn't wind up on top of the bed, all is good.

No doubt BooClownCat finds living at Wit's End Comedy Club a textbook perfect chaotic mosaic cathouse. She has her own toys and furniture, which would please any cat. On top of that, there are dogs small enough and docile enough to rule, bird feathers to pluck, snakes to catch, crickets to munch on, millipedes to roll around like marbles, mice under the bed and ghosts in the ceiling. Or maybe there are mice in the ceiling and ghosts under the bed. Every cat should be so lucky.

BooCat Unleashed: The Movie

68

"*Category (cat-a-gory): Leftovers from a successful cat and mouse hunt.*"
(Whimsy by Barbara Sharik)

Good friend Tom C. sent me an e-mail about a sunset he viewed January 11, 2010. He wrote: "I came home, after an inspection of our grass fields near Mer Rouge, through Collinston and across the east to west Perryville road at about 5:30. The sunset was gorgeous. A clear blue sky (the color of the second dozen eggs immersed in blue Easter egg dye) as background to a web of jet contrails of fuchsia fading to coral."

Tom wrote about how insignificant the human race is and said

> Unbelievable arrogance of some to think we are anything more than a fart in the ocean when it comes to affecting the earth's environment. Statistical analysis is a wonderful tool, which can be used or abused. Trends can be recognized and their paths projected when input sampling is taken properly with integrity. Selective sampling to "prove" a predetermined conclusion results in fraud to advance the agenda of the political socialists now in power.

BooCat Unleashed

Tom C. and I have humorous conversations. He has one of the best senses of humor of anyone I know. We also have deep philosophical discussions on an array of subject matter.

Being a believer in man's abuse of this earth, I chose not to comment when he wrote "Global Cooling or Warming - Which is It?"

What I told him was that I saw that exact same sunset. I even considered stopping my car, digging out my camera—the criss-crosses from the jet contrails appeared more heavily webbed than usual, the colors beautiful. I suppose I should have stopped and snapped. The beautiful moment could have been captured for more enjoyment than just a memory.

I continued my missive advising Tom that I was scheduled to have some reparative female type surgery on the morrow of the writing of this e-mail; that the Humpty-Dumpty doctor was going to put me back together again. I jokingly added that I trusted the physician would come prepared with a lot of superglue, band-aids and maybe even a roll of string for tying up loose ends, as the list of repairs is fairly long.

I told Tom I'd let him know how I fared as soon as I did (fare that is), and added that I was writing a warm and fuzzy book titled "*BooCat Unleashed.*" I explained that the heroine is my black BadBooCat. I recommended he watch for the movie coming to a theater near him soon.

I supposed this was a good time to undertake such a project—when because of upcoming surgery, I'd have more time on my hands than asked for.

Tom responded:

> Sounds as if you are going to the paint and body shop for repairs to a fare-the-well. Certainly hope things go well, and recovery is swift.
> I am eagerly awaiting *BooCat Unleashed* —I usually pass on the movies based upon books I have enjoyed. Nearly always ruins a good story when the screen adaptation is filled with filthy language and gratuitous nudity. Boocat doesn't deserve that kind of misrepresentation, although I'm sure she is comfortable in her own skin.
> Upon re-reading my hurried, un-proofed global cooling

missive I realize I could have done better with a little revision or two.—I meant to say, "...second dozen eggs after immersion in blue Easter egg dye."—And—my sainted mother would have preferred "butterfly's belch" to my crude "...fart in the ocean...," but when Al Gore is lurking in the nether regions of one's mind it is difficult to suppress even a very tiny puff of flatulence. Wishing for great good fortune with your surgery, TC.

Of course I had to counter to the chat about the movie and Tom's revisions. I wrote that he had made several good points regarding movies-made-from-books. Movies rarely do the books justice. I always prefer to read the book first and quite often, I never bother to see the film.

In the case of BooCat's book/movie, I told Tom the only "filthy language" probably would be the scene where Boo knocked down the curtain, rod and all, while gazing longingly out the window (my fault more than hers because no one was supposed to breathe when near the precariously hung rod, of which she was unaware)—and when I attempted to rehang the rod, I bumped the antique decorative hand-painted plate hanging on the wall above the windows and it fell, beamed me in the head, bounced beautifully in ballerina style floating one stroke faster than I could reach, and broke upon impact with the floor. Boo heard her mom (me) spout off a few naughty words as a result.

Commenting on his mention of nudity, I told him, that would be SnowBird the white dove. BooCat had plucked several more tail feathers from the sweet hapless bird from between the birdcage bars. BadBoo has what I call Boo's Bounty—a little pile of white bird feathers stacked on the floor.

At this rate, I told Tom, unless I can teach BooCat some manners—unleashed as she is, a fury in her own right—the poor bird will wind up starring in the nude scene.

In any case, I explained that the BooBook is my latest fill-in-the-time project. Because I can only pick up two channels on my TV since the conversion from analog to digital—and the second channel is actually just a weather map with no written or spoken script, I have time on my hands.

I explained too that what with having four days off for Christmas—when I started the BooBook, and then four off for New Years when I continued it—what with the pending surgery, I definitely should be able to make a dent. Make a dent isn't really a good choice of expression. I should be able to fill some pages with the overflow filling my head since BooCat moved into my home and my heart.

I found my insecure self adding that whether it winds up with any redeeming virtues, only time will tell, but it keeps my mind working and makes me happy. I have to remind myself a book can't be written in a couple weeks and that I must stop being impatient. I've gotten spoiled writing newspaper and magazine columns in six-hundred words or less. They come easy. Someone as long-winded as me thinks, speaks and writes in six hundred words or less on a regular basis.

And to Tom's amusing revisions, I said that I liked them—especially what's perceived as Mom's preference—*butterfly belch*—or perhaps, even more refined, call it a *butterfly burp*—as babies are burped and grown men who "fart" also "belch." So burp is better. I told him I was sure his mom would agree.

Naturally, I thanked him for the well wishes regarding the surgery, adding that traveling the last lane isn't always as much fun as I make it sound when I write my columns. Which, as a senior, he understands only too well.

Regarding the Academy Award winning upcoming *BooCat Unleashed* book-into-movie, Chuck said: "If they make a movie about your cat it will have to be a cartoon."

Don't Eat the Yellow Snow

"Advice to Cat-People: Never bring work home from the office if your cat likes to sits on your computer and you can't bring yourself to move him."
(Barbara Sharik)

Ranting and speaking out on various subjects becomes easier as I age. Sometimes I see myself sounding like a cross between Erma Bombeck and Maxine. I put together a book of cartoons back in the 1980's and called it *It's Barbara's Business!,* and if I'd had the right contacts, you'd be reading Barbara instead of Maxine. My caustic Barbara cartoon said the same stuff back in the 1980's that Maxine is saying now in the 2000's.

You snooze you lose.

In real estate it's all about location, location, location. In real life it's all about contacts, contacts, contacts.

The ranting and raving, having an opinion on everything, is a human condition, the nature of men and women the world over. I've been around so long and been through so much, I consider myself at the point when life generally underwhelms me rather than overwhelms. I usually regard myself beyond being surprised by humanity.

Almost.

And then along came Jones. Big talkin', slow walkin' Jones. And I am surprised all over again. Not necessarily a student of human nature, I do find myself taking notes for future references. It all started with the snow storm of 2010. People began to believe the map had shifted and they weren't in Kansas anymore—nor were they in Washington D.C. or the state of Maryland or Pennsylvania. They were having delusions of being in Buffalo, New York or Butte, Montana instead. Maybe even the Artic Circle.

In fact the Friday prior to Valentine's Day, 2010, we had snow. Real snow. Not just the dusting of a few weeks earlier, but enough to close schools and some businesses. Right here in the deep sunny South. Not to mention in many other places around the country. Some as surprising as the snowfall in Louisiana; some not so surprising.

I rushed outside and took early morning photos. The white fluffy flakes were falling thickly even as I snapped. The flash turned the snowflakes into mini-twinkling fairy lights in most of the pictures.

Because it was still fairly dark—the sun rarely shines during snow flurries—I planned to go back outside an hour or so later to take more photographs when the sky lightened up. I had no desire to make snowmen or play in the snow; but I thoroughly enjoy snapping pictures. The landscape was beautiful.

As I sat drinking coffee and typing, BooCat nibbling kitten chow, Rosie and TacoBelle still in bed, I noticed an overall lightness emerging. There was a glow coming through the pink sheers at the window in my office, casting a lovely color across the floor, joining with the pink area rug. The whole room was pretty in pink. I slipped on my jacket, grabbed my camera and opened the door.

Whoa!

Bummer. The snow stopped falling and the temps warmed so much, the lovely white stuff was already in a state of meltdown. I was glad I'm an early riser. Had I waited till most people rise and shine, I would have missed the whole snow scene.

That's the sunny South for you—a blizzard of a snowstorm come and gone in a couple hours. The old adage that if you don't like the weather, wait a few minutes really does fit. It's so changeable.

My sister Jan lives in Maryland not many miles from our nation's capital. She reported 50 inches of snowfall. My granddaughter Alisha and daughter-in-law Cindy just across the Maryland state line and

69 / Don't Eat the Yellow Snow

the Mason-Dixon Line, in Pennsylvania, recounted their snowfalls in feet rather than inches.

So with two-and-a-half feet of snow burying and blocking in cars on the east coast, requiring the overuse of shovels and snow blowers, keeping folks inside their homes, preventing them from work or school, and in fact creating a huge case of cabin fever, Jan posted photos on her Facebook page validating just how deep the snow was at her house in southern Maryland.

A networking website, people chat. They stay in touch. They make comments. They announce things. It's a great source for friendship new or renewed. People with like interests end up meeting and becoming friends—I've met more bird people than I ever dreamed were alive and well all across the globe. It's been great. I've rekindled friendships long lost and newly found from high school and beyond. Practically my whole graduating class is united on Facebook. I've rediscovered long lost cousins, kissing and otherwise, previously lost due to years and miles.

Personally, a great plus is that practically everybody who lives and works in Morehouse Parish where I live, stays connected daily. I wish everybody I knew was signed up on Facebook. What often happens is one person makes a statement and a passel of other people comment. Often benign, occasionally political and emotional issues rear their heads. Jan made a trite but humorous remark on her Facebook page, referencing the snow pile covering cars and roads and houses and trees: *"Global warming, my butt!"*

The comment was the stuff normal folks would read and chuckle. A commentary on the huge amount of snowfall; but certainly not meant to support or discount Global Warming.

The controversy those four little words elicited was unbelievable. Immediately mounting the threshold, climbing upon soapboxes and standing front and center on stage, the pro- and the anti-believers in Global Warming set about to make their cases. I've seen responses mushroom before when certain subjects such as Healthcare Reform, were put forth, but none any more volatile than those about Global Warming.

Attempting my usual bit of tongue-in-cheek jest I advised Jan: *With all that snow your butt will need a little Global Warming.*

And still the radicals did not cease. Humor didn't stop the anger extended by the anti-Global Warmers. They were on a roll. They were jumping with joy. They had their proof positive that global warming was a lie made up by liberals. Curse that Al Gore guy. Who needs Polar Bears anyway?

In a nutshell, they were declaring: See. It's snowing. If global warming was real there wouldn't be all this snow piling up on the cars, in the streets and down the block!

This was the reasonong put forth with froth dripping from rabid computer keyboards. Their responses were so hostile. They also took this opportunity to blast any- and every-one who opposed their belief that none of what is wrong with Planet Earth has been caused by anything mankind has done.

Many played the God-card. God wouldn't let earth, climate and environment be damaged by people. People can do whatever they want and it doesn't matter. They will just pray it away. The attitude is that God is omnipotent and he'll clean up after us no matter what we do. Besides, who cares about tomorrow? Tomorrow they will have relocated. These particular zealots planned to rise up and spend eternity in Heaven, leaving this messy planet behind. It's like I'm throwing these blue jeans away tomorrow so I might as well use them to paint in today. When End-Time comes—and it's been on its way for a very long time—nobody's going to need Planet Earth any more anyway. A weird brand of illogical logic. But when it comes to Faith, common sense never enters into the equation.

The people who begged to differ didn't stand a chance. They didn't have irrationality backing their responses. Irrationality is pretty strong stuff. It's the substance squeaky wheels are made from. It speaks and squeaks loudest.

You see, these people came crawling out—or maybe I should say clawing out, from under. Anti-Global Warming people are an angry bunch, contending nothing man has done has contributed to the climate changes being experienced worldwide. The pro-Global Warmers defended the problems being experienced, like ice melting at the Poles leaving Polar Bears with insufficient habitat and the changes in weather patterns overall.

There were many remarks appearing on Jan's Facebook regarding the cold weather and global warming. Misunderstanding the concept of global warming and its effects on climate change, many folks took this venue to declare the cold and snow validated their case against the authenticity of it; proof positive and a clear indication there's no such thing. They were taking the snow and cold versus global warming figuratively, missing the point that all these unusual snowstorms, the out of the ordinary weather patterns that are shifting—that is what Global Warming represents. You can still have cold weather even with the thing called Global Warming. So many people open their mouths and remove all doubt. In these cases, ignorance is bliss.

With Jan's innocuous remark sparking controversy from both proponents and non-believers of the Global Warming issue and becoming so heated and so lengthy it ramped up my emotions. I had to comment, advising: *Here's my two-cent's worth. I don't expect any change.*

Okay. I'm as bad as the next outspoken extremist even if I chose not to call myself a radical. What got my goat uppermost was the vehement denial that people are in any way responsible for environmental damage. Whether or not Global Warming is real, damage to our world is.

I wrote:

> This discussion has melted down to the level of the bullfighting controversy. Bleeding heart liberals emotionally feel bullfighting is cruel; thin-the-herd pragmatists shrug and declare why else you think God made bulls?
> Whether or not you believe in God or global warming is not the issue. Mankind—who isn't kind at all—has stewardship of this planet and we may be running out of do-overs. The motel checkout time is liable to catch us with our britches down. Due to the duplicitous nature of man, selfishly with a shoulder shrug, some aren't worried about future generations because they believe they're going to a better place anyway.
> Stop drawing lines. Recognize the joint necessity to save us from ourselves. Thomas Paine said, "The world is my country and to do good is my religion." There are two sides to every issue but we've only got one world. Stop arguing incidentals. Take care of what is important: our planet. All the rest is just dirt in the wind and a pile of garbage.

BooCat Unleashed

BooCat, the pups and I, we understand. We recognize a need for lifestyle changes.

Thinking back to when we heard less about toxic runoff, pollution, greenhouse gasses, emissions control, agent orange, loss of rain forests, extinction of species, I remember when Mom made Snow Ice Cream.[§]

Adding sugar, vanilla and a bit of milk, it was such a treat. Now we must avoid more than just the yellow snow. So, how can I recommend making it now? Now, instead of snow, you would have to use shaved ice. Because now, there is no such thing as fresh-fallen snow. It's tainted. We cannot feed our children snow ice cream because of toxic waste, acid rain, radioactive particles and all manner of contamination.

This certain faction of people may not believe mankind is doing damage to our world. They may not believe in Global Warming. They may see nothing wrong with one species after another going extinct. They may selfishly live only for themselves, day by day, year after year, but would they dare eat a bowl of snow ice cream today? What conclusion would they come to by comparison based on having eaten a bowl before it was poisoned by the crime of not caring?

---

§ Snow Ice Cream #1
8 cups snow (or shaved ice)
1 (14 ounce) can sweetened condensed milk
1 teaspoon vanilla extract
—Forget the toxic snow. Place shaved ice into a large bowl. Pour condensed milk over and add vanilla. Mix to combine. Serve immediately in bowls.

Snow Ice Cream #2
1 gallon fresh-fallen snow (or shaved ice)
1 cup white sugar
1 tablespoon vanilla extract
2 cups milk
—When it starts of snow, place a large, clean bowl outside to collect the flakes. When full, throw it away and replace it with shaved ice because there is no such thing as fresh fallen snow—it is all contaminated. Into the shaved ice stir in sugar and vanilla to taste, then stir in just enough milk for the desired consistency. Serve at once.

69 / Don't Eat the Yellow Snow

No doubt about it, our politicians are so busy worrying about changing the time back and forth, that half of them have elected to join the blind who refuse to see and accept that we can no longer eat snow ice cream. 'Tis a sad commentary.

Ah, let *them* eat ice cream.

Now we have acid rain. Chemical runoff. Air pollution in every breath we take, every bite we swallow, everywhere we turn. Environmental changes. Of course man is responsible. Who else is to blame? Even animals know better than to mess in their nests.

Since sister Jan innocuously started the whole Global Warming diabolical debate whether she meant to or not, let me tell you something about her. She obviously takes after the alien that kidnapped Mom and beamed her up to a large constellation located on the celestial equator between Leo and Libra, containing the binary star Spica. It was at this Virgo cluster lying near the North Galactic Pole about sixteen billion light-years from the Earth, containing about three thousand galaxies, that the alien exposed Mom to off-the-wall genes, thereby rendering my sister and I different as night and day.

Despite our personality, general outlook, and political differences—Jan's perceptions varying from mine by about one-hundred-eighty degrees—I couldn't ask for a kinder, gentler sister. Okay, I could ask, but I wouldn't find one any better. For that I thank my lucky stars. Or maybe I should be thanking Mom's lucky stars along with the alien abduction.

Considering our vast dissimilarities, Jan probably doesn't put much store in the alien theory and instead might consider the older-sister-was-adopted hypothesis. We're both brimming with intelligence—alien or otherwise—with a constant thirst for knowledge; which we can attribute to our real parents, adoption and kidnapping aside. And there it ends. Jan's a moderate Democrat and so am I except that our definition of moderate varies considerably.

Actually, I'm a moderately liberal Democrat. I'd say she's a tad more moderately to the right. As an old geezer gal I believe a lot of right is wrong. I've asked Jan not to let my liberal, easygoing, anti-war, peacenik, occasionally unrealistically optimistic outlook irritate her. Indeed, she probably won't find this funny at all.

I recognize my weaknesses for what they are. I'm easily swayed and even wishy-washy at times, seeing both sides of issues. Also, I dislike hurting feelings and sometimes agree when I ought not. It doesn't help that I'm half deaf so when I nod in agreement, it may not be at what someone said, but rather at what I heard.

If I say yes and it should be no, maybe I forgot my hearing aids or perhaps the batteries need changing. Like the mule, get my attention before telling me stuff. I don't do signing but I read lips.

Between fifty years of suffering from Tinnitus and Meniere's disease surgery caused hearing loss sometimes it's easier to nod rather than ask for a repeat. Easier, but not necessarily right. I'm usually not being flip, but I make a lot of jokes about stuff because I handle everything better with a smile than a frown.

In any case, if I smile when I ought not, don't get annoyed with me. Getting angry never made me feel better and it won't do much for you either. Now, getting even, that's a whole different subject.

Joan Baez sang a song about some days being diamonds and some days being rust. I recall the diamond days very well, but nowadays, I'm having to fight rustiness. In other words, I've slowed down and it didn't take me long to learn about the only thing that removes rust stains is laughter. I've discovered if a little rustiness shows up in my life—creaky joints, extra poundage, mind not so sharp, broken bank account—laugh. It may not do much for the stains in my sink but it does wonders for my constitution.

Thus my motto is that if it can be cried, it can be laughed, or as Kinky Friedman says, "Anything worth cryin' can be smiled." Which includes even being deaf and having an alien for a sister.

By the way, my alien sister has five full grown cats and over thirty birds of all sizes, shapes and colors. She is owner and operator of *Home is Where the Heart Is Bird Rescue Service* and is on the board of directors of another bird rescue organization spanning several states.

Her cats interact with her birds and nary a drop of drool or a stolen tail feather comes to pass. I wonder if it has to do with alien know-how? Maybe I need to send BooCat to Jan's house for a week's worth of BooCamp—I mean Boot Camp.

The Cat Toy

70

> "You know you're way past redemption and that you love your cat too much when you pass around 8 x 10s of said cat at the office; have 13 x 19" 'Hang in there BabyBoo' posters made; open up a Facebook page titled BooCat Unleashed and upload tons of cat photos to her page (and on July 12, 2010, BooCat had 100 'friends'—one week after her Facebook page was set up); and email cat photos to everybody you know."
> (Barbara Sharik—Guilty as Charged)

It's official. I'm a genuine life-sized cat toy.

Due to a little added bonus, some unexpected problems, I wound up having to stay over at the hospital an extra night and partial day following what was to be one day-surgery. Therefore, my fids missed me. TacoBelle and Rosie have spent a few nights away from me over their lifetime, but this was a first for BooCat.

"She made up for missing you, didn't she?" Chuck said the next day after I told him about her reaction to my coming home.

I arrived home with three hospital bracelets still attached to my left wrist: the main identification bracelet and two informational brightly colored armbands with tails.

The bright yellow one read *Fall Risk*. The other, radioactive red, was inscribed *Allergy*.

Both were wrapped loosely and one sported a three-inch tail, the other four-inches. That evening when we went to bed and BooCat discovered these colorful tails draping my left wrist, she claimed them as her private toys. And because they were attached to me, I was included in the game playing.

She batted, chewed and twirled them ever so gently until she grew tired and sleepy. I contribute her gentle play being because the colorful tails appeared to be a part of me, in her little cat's eye.

She snuggled next to me, resting her head in my hand, her warm body up next to mine. Taco, in her usual Chihuahua Curl, was a few inches lower, cuddled so close she was practically underneath my body. And while under normal circumstances neither Boo nor Taco dared touch each other during the night, perhaps because of the harrowing lonesome night they all spent the night before, for once they were okay with physical contact. Even a wisp of hair could not have been slipped between any of us.

Rosie was partially beneath my knees on the right hand side of my weary surgery-savaged body. Nary a single one of these pets had ever slept any closer than they were at that moment.

Several times during the night BooCee woke up and chewed gently on the bracelets that transformed me into a human cat toy, only to fall back fast to sleep.

She slept the whole night resting close, with her head in the palm of my hand. The several times she woke I whispered to her, *"Sweet baby Boo. My BooBaby. Good baby,"* petting her softly. My whispered words were as much to comfort her as my own self.

Planned as a day surgery, I should have been headed back home by six that evening.

Instead, shortly after returning to the recovery room, my throat and neck began to swell.

It was affecting my speech and my breathing. My designated nurse took charge, but I could hear fear in her voice. She placed an ice bag on my throat and located the anesthesiologist. She was fearful, as I was also, that it was a reaction to the narcotic medication I'd been administered.

The anesthesiologist determined a tracheotomy wouldn't be needed; and in fact, he deemed it "trauma." The air tube had injured the inside of my throat, and even abraded my lip. Chuck had wiped dried blood from my lips when I was first brought back to the room.

I laughed, when I could, and said the anesthesiologist attempted a tonsillectomy, a uvula-ectomy and removal of my adenoids. Which might have been beneficial for my sleep apnea—of which, was very evident all that night through.

I awoke gasping time after time when I stopped breathing time after time. Not planning to spend the night of the surgery, I didn't even consider bringing my CPAP breathing machine.

I was moved from the recovery room into the main hospital and was monitored throughout the night. The ceiling light stayed on and someone was in and out every few minutes. But come morning, it was good to be released and allowed to return to home sweet home and my lonesome fids.

I was due back to the doctor's office the next day, Friday. I barely got home when it was time to turn around and go back. But, except for my throat and lip hurting, I wasn't in much distress. I determined I'd pick up a bottle of Tylenol the next day on the way back to the doctor's office and get some safe pain meds into my body.

I didn't trust the narcotic pain meds prescribed. I've never been good with narcotic-based pain relievers over the years. I'd never make a good drug addict. Years ago Demerol caused my blood pressure to bottom out as the doctors termed it, scaring them right along with me as they played like Dr. House and restored me to safety.

Morphine makes me throw up and someone who has just had their insides stapled and glued back in place didn't need to be doing that.

I've had at least a dozen too many surgeries during my lifetime. Each time I have another I swear it's the last. And then something else breaks and surgical repair is necessary. But I'm still puttering along and intend to keep going for a long time to come.

Earlier, before I gave it up and went to bed that first night home, I stood over the computer keyboard, typing a short message to several friends and loved ones. Usually, under normal circumstances, when I sit in my desk chair to type, BooCat leaps on the chair-back and settles in just inches from my shoulders.

Due to the type reparative surgery, sitting down wasn't something I wanted to do at that moment. The strain of getting up and down was difficult and I was experiencing a great deal of discomfort. I planned to quickly type a few sentences, then make my way to the bedroom and read myself to sleep. My body was very tired.

As I leaned over typing, Boo leapt from the ground up to the back of the chair per normal. There normal stopped. Although I was several feet away from her and not seated in the chair, when she landed on the chair-back she did what any cat who was too far from its mom would do—she leaped through the air and landed on my shoulders. We're talking several feet. DareDevilBoo would have gotten a big hand at the circus with that feat.

I felt one set of rear claws lock into place—in my skin. Keeping her from falling off the precarious precipice, I reached up and steadied her. If a cat can sigh, she did. She wanted to be next to her mom and was bound and determined no matter the cost or mode of travel.

Yes. She missed me. It was shortly after that unusual move that I decided it was time for the crew and I to go to the bedroom and make ourselves comfy.

That was when Boo discovered the wrist bands and converted me into a human cat toy.

I had to return to the doctor's office the next morning so that what the physician referred to as packing (bandages) could be removed. A catheter was left in place. Because of the aforementioned problem tolerating narcotic pain meds, I had Chuck stop along the way to buy a bottle of Tylenol. Extra-strength. I took two.

Several hours later I took two more. I wanted to get them into my system so I'd feel better. As a precaution, Dr. Robert Marx, my doctor, said not to take aspirin or any product containing aspirin. Aspirin is a blood thinner and not recommended for surgical patients.

When I returned home again, again there were three very happy fids. They met me at the door and herded me to a chair in the living room. I plopped the coccyx pillow down in my favorite chair that good friend Mona Hayden, publisher and editor of the *Louisiana Road Trips* magazine had gotten me from a medical supply store. Then I gently eased into the chair on the pillow—what a blessing—and before I settled properly, there were three babies vying for the main lap.

If you want to be loved, get a pet. If you want to be overwhelmed with love, get several.

I had an appointment to return to the doctor's office the upcoming Monday, Martin Luther King Day. At that time the catheter would be removed. Then I'd again return for a check up the following Thursday. It's approximately seventy-five miles one way and at three-dollars a gallon gasoline, I was sure burning up the roads and the fuel. Yet, all in all, I was feeling fairly well.

How grateful I am to Chuck—a champ. I had an e-mail from Mona kidding me about having an ex-husband caring for me. She said, "One of my friends asked who was taking care of you and I said your ex. She said, 'Oh hell, she'd better make sure he hasn't taken out a big insurance policy on her!!' I laughed for ten minutes! Better check ole Chuck out!! Haha."

I wrote back "Who else can I boss around if not my ex? What's he gonna do, divorce me? Hah!"

That next day I had a bad morning. I woke up feeling shaky, took a shower and put some clothes in the washer (which caused Chuck to start telling me that I shouldn't have done that but I explained I put them in a few at a time. No heavy lifting). He wound up putting them into and out of the dryer. Did I say he's a gem? Yes. He is.

Suddenly, I felt the mother queen of all hot flashes—like I was going to go up in flames. I was unable to drink even half my cup of coffee. Chuck came and checked on me about that time. I went to bed—took off my warmest fluffy robe and tried to get cool, slipping on a summery gown instead.

Within a short time I was shivering. My regulator was busted.

I dozed off reading and shivering. The fids came and snuggled, which helped me warm up. I didn't have the strength to get up to put on the warmer robe again.

I knew I was going to be okay. Apparently there are just going to be days like that. I'm so used to doing whatever needs doing when it needs it, it's a metaphysical slap in the face when suddenly the rug slips out from under me. I was missing my independence.

Later I got up and microwaved steamed veggies and nibbled on them. I checked e-mail before giving in (but not giving up) and returned to reading from a prone position. I figured that's probably the turning point and from that moment forward, I'd be better.

Wrong.

There were new wrinkles each and every day. This must be why

Doc said it takes six weeks for surgery recovery At this point, it was less than a week.

Impatience isn't a virtue.

The good thing on Monday was having the catheter removed. I thanked God and greyhound and BooCat and whoever else needed a note of appreciation.

Another e-mail from Mona advised: "Also, if you don't know this, anesthetic from surgery will stay in your body up to 3 weeks, making you moody, sleepy, and generally out of sorts. So there, sugar, you now have an excuse if you want to go off on anybody!"

Good friends are worth more than anything money can buy. Mona has a magic way of cheering me up.

Evidently the coccyx pillow helped because I soon fell asleep sitting up in the chair, only to wake up around six when BooCat leapt into my lap. I took two more Tylenol, turned on the news.

The Tylenol hadn't had time to even dissolve when the television newsman advised of a Tylenol recall. Go figure. What are the odds? I didn't have any Tylenol in my household. I spent seven bucks on a bottle of Extra Strength. I started popping them in the name of pain relief, only to find out that my brand new bottle was among the lot number being recalled.

Recalled the same day I started taking them. The exact same day. If it had been a lottery ticket, I'd be counting my winnings.

The anchor reported McNeil-PPC, the Johnson and Johnson division that manufactured the recalled products (also recalled were Motrin, Rolaids and Benadryl at the time of the broadcast), received a *"small"* (70) number of complaints that included nausea, stomach pain, vomiting or diarrhea. Just the things I wanted to avoid; the reason for not taking the prescribed Percoset.

Can you believe the luck?

According to sources at McNeil, a small number of the recalled drugs were found to contain small traces of a chemical called "2,4,6-tribroanisole" (TBA), which is applied to wooden pallets that are used to transport and store packaging material.

Quoting the news report, "Mc Neil said consumers who purchased from the lots included in its recall should stop using the product and contact McNeil Consumer Health care for a refund or replacement."

Also "The company said consumers with medical concerns should contact their health care provider."

Urologist Dr. Marx, my surgeon, said Tylenol smelled funny to him going in *"and smells worse coming out."* Therefore, he said he doubted he would have noticed the odor reported by the original complainants. I agreed. Meds mostly have a medicinal odor that is not always pleasant to the olfactory gland. I've taken so few Tylenol, I didn't recognized whether it smelled right or not.

I didn't get ill. I originally planned to call the 800 number for a refund when I felt up to it. It's probably too late now. I never quite felt up to it while recovering; not that I have, it's probably too late. My bottle is sitting here in front of my monitor as a reminder but instead of reminding me to call, it's blended in with the background.

Another missive from Mona, this time in response to the Tylenol debacle. She wrote: "So you survive serious surgery and end up getting killed off by bad Tylenol!!! LOL If it wasn't so serious, it'd be funny!! You know, I think those anesthesiology people could be more careful when they insert the tubes. Catch one on a bad day and you're in trouble!"

And at the same time as the Tylenol recall, there was another recall in dog food. This for Salmonella found in dog treats distributed by Merrick Pet Care. The Food and Drug Administration (FDA) warned consumers not to use certain beef dog treats because they may be contaminated with salmonella: *Merrick Beef Filet Square for Dogs.*

Salmonella can affect both animals and humans. Humans can become ill after coming in contact with the tainted treats or any surfaces exposed to these products.

Several years ago thousands of pets were sickened and died from contaminated dog and cat food imported from China. Melamine-tainted wheat gluten was added to the pet food, contaminating it. Wheat gluten is a natural protein used as a binding agent in pet food to thicken the gravy. By adding melamine to the wheat gluten, the product was made to appear to have a higher protein level than it did, FDA officials said. It was deliberately added, in other words. And the bottom line was about money. It's always about money and making a profit.

What happened was that dogs and cats across the country suffered kidney failure after eating the contaminated food. While there is no coordinated national tracking system to monitor the number of pet deaths, the FDA said approximately 1,950 cats and 2,200 dogs died after eating pet food made with tainted wheat gluten. This was the largest pet food recall in U.S. history. The melamine-tainted wheat gluten forced pet food makers to recall more than 150 brands of dog and cat food during 2007.

Since then, there have been too many other incidents. It's an ongoing problem. Authorities attempt to stay on top of the problems that keep rearing their ugly heads, but they keep rearing none-the-less. Perhaps the staying-on-top method is flawed.

We must go lightly through the woods.

In the Eye of the Beholder

71

"I've learned to type with one hand so I can pet BooCat with the other."
(Barbara Sharik)

I call my newspaper humor column "Life in the Last Lane." And while I'm not exactly running full speed ahead, I am still traveling. It's just that it is getting harder to maneuver this old bod—as evidenced by my necessary surgery. It's getting more and more difficult as time and the elements erode body parts.

Funny I should use the term erode body parts. A couple months after Retail Surgery, I've discovered Acid Reflux has eroded my esophagus and created something termed Odynophagia. If it's not one thing, it's three.

I've always figured I could live with malfunctioning body parts so long as my mind retained alertness. I'm pleased my mind is still functioning, but I have to admit, I misspoke regarding the broke-down body parts.

When every joint ached every morning of every day, and I had no health insurance, it wasn't always a positive. I found myself counting the years until I qualified for Medicare. That wasn't necessarily going along with the half-full glass of V-8 sermon I've been preaching for years. A bit of negativity peered from beneath the wart of worry developed from being poor.

Decrepit means weakened or worn out by age, infirmity or long use. Decrepitude means a state of deterioration due to old age. And deterioration means to make or become bad or worse.

Decrepit is my new favorite word. My tongue gets wrapped around my eyeteeth so I can't see to properly pronounce deterioration, or I'd add it to my favorite words too. There are too many a, e, i and o's conglomerated in it.

Now there is a word: Conglomerated. A number of things forming a heterogeneous mass. Heterogeneous just means diverse in character or varied in content. This could go on forever.

My fourth grade school principal once stood in the lunchroom line beside me and told all us kids we should learn at least one new word every day. He gave us the word eventuate. He said it meant when something would happen and used it in a sentence: "When and where will the kiss eventuate?" Needless to say, the word, and especially used in conjunction with kissing, made an impression on a group of fourth graders.

Conjunction: The action of joining; the condition of being joined.

But back to my personal favorite, decrepit. In relation to my old self, some days I wake up feeling very decrepit and it is a confusing thing. You see, my mind is still eighteen—and I hope that isn't from lack of use—but my body feels older than dirt. It's betraying me on a daily basis.

It's a fact, becoming an old geezer gal isn't everything it's cracked up to be. It was more fun getting old at eighteen than it is at sixty-plus. From time to time it seems traveling life in the last lane, the best part is the senior discount at Popeye's Fried Chicken. I mean, ten percent is ten percent.

People used to say after forty it's patch-patch-patch. I didn't notice a whole lot of patching going on at that time in my life, but by golly, since hitting the sixty milestone it has been all about re-re's. If it can be redone, it needs to be. It is relocation, rerun, repeat, replacement and removal.

Body parts have relocated. There is a degree of drooping whereby the upper part is merging with the lower part. The jowls sag onto the neck, the neck onto the chest, the chest onto the belly, the belly obliterates the waist, and before I knew it what with everything going south I went from a size eight shoe to a size ten.

My ears require regular reruns and repeats. It is so embarrassing asking folks to rerun that by me again with a repeat, please. Sometimes I just nod and smile and hope it's the right response.

Then there are the replacement and removals. I haven't had my knees or hips replaced yet but they are bone-on-bone so it is just a matter of time. There is a whole lot of snap, creaking and popping going on every time I move. The removal, that's been underway for awhile, like hair; non-voluntary strands leaping into outer-space causing an embarrassing thinness of tresses.

There is removal of useless innards and odd growths; everything except excess deep skin. That seems to have moved in for the duration. I've become very fluffy. It could be the Blue Bell Homemade Vanilla Ice Cream I'm addicted to. Once on the lips, twice on the hips.

I know my Use-by date is fast approaching. Ah, and to think I used to be a Babe. Now I'm just plain decrepit.

Thus it is, that sometimes when I found myself sitting on the side of the road, watching life speed by, my thoughts wandered and I wondered. Especially when it took every bit of grit God gave to keep on keeping' on. And I speculated whether or not there is really a logical reason to believe in a Supreme Being.

Of course there are emotional reasons. But it's tough to have faith that nothing is something just because it's reassuring to do so.

I know. I know. Faith. You have to have faith.

But, how can I believe in a Supreme Being when such a being cannot be proven scientifically or otherwise? If not scientifically, then logically? Or if not logically, then why not at least fairly and evenly? You know, like why can't there be a giant miracle in the sky for all mankind to witness simultaneously so we wouldn't have to depend on one man's ceiling being another man's floor?

The crux of the matter is that it's impossible to prove the nonexistence of a thing. Yet, preachers and children and warriors of God alike expect us to do just that or else they damn you and your soul for all eternity to the worst perdition imaginable, declaring that "Absence of proof is not proof of absence."

Using fear tactics to force people to believe in a loving God just goes against the common-sense grain. It is an oxymoron to top all oxymoron's and is, in fact, moronic. Yet fear is the bottom line. From one side of the preacher's mouth comes the words: "My God is a loving God," and from the other comes the threat of plagues, wrath, wars forever, and burning eternally in hell if someone fails to believe in this loving God.

Say what? Sort of like the old song :"Love and Marriage"—singing "You can't have one without the other." I can understand the love and marriage ideology, but I sure can't wrap my brain around all the hate, suffering and war being the standard quid pro quo in connection with a loving God.

So, besides the miracle in the sky, I'd also appreciate the elimination of suffering and the abolition of blind hate. I would like a world full of pure unadulterated happiness; sufficient love to go around and a peaceable kingdom so peace-filled that men wouldn't have to kill each other and have wars just to prove God is on their side.

I recall seeing an interview of a man who had been bitten by one of the largest, deadliest and most poisonous of all snakes, a fer-de-lance. He lived.

These venomous vipers are usually fatal to humans. Average length is six-feet, they have large speckled eyes with vertically elliptical pupils and a broad triangular head. The body is covered with gray or brown velvety scales. Ferocious and deadly.

During the interview the survivor said that everybody kept telling him he should be so grateful to God for saving his life.

In a very infectious Aussie accent he spouted back that he told each and every one of the people telling him to praise God, that the ones who he was grateful to were the doctors and nurses.

He said, "They were the ones who saved my life." Then he added, "God should not have let me get bit in the first place."

That is what I mean too. If there is a God and he is so loving, why must there be suffering of little children? Why must there be so much hate?

Of course the answer is that no one should question God. Sorry Charlie. I've got a brain and it behooves me to use it. If I don't want to get hit by a train, I'm not going to sit on the tracks. I'm not putting my faith in the engineer's rapid responses nor the train's brakes. And I'm not putting my faith in an unseen entity that allows so much evil.

This could apply to the horrible Haitian earthquake of January 2010, and the Twin Towers 9/11 bombings, and the Holocaust—unless these were just God's way to thin the herd.

Religion as preached by man makes a mockery of the possibility of a God. More evil is done in the name of God and religion than anything else. Religion tends to breed fanatics.

Who claims to hear the voice of God speaking to them, telling them what to do—some instructions so vile, so evil, so cruel, so deadly? It's not the non-believer, or doubter, I can tell you that. The people who claim to hear God's voice in their ear are the people in asylums and sitting on death row and not to mention the wealthy evangelicals taking the food from the table of the poor so they can drive BMWs and wear gold and diamond jewelry and have their suits and shoes handmade.

I believe these voices heard are a direct result of radical religious training and upbringing taken to the extreme—the Bible taken literally. And why not? Everything that is written is supposed to have happened. If you are a believer, you aren't supposed to pick and chose what to believe and what not to. That isn't exactly kosher. It is either all real or it all is not. Bear in mind, the word of God as we know it, has flowed from the pen of mere man. That should say it all. Men have been pulling the wool over other men's eyes for all eternity.

Because the Bible is full of killing and warring all in the name of God, you take a weak minded person, and these hateful sermons push them over the edge. Far too often. Sometimes BooCat and I just have to put on our big girl britches and get on with what we feel is right and not worry what other folks think of us. Going with the flow is the easiest choice, but not always the right one.

For confirmation, check out Bill Mayer's documentary *Religulous*. It is an eye opener.

Sweet Baby BooCat

Retail Surgery

72

"Animals are not respecters of good looks, intelligence, prestigious honors, or fashion sense. They remind us regularly of our real place in the food chain."
(Baxter Black)

I slowly undressed, getting ready for a shower following surgery. I was home and happy to be here. Despite the Tylenol fiasco, I wasn't really hurting as bad as I feared, but my mind was running full-speed ahead.

My life has been good for the most part. Some years have been better than others. My credo is to keep a smile on my face and laughter in my heart, and don't ask for more than I can have. There have been times when it appears Mother Nature is hopped up on her PMS cycle and I have to remind myself life isn't about waiting for the storm to pass, it is learning how to dance in the rain.

Always the mysterious, all-knowing "they" say don't bother to complain because it does no good. And no one wants to hear it anyway. Instead of complaining, I try to see the bright side of every situation and make the best of it, philosophy that comes from years of subjection to all things good and bad. It's an acquired attitude of choice. I'm not an expert at it, but I keep trying, based on the children's lesson that if you don't succeed at first, then try, try again.

Someone once asked if I was afraid of anything. It took me about two seconds to say: Losing my mind and tornadoes.

A mind is a terrible thing to waste and a worse thing to lose. I'm handling the effects of aging on my body, but losing one's mind is a fearful prospect. I know mindless people.

I remember old people—before I became one—saying the first thing they read in the newspaper are the obituaries. Now, I do too. Not just to see if I know the deceased—living in a tightly-knit and relatively small population-wise area, I do know so many—but truthfully, it's to see how old they were when they stepped on that rainbow. It is very scary to see so many deceased circling all around my current age. I want to hang around another twenty-plus years. With a sound mind of course.

My other fear, tornadoes, is because of the uncertainty connected, coupled with the absolute fury they unleash. Tornadoes drop down from the sky in an instant, wreaking uncontrollable havoc in every sense of the word. You can run but you cannot hide. And guess what? They aren't just in Kansas any more.

I long associated tornadoes primarily with *The Wizard of Oz* and Dorothy and Toto and Kansas. For half my life Dorothy and dog were the only people I knew who had ever been in a tornado and it didn't go all that bad for the two of them after it was all said and done.

Then I moved to Jones, Louisiana.

That first November in 1969 the roof of the house had to be replaced due to tornado damage from a middle-of-the-night tickle of a tornado. Fortunately, the tornado passed over high enough it only moderately damaged the roof and sucked water inside closed windows—that have rattled ever since. It did not drop down low enough to wipe out the entire house. We were lucky. Thousands of people year after year are not.

I've witnessed neighboring houses, communities and towns, suffer damage and loss of life over the years. One need not go farther than a mile or two to find the damage, year after year, season after season.

Yes. It scares me. If I were to relocate I'd like to find a tornado-free place to go—if such an animal exists. TacoBelle has gotten more nervous over the years when it storms; I probably made her spend too much time sitting in the safety of the bathroom and she picked up on my uneasiness. Rosie has exhibited a slight increase in anxiety this past year, but it seems more a follow-the-ChiChi-leader than anything else. BooCat would probably go outside and dance naked in the rain given the chance. While she is sometimes jumpy she does not heed to the side of caution. She is fairly fearless.

I'm fearful because I know what can happen, but I don't let it drive me. We take cover when the weather radio says a tornado will pass over Jones at such-and-such a time. Between my weather radio, police scanner and the television, I keep one ear tuned to the possibility of danger.

I recall coming home from the newspaper one evening—due to the threatening weather my editor sent me home a little early. I got a few miles down the road when the meteorologist broke into the radio station I was listening to and advised a tornado was picked up on radar by the National Weather Station in Jackson, Mississippi. At that moment it was passing over the town of Beekman and would reach Jones in twenty-minutes.

I would reach Jones in twenty-minutes too.

I was just a few minutes away from Oak Woods where Mom was, so I stopped there. The nurses had all the residents lined up in the hallway; this storm was a very severe and real threat. I stayed in line with Mom until the all clear was given. At home, I found no damage.

But living with this type threat every time a cloud blows up, is hard on the nerves.

I tell myself, laugh-lines make women prettier and men handsomer. Frown-lines are just smiles upside down, waiting to be reversed.

So, sitting in the bathroom in anticipation of my first shower following surgery, I peered in the mirror and wondered what the heck happened? Who is that old woman staring back at me? I think like a thirty-five year old, but look every bit sixty-five. Gray hair. Wrinkles that don't hurt but joints that do.

I've reached a time in my life when I look better clothed than not. I have loved life and lived it nearly to the fullest. But now I'm tired. That doesn't mean I'll stop doing, it only means I'll not be doing quite as much at the pace I once did it. In other words, I guess it's time to slow down.

I take with me superb memories, but I also take with me my share of tears. I try to never dwell on the tears, but instead dwell on the superb. It is always my choice. I do believe misery is optional. So is happiness. I choose happiness. I choose joy. Forever and ever, I choose laughter.

The first things I removed as I sat contemplating were my footy-socks. Leaning over was not an option, and with bad knees and hips and back—aye yes, everything is bad in its old age—I managed to sort of slip the first sock off by stepping on the toe with the opposite heel and tugging. It worked. No mishaps. Even being unbalanced—physically mind you, we're not getting into anything mental—I took them off and left them lying in the center of the bathroom floor.

I sat on the toilet seat and tackled the task of removing my pajama bottoms. BooCat entered the bathroom; her usual curious-cat self. Not much goes on in this household of which she isn't aware. Actually, maybe *nothing* does. Seeing BooCat reaffirmed my choice of joy, of happiness and laughter. She makes me laugh. She gives me joy. I'm old and damaged, but I'm happy.

I saw her walk over to the little sock pile, and as she straddled it, her nose dipped down. When she lifted her head back up, a sock was in her mouth and she kept going, full-speed ahead.

"Bring that back, BooCat!" fell on deaf ears. Of course. Like a human kid, this fid hears what she wants to hear.

You probably had to have been there to see her stealth move in action. It was really cool. Now you see it. Now you don't.

I had to assume I'd eventually find the missing sock. I turned my need-to-find-it-now button off. What I needed now was to take a shower; wash some of the funk from surgery off my body; ease sore muscles with streaming hot water.

The sock could wait.

Wrapped in a wooly-warm robe after the gratifying shower, I made my way into my bedroom, and sure enough, there in the middle of the bed was the missing sock. So long as BooCee keeps delivering her prey to the center of the bed, I shouldn't lose anything important that she spirits away.

On a lighter note, as I sat drying off following the shower, it popped into my head that instead of trying to explain the type surgery I had to everyone—and everyone did ask because we Southerners will talk to anyone about anything all the time; nothing is sacred. Instead of talking about cystoceles, rectoceles, bladder slings and pelvic floor

401

reconstruction, I simply declare that I had *Retail Surgery*.

Let the double entendre speak for itself.

At the checkup following my original *Retail Surgery* humorous breakthrough, I jokingly told Dr. Marx's nurse the name I had come up with. She immediately told Dr. Marx when he walked into the examination room. He laughed out loud and asked if I would mind if he used the term.

I gave Dr. Marx a book in appreciation and inscribed it: *When it sticks and it shouldn't, use WD-40. When it doesn't stick and it should, use Duct Tape. And when everything goes South and it shouldn't, use Dr. Robert Marx.*

He said he enjoyed the book, adding that I'd written more on the first five pages than he's written in five years.

I'm not a proponent of everything happening for a reason—some happenings are non-reasonable, but I do believe so long as it happens, make it a convenience. Turn it into an opportunity. While I am off mending from surgery, I am penning this BooBook.

A Moment in Time Remembered Forever

73

"You're only a dog, old fellow; a dog, and you've had your day; But never a friend of all my friends has been truer than you always."
(Julian S. Cutler, *Roger and I*)

Closing out the old, bringing in the new might be a good way to describe this memory leftover from Christmas 2008. Especially if you are one of those folks who send Me-Me letters in with your Christmas cards. You know the letters I am referring to: it's all about me and what I did during the year just past.

Sometimes I do if I'm in the mood and if I have something worth sharing. In some cases, these once a year Me-Me letters is the main time a few of my friends and I catch up. Cousin Rick called and said he missed my Christmas Catch-up letters when I didn't include one in with my card. So, that year I decided I'd do one up and share it with Rick and anyone else interested enough to read it.

I really wish I had been wise enough to have written a Christmas letter every single year, year after year. What a perfect diary the letters would have made. Memories and milestones memorialized for anyone who might care. Good family archives. Why, a hundred years from now some distant relative might have whipped out a whole collection of my Me-Me Christmas letters and had their worth declared on *Antiques Road Show*.

In the letter of 2008 I told how I had spent a whirlwind year, how it was like being on one long road trip, and how time flew. Not necessarily because of fun, but because I was more mature. As a Geezer Gal, my days (and nights) flit by like a hard candy Christmas. One minute it's Friday. Next, it's Monday. Busy all day at work, I come home, plop in front of Antiques Road Show, wake up later, go to bed to read myself back to sleep. For some reason, reading-self-to-sleep isn't necessary when sitting upright watching television, but it is when reclining in bed at bedtime. Go figure.

I wrote that things hadn't much changed in a year's time. I still watched more of the inside of my eyelids than television shows, explaining how the next thing I know the alarm is singing and there I am, night-light still lit, eyeglasses propped on my nose and my book lying open across my chest. What I wondered was how did it go from ten-thirty at night to five-thirty in the morning in five minutes? Talk about flying time.

Now, I have BooCat sleeping on my feet when I wake up at five-thirty unless it is one of her wake-me-up mornings. In which case she will likely be stretched out on my chest with her head tucked beneath my chin with her purr-motor fully engaged.

In 2008 I told everybody my routine was to wash clothes, change sheets, vacuum, and mop on weekends and how immediately thereafter, it is time to do it again. To avoid talking to myself, sometimes I ask TacoBelle and Rosie where did the week go? They don't know. They had been napping and took no notice. Ah, the luxury of being pampered pets. This year, BooCat joins those ranks.

My 2008 Christmas letter read:

> As I moved through December, it seemed like I just mailed Christmas cards. It is time to do it again. I barely had time to answer everybody's Christmas letters in between.
>
> I remember Christmas was good last year. It wasn't quite so good this year since Mom passed away Nov 21, 2008 a couple weeks after her eighty-fourth birthday; a few days before Thanksgiving.
>
> Several hours earlier, thirteen-year-old Hershey Cat also died. Maybe he decided she needed company on her journey to the other side of the rainbow. Mom was laid to rest beside my late son Tony Tubbs November 24, 2008 at

73 / A Moment in Time Remembered Forever

New Hope Baptist Church Cemetery in Jones, Louisiana.

Prior to that, the year whizzed by as fast as the days, nights and weeks do. I did the usual stuff—attended meetings, worked the polls, spent four days a week as Bonita's village clerk and one day a week as journalist and humor columnist at the Bastrop Daily Enterprise. I penned monthly columns and was guest speaker at clubs, organizations, and a state convention, based on my humor columns. It's terrific that people think I'm funny. I'd rather be funny than rich. See? I'm a laugh a minute.

Catching up, I got a flu shot followed by the flu a couple months later in February, along with some other health stuff that reminded me I'm finally too old to die young.

March brought a snow storm with blinding flurries right out of the blue. It was beautiful to behold from behind closed doors in a warm house. We rarely get snow that sticks. That's why the Canada geese come by the thousands and winter here every year. We also had nasty-bad, floodingly-wet weather leftover from Hurricane Gustav the end of August, first of September.

In April after boo-coo years, I traded in Trusty-Dusty, my 2000 Blackberry Saturn, for the 2006 Chevy Impala XYZ (or some such letters). If I would have known the cost of gas would go out the window and electric bills would rival the national debt, I might have kept Dusty a while longer. Dusty was paid for.

Rosie the Doxie was six-years-old at the time she suffered a second bout of Canine Intervertebral Disc Disease but recovered without the purchase of a doggie cart. Mom's Gizzy (aka: Gizzard), a deaf, dumb, blind Peke just turned fourteen; Alpha dog, TacoBelle is ten, and Cockatiel George, sixteen and a-half, Snowbird is eight. We are a household of old geezers.

I had seven yard dogs spayed; two to go. A lot of my life revolves around my pooches. Out of all of them, I only have one named NoNo-Bad Dog. Unfortunately, I also have one named CrazyGracie.

There were forty-plus hummingbirds at one time at the

feeders, a pair of Orchard Orioles gleaning the branches of the Lady Banksia rose bush, a Dark-Eyed Junco on the patio, fascinating Shrikes hunting overhead, Purple Martins dive-bombing for mosquitoes, along with the standard yard birds—sparrows, doves, mockingbirds and the like. So I did a lot of bird-watching.

In a nutshell, that was 2008. Merry Christmas, one and all.

I didn't send out Christmas letters in 2009. I should have so I could have told everybody about BooCat. I reckon everybody will just have to read the book or see the movie.

Thinking about my Christmas epistle and that now Mom is lying to rest beside my son, Tony, reminds me that at the time he was killed in a tragic traffic accident, his daughter Alisha was only three years old. She and her mom Cindy moved back east and settled in Pennsylvania. I don't recall how soon afterward Theresa and I made a trip to visit Cindy and Alisha, my sister Jan and her family and brothers Jimmy and David and their families, but Alisha was still very young and her loss still achingly new.

We were at an ice cream stand where Alisha walked over toward a trash barrel to discard something and a yellow jacket stung her hand. She cried like her heart was breaking. Mine was, with every tear she shed. I put my arms around her and lifted her, kissing and cooing granny love words.

With tears streaming down her pretty pink cheeks, her sobs slowing to a hic-cupping few, she lifted her hand up into the air, looked skyward and said, *"Daddy, kiss my hand."*

She had been told her daddy had gone to heaven, because what else do you tell a child of three who was the apple of her Daddy's eye, inseparable and adored. Therefore, it was quite natural for her to think he could kiss the bee sting and make it all better, so she lifted her hand skyward.

To this day, I can see and hear her sweet words from that tender, heart-wrenching moment. We never know what tomorrow will bring.

73 / A Moment in Time Remembered Forever

There are no promises. A baby child should not lose the father who loved her beyond words.

Tony stopped by to see me on his way to work that morning. And when he left he hugged me and told me he loved me. By the time I could have counted to sixty, he was gone.

Gone in sixty-seconds.

I try not to mourn his loss so much but rather I rejoice his having been.

Epilogue

> "There's no question about this. I know too well his look of despair and disapproval when I have just thought that he must be left at home."
> (John Steinbeck, *Travels With Charley*)

A few weeks ago while shopping, a stranger asked, "How's Boo-Cat?" He had read about her in my newspaper columns and the *Louisiana Road Trips* magazine. I told him she is still a Wild Child, and that by the way, Rambunctious might've been an appropriate name—Rambo for short. It wouldn't have mattered that it wasn't girlie. After all, BooCat isn't exactly a girlie kind of cat most of the time anyway.

Then, because he seemed to honestly care, I told him how, when all the games are finished, she climbs onto my lap and purrs—that she has an automatic purr-button and her purrs are contented purrs. Pet her, pick her up, just touch her and she purrs. No batteries required. The only time she doesn't purr is when she is sound asleep.

I qualified the "sound" part of sleep, because I have heard her cat-nap and purr simultaneously.

He told me he has a cat named "Psycho," adding that he understands where I am coming from when I write about BooCat and her unusual personality and kitty quirks.

He smiled and walked away. I was left standing in the middle of

Epilogue

the store smiling too. My BooCat. She even has me talking about her to complete strangers in stores. Yes. Silly old woman with a cat fits me now. And it is all good. All good.

No more empty spot in my heart. BooCat fills it to overflowing.

Example would be how first thing in the morning, after a night of sleeping on my feet or in the crook of my arm, BooBaby traipses up my body with light-weight kitty paws. The gait could be described as prancing. Then she plops down on my chest and tucks her head beneath my chin. Next, she stretches out and purrs.

Can anyone imagine the happy glow she brings to an old lady's otherwise mundane life?

I stroke her. She enjoys. She is so thrilled by the early morning attention, so that the more I pet the more she rubs her head beneath my chin. I whisper softly for her ears only. I tell her how sweet she is, how good, how beautiful. She preens with delight.

I don't know who rescued who. All I can say is that this is a great way to be awakened each morning. This is the beginning of a most pleasant, loving part of my BooCat as she matures.

Another encouraging sign of calm maturity moving into BooCat's personality happened New Year's day. TacoBelle was snuggled beneath the covers still in bed, I was sitting in my home office at the computer and Rosie was snoozing on the hot-pink shag rug covered up with a hot-pink wooly throw, when BooCat meandered over to her side. She managed to pull part of the throw off Rosie's head, awakening her.

Next she began grooming Rosie. She licked her chest, her neck, her inner and outer ears, back down to her neck again. She licked and licked for a good fifteen minutes.

Judging by the look on good-natured Rosie's face, she was making every effort to be patient, waiting for the bath to end. When it seemed the end would never come, Rosie took things into her own hands—err, paws—and stood up, which isn't all that far up since her legs are so short even BooCat is taller. She inched away just a tad.

"Tad" is Southern for a tiny bit.

Boo looked at her, like, *Where are you going? I'm not done yet.*

Almost in slow motion, Rosie snuck to the other end of the throw. She nonchalantly sat down. I saw her out of the corner of my eye, peering out of the side of her eye at BooCat. When she looked over at BooCat, she found BooCat looking right back at her. It was a *"Yikes!"* moment.

Caught in the act of checking out Boo, Rosie immediately turned her back and scooted underneath the cover at the opposite end, leaving BooCat sitting all alone.

Written all over her face, Boo was not a happy cat.

So, what did Boo do? Did she get mad? Why, no. She just crawled under the cover with Rosie and started licking again.

It was one of those *"you can run but you can't hide"* moments.

Poor Rosie. When BooCat adopted her as her own private pet she meant business. This was a positive even if it did wind up annoying Rosie. Instead of starting a fight with her, rough-housing, or body-slamming her, she lovingly groomed her.

Therefore, I am trusting eventually the pleasant and playful side of Boo's personality will even out her insecure and bossy temperament. After all, she is still just a baby and needs her quiet time and gentle petting and caring words to tell her what a good kitty she is. And she really is. Not to mention, she's purr-fectly Boo-tiful.

BooCat gives me laugh lines. She has found a permanent home and I have found another piece of my heart. It is a good thing human hearts are expandable because sweet BooCat has moved into mine and she is a purr-fect fit. She will never feel like an orphan again. I love this cat. I will no longer have time to feel like an old decrepit geezer gal; I have to stay young to keep up with my young whipper-snapper BooCat.

Sure, some might say BooCat is just doing what cats do, indicating she's just an ordinary cat. There is nothing ordinary about BooCat. Besides, BooCat doesn't even know she's a cat, much less an ordinary cat, which is part of what makes her so special.

BooCat thinks she's just like Rosie and TacoBelle. And both Rosie and TacoBelle believe they are little furry human beings. And who am I to burst all these bubbles?

At day's end, all played out, there I am, bound up with my breathing machine, book in one hand when BooBaby climbs onto my chest. She tucks her head beneath my chin. Surrendering herself to Morpheus, she purrs herself to sleep. My hand rests on her back offering her security while providing me comfort.

Epilogue

Like poetry in motion, having BooCat in my life takes it full circle. A good beginning and a better ending.

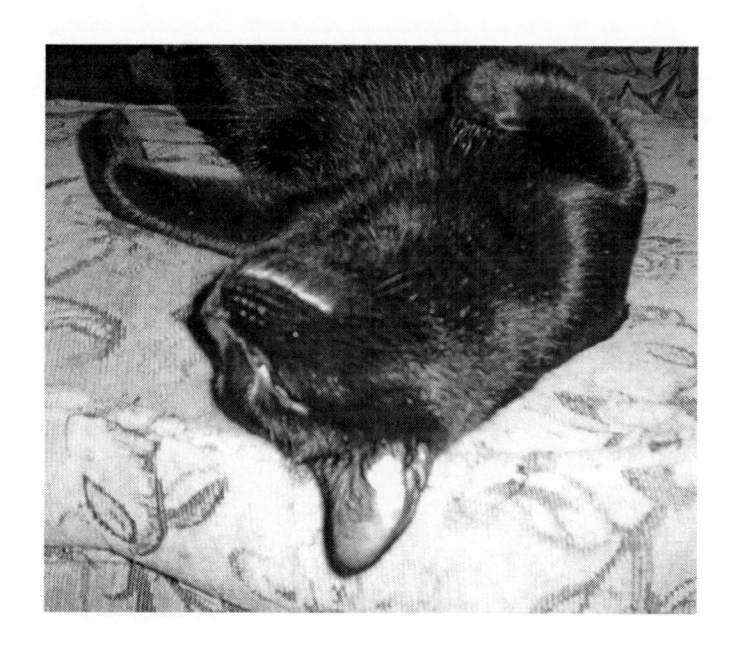

The Beginning

Bibliography

About Cats
Bleecker, Arline. *The Secret Life of Cats.* Globe Communications Corp., 1995.
The Cat Fanciers' Association Cat Encyclopedia. Simon & Schuster, 1993.
Hempel, Toby. *Cat Lover's Handbook.* Globe Communications Corp., 1997.
Richards, James R., DVM. *ASPCA Complete Guide to Cats.* Chronicle Books, 1999.
Vine, Louis L., DVM. *Common Sense Book of Complete Cat Care.* William Morrow and Co., 1978.
Waring, Philippa. *A Dictionary of Omens and Superstitions.* Souvenir Press, 1978.
Warner, Matt. *Cats of the World.* A Ridge Press Book, Bantam Books, 1976.
Wilkins, Kelli A. *Cat & Kitten Care.* TFH Publications, 2005.

About Dachshunds
The Complete Dog Book, 17th Edition. American Kennel Club Inc., 1985.
Gordon, Ann. *The Dachshund, A Dog for Town and Country.* Howell Book House, 2000.

About Chihuahuas
Coile, D. Caroline, Ph.D. *A Complete Pet Owner's Manual.* Barron's, 2003.
Gerstenfeld, Sheldon L., DVM, with Shultz, Jacque Lynn. *ASPCA Complete Guide to Dogs.* Chronicle Books, 1999.
Pisano, Beverly. *Chihuahuas.* TFH Publications, 1998.
Terry, E. Ruth. *The Chihuahua, An Owner's Guide To a Happy*

Healthy Pet. Howell Book House, 1996.

About Pekingese
Pisana, Beverly. *Pekingese.* TFH Publications, 1997.

Animal Quotes
Black, Baxter. *Horseshows, Cowsocks & Duckfeet.* Three Rivers Press, 2002.
Friedman, Kinky. *Cowboy Logic.* St. Martin's Press, 2006.

Cat Poem
Kliban, B. "Love to Eat Them Mousies."

Birds
Burton, Robert. *National Audubon Society North American Birdfeeder Handbook.* Dorling Kindersley, 1992.
Kaufman, Kenn. *Kaufman Field Guide to Birds of North America.* Houghton Mifflin Company, 2000.
National Geographic Field Guide to the Birds of North America. Fifth Edition. National Geographic Society, 2006.
Purple Martin Conservation Association, http://www.purplemartin.org.
Thompson III, Bill, and the Staff of *Bird Watching Digest. Louisiana Bird Watching, A Year Round Guide.* Cool Springs Press, 2004.

Monarch Butterflies
http://www.MonarchButterfly.org.

Acknowledgment

Writers are inspired in many ways, but most often by the people around them. In this case, I was not only inspired by the people around me, but by the animals filling my yard, my home, my heart.

Let's get the people out of the way first: The constant encouragement offered by Chuck Babb (plus running me back and forth to the doctors during my health meltdown); Wes Helbling (good friend and co-staff writer at the newspaper); Rose Ross (devoted cat person, fellow artist and book lover, best friend and Irvin High School Class of 1962 classmate); and Mona Hayden (publisher and editor of *Louisiana Road Trips* magazine, confidante and good friend); cannot be overlooked. Without their support, *BooCat Unleashed* would still be just an idea knocking around in my old grey head.

There are folks like Tom Carpenter who provided fodder for my mill (and a working outside TV antenna). Thank you Sue Reppond Glass. I'm so glad you had so many pets you didn't know what to do. That's how I ended up with BooCat.

And always, so much love to daughter Theresa. And to Carla and Lance McGee. Not to mention love forever to granddaughter Alisha and her mom Cindy Tubbs.

Special thanks to Dr Robert White and Elizabeth, veterinarian and assistant extraordinaire. If it weren't for Elizabeth, who made the adoption happen there would've been no BooCat and Barbara merger.

Then there are sisters Jan Sharik Baker and Michele Sharik who were with me when I started this amazing journey with this amazing cat. And about this time, along comes Reinhard Hollink and the heart expands a little larger to make room for another somebody to love.

Of course I'm appreciative of all the various folks who made appearances in the book: These include my beloved loved ones who are

Acknowledgment

gone but never forgotten: my son Tony Tubbs; my once in a lifetime soulmate Jon McNeil, Mom, Phyllis Geoghan Sharik and Dad, Michael Sharik.

There are others who read most of what I write and some actually rave about what they've read: "Cuzin" Mike Sarik, Johnny "Megabucks" Wink, Melba Davis, Tammi Garner, Mayor Mike Lytle and Mayor Floyd Baker, plus a handful other loyal fans. Correction: At least two handfuls.

Humorous and grateful smiles are extended to both of BooCat's self-proclaimed Number One Fans: Ann Wilson Hamilton and Lila Wolfe. Any celebrity can have fans but only BooCat has two Number One Fans. Special thanks to Dorothy Ford, Morehouse Parish Humane Society board member and Bastrop-Morehouse Chamber of Commerce Director. She has more cats than you can shake a stick at.

Then there are the animals, some still here: TacoBelle, Rosie, George, SnowBird, Cheeto, Buddy and about a dozen rescue yard dogs; plus some wandering around Rainbow Bridge awaiting crossover time: Hershey Chocolate and Sterling Silver, Granny's Gizzy, Boyo, and Candy.

And of course BooCat, without which there would be no *BooCat Unleashed* book.

About the Author

Barbara Sharik was born in Glen Burnie Maryland, lived around the United States and overseas and now makes her home at Wit's End Comedy Club in Louisiana with young dogs, old dogs, and several stupid dogs, a couple birds and fish and a thrice rejected, emotionally conflicted cat named BooCat.

She writes a weekly humor column "Life in the Last Lane" in the *Bastrop Daily Enterprise* newspaper and monthly humor column "Runnin' the Roads" in the *Louisiana Road Trips* magazine. Besides having published several books of poetry, a couple volumes of short stories, a humorous novel, a collection of cartoons, seven annual compilations of collections of her newspaper and magazine columns, she was published in *Dark and Stormy Rides Again* (Penguin Books) and in the *World's Best Short Stories (of all time)* (Quality Paperback Books).

Active in civic affairs, she currently serves as president of the Morehouse Parish Tourism Commission, secretary of the Jones-McGinty Water System, member of the Morehouse Sales Tax Commission, founding board member and curator of the Village Museum. She served for eight years as a Justice of the Peace and has been a Notary Public since 1970. She is the town clerk for the Village of Bonita where she has worked since 1996. Previously she was in banking.

About the Author

One year she was among eight finalists in a Jay Leno Comedy Challenge. Occasionally she is called upon to speak before organizations and groups where she delivers her own brand of humor.

To purchase copies of *BooCat Unleashed*, mail $20.00, plus $5.00 postage and handling, to:

It's Barbara's Business
Barbara Sharik
16813 McGinty Road
Jones LA 71250

Or email:
Lifeinthelastlane.sharik@yahoo.com

Or call:
318.823.2668

Please visit:
BooCat Unleashed on Facebook